42

Social History of Canada

H.V. Nelles, general editor

Bushworkers and Bosses:
Logging in Northern Ontario, 1900–1980

The lumberjack – freewheeling, transient, independent – is the stuff of
countless Canadian tales and legends. He is also something of a dino-
saur, a creature of the past, replaced by a unionized worker in a highly
mechanized and closely managed industry. In this far-ranging study of
the logging industry in twentieth-century Ontario, Ian Radforth charts
the course of its transition and the response of its workers to the
changes.

Among the factors he considers are technological development,
changes in demography and the labour market, an emerging labour
movement, new managerial strategies, the growth of a consumer society,
and rising standards of living. Radforth has drawn on an impressive
array of sources, including interviews and forestry student reports as
well as a vast body of published sources such as *The Labour Gazette*, *The
Pulp and Paper Magazine of Canada*, and *The Canada Lumberman*, to shed new
light on trade union organization and on the role of ethnic groups in the
woods work force.

The result is a richly detailed analysis of life on the job for logging
workers during a period that saw the modernization not only of the work
but of relations between the workers and the bosses.

IAN RADFORTH is Assistant Professor of History at the University of
Toronto.

IAN RADFORTH

Bushworkers and Bosses: Logging in Northern Ontario, 1900–1980

UNIVERSITY OF TORONTO PRESS
Toronto Buffalo London

© University of Toronto Press 1987
Toronto Buffalo London
Printed in Canada

ISBN 0-8020-2639-7 (cloth)
ISBN 0-8020-6653-4 (paper)

Printed on acid-free paper

Canadian Cataloguing in Publication Data

Radforth, Ian Walter, 1952–
    Bushworkers and bosses

    (The Social history of Canada ; 42)
    Includes bibliographical references.
    ISBN 0-8020-2639-7 (bound). – ISBN 0-8020-6653-4 (pbk.)

    1. Loggers – Ontario – History. 2. Trade-unions –
    Loggers – Ontario. 3. Logging – Ontario – History.
    4. Logging – Ontario – Technological innovations.
    I. Title. II. Series.

    HD8039.L92C37 1987   331.7′634982′09713   C87-094766-4

Social History of Canada 42

COVER: Pulp cutters felling with a crosscut saw, near Capreol, c. 1922
University of Toronto Archives

This book has been published with the help of a grant from the Social Science
Federation of Canada, using funds provided by the Social Sciences and
Humanities Research Council of Canada, and a grant from the University of
Toronto Women's Association.

FOR FRANCA

Contents

Acknowledgments

I am not a lumberjack. Nor am I a northerner. But with the generous assistance of countless people I have come to know something of the northern Ontario region and its history. It is a pleasure to acknowledge the help I received from many individuals – bushworkers and bosses alike – who opened their doors to me and generously shared their recollections. It took little probing to set them reminiscing, because they have vivid memories of winters spent in the bush. I hope this book does justice to the lively past they recall. Two men not only spoke frankly about their own experiences, but also opened their papers to me: C. Ross Silversides, a consulting engineer and forester now living in Prescott, Ont., and Tulio Mior, long-time president of the Lumber and Sawmill Workers Union local 2693, Thunder Bay. For assistance in arranging interviews and for their warm hospitality, I thank Gwenda Hallsworth of Sudbury, Jean Morrison of Thunder Bay, and Helmi Vanhatalo and Hilkka Vuormies of Sault Ste Marie. Varpu Lindstrom-Best introduced me to several Finnish old-timers and generously provided translations of dozens of Finnish documents.

Numerous archivists, librarians, and technicians gave me courteous assistance. I thank especially the staff members of the Forestry Library, University of Toronto, who cheerfully hefted dozens of dusty volumes from the back room, and Harold Averill of the University of Toronto Archives who brought to my attention sources that I otherwise would have missed.

My arguments have been sharpened by discussions with many perceptive scholars. This book began life as a PHD dissertation prepared for the Department of History, York University. I received sound advice and unfailing support from my supervisor, Irving Abella. And I benefited from the cogent criticisms of my examiners: H.V. Nelles, Tom Traves, Norman Penner, Leo Panitch, and Terry Copp. Over the course of several years my friends in the Labour Studies Research Group made many helpful suggestions, and our meetings have been an invaluable source of intellectual stimulation. Craig Heron, Ruth Frager, and James Naylor made special contributions for which I am sincerely grateful. I also benefited from lively discussions of portions of the manuscript which I presented to groups at York University, at Glendon College, and at the universities of Toronto, Ottawa, and Victoria. I greatly appreciate the suggestions of those who took time from their own busy schedules to read parts or all of the manuscript: Allan Greer, Carmella Patrias, and Craig Heron. Naturally I take full responsibility for what follows.

During the course of researching and writing, financial assistance was provided by the Fellowships Division of the Social Sciences and Humanities Research Council of Canada and by the University Research Program of Labour Canada. For their encouragement and efficiency I take pleasure in thanking people associated with the University of Toronto Press, in particular series editor H.V. Nelles, editor Gerry Hallowell, and my copyeditor Catherine Waite.

I benefited enormously from the shrewd scholarly advice and constant encouragement of Franca Iacovetta. At times she helped speed production; at other times she distracted me from my work. For all this and much more I am deeply grateful. This book is for her.

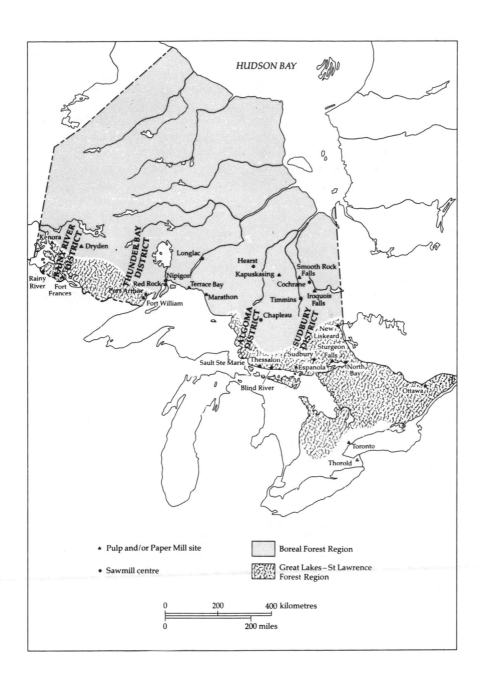

HUDSON BAY

Kenora
Dryden
RAINY RIVER DISTRICT
Rainy River
Fort Frances
THUNDER BAY DISTRICT
Longlac
Hearst
Kapuskasing
Smooth Rock Falls
Nipigon
Red Rock
Terrace Bay
Cochrane
Fort Arthur
Marathon
Fort William
Timmins
Iroquois Falls
Chapleau
ALGOMA DISTRICT
New Liskeard
Sturgeon Falls
Sudbury
SUDBURY DISTRICT
Sault Ste Marie
Thessalon
Espanola
North Bay
Blind River
Ottawa
Toronto
Thorold

▲ Pulp and/or Paper Mill site   Boreal Forest Region

● Sawmill centre   Great Lakes–St Lawrence
                                       Forest Region

0   200   400 kilometres

0   200 miles

Andy Blais, employee of Temagami Timber Company, with canthook, near Goward, 1956

Pulp cutters leaving camp, 1949

Alton Morse, manager of the Devon Lumber Company, taking two lumber company owners into camps near Chapleau in the mid-1920s

Loading pine logs with a jammer, near Thessalon, *c.* 1916

Hauling pine sawlogs on an iced logging road at camp 41 of the J.J. McFadden Lumber Company of Blind River, 1953

River driving on the Mississagi, 1949

Tote teams loaded with supplies leaving Thessalon for camps to the north, *c.* 1920

Julius Gilbert baking bread at Abitibi's camp 15 near Iroquois Falls, *c.* 1945

Finnish cookees sound the dinner gong at an A.E. Wicks camp near Timmins, 1929

Camp blacksmith for William Milne and Sons Company, Ltd, near Temagami
Lake, 1955

'Dinnering out' – a hot lunch in the woods, 1949

Saturday night diversions, pre-World War I

Bucking with a Swede saw near Longlac, *c.* 1949

Hauling crew with a Lombard Steam Log Hauler, *c.* 1914

Hauling a sleigh train with a Linn gasoline tractor, near Chapleau, *c.* 1925

Hauling logs with an early-model track-type tractor near Chapleau, *c.* 1929

Striking bushworkers outside the Finn Hall at Nipigon, 1935

Mounted police patrol Lumber Workers' picket line at the barns of the Pigeon Timber Company in Port Arthur, 1933

Removing the bodies of Viljo Rosvall and John Voutilainen, organizers for the Lumber Workers Industrial Union of Canada, Onion Lake, 1929

Activists from the Lumber and Sawmill Workers Union at the Lakehead, *c. 1953*

The type of single bunks demanded by the Lumber and Sawmill Workers Union in 1946 – shown here in an Abitibi camp near Iroquois Falls, 1954

New diversions, Abitibi camp, *c.* 1963

Abitibi's central camp 39, near Smooth Rock Falls, c. 1959

Cable yarding – moving logs by diesel engine and steel cables – near Marathon, 1952

Moving pulpwood with a Blue Ox skidder, near Espanola, 1959

Timberjack's articulated skidder with a load of logs, c. 1978

Transporting pulpwood with an articulated Koehring-Waterous Forwarder, 1966

Converting tree-lengths into eight-foot logs using a semi-portable slasher, near Iroquois Falls, *c.* 1975

Felling spruce with a Feller-Buncher, *c.* 1980

Shears and felling head are featured in this shot of a Feller-Buncher in action, *c.* 1980

Powersaw operator wearing protective gear, *c.* 1978

BUSHWORKERS AND BOSSES

Introduction

Few jobs in Canada have a more secure place in our folklore than that of the woodsworker. For many years the roistering lumberjack of the snowy northern woods was one of Hollywood's favourite characters in movies with a Canadian setting. Children still learn about the exploits of Paul Bunyan and his Ottawa Valley counterpart, Joe Monteferrand. Given the importance of the north and the Canadian Shield in our national mythology, it is little wonder that the lumberjack has captured the imaginations of Canadians over the years.[1]

Until the mid-twentieth century, the familiar image of the lumberjack – hardy axeman, knee-deep in snow, forcefully chopping at the trunk of a tall, straight pine – closely corresponded to the realities of the Ontario bushworker's calling. During the past three decades, however, the woodsworker has moved sharply away from the popular stereotype. A visit to the northern woods in the 1980s reveals few axes wielded by brawny men. Today's loggers fell trees with chainsaws or with gigantic, hydraulic-powered shears that cut down jack pines as easily as garden clippers snipping grass. Rather than shouting commands at horses pulling sleighs loaded with hay, woodsworkers now operate powerful diesel equipment which carry heavy loads across muskeg and rock in summer and winter. No longer do most bushworkers spend Saturday nights sharing stories and playing cards in the bunkhouse; most now live with their families on the weekends. Once a seasonal work force of foot-loose men enjoyed a great deal of independence on the job. Now most loggers are employed by big corporations and see woods work as a career. They accept as a matter of course both the security and the constraints that come with their unionized but more closely supervised and regulated jobs.

This study explores the transitions in the work-world of Ontario's twentieth-century woodsman. For the period of comparative stability that lasted into the 1940s, it involves a close examination of the traditional woods-worker's way of life, especially his work – the organization of tasks, the knowledge and skills required on the job, tools and equipment, and the forces in the workplace that promoted independence or solidarity. For the post-war period of rapid innovation, similar topics need to be explored, but here the focus is on the causes and processes of change. Throughout, an attempt is made to see how bushworkers and their bosses responded to one another thus shaping social relations in the woods. In pursuing these issues a number of related questions are addressed. Who were Ontario's seasonal woodsworkers and how were they recruited? What was it like to live in a winter bush camp? How did bushworkers protest their lot, and what kind of union structures and methods did they choose? Who was responsible for innovations in logging techniques, and how were new methods diffused throughout the industry?

Research has led to the central conclusion that, while management has always predominated, throughout the twentieth century bushworkers themselves have played a vital, though often unwitting, part in shaping the pace and nature of transformations in Ontario's logging industry. Before World War II, there were almost always plenty of men who, desperate for winter work, snapped up logging jobs however low the pay and poor the living conditions. Given these labour-market conditions, neither management advocates of woods mechanization nor unionists could make much headway. Employers simply did not need to introduce elaborate equipment, provide comfortable accommodations, or pay wages adequate for the support of a family. But after World War II, in the wake of broad demographic, economic, and social changes, far fewer men were willing to work in remote bush camps, and many of those who did joined a union that helped raise the standards of their working conditions and their pay. As a result, employers who hoped to profit from booming markets felt compelled to introduce new, sometimes radically different, labour policies, work routines, pay schedules, and tools and machinery. Yet, management's innovative strategies did not go uncontested; collectively and individually, woodsworkers' behaviour shaped the actual course of change.

Residents of northern Ontario have long appreciated the importance of the logging industry to the well-being of their resource-based economy. In most years prior to 1950, forest operators offered 20,000 to 35,000 jobs during the winter, when work was scarce in other industries.[2] As late as 1978, some 10,000 people worked in the Ontario logging industry and indirectly their labour provided jobs for more than 150,000 men and women.[3] More recently, growing numbers of Canadians, even in urban centres far from the logging camps, have become interested in forest-related issues. Scarcely a week goes by when there is not news of a clash between environmentalists and logging operators, a prediction of timber famine with consequent loss of jobs, or a new twist to the Canadian–American trade dispute over the alleged subsidization of crown timber. Yet there has been little serious academic study of the Canadian forest industry, especially the primary sector. A half century ago the dean of Canadian forest historians, A.R.M. Lower, published a pioneering survey, *The North American Assault on the Canadian Forest* (New York 1938). More than a decade ago, in the impressive study *The Politics of Development: Forests, Mines, and Hydro-Electric Power in Ontario, 1849–1941* (Toronto 1974), H.V. Nelles updated one of Lower's themes – the political economy of the forest industry. And Lower's interest in the failure to conserve Canada's forests has been recently followed up by R. Peter Gillis and Thomas R. Roach in *Lost Initiatives* (New York 1986). But scholars have been slow to take up another of Lower's themes, the changing way of life in the bush.

Even if we add to the bibliography of forest history by including studies of developments in the United States there are virtually no published monographs that focus on what has been happening within the logging industry during the twentieth century – how workers and employers interacted or how choices were made about logging techniques. This lacuna is all too evident in the recent and otherwise comprehensive survey of U.S. forest history, *This Well-Wooded Land*. Because of the nature of the literature in the field, the authors highlight the actual work of woodsmen only in early chapters on nineteenth-century lumbering; by the post-World War II period, the loggers all but disappear from view.[4]

The questions addressed in *Bushworkers and Bosses* fall chiefly within the rubric of the new labour history, particularly that branch of it primarily concerned with work rather than community.[5] The transiency of the logging work force and the ephemeral nature of the woods camp require that the focus be on the point of production rather than on working-class politics, community, or family life.

In raising questions related to the transformation of work, this book seeks to draw on the labour process debate that has recently raged among sociologists and historians.[6] Since the publication in 1974 of Harry Braverman's provocative study, *Labor and Monopoly Capital: The Degradation of Work in the Twentieth Century*, scholars have squabbled over the causes, course, and consequences of technological and other changes introduced in industrial workplaces. In explaining the shift to new methods, some studies have emphasized the role of new managerial concepts for organizing and motivating workers, while others have pointed to structural factors, such as changing product and labour markets. Some authors have argued that capital had its way; others point to the compromises and retreats forced on management by workers. In assessing the impact of new methods, some scholars see a process of deskilling and degradation, where others find a more complex picture of re-skilling and deskilling, welcome opportunities, as well as degraded jobs. These fascinating and important issues have shaped the approach taken here, and this book stands as a case study which advances arguments about the labour process on the basis of evidence gained from research on one industry in one region.

Studying the logging industry serves to highlight the contrasts between the experience of resource workers and those of the more intensively scrutinized craftsmen in the late nineteenth century or mass production workers in the early twentieth.[7] From the perspective of workers and bosses alike, outdoor work in the woods different profoundly from activities within factory walls. As Canada's staples historians emphasized a half century ago, the patterns of development in resource industries are greatly influenced by geography and by the characteristics of the staple itself.[8] A central contention of this study is that managers and workers in this primary resource industry have continually had to confront the challenges and opportunities posed by the geography of the Canadian Shield, the changing weather and seasons, and the particular characteristics of the region's coniferous forests.

Readers will have already grasped that in explaining developments in logging, the argument advanced here places great weight on structural factors, especially those related to the material environment and changing labour markets. However, it must be stressed that cultural factors also influenced the shifting relations between bushworkers and bosses. This book points to the key role played by radical Finnish immigrant bushworkers in shaping not only labour relations in the industry but also the broader transformations in the woodsworker's world. Without the Finnish presence, the bushworker's union might have emerged much later than it did, and mechanization could well have been delayed or taken a rather different course. Only by understanding Old World cultural influences in combination with the experiences of these immigrants can we understand why the Finns played such a crucial part in building a bushworkers' union. In other words, this study examines how work affected the Finns and how the Finns affected work. In so doing, it provides a window on immigrants at the workplace.[9]

While the stuff of institutional labour history – strikes, trade-union

growth and political machinations among union leaders – forms a significant part of the story presented here, it is by no means the whole tale. For
instance, the bushworker's habit of jumping from camp to camp in search
of superior working or living conditions will be seen as a vital, individual-
ized form of worker protest. Moreover, trade-union developments are
related to the broader theme – transformations in the workplace. This
approach serves to reveal the wider – and usually unintended – consequences of union activities.

Some comments on the limits of this study are in order. First, it should
be noted that it is an examination of the primary sector of the forest
industry and not sawmills or pulp and paper plants. Secondly, the study
concentrates on the operations of the larger lumber companies and the
pulp and paper corporations. This approach is appropriate because they
made up the most dynamic sector of the industry in terms of labour
protest, union development, and managerial innovations. Moreover, the
sources concerning these larger firms are more complete. Thirdly, it must
be stressed that this book deals with the northern Ontario region – that
part of the province lying north of the line of the Mattawa and French
rivers, where the great bulk of the province's logging activity in the twentieth century has taken place. In the parlance of the industry, Ontario
logging is part of the Eastern Canadian Region, that is, Canada east of the
Rockies. Within this so-called eastern region, however, patterns of labour
recruitment and labour organization varied markedly. To a significant
degree in eastern Canada, Ontario led the way in unionization and mechanization. Hence, it makes sense to study Ontario separately, although we
are certainly in need of similar studies of other provinces. Even within the
northern Ontario sub-region, forest sites and methods of exploitation have
differed widely. A more powerful lens held over one particular district
might well reveal patterns other than the ones stressed here.

Finally, a note on language. Just as logging techniques have changed
during the twentieth century, so, too, has the vocabulary of those in the
industry. Ontario's forest workers have frequently been called lumberjacks, but with the rise of pulpwood logging early in this century, the term
lumberjack more frequently came to refer to only those men felling and
handling logs destined for sawmills. More recently, the term has been
virtually abandoned. Also throughout this century, bushworker and
woodsworker (or bushman and woodsman) have been used to designate
manual workers in both the pulpwood and sawlog sectors. A lumberman
was usually a lumber company owner or boss. Only Canadian forest
workers on the west coast used to be called loggers, but during the last

three decades, as working and living conditions in the Ontario bush have begun to resemble those in the west, woodsmen here have taken to calling themselves loggers. This study maintains these various distinctions. Furthermore, masculine terms such as bushworker or woodsman have been used intentionally. Although a few women worked as cooks and laundresses, virtually none harvested timber until the late 1970s when perhaps a half-dozen women became logging equipment operators. The bush camp was a male world, suffused in every respect with a keen sense of masculinity.

This book is organized partly chronologically and partly according to theme. Chapter 1 provides a backdrop by briefly describing the geography and forests of northern Ontario, the rise of lumbering in the nineteenth century, and the changing economic fortunes of the province's forest industry in the twentieth century. The following four chapters, which deal with logging in the period before 1945, examine in turn the work force and its recruitment, labour processes in the forest, management's attempts to alter those processes, and, finally, camp life. Chapters 6 and 7 explore the growth and consolidation of the labour movement. The following two chapters describe managerial responses to the higher post-war logging costs, including renewed attempts at labour recruitment, improvements in camp conditions, closer supervision, and mechanization. Chapter 10 analyses labour processes in mechanized logging operations, and chapter 11, the responses by loggers to the new kinds of work. A brief conclusion follows.

1

Northern Ontario and the forest industry

Ontario's forests stretch seemingly countless miles across the ancient rock, deep muskegs, rolling hills, and clay flats of the Canadian Shield. Black spruce, white spruce, red pine, white pine, jack pine, balsam fir, aspen, poplar, and birch – these species grow in a profusion of combinations and patterns between the lakes, streams, and rivers that drain the woodlands and for centuries provided the only means of access to much of that vast, thinly populated hinterland. Snow-covered, frozen solid, and periodically whipped by arctic gales throughout half the year, the scene is transformed during the summer into an array of mosquito-infested bogs and hot, dry tinder-boxes, all too ready to be set ablaze. Lawren Harris – who knew this country well, as his paintings vividly attest – captured the north's outstanding feature when he spoke of 'the endless diversity of her expression.'[1]

Not surprisingly, Canadians over the years have viewed this diverse forest country in a variety of ways. Long the preserve of Indian trappers and strong-backed voyageurs, by the 1850s the fringes of the Shield had become an agricultural frontier for land-hungry Upper Canadian farmers. But after years of tilling the stony ground of the Ottawa-Huron tract, many eventually concluded that it was a thankless task in a God-forsaken land. To nationalist myth-makers of the late nineteenth century, however, this same country was responsible for moulding Canadians into a hardy, ruddy-cheeked people made of sterner stuff than our effeminate neighbours to the south. 'We are the Northmen of the New World,' cried Robert Grant Haliburton. By the turn of the century, businessmen and provincial officials promoted northern Ontario – the New Ontario – as a rich treasury of resources, recently unlocked by modern technology and ready for the taking by men of spirit and audacity. Canadian novelists, on the other hand, have warned that people's attempts to subdue the north have ultimately been destructive to both humanity and nature, a theme that echoes through the writings of historian A.R.M. Lower.[2]

Throughout the years the varied terrain and forests of northern Ontario have also been put to many uses. In the northern woods, the recreationist has found welcome relief from urban pressures, the farmer a source of cordwood to warm his home, the pulp and paper executive a supply of pulpwood to feed his mill and make possible a return on investments. Moreover, the forest industry itself has manufactured a remarkable range of products. Primary forest products have included sawlogs and pulpwood, mining props and telegraph poles (see Appendix 1). For more than a century, small sawmills have been cutting lumber for local builders, while large mills have sent vast quantities of timber to distant markets. By the 1970s, provincial mills were manufacturing huge quantities of studs, plywood, particleboard, as well as enormous volumes of such products as newsprint, tissues, brown paper bags, and cellulose. In most years since the mid-1920s, production in Ontario's primary forest industry has topped 500 million cubic feet, at least one-sixth of the total Canadian output (see Appendix 2).

FOREST COUNTRY

Northern Ontario is only one part of the Canadian Shield, an enormous expanse of Precambrian gneisses and granites that comprises most of Quebec, Ontario, northern Manitoba and Saskatchewan, as well as much of the Northwest Territories. Roughly shield-like in shape, it is centred on Hudson Bay and penetrated by James Bay, towards which most of northern Ontario's long, meandering rivers gently flow. Shorter streams plunge southward from the height of land towards the Great Lakes. They are broken by innumerable rapids and falls, for this is the most rugged part of the province. The Rainy River district is more level, but its landscape is strewn with countless freshwater lakes. Muskeg, a combination of water and vegetation, occurs in many areas and especially north of latitude 50°, in the region known as the Hudson Bay lowlands.[3]

In northern Ontario agriculture is largely confined to a few pockets: the level ground along the north shore of Lake Huron, the area around centres such as Sudbury and Thunder Bay, and the flat, poorly drained clay belts, near New Liskeard and Lake Abitibi. Most of the Shield country cannot be successfully farmed because of the rocky outcroppings and coarse, acidic soil. Prospects are made worse by the high risk of early frosts. In contrast to southern Ontario, with its warmer climate and superior farm lands, the north never had to endure a major land-use conflict between settler and lumberman. From an early date, the Shield country was looked on principally as a mineral- and timber-rich resource hinterland.[4]

The forests that thrive in Ontario's north belong to two recognized regions.[5] Most of northern Ontario falls within the Boreal Forest Region, the largest of Canada's eight regions. It forms a broad belt across much of the country, from Newfoundland to the Rocky Mountains. White and black spruces are the predominant species, although other conifers such as tamarack, balsam fir, and jack pine are also common, as well as some broadleafed species – white birch, trembling aspen, and balsam poplar. Wherever wet, organic soils are found in the boreal region, black spruce are ubiquitous – unless they have been recently logged off. The heaviest stands are in low-lying areas along the north shore of Lake Superior. In the more northerly areas the trees grow smaller and farther apart, until they peter out at the fringes of the tundra. Jack pines prevail in sandy, well-drained soils throughout the region, as well as on the high, rocky ground along Lake Superior's northern shore.

A smaller proportion of northern Ontario's forests are in the Great Lakes–St Lawrence forest region. Four distinct pockets are visible. In the Sudbury–North Bay area, where smelter fumes have destroyed or reduced growth, hardy pioneer species such as trembling aspen and white birch struggle to survive. To the north, in the Temagami district, white, red, and jack pine are the characteristic species growing in sandy soils in areas where periodic fires prepared the way. In the rugged Algoma district there is a wide mixture of hardwoods and conifers: hence the region's popularity with camera-carrying tourists during the autumn colour season. On the upper slopes of the area's many ridges grow pure hardwood stands. Lower down, on the southern slopes, are forest of eastern white pine; on northern slopes grow yellow birch, white spruce, balsam fir, sugar maple, and eastern white cedar. Finally, in the Rainy River area eastern white and red pine as well as hemlock can be found.

These forest classifications imply a static environment, whereas in reality forests continually undergo changes as a result of competition among species and the impact of disturbances such as fire, wind storms, and harvesting.[6] Furthermore, twentieth-century foresters have intervened in the succession process by introducing silvicultural techniques that speed up the growth of commercially valuable species. In some of the more carefully tended areas, foresters have planted conifer seedlings, removed weed species, sprayed bush, and thinned the second growth. Yet, even where exceptional amounts of time, effort, and capital have been spent, there is no guarantee that the desired species will grow in abundance. Each site has its own specific characteristics that impinge on growth rates and patterns. In northern Ontario, nature is fragile, unpredictable, and constantly changing. The variety of these forests, the variations in terrain, the extremes of climate, and the variability of the weather, together form an environment that has demanded innovation and creativity from those seeking to exploit its wealth.[7]

THE RISE OF LUMBERING

The forest industry's roots reach deep into the province's history. In the late eighteenth century, when loyalists and British immigrants began settling the more accessible and hospitable southern rim of what is now Ontario, they found a plentiful, indeed forbidding, forest cover that had to be cleared before farming could begin. Although the task of clearing appeared enormous to early pioneers, trees provided valuable sources of heat, construction materials, and potash. The forest resources made life more bearable and helped stimulate local commerce.[8]

In the earliest decades of the colony's history, however, Upper Canadian settlers found that there was little external demand for the region's abundant forest resources. The value of their wood could not bear the costs of overseas transportation to the distant timber-importing areas. The take-off of the British North American timber industry occurred as a result of the Napoleonic wars. Following France's defeat at Trafalgar in 1806, Napoleon sought to cripple Great Britain's economy by closing European ports to British shipping. Cut off from nearby Baltic timber which had long supplied their construction and mining industries, as well as the strategically significant shipyards, the British saw wood prices soar. Eager to profit from these circumstances, British timber merchants turned to the colonies, especially New Brunswick and the Ottawa Valley in Upper Canada. Meantime, to finance the war effort, the British government raised the tariff on many items, including timber. As a result, by 1810 colonial timber was substantially protected in British markets. Although the imperial government reduced the tariffs on colonial timber in the 1820s and 1840s, before eliminating them entirely in 1866, the protection had been substantial enough to help establish a permanent British North American timber industry.[9]

Though subject to periodic price fluctuations, British demand for colonial wood generally remained strong throughout the pre-confederation era. In a rapidly urbanizing and industrializing Great Britain, Canadian pine, oak, tamarack, and elm served countless purposes, such as mining props, railway ties, and construction timbers. Strong, durable red pine was in particular demand in the shipyards, while a market for eastern white pine, which is light and easily worked, was found in the moulding industry. And thus, the Canadas and New Brunswick annually shipped vast quantities of square timber and deals.[10]

As staples historians have stressed, the transatlantic timber trade linked the well-established import houses of metropolitan Britain to substantial merchant wholesalers in ports such as Saint John, NB, and Quebec City. They in turn established commercial ties with rafting firms, general merchants, and timber producers operating upstream in the forest hinterlands.[11] Although the cost of timber cutting in the backwoods was not necessarily high and hundreds of producers scrambled to supply the market, production was dominated by a few substantial businessmen. By the early 1850s John Egan, the king of the Ottawa, employed 3,500 men in a hundred establishments and spent $2 million annually on supplies and wages.[12] Like most other Canadian operators, Egan's timber came from crown land. Lumbermen found it convenient to obtain provincially issued timber licences that enabled holders to harvest the timber without having to purchase the land itself.[13]

At about the time of confederation, the trans-Atlantic timber trade began a sharp decline. Baltic competition in open British markets and the collapse of wooden shipbuilding in Great Britain combined to fell a once thriving and giant industry. Fortunately for producers in Ontario's forest industry, however, rising American demand for sawn lumber filled the gap. Forest depletion in areas directly south of the province, and improvements in transportation stimulated the growth of a north-south trade in pine lumber.[14]

Until the late nineteenth century, lumbermen found plenty of pine to harvest in central Ontario, on the fringes of the Canadian Shield. By the 1880s, however, these resources had been largely exhausted, and so operators acquired crown land timber limits in the Shield country to the north. Some lumbermen floated logs long distances to established mills along the Ottawa River and southern Georgian Bay. Others, many of them younger and less financially secure, constructed sawmills along Lake Huron's north shore, in the Shield country itself. A third group, composed of American mill owners, towed booms containing enormous quantities of northern Ontario timber to their big mills in Saginaw, Bay City, and other Michigan centres.[15]

In the last years of the century, conflicts developed among these groups, for Georgian Bay mill owners grew alarmed by the u.s. Dingley tariff of 1897. It protected American importers of logs, while setting tariff rates that barred the entry of Canadian sawn lumber. Fearing they might be compelled to close their mills, western Ontario lumbermen demanded retaliation. However, it was impossible to do so by raising Canadian tariffs because the Dingley tariff provided that any retaliatory foreign duties on logs be automatically added to the tariff against imported lumber. A group of Canadian millowners who were almost wholly dependent on American markets turned to the Ontario government. In 1898 they succeeded in persuading the provincial government to use its authority as a landlord and prevent the export of unprocessed pine sawlogs cut on crown land. This so-called manufacturing condition contained in Ontario timber licences pressured American sawmill owners to stop importing logs and build or purchase mills on the Ontario side. It also set the stage for the provincial government's more interventionist role in the forest industry of the twentieth century.[16]

ASSAULT ON NEW ONTARIO

As the twentieth century began, many Ontario businessmen, politicians, and officials hoped it was the dawn of a new era when the resources of the Shield would fuel the provincial economy and expand investment earnings. 'The resources of New Ontario in soil, minerals, timber, water powers and other raw materials of civilization,' the minister responsible for crown land confidently asserted in 1899, 'are extensive and valuable and quite capable of becoming the home of a hardy, thrifty, and prosperous people, many millions in number.'[17] H.V. Nelles and others have shown how businessmen and their government allies worked hard, if not always scrupulously, to realize the dream. As it turned out, profits derived from the silver veins of Cobalt and the gold fields of Kirkland Lake and the Porcupine proved higher than most ever dreamed possible. The wealth flowed freely – mainly to investors living in Toronto, Montreal, and the eastern United States. In the forest sector the development process lacked the drama of Cobalt, but it was no less vigorous.[18]

During the first decade it was the traditional lumber sector that grew spectacularly. Demand for construction materials soared during the general economic boom, and northern Ontario's forests offered some of the best remaining stands of accessible pine. These factors, along with railway building projects that opened up additional forests, brought American lumbermen to the province. 'I followed the pine trees that were disappearing in Minnesota and came to Canada in 1902,' recalled J.A. Mathieu, as he looked back on more than a half century of lumbering in the Rainy River district.[19] In the years 1896–1910, pine production in the province topped 125 million cubic feet annually (see Figure 1).

Ontario's lumber industry took a severe beating in the economic slump of 1913–15, and recovery was only partial. Few first-rate stands remained in the province, and so investors turned elsewhere. The industry struggled through the 1920s, drawing increasingly on less valuable species such as spruce and hemlock. But the Great Depression brought a nearly total collapse. In the early 1930s the province's red and white pine harvest dropped to less than 10 million cubic feet and total lumber production was valued at under $10 million (see Figure 1). Once thriving sawmill centres became ghost towns.

The provincial lumber industry started to recover during the late 1930s, and soon after World War II a process of reorganization and adjustment was well under way. As producers in the southern United States increasingly supplied Ontario's traditional markets in that country, the industry here became more oriented towards a few centres that were comparatively remote from the new suppliers. By the 1970s Toronto, Detroit, Chicago, and Minneapolis were buying the lion's share of the province's output. In the post-war period, Ontario's more important solid wood product was studs or two-by-fours used in the construction industry. Beginning in the 1950s, however, veneer and plywood production became significant. And in later years, a substantial particleboard sector emerged.[20]

The size of Ontario mills underwent a similar transformation. After the closure of the province's large sawmills in the early 1920s, the average output per mill fell to about one quarter of what it had once been. This held true until the 1970s when companies began building enormous mills, some cutting well in excess of 50 million feet annually. Owners hoped to take advantage of economies of scale, and they automated their mills in a drive to reduce labour, optimize yields, and increase quality control. New equipment such as chipping machines, high-strain band mills, and thin-kerf circular saws enabled companies to profit from cutting small-diameter logs. Full-tree logging methods, where entire trees, rather than logs are brought out of the forest, and new provincial regulations further encouraged lumbermen to make use of smaller trees and less desirable species, and to get more from each tree. Moreover, the growth of a chip market at pulp mills and particleboard plants made it profitable. By the end of the

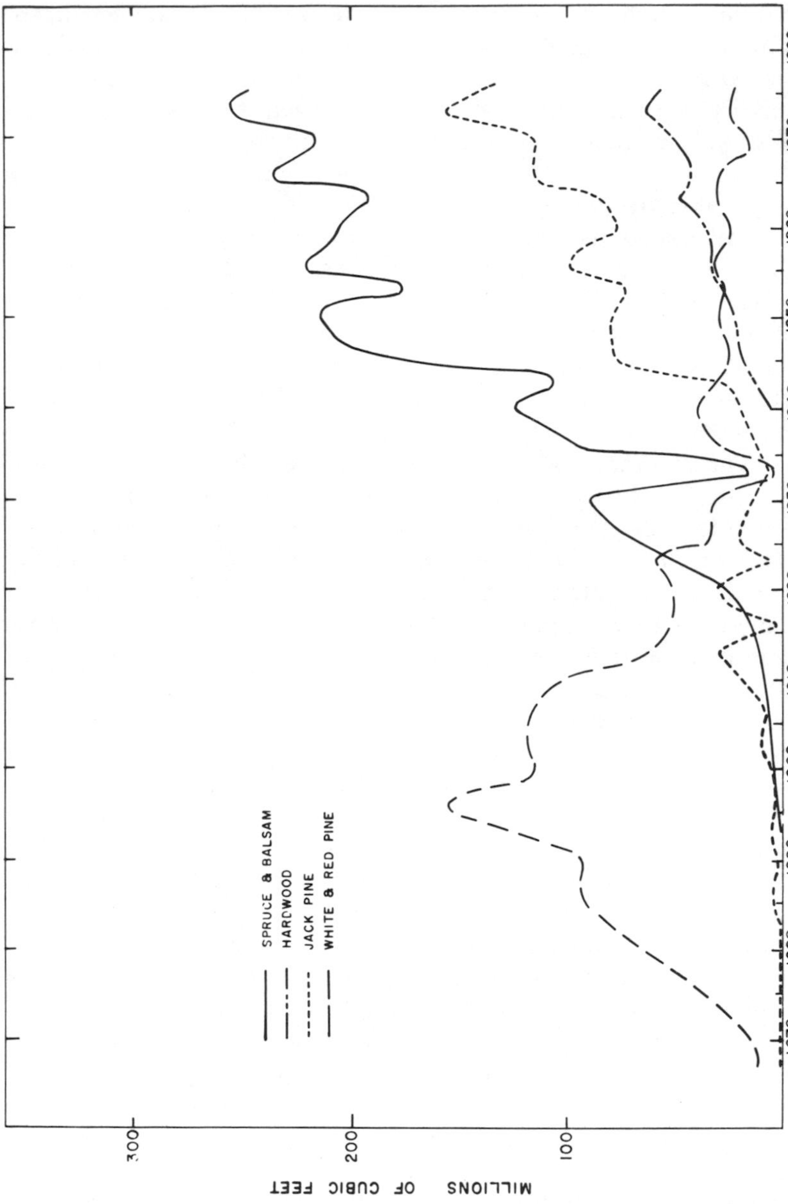

FIGURE 1 Ontario crown land wood harvest 1867–1976. SOURCE: From Clifford E. Ahlgren and Isabel F. Ahlgren, 'The Human Impact on Northern Forest Ecosystems,' in Susan L. Flader ed., *The Great Lakes Forest: An Environmental and Social History* (Minneapolis: University of Minnesota Press 1983)

1970s lumber production was at an all-time high, and huge, integrated forest products firms were processing and selling a growing share of the timber harvest.[21]

More dramatic than twentieth-century developments in the lumber sector has been the emergence of a very substantial northern Ontario pulp and paper industry which supplies newsprint and other products for the huge American market. At the turn of the century, promoters of the New Ontario held great hopes that such an industry would develop. A Department of Crown Lands pamphlet in 1901 insisted: 'Not only has Ontario an almost limitless supply of the right kind of material (which is readily available) but she has also extensive water power and suitable labour, both important factors in the successful manufacture of paper.'[22]

Given the circumstances of the time, such confidence appeared justified. Demand for paper, especially newsprint, was soaring in late nineteenth-century North America. Rapid population growth in the United States, advances in literacy, and the expansion of newspaper advertising contributed towards an 80 per cent increase in American newspaper circulation in the period 1870–1909. By the late 1890s, many U.S. newsprint mills were running short of cheap, convenient supplies of pulpwood. In the mean time Canada was producing more pulpwood and woodpulp than its mills could absorb and exporting the difference to the States. Not surprisingly, American pulp and paper producers began to consider Ontario forests as a major source of supply for their mills. Some also began to investigate the possibility of constructing mills in northern Ontario, a proposition with obvious attractions given the savings involved in transporting manufactured pulp and paper products rather than heavy, bulky logs. Abundant water supplies and hydroelectric sites in the north added further inducements. So, too, did Ontario government policies that included generous long-term leases to crown land timber and a 1900 order in council which extended the export restrictions to pulpwood cut on crown land.[23]

The beginnings of a northern Ontario pulp and paper industry were made at the turn of the century. To the irrepressible American entrepreneur Francis Clergue goes credit for constructing a pulp mill that was to become the model on which others were built. In 1892 the Ontario government granted him a twenty-one-year lease for cutting rights to fifty square miles of crown forests. Using the lease as collateral, Clergue was able to persuade American investors to provide the capital for building a pulp mill beside the rapids of the St Mary's River at Sault Ste Marie. The mill began producing groundwood pulp in 1895. Three years later the Sturgeon Falls Pulp Company started grinding at its mill on Lake Nipissing and in 1905 the Spanish River Pulp and Paper Company went into production at Espanola.[24]

Boosters of the New Ontario found this rate of expansion disappointing and blamed U.S. paper tariffs for the poor results. Fortunately for Canadians, they had a powerful ally in the lobby of U.S. newspaper publishers, which mobilized against the tariff. In 1911 Congress reduced the tariff on newsprint, and two years later the Underwood tariff entirely eliminated such duties.[25] These developments triggered a rapid expansion of Canadian pulp making and newsprint production, as existing mills increased their output and new ones went into production. In northern Ontario large plants began to rise at Dryden in 1911, Iroquois Falls in 1912, and Smooth Rock Falls in 1918. While the Abitibi Pulp and Paper Company's plant at Iroquois Falls was under construction, the Ontario government was enthusiastic about the enormous scale of operations designed to 'produce 150 tons of pulp and 200 tons of paper every 24 hours.' Not only would the Company 'give employment to from 1,500 to 1,800 men,' but it would also 'give contracts for taking out pulpwood and buy wood from . . . settlers.' The appearance of these plants marked the beginnings of paper-mill towns, resource communities heavily dependent on the fluctuating fortunes of a single industry and the payroll of one firm.[26]

Canada's newsprint production, which in 1913 stood at 350,000 tons, soared during World War I. By 1920 it had reached 876,000 tons. Prices rose even faster. Newsprint, which sold at the Iroquois Falls mill for $37 a ton in 1916, fetched $103.50 in early 1921. Spot prices on the open market topped $300 a ton, as publishers sought to meet their readers' thirst for news and their advertisers' hunger for space. In late 1920 the bubble burst. A sharp recession set in, newsprint prices tumbled, and for a few months in 1921 several of the largest mills closed.[27]

Business soon picked up. During the mid-1920s capitalists in the United States made huge direct investments in Canadian plants that were thrown up in response to the surging American demand for newsprint. By 1926, 13 per cent of all U.S. direct investment in Canadian manufacturing was in the wood and paper sector, and approximately four-fifths of the newsprint produced in Canada was exported to the United States.[28] Each new mill – at Fort William, Port Arthur, Kapuskasing, and Kenora – represented a large investment, with funds raised through bond issues and stock offerings. Promoters expected the new mills would be paid for by their future earnings, calculated on the assumption that the plants would run at close to full capacity and that prices would hold steady. However, with every new paper machine installed, prices slid.[29]

The industry tried two approaches to ward off catastrophe. Companies joined together to form cartels. But each time this was tried at least one firm proved willing to undercut cartel prices. A second approach was corporate consolidation; executives hoped to carve up the market and fix prices. Despite such efforts, the depression brought disaster. Mills operated at less than half capacity and prices plummeted. This combination proved devastating for an industry burdened with extremely high fixed capital commitments. The companies' heavy dependence on bonds and preferred shares made for unbearable debt loads. Firms fought viciously for the remaining markets, but the industry could not survive in its existing form. Big corporations like Abitibi and Great Lakes fell into receivership. By 1932 companies with more than half the industry's rated capacity had passed into receivership or undergone substantial reorganization.[30]

In the late 1930s the Ontario and Quebec governments enjoyed some success in stabilizing the industry. By delegating authority to a newsprint producers' cartel, the provinces helped the big corporations to save themselves. The Ontario government also played an active role in reorganizing the bankrupt Great Lakes Paper, and in the 1940s, Abitibi. By the late 1930s such measures, along with improved demand, brought some growth and stability to the troubled industry. However, it took the stimulus of war production and hopes for post-war expansion to trigger substantial improvements in its fortunes.[31]

Towards the end of World War II newsprint prices began to rise sharply, and by 1948 they had reached levels not experienced since the mid-1920s. Canadian mills produced at an all-out pace. Although firms built few new mills in eastern Canada, they updated old equipment and installed new paper machines. In Ontario capacity rose by 49 per cent between 1950 and 1959.[32] Predictably, as all this new equipment came on stream, operating hours were cut back and real prices of newsprint declined although only slightly between 1962 and the early 1970s. The industry's problems in Ontario, however, were not merely the result of increases in capacity; they had more to do with a massive increase in the newsprint production in the southern United States. Operators there enjoyed significant cost advantages – dense, accessible, fast-growing forests, cheaper labour, and efficient new mills.[33] During the 1950s Ontario had managed to maintain its one-fifth share of American newsprint markets, but throughout the 1960s the province lost ground and was increasingly confined to the Midwest. Nevertheless, the total capacity in Ontario newsprint mills rose by about two-thirds in the period 1950–69.[34]

Much more spectacular than post-war developments in newsprint was the rise of Ontario's kraft sector. During the inter-war years a revolution in shipping and packaging had created a great demand for coarse, brown kraft papers in the United States. Until World War II southern U.S. producers and Scandinavian exporters had supplied these rapidly growing markets. Ontario had but one kraft mill, at Dryden. During World War II, however, Scandinavian supplies had been disrupted and U.S. kraft pulp users had encouraged the development of more reliable North American sources. In the post-war period six new kraft mills were established in northern Ontario. Despite stiff competition from British Columbia and southern U.S. sources, Ontario mills proved able to compete in the Midwest. By 1980 the province's kraft pulp exports had risen to a level forty times that of 1950, and kraft pulp production had become almost as important to the northern Ontario economy as newsprint.[35]

CHANGING STRUCTURES AND NEW CHALLENGES

From the start, northern Ontario's pulp and paper mills represented far more substantial investments than sawmills, and that pattern persisted. Statistics from the mid-1920s illustrate the relative size and importance of these two sectors in the provincial economy. In terms of the volume of timber cut, the pulp and paper industry had quickly outpaced the pine lumber business. And though there were many more sawmills than pulp plants, the latter had more men employed, produced more valuable goods, and represented a much larger capital investment. In 1924, for instance, Ontario's 720 sawmills employed 8,828 people, while the province's 46 pulp and paper mills provided jobs for 9,874. Ontario sawmills produced goods valued at a total of $38,285,598, while gross value of production in the pulp and paper sector was nearly two-and-a-half times that amount. Most striking is the difference in levels of capital investment in the two sectors: the province's sawmills represented an investment of $53,039,659 while the equivalent figure for the pulp and paper sector was $160,766,866. This overall pattern remained unchanged for many years (see Table 1).

The two branches of the forest industry also had contrasting mill production techniques and organization structures. In the middle decades of the nineteenth century, Ontario's lumbermen had introduced a form of the continuous-flow production system in the big sawmills. Yet the transition was not very dramatic, for sawmilling equipment simply replaced manual operations and maximum cutting speeds were soon attained. As Alfred Chandler points out in his classic study of business organization,

TABLE 1
Ontario sawmill and pulp and paper industries

Year	Estab-lishments	Capital Investment ($)	Employees[1]	Value of Products ($)	Rank[2]
1922					
Pulp and paper	39	133,749,364	8,542	62,998,985	3
Sawmill	607	43,086,333	8,076	30,477,737	9
1924					
Pulp and paper	46	60,766,886	9,874	106,141,210	4
Sawmill	720	53,039,659	8,828	38,285,598	10
1926					
Pulp and paper	45	167,788,862	10,312	80,960,073	4
Sawmill	676	50,578,550	7,640	30,875,908	12
1928					
Pulp and paper	43	220,281,502	10,993	29,718,660	5
Sawmill	923	48,963,426	10,948	31,422,230	19
1930					
Pulp and paper	41	221,466,576	10,211	68,036,733	5
Sawmill	874	46,486,317	9,239	24,714,168	23
1932					
Pulp and paper	38	190,427,742	7,863	44,027,587	3
Sawmill					
1934					
Pulp and paper	37	175,728,071	8,466	40,716,443	5
Sawmill	765	16,755,696	3,881	9,812,710	36
1936					
Pulp and paper	34	170,720,720	9,145	59,166,958	5
Sawmill	710	18,405,850	4,785	13,068,688	35
1938					
Pulp and paper	37	174,219,617	9,637	60,946,197	6
Sawmill	670	19,940,747	4,915	14,432,476	34

SOURCE: Canada, Dominion Bureau of Statistics, *Census of Industry* 1922-38

1 Does not include woods employees
2 Rank of pulp and paper or sawmills in terms of total value of production and in
  comparison with other Ontario manufacturing industries

The Visible Hand, this kind of mechanical industry was not at the leading
edge of the managerial revolution. He explains that since the speed of

production was limited, and the energy used did little more than power the machines, 'the requirements for coordination and control remained relatively simple.'[36]

By contrast, in Ontario's pulp and paper mills, production processes and organization were of another order entirely. The application of chemicals and enormous quantities of hydroelectric power resulted in high-speed, high-volume production. In 1927, for instance, 44 pulp and paper mills consumed thirty-two times as much electricity as 642 sawmills.[37] As Chandler explains, in this type of modern mass-production industry, the increased 'speed and volume of production put a premium on developing plant designs to assure the maximum use of equipment' thus ensuring 'a steady and smooth flow of the maximum amount of materials through the production process.'[38] In such industries, firms developed managerial hierarchies to coordinate the flow of material goods and became characterized by comparatively complex managerial structures. To use Chandler's typology, while most twentieth-century lumber firms still resembled the traditional enterprise, pulp and paper corporations were modern business enterprises. Even during the late 1970s, in dozens of lumber firms, the owner still oversaw production and distribution. For decades these responsibilities had been carried out by salaried managers in the pulp and paper corporations.

The distinctions between the two sectors only began to blur in the 1970s with the emergence of huge, integrated forest-products corporations that produced lumber as well as pulp and paper. In 1969 E.B. Eddy Forest Products, a firm with roots in the Ottawa lumber trade of the nineteenth century and the pulp business in the early twentieth century, purchased the Espanola pulp and paper mill and began operating a sawmill next door. The Great Lakes Paper Company started up a particleboard mill in 1975, and later the firm's name was changed to the more appropriate Great Lakes Forest Products. Most dramatically of all, in 1974 Abitibi obtained a controlling interest in Price Company, once a giant of the Quebec timber trade. The two firms were fully amalgamated in 1978–9 under the name Abitibi-Price, Inc. Integration increased in 1979–80 when Great Lakes Forest Products was purchased by the giant Canadian Pacific empire and when Olympia and York Investments of Toronto gained a controlling interest in Abitibi-Price.[39]

Some of the big new firms were branch plants of American-based multinationals. During the late 1970s this group included Kimberly-Clark of Neenah, Wis., with northern Ontario mills at Terrace Bay and Kapuskasing; Boise Cascade of Boise, Idaho, with mills at Fort Frances and Kenora;

and American Can of Greenwich, Conn., with its mill at Marathon. In the 1970s it was estimated that foreign, mainly American, interests owned about 44 per cent of the Canadian forest industry, and in Ontario, land licensed to pulp and paper firms was split equally between Canadian and non-Canadian firms.[40] Large Canadian-based corporations in the forest products field of the north included Abitibi-Price of Toronto (Ontario mills at Thunder Bay, Sault Ste Marie, Iroquois Falls, and Smooth Rock Falls); Domtar of Montreal (Red Rock); Consolidated-Bathurst of Montreal (Dryden); E.B. Eddy Products of Ottawa (Espanola); Great Lakes Forest Products of Thunder Bay (Thunder Bay and Dryden); and MacMillan-Bloedel of Vancouver (Sturgeon Falls). In a class by themselves were Spruce Falls Power and Paper Company (Kapuskasing), controlled by the publishers of the New York *Times*, and Ontario Paper Company (Heron Bay and south at Thorold), owned by the publishers of the *Chicago Tribune*.[41]

The corporate activity of the late 1970s coincided with widening doubts about the viability of Canada's forest sector. Various government-sponsored studies suggested that the future of the Ontario industry was not promising.[42] One study prepared in 1980 by Lakehead University, Thunder Bay, for the Ontario Royal Commission on the Northern Environment argued that existing mills faced severe cost disadvantages in comparison with major competitors elsewhere. In the newsprint sector, total labour costs in the 1970s were unusually high because of old mill equipment which required significantly more labour input per ton of newsprint than the newer mills of the southern United States. The average cost of transporting newsprint from mill to market was also higher for the Ontario producers. And in both the newsprint and kraft pulp sectors, wood costs were far greater in northern Ontario than in either British Columbia or the southern United States. The study recommended that equipment be modernized, but it warned against increasing capacity since wood supplies would be inadequate.[43]

Indeed, there was a growing concern that wood shortages, high wood costs, and obsolescent equipment would result in a decline of the Ontario forest industry. A federal study in 1978 summarized the problems confronting large sectors of the Canadian pulp and paper industry: 'Accelerated modernization and rationalization programmes as well as favourable forest management currently underway in Europe, the favourable economics of locating new capacity in the United States, and the concerted drive to develop the forest resources of the developing countries.' In the 1980s, businessmen, politicians, foresters, and journalists increasingly drew public attention to the environmental and economic crisis developing in Canada's forests. 'Years of complacency and shortsightedness are now coming home to roost,' declared Royal Bank of Canada President Rowland Frazee in 1980; 'already there are wood shortages in some parts of Canada.' Books intended for wide audiences exposed the problems. In *Cut and Run* Jamie Swift explored the development of what he refers to as 'an institutionalized lack of concern for all the benefits [the forest] has to offer.' In his *Heritage Lost* Donald MacKay set out in non-technical language the positions of professional foresters. As this crescendo of comment and criticism made clear, enormous challenges lay before the industry.[44]

The material environment of the north and the expansion of forest enterprises are only the beginning of this study of the forest industry. The men in the field – bushworkers and bosses alike – actually produce the raw materials on which the industry depends. Woodsworkers, their supervisors, and managers surmounted the problems posed by the varied terrain and forests of the Shield. As employees of family lumber firms or giant corporations, they had to work within the existing structures. When the industry went through periods of expansion or contraction, logging operators and their crews felt the consequences directly and had to adjust to changes.

2

A seasonal labour force, 1900–1945

Throughout the first half of the twentieth century, production processes in the Ontario forest industry were a curious hybrid. The organization of work in the province's larger sawmills was characteristic of industries transformed in the nineteenth century by the first Industrial Revolution, which was shaped by coal, iron, and steam. Well before the turn of the century, these sawmills had relied on steam to power giant circular saws and other pieces of equipment that moved the wood through the mill virtually untouched by human hands. Almost from its start, the northern Ontario pulp and paper industry had been a modern science-based industry, using the latest technological and chemical advances developed in corporate laboratories. The industry was affected early by the second Industrial Revolution which saw large corporations experiment with innovative techniques and create the new mass-production industries in steel, auto, chemicals, electrical goods, as well as pulp and paper. And yet in their logging operations, even as late as 1945, lumber companies and pulp and paper firms clung to time-honoured methods that depended heavily on learning-by-doing, the strength of men and horses, and natural factors, such as the friction-reducing qualities of snow and the flushing power of the annual spring run-off.[1]

Here, then, is a striking example of what scholars examining other industries have called combined and uneven development. By recognizing the unevenness of development among different industries, different sectors of industries, and even within single firms, historians have revised conventional interpretations of industrialization that generalized too widely about distinct stages of development.[2] Certainly, within the Ontario forest industry of the early twentieth century, the secondary manufacturing sector was far more technologically advanced than the primary sector which, woods officials frequently complained, remained in a primitive state. In 1918 one manager insisted that, 'Medieval methods must be improved to put the woods end on a scientific basis, comparable with the mill.'[3] Thirty years later the problem remained.

A SEASONAL INDUSTRY

Throughout the first half of this century, Ontario logging operations were conducted overwhelmingly out of winter camps. To be sure, a small proportion of the cut was made by settlers who supplied the industry from their own woodlots or homesteads.[4] Nearly three-quarters of the total harvest, however, was the work of seasonally employed wage earners. Each fall, bosses would hire men, send them to camps scattered throughout the forest, and the employees would spend the fall and winter felling trees, sawing logs, and hauling them out of the woods. Since the early nineteenth century, Ontario lumber firms had been using this system, and it was adopted by the new pulp and paper firms when they began their woods operations.[5] Even the biggest firms, which hired as many as 2,000 bushworkers each year, relied on a decentralized camp structure. They simply divided their men into groups of 50 to 125 and sent them off to the many camps spread throughout the companies' vast timber limits.

Ontario logging operators found production costs were lowest when they took advantage of nature. It was far cheaper to house workers in rough, temporary camps within walking distance of work sites than to build expensive roads or railways into ever-moving cutting areas. Crude, stump-filled roads were adequate for transporting logs from the backwoods. In the heart of winter, when these rough roads were covered with snow and ice, they became slick surfaces over which horses could pull sleighs heavily laden with logs. In springtime, even small creeks could carry large quantities of logs when river drivers effectively marshalled the run-off.

Because of the industry's dependence on nature, the demand for woodsworkers was highly concentrated in the fall and winter when the most labour-intensive logging activities took place. According to figures collected by the Dominion Bureau of Statistics, in 1920 the number of Ontario woods employees on wages peaked in February when 19,099 worked in the forest, and fell to a low in July of 6,551. The average monthly employment from April to August of the same year was 7,430, whereas the average for September to March was nearly two-and-a-half times the summer figure. A quarter century later, a Canadian Pulp and Paper Association study found that the number of regular employees in Ontario pulpwood camps was three times higher in November than in April. The study also noted that the Canadian logging industry had a larger seasonal fluctuation in employment than farming or construction – industries well known for their sharp seasonal variations in labour demand.[6]

Fortunately for employers, there was usually an abundant supply of labour available in Canada during the late fall and winter, when outdoor activities in farming, construction, and various other industries were curtailed. In the pre-industrial economy of the first half of the nineteenth century, winter had spelled disaster for thousands of labourers thrown out of their jobs on the farms, wharves, and transportation projects of British North America.[7] Despite the ever-quickening pace of industrialization in post-confederation Ontario, winter unemployment persisted.[8] Yet the desperate plight of the jobless in winter amounted to an opportunity for woods employers and reinforced their commitment to traditional logging techniques. With the notable exception of the early years of the depression, in nearly every winter before 1945, operators in Ontario offered logging jobs to some 20,000 to 30,000 men (see Appendix 2).

PART-TIME WAGE-EARNERS AND PROFESSIONAL BUSHWORKERS

Employers drew on three major sources of labour. First, they turned to the seasonally unemployed general labourers, many of whom were recent immigrants. The early twentieth-century boom that saw the west settled and northern resources developed attracted hundreds of thousands of immigrants to Canada. Already uprooted by demographic and economic changes in Europe, and drawn via the commerce of migration into an international labour market, thousands of British and European men and women arrived in search of jobs that would permit them to save money, and perhaps fulfil the dream of owning a farm in Canada or back home. Canadian immigration policy was ostensibly aimed at attracting agriculturalists. But in practice thousands of European immigrants became industrial workers, a situation applauded by influential Canadian industrialists – especially employers in the labour-intensive resource industries. They welcomed a large and hence cheap supply of labour.[9] Most of these newcomers were classified as unskilled. By the 1930s, unskilled workers made up 40 per cent of Canada's labour force, forming the largest occupational class in the country.[10]

In the summer there was usually a comparatively strong demand for labourers on the farms, docks, construction sites, and railways. The bunkhouse men travelled from the mining towns of the Kootenays to the track-laying projects of the Ontario Shield country in search of work. But with the onset of cold weather, most labourers in outdoor occupations found themselves jobless. The thousands who had too few savings to return to Europe drifted into the cities of Canada where they joined others in a desperate struggle to survive.[11] Canada's first reasonably accurate unemployment statistics, which date from the 1920s, indicate that the number of unemployed doubled or tripled between August and December of each year.[12] Before World War II the jobless in Canada had no government unemployment insurance scheme to fall back on; charity was demeaning and the handouts irregular. It was in winter, when Canada's unskilled workers were at their most vulnerable, that logging operators needed the most men. Here lay a huge and easily exploited labour pool on which operators could, and did, draw heavily.

The second source of seasonal labour for Ontario logging operators was agriculturalists. Large numbers of farmers, their sons, and their hired hands needed wages in winter when there were few ways to earn income on farms. In the nineteenth century it had been common for the sons of southern Ontario farmers to seek work in the lumber camps each winter. In the twentieth century fewer young men left prosperous southern Ontario farms for logging jobs, but significant numbers of agricultural labourers from the Prairies sought employment in Ontario's logging camps. In the early years of this century, winter logging was a way to earn cash for homestead improvements. By about the beginning of World War I, however, many who migrated from the west were permanent wage-earners who worked seasonally in agriculture and lumbering. Thousands of agriculturalists also travelled to logging camps from the more marginal farms of the Shield country, eastern Ontario and Quebec. They were part of Canada's widespread agro-forest economy.[13]

On the surface, logging appears to have offered opportunities for struggling farmers, an interpretation long stressed by historians. In fact, however, many of these part-time wage-earners were caught up in a structure of capitalist under-development that brought them few rewards.[14] Employers drew on this seasonal labour force as they required, and then left the jobless to fend for themselves in the summer. Winter wages helped these men and their dependents survive, but they were inadequate to maintain families throughout the year. By offering woods jobs, forest companies encouraged people to remain on their marginal farms. In this way, operators may well have helped to perpetuate a system that entailed endless toil and poverty on the treadmill of the agro-forest economy. The consequences of logging on farm communities need further study. It seems likely, however, that the effects may have been similar to the kind of impoverishment Allan Greer has found in the districts of Lower Canada from which seasonal fur trade labourers were recruited.[15] From the point of view of woods employers, this system offered obvious advantages, though no doubt many operators remained oblivious of the wider consequences as they eagerly drew on a seemingly bottomless pool of farm labour.

A third source of labour consisted of so-called professional bushworkers who depended on logging wages as their chief or only source of income. In the lumber sector, many men would work in a sawmill during the summer, when most of the sawing took place, and then find jobs in the same company's logging camps in the winter. The neat dovetailing of manpower needs in sawmills and logging operations can be seen in Dominion Bureau of Statistics data. For instance, in January 1919 some 18,712 worked in Ontario's woods operations and only 3,078 in sawmills; in July of the same year, 6,551 men were active in woods or river operations, but 14,085 found jobs in mills.[16] Although the year-round employees enjoyed comparative job security, they faced a trade-off. Such employees remained constantly in the shadow of the company, many of them living in company houses in summer and company camps in winter. Ken Collins, who worked during the 1920s in the woods operations of Indian Lake Lumber Company of Osaquan, Ont., recalls how he rejected this kind of domination: 'I could not see myself becoming a permanent member of a community that was ruled and dominated by the lumber company and where practically every aspect of one's life had to have the approval and sanction of the Company.' Collins left Osaquan and sought work elsewhere.[17]

In other sectors of the forest industry this seasonal dovetailing of labour did not take place. During the boom years at the beginning of the twentieth century, choppers wielding broadaxes hewed millions of railway ties each winter. No further processing was required, and so there were few summer jobs in this sector. Pulpmills usually ran steadily throughout the year and were manned by more or less permanent employees, many of whom had highly specialized skills. Seasonal bushworkers stood apart from the higher-status, sedentary mill work force. Some professional bushmen, as they were known in the industry, found work on the river drive, but labour demands for the drive were not large. Abitibi provided summer jobs at fire-ranging for their camp foremen, timekeepers, and camp clerks – staff who were harder to replace and whose loyalty was essential to efficient operations.[18]

During the slow season, however, most pulp cutters failed to find employment in the industry. Some rejoined their families and survived on winter savings and the produce of their gardens. Others descended on the boarding houses, brothels, and bars of cities such as Sault Ste Marie and Port Arthur. When money ran out, they would head for a shack in the woods. Some lived in lonely isolation. Others clubbed together. A Jesuit missionary who worked among the lumberjacks of Algoma explained that it was customary for some men to form 'un groupe, se procurent quelques provisions, de la farine, des fèvres, du lard, du thé, du tabac ... et vont camper sur le bord d'un lac. S'ils trouvent un vieux *shack* abandonné, ils le réparent, le nettoient un peu et s'y installent tant bien que mal.'[19] These men were as desperate for work each winter as the bunkhouse men and the struggling agriculturalists.

It is difficult to gauge the relative importance of each of the three major sources of woods labour. It is harder still to determine whether recruitment patterns differed from district to district and to trace changes over time. Before the end of World War II, it appears there was only one attempt to measure the Ontario woods labour force and that study examined only the pulpwood sector. In 1941–2 the Pulpwood Committee of the Canadian Pulp and Paper Association prepared a Woods Labour Inventory Report, based on some 25,000 employment records cards, as well as questionnaires sent to operators.[20] Although wartime labour shortages had already begun to occur in 1941–2, and not all operators fully answered the questionnaire, industry spokesmen believed the report's fundamental findings to be sound. It showed that 50 per cent of Ontario's woods labour force were residents of the province, and the great majority of these workers – some 85 per cent – worked in the district in which they lived. Of the 10,000 workers who came to Ontario from other provinces, 4,600 were from Quebec, 2,800 from Saskatchewan and 2,200 from Manitoba, with small contingents from each of the other provinces. Farmers or farm workers made up about 50 per cent of the total labour force. As the report noted, another 20 per cent came from 'other industries such as building and highway construction where employment opportunities are low in the winter months.' The remaining 30 per cent were classed as professional woodsworkers. Unfortunately, the lack of any similar studies of the lumber sector and for any other year makes it impossible to draw strong conclusions from these statistics, but they provide at least a rough guide.

Throughout the early decades of the twentieth century, when management commentators discussed the sources of woods labour, they often lamented the decline of the old, reliable farmer-lumberjack and the industry's growing reliance on general labourers, especially foreign-speaking immigrants. 'It will not be long,' prophesied the *Canada Lumberman* in 1908, 'before the good old camp days are gone, when a lumberjack took pride in his work, and the camp will be manned by foreigners who have no interest in their work and never become expert.' In the early boom years commentators believed that increasing job opportunities in other industries were drawing men who otherwise would have found their way to the lumber camps. As the *Canada Lumberman* complained in 1903, too many good men 'prefer remaining in the bosom of their families, providing they can get steady work, to undergoing voluntary exile in the shanties.' As a result, the idle class had 'stepped in eagerly to fill up the gaps, only to drop out, many of them at the first opportunity.' At the 1907 general meeting of the Ontario Lumbermen's Association, the president stated that the deterioration in labour quality had been 'largely caused by the native labour going west and taking up farms and having been replaced largely by foreign labour, which you all know is very unsatisfactory in the woods.'[21]

Later observers blamed World War I for the changes. 'When the lumberjacks came out of the bush this spring,' declared the *Canada Lumberman* in 1916, 'they were met all over the country by recruiting officers who offered strong inducements to enlist. The result is that large numbers of sturdy choppers and teamsters have joined the colors.' And after the Armistice, observers explained that woodsmen remained in short supply because during the war shantymen had 'gained a thirst for city life.' The Board of Home Missions of the Methodist Church confidently attributed the changed supply of woods labour to another outgrowth of the war, prohibition. A report cited one lumberman who maintained that 'in the old whiskey days,' the drunken lumberjack was compelled to return to the woods after 'some hell-hound got his roll.' But now that he was 'emancipated from the slavery of liquor,' he had a year-round job, lived with his wife and family, and had become a respectable citizen.[22]

Whatever the reasons for the perceived decline in traditional sources of labour, by the 1920s operators were no longer merely lamenting their increasing dependence on foreign-speaking immigrants, they were vigorously recruiting such newcomers. Officials of the Canadian Lumbermen's Association kept the federal Immigration Branch abreast of the needs of the industry, and they also recruited directly in Europe. For instance, 1,042 woodsmen from eastern Europe were among new arrivals at Quebec between 1 Sept. and 30 Nov. 1923, some 245 of them destined for the McFadden Lumber Company near Blind River, Ont., and 160 for the Hope Lumber camps.

Far more immigrants found their way to the logging camps without this kind of direct employer assistance. But the addition of several hundred men at one time to an employer's labour supply certainly compensated for any labour shortages. Moreover, it helped discipline other workers. In December 1923 the *Canada Lumberman* explained that lumber camp operators had been troubled by hold-outs who refused to accept jobs until employers offered higher wages. In response, operators, 'who had exhausted about all the patience they owned,' succeeded in importing several hundred 'big-boned and husky' Poles. Not only were these men apparently quite capable in the bush, but their presence paid off in other ways: 'with the arrival of the importations, the lumberjacks, who had previously been inclined to hold out, reconsidered in many instances their prospects. In not a few cases, the made-over plans led them to the employment offices or the shipping boss and they joined the procession to the woods.'[24] Unwittingly, immigrants served as powerful ammunition in the operators' battle to man their camps cheaply.

A MIXTURE OF TONGUES

The ethnic composition of the woods work force in Ontario reflected the diverse sources of labour recruitment. 'If we are to stop in the average logging camp today,' observed an American visitor to northern Ontario in 1913, 'we would find a mixture of tongues – Pollocks, Hungarians, our Canadian friend with his rich colonial accent – our friend Baptiste is also there.' Indeed, in any year after the turn of the century, visitors to camps located anywhere in northern Ontario could expect to find European immigrants. In the northwest, recent arrivals from Scandinavia and Finland were more numerous than in the northeast, where French Canadians predominated. In 1929 Abitibi reported that the work force at Iroquois Falls was 52.1 per cent French Canadian, 8.19 per cent English Canadian, 12.7 per cent Scandinavian, and 26.3 per cent middle European.[25]

Some camps were entirely manned by members of one ethnic group. Finnish pulpwood contractors near Port Arthur and along the Algoma Central Railway tended to hire their own countrymen, who preferred to work with men who spoke the same language or shared a similar background. But in most camps there could be heard 'a mixture of tongues.' Certainly the reports of third-year Forestry students from the University of Toronto who, beginning in 1908–9, annually visited Ontario logging camps, indicate that ethnic diversity prevailed among bushworkers. For instance, a 1921 student report on the Shevlin-Clark Lumber Company camps near Fort Frances categorized the labour force as being 10 per cent Swedish, 20 per cent English and French Canadian, and 70 per cent 'Russian, Austrian, Polish and Central European.'[26]

Operators tended to have preferences for certain ethnic groups. Although such attitudes were ostensibly based on the employers' knowledge of the characteristic work habits of each group, they in fact reflect the widespread prejudices and perceptions of the era. The Anglo-Canadian's hierarchy of preferred immigrant groups closely resembled the operators' preference ladder for woodsworkers. At the top were the whites – English and French Canadians, as well as northern Europeans. Canadians of British descent dominated supervisory positions and the better-paid, specialized jobs such as blacksmithing and tending the camp's horses. It paid to know English, to be familiar with the system, and to share the ethnic background of the boss.[27]

Most woods operators believed French Canadians made the best woodsworkers on account of their skills and docility. One woods supervisor explained: 'with his long experience in the shanties and his aptitude for doing all kinds of work for which he has to use an axe, saw and horse, such as clearing land, making firewood, building roads, his winters spent in the shanties with his parents, has given the French Canadian woodsman a training which places him among the best of Eastern Canada.' As an added bonus, managers agreed that French Canadians required nothing luxurious in the way of accommodation and 'eats generally everything put on the table.'[28]

Woods managers ranked Finns among the best producers and cutters in the logging camps. While not as energetic as the French Canadians, Finns were considered to be more steady and consistent. Studies also showed that Finns were better at cleaning up their cutting area, which facilitated subsequent steps in the logging process, and that they kept their camps tidier. Nevertheless, managers held that there were drawbacks to hiring too many Finns – they were 'very susceptible to all labour movements and untrustworthy where they are in a majority.' Operators also complained that Finns used too much butter and sugar, and cost 15 per cent more to feed than French Canadians.[29]

Other European groups had less distinct reputations. Scandinavians were highly regarded partly because of their physical characteristics and partly on account of the woods experience they brought with them from their homelands. On the other hand, it was reported that eastern Europeans were 'very clumsy in their first attempts in ... bush operations.' Bosses usually assigned them heavy, unpopular tasks, such as road clearing and log piling, at least until the newcomers had gained Canadian bush experience. Such tasks fit with prevalent stereotypes. Few southern Europeans toiled in the bush, with the exception of Italians who sometimes worked for contractors in charge of constructing logging roads and camp buildings.[30]

At the bottom of the pile were native peoples. 'They will work for a time and then take a rest while spending the money they have earned,' said the *Canada Lumberman* in 1911. 'There is no telling how long an Indian will stay on a job.' Yet on river drives the Indian's skills gained him a high reputation. Certainly the reports of the federal Indian Affairs Branch indicate that men from many bands throughout northern Ontario sought winter jobs in the logging camps.[31]

Undoubtedly, workers in the less-preferred groups often found it more difficult to get good bush jobs. They could only hope that the demand for bush labour would be great enough to compel operators to hire anyone they could find. Their experiences, however, have gone largely unrecorded. An exception is the case of a Swedish-speaking Finn who later recalled how hard it had been for Finns to find work in northern Ontario during the 1930s, when jobs were scarce and his countrymen had a reputation for labour agitation. But because he could speak Swedish, he was able to pose as a Swede and secure a job.[32] Not all Finns could do this. One of the chief reasons anti-communist Finns formed the Loyal Finns of Canada in 1931 was to make it clear to Canadian employers that not all Finns were radicals.[33]

RECRUITMENT

Recruiting a woods labour force each fall and winter was a huge undertaking. Thousands of men had to be hired and transported to the camps. Even though most years there was an abundant labour supply, the sheer size of operations made the job a daunting prospect for woods managers. In 1928 Abitibi estimated that only 10 per cent of its work force could be expected to return the following year.[34] The company's Labour Bureau had to find several thousand workers annually – many a corporate headache resulted from problems encountered in assembling a labour force.

Logging operators recruited labour in a number of different ways.

Often the employer needed to do little, for bushworkers in need of work would seek out the foreman, personnel officer, employment agent, or whoever else was responsible for hiring. Sometimes foremen demanded bribes from the woodsworkers before they would sign men on for the season. The 1916 report of the Ontario Commission on Unemployment noted that fraud was a common occurrence.[35]

Of course, bribery was not evident everywhere; indeed, in many operations the core of the camp crew consisted of the foreman's personal following. He would offer work year after year to men he knew and favoured, or whose work he admired. In small and medium-size firms, the manager relied heavily on his foreman to find workers and make the necessary arrangements for their arrival in the logging woods. A letter dated 19 Aug. 1898 and addressed to Thomas Kirby, a foreman living in the off season in Parry Sound, illustrates how much the woods superintendent of the Collins Inlet Lumber Company relied on his foreman:

I would like to have you here with your men not later than next Thursday the 25th or earlier if possible. Get about forty men now, & we will enlarge to fifty men a little later or when you get going good. There is several men here that will go in. Don't pay any fares unless you charge the parties up with same. Woods will be able to go blacksmith for you. Try and get a good Cook. Men are very plentiful. If you can get a handy man that can build a dam bring him along. Wages will be governed by what is paid other places for men, so we will arrange them the same as other years.[36]

Hiring was more complicated in the big firms. Wherever possible they relied on the foreman or jobber and his personal following. But increasingly, as firms grew and labour relations problems developed, hiring became the responsibility of central personnel departments located at district headquarters. By the late 1930s, several Ontario firms used mechanical means to sort through thousands of personnel records in their woodlands offices. One of the purposes was to keep track of crews so that efficient, co-operative men could be assigned to foremen with whom they had worked previously. Since employers held that improved productivity and labour relations resulted from using the card system, managers eagerly took advantage of this bureaucratized form of a customary practice. This innovation was in line with depression-era trends throughout North American industry. Anxious to avoid the threat of unionization posed by a revitalized labour movement, corporations relied increasingly on central personnel departments to weed out union agitators, and to reduce employee complaints about the arbitrary hiring and firing practices of foremen.[37]

In all but the worst years of the depression, most logging operators had to allocate considerable funds and energy to the often frustrating task of recruiting workers from far afield. Some companies sent representatives to hire bushworkers in areas where woods manpower was likely to be found. An Ontario government official at Pembroke noted in 1919 the prevalence of 'alleged salaried representatives of various lumber companies ... the majority of whom will adopt almost any means, fair or unfair, to entice workers to join up with their companies.' In a small operation like the Plaunt Lumber Company of the Sudbury district, it was the owner's son who went in search of workers. Bill Plaunt recently recalled how, as a young man, he used to travel each fall to Glengarry County where he would explain his needs to a local priest. As parishioners left the church after Sunday mass, the priest would select the men whom he felt needed the work and could be spared from farm duties. Early in the century Rat Portage Lumber Company relied on the woods superintendent or walking boss to round up crews for the firm's Lake-of-the-Woods operations. As a Forestry student explained, 'the walking boss got the crew together and gave them booze. They arrived in a happy but irresponsible condition,' and so supplies of Perry Davis Painkiller became 'almost depleted during the first week as it is counted a good thing to "sober off" on.'[38]

More commonly, however, companies relied on employment agencies to find them bushworkers. Before 1918 private agencies did virtually the whole job. For many years several Ottawa agencies, such as D.A. Martin or D'Amour's, had specialized in handling the large numbers of lumberjacks who descended on the capital annually in search of jobs. 'In the 1870's, as nowadays,' remarked the *Canada Lumberman* in 1903, 'Ottawa was the great employment bureau of Ontario and Quebec, if not the whole Dominion. Men flocked to the Capital from all parts of Quebec as much as political favour seekers do today.' When logging districts were opened in north-western Ontario, large numbers of bushworkers were also recruited at Winnipeg. By 1919 there was at least one registered private agency in every northern Ontario lumbering centre.[39]

These private employment agents played on the vulnerability of jobless woodsmen. Agents often overcharged bushworkers, and in describing pay in conditions, they exaggerated. 'The complaint that Private Employment agents, particularly in Ottawa misrepresent conditions re bush work ... is undoubtedly justified by the facts of the case,' observed one Ontario government official. Sometimes agents sent job seekers to positions for which they were unqualified. Employment agent Louis Goldstein of Massey not only was guilty of this, but he charged double the legal fee. Apparently he made immigrants from Sudbury and Sault Ste Marie pay two dollars each for jobs they could not perform. Several of the men who had insufficient money to return home by train had to walk over fifty miles through the woods. Goldstein was fined seventy-five dollars plus court costs. According to the report of an Ontario employment agent inspector, the Reliance Agency of Sudbury, which hired bushworkers through a Montreal branch, deducted two or three dollars from each worker's wages, and tacked on spurious board and storage charges.[40]

Although many bushworkers were victimized by unscrupulous employment sharks, some workers were able to turn the system to their own advantage. Ever since the mid-nineteenth century, it had been customary for lumber companies to advance employees money to cover transportation costs from Ottawa. In the twentieth century employers provided hiring agents with funds to cover railway and in some cases accommodation charges *en route* to the camps. Agency personnel often accompanied the men to ensure that they used the advances for the intended purposes. In other instances, the agent held baggage as security. Sometimes, however, bushworkers would submit phony baggage, take the advance, and disappear. A North Bay agent told one inspector about the 'bonfires which he had built in his backyard out of bogus baggage which some of these men carry with them in order that they may get transportation over distances.'[41]

Employers had to pick up the tab for these lost fares, something they resented. Recovering fares through the courts was impractical. 'You might as well sue a table leg,' was one lumberman's assessment of the chances of getting funds from penniless workers. In 1930 an exasperated C.B. Davis, woods manager of Abitibi's Iroquois Falls Division, described his fruitless attempts to deal with the problem:

Seven of our men jumped and went to Cochrane. We had them arrested in Cochrane. The man who arrested them said 'you either come through with the fare or go to jail.' This was in December. They said: 'fine; we will got to jail; that is where we want to go anyway. . . .' What are you going to do about it? You put them in jail, but what of it? It does not help you out any; it does not get you your money back because the men are content to stay there . . . what good does the whole thing do?[42]

Operators complained that they, too, were cheated by employment agents. 'Their only object,' explained one manager, 'is to make money; most of the time to the detriment of the Companies. No matter for them the class of men they are hiring and how long they will stay in the bush; as long as their recruiting list bears a great number of names and that the amount of compensation is high, they do not care what may happen.' Another operator opined: 'If something could be done in the way of getting pulp operators together with the Labour Bureaux, so that the available supply could be apportioned to the people who need it, it might help us out a great deal.'[43]

After 1917 the government became increasingly involved in the woods labour market. Although the Canadian government had previously participated in distributing immigrants and harvest workers, no level of government had had much presence in the logging industry. The Employment Offices Co-ordination Act of 1918, which established a national network of labour exchanges financed jointly by the federal and provincial governments, brought substantial government intervention to the manpower field. Officials maintained that the departure was necessary in order to coordinate wartime manpower requirements and to minimize unrest during post-war reconstruction. As in other industries, woodsworkers and employers were encouraged to register with the government offices in major centres throughout Canada. Employment Service personnel would then attempt to match applicants to job openings. During the years 1918–20, when there were war-related bush labour shortages, woods-bound workers registered with the service were given cut rates on the railways. Soon, the Employment Service was handling thousands of bushmen and servicing hundreds of forest companies.[44]

Government-run offices eliminated many of the complaints of those who relied on the Service, but not all. Some bushworkers proved reluctant to register. In 1920 officials of the Indian Lake Lumber Company maintained that their employees avoided it because 'they don't like filling out forms in a government office.'[45] At a time shortly after the passage of the Conscription Act and the Anti-Loafing Law, it is understandable that many workers might have been hesitant to register with government officials.[46] Moreover, unlike the Employment Service, private agents could advance transportation costs, and so many bushworkers continued to register with them. The unfortunate were still snagged by sharks who advanced money for whiskey, got the men drunk, and then packed them on a train headed in the direction of the camps.

Employers, too, continued to rely at least partially on private agents.

Alton Morse of the Devon Lumber Company explained to provincial officials that while he had made a great deal of use of the Employment
Service, he had found private agencies better at securing men on short
notice. He also pointed out that private agencies advanced funds to penniless lumberjacks, 'something the government cannot do.' Morse added,
however, that once the agents with whom he dealt had found the men and
advanced funds, the recruits were handed over to the Employment Service so the firm could then take advantage of the cut-rate railway fares.[47]

Labour recruitment was much more troublesome for employers, and a
great deal more lucrative for agents, because of the high mobility rates of
woodsworkers. Companies continually had to hire new men because so
many woodsworkers would quit their jobs before the logging campaign
was finished. Bushworkers did so for a number of reasons. Sometimes ill
health or a family crisis would require them to return home early. Many
left the camps at Christmas in order to enjoy the holiday season. Since the
woodsworker tended to quit as soon as he made his stake, in a season
when wage rates were comparatively high he might do so well before the
camp break-up. Many bushworkers would resign and look for jobs elsewhere as soon as they became fed up with the food, their camp mates, or
the boss. A binge in town provided much-needed relief. Woodsworkers
paid on a piece-rate basis were particularly likely to move from camp to
camp in search of superior forest conditions that would enable them to
produce more wood and earn money at a faster pace.[48]

Labour turn-over increased when bush jobs were relatively plentiful and
woodsworkers could count on being rehired. During the boom years just
after the turn of this century, lumberjacks became so restless that lumbermen coined the term jumper to refer to the men who jumped from camp
to camp. 'Lumbermen report that they are unable to keep their men at
work in the woods,' reported the *Canada Lumberman* in 1901. 'They are very
unsteady and will leave at the slightest provocation, knowing that their
chances of securing employment elsewhere are good.' During the slump
of 1907–8, however, the *Canada Lumberman* observed that 'fewer men had
jumped their jobs.' Turn-over rates rose again towards the end of World
War I, when bush labour shortages became acute. At that time logging
operators said they had three crews: 'one at work, one leaving, and one
coming into camp.' An exasperated operator complained that the woodsmen 'don't know where they're going, but they're on their way!' At least
some employers realized, however, that jumping was a form of labour
protest in which bushworkers engaged whenever employment conditions
permitted. 'While the lumberjack is unorganized,' said the manager of the

Spanish River Mills Company in September 1919, 'he cannot go on strike in the way various unions have been doing; yet he goes on an individual strike quite often.'[49]

As it turned out, the restlessness of 1917–20 was short-lived. Labour settled down during the recession that began in late 1920. A future dean of forestry who visited the Schroeder Mills and Timber Company operations near Pakesley in 1921 found that labour had suddenly become plentiful and stable, while wages had fallen. 'The firm does not need to worry about men leaving this year,' wrote Gordon Cosens. 'A great many of them do not have the chance to stay more than a day or so, as he [the boss] can afford to let all the men who are not suitable go.' If the labour market did not solve the turn-over problem, companies tried techniques like providing better grub or switching from company-run camps to ones run by jobbers or sub-contractors. Two Forestry students observed after a visit to Abitibi's Iroquois Falls operations in 1928–9 that while the 'Company camps lack the personal element,' in the jobbers' camps there was 'a sort of esprit-de-corps . . . and consequently the constant stream of men to and from the camps was not so apparent.'[50]

THE LURE OF THE BUSH

Why did men respond to the offers of hiring agents and logging operators? The vast majority of men doubtless accepted logging work because it offered them the best opportunity to earn wages during the winter when other options were limited. Logging could be quite lucrative. Earnings depended on the district in which a fellow worked, seasonal fluctuations in wage rates, the skills of the individual, and the type of payment offered. Woods wages generally increased from east to west, both across Canada and within Ontario. A December 1900 report in the federal government's *Labour Gazette* shows that log cutters in New Brunswick made $24 a month; in Quebec, $18 to $26; in the Ottawa Valley and Georgian Bay districts, $24 to $26; and in Rainy River district, $26 to $30. Manitoba woodsmen earned $26 to $32, while British Columbia log cutters were paid hourly rates, fallers getting 27½ cents to 35 cents.[51] At least until the depression, this regional differential was maintained in logging and in many other industries.

Within each region, wage rates in the woods had always risen and fallen with the general business cycle, and they had been strongly affected by the changing levels of demand for timber and woodsmen. In an early issue of the *Canada Lumberman*, it was reported that in 1881, wage rates in lumbering were 25 per cent higher than in the previous year and 50 per cent above rates in the heart of the depression two years earlier. In February 1901 the president of the Ontario Lumbermen's Association noted that over a twenty-four month period, wages had advanced from $16 to $26 per month. Appendices 5 and 6 indicate that similarly abrupt fluctuations continued to occur for decades. Since the cost of living did not fluctuate as widely, the woodsmen's chances of making good earnings were far better in some years than in others.[52]

The size of the bushworker's stake also depended on his skills and bargaining power in the labour market. In the old square timber camps, wage differentials between skilled and less-skilled workers had been substantial. In December 1891 highly skilled hewers, men who wielded a broadaxe to hew the logs into giant, square sticks, commanded monthly wages of $35 to $40, while ordinary log cutters made $20 to $22 and general hands $16 to $20.[53] In the great majority of Ontario sawlog operations during the first half of the twentieth century, differentials among production workers were far smaller. During the late 1920s, for instance, general hands earned approximately $30 to $32 per month, while choppers and sawyers made $35 to $40. Service employees did earn more, particularly cooks who in the 1920s made two or three times the monthly wages of choppers (see Appendix 6). Thus, a young man looking to make a big stake in sawlog camps in the inter-war period was likely to do far better if he could land a job as a cook. However, with only one cook to every sixty men, such openings were comparatively few.

A substantial proportion of bushworkers, particularly in the pulpwood sector after World War I, were paid on a piece-rate basis, and thus earnings varied enormously depending on the skill of the individual and the forest conditions where he worked. Though it required experience, good fortune, a little savvy, and a great deal of hard work, some piece-work cutters made substantially more than those paid on monthly wages. A 1944 Ontario Forest Industries Association report indicates that top producers earned nearly double the average amount paid to piece-work fellers.[54] Another study, presented to the Canadian Pulp and Paper Association, Woodlands Section, shows that in one large pulpwood operation employing 3,108 men in 1935–6, the top 23.4 per cent of the choppers cut an average of 2.67 cords per man-day and made $3.42, while the overall average was only 2.14 cords and $2.72 per day (see Appendix 7). Of course, both studies also indicate that a significant proportion of piece workers made abysmally low wages. According to the 1944 report, while the average pulp cutter in the Hearst district earned $4.29 per day and top producers got $8.69, the lowest producers made only $2.05. The Woodlands Section study shows that the bottom 8.9 per cent of the workers cut on average less than a cord per day and made wages of $1.32 or less. After deductions for meals, clothing purchases, and so forth, these men received only paltry rewards for a sojourn in the bush.

On the basis of available wage-rate data, it appears that the majority of woodsmen did not fare well in comparison with workers in other Ontario industries. Unfortunately, it is difficult to make meaningful comparisons, in part because monthly paid woodsmen received free board whereas workers in most industries did not. Although logging operators in the inter-war years usually charged piece workers 75 cents to $1 per day for board, it is impossible to put a dollar value on board because it had such different values for various categories of workers. It was worth much more to the immigrant sojourner who otherwise would have had to pay for a room in a boarding house than it was to the farmer's son whose alternative was staying at home. Calculations are further complicated because people in most industries worked intermittently and their actual earnings averaged far less than reported monthly pay rates. In the winter, woods work was comparatively steady, as long as the weather held and ill health and accidents were avoided. But if it is assumed that all employees worked a full month, then it can be seen from Table 2 that the wages choppers received ranked well below other categories of blue-collar workers. Perhaps more appropriate comparisons can be made with agricultural labourers, for they too received board. Table 3 compares monthly wages of western Canadian harvest workers, summer wages of male agricultural labourers in Ontario, and those of Ontario choppers. Obviously, western harvesters were comparatively better paid, though it should be noted that their season lasted only two months a year. Monthly wage rates for Ontario choppers and farm workers were similar, both being very low.

Given this level of wage rates, a seasonally employed woodsworker paid on a monthly basis could not have been the sole support for a family of average size living in urban Ontario. According to Michael Piva's study of the cost of living in Toronto, a family of five in 1921 would have required $1,655.29 per annum in order to rise above the poverty line.[55] In the summer of 1921 a river driver made about $70, and in the autumn of 1921, after a wage cut, first-class choppers and teamsters were paid approximately $32 per month. Thus, a professional woodsworker, employed the maximum number of months possible that year, would have grossed $364. From this figure there would have been deductions, such as the compulsory one dollar a month medical fee, and he probably would have been

TABLE 2
Monthly earnings of groups of Ontario workers

Occupation	Monthly earnings ($)
1914	
Carpenters (Toronto)	79
Sawyers in mills (Ontario)	60
Building labourers (Toronto)	56
Common factory labourers(Toronto)	48
Railway sectionmen (Toronto)	36
Choppers	26 (and board)
1926	
Carpenters (Toronto)	150
Metal mine machinemen (Ontario)	114
Mining labourers (Ontario)	90
Carpenters' labourers (Toronto)	80
Sawmill labourers (Ontario)	72
Choppers (Ontario)	35–40 (and board)

SOURCE: Canada, Department of Labour, *Wage Rates and Salaries* 1914, 1926

TABLE 3
Monthly wage rates with board included

	Western harvesters[1] ($)	Ontario farm workers[2] ($)	Ontario choppers[2] ($)
1921	81	40	70
1922	75	37	26–32
1923	79	38	353–40
1924	71	36	40–45
1925	86	34	30–35
1926	71	34	35–40

SOURCE: 1 John Herd Thompson, 'Bringing in the Sheaves: The Harvest Excursionists, 1890–1929,' *Canadian Historical Review* 54:4 (1978) 482
2 Canada, Department of Labour, *Wage Rates in Canada* 1921–6

docked at least a few days for ill health. Even if he made no clothing or tobacco purchases while in camp, at best he would have sent home $350 – far short of the amount required for a family to live on decently in Toronto. Of course, it was possible to survive on less than this, especially outside cities. And the woodsman might have been able to secure short-term work in other industries during the three-month period when there was no work to be had in the bush. Even so, the shortfall was enormous.

Notwithstanding the often poor wages earned by bushworkers, there were always plenty of men willing to do the job. For the immigrant sojourner, the logging camp at least provided food and accommodation during the slack winter period in the construction industry. And there were few opportunities to spend money in a logging camp – as long as poker games could be avoided. For the agriculturalist whose money-making opportunities on the farm were strictly limited in the winter, logging meant the chance to earn at least a little cash. And no doubt, for many young Canadians, there appeared to be no alternative to winter woods work, so circumscribed were their lives. Bob Taylor, who left his Ottawa Valley farm for a logging camp in 1903 when he was sixteen, recalled much later: 'In those days there were no factories to work in as there are now so the young fellows went into the bush.' The paucity of options was stressed by C.B. Davis, woods manager for Abitibi in 1930. 'Woods labour is not woods labour by choice ... woods labour is woods labour by force of circumstances.'[56]

Yet not everyone turned to bush work out of sheer desperation; some men loved the woods and eagerly sought logging jobs. Forest work offered them more than just an income; it was an appealing and satisfying way of life. They liked the freedom of working outdoors close to nature, in much the same way they enjoyed hunting and fishing. When retired pulp cutter Arvi Tuuamen isn't on a fishing trip, he likes to reminisce about the Algoma pulpwood camps where he worked in the 1930s. 'I tried mining,' says Tuuamen. "But I couldn't stand being cooped up underground in the dark. Cutting pulpwood in the open air was for me.' Many old-timers thrive on telling tales of the camps: the visits of bears, practical jokes played on greenhorns, and a hard job completed in record time. Jim Mac-Donald, who knew the bushmen well, writes: 'Camp life was like a fever that some could not escape.'[57]

Many a farm lad must have longed for the day when he would be old enough to work in the camps, to experience at first hand the life his father and brothers had been describing. Setting off for the first time to the pineries was a rite of passage, a sign of approaching manhood. Some married men liked to escape to the camps in order to avoid the responsibilities and petty irritations of home life; pulp cutters did not have to listen to crying children or see dirty dishes. According to lumberman and historian J.P. Bertrand, in northwestern Ontario logging camps there were 'lots of widowers' who, 'not being able to get along with their mates, sought solace in the company of men, hard work, good food, and enjoyment of outdoor life.'[58] Writing in 1922, Edmund Bradwin reflected:

Lumbering is still, perhaps the most romantic of all frontier works in Canada. From the week in early fall when the first camp operations begin, on through the cutting season of autumn woods, gorgeous in changing tints, into the snows of early winter, followed at the new year with the sleigh haul that ends with the break-up only when the logs of the great skidways have been landed at the dump – these differing activities of the woods embody for strong-limbed men a distinctive fascination that does not vanish with succeeding generations.[59]

It would be unwise, however, to exaggerate the romance of logging, for however fascinating bush work might appear from afar, activities were dangerous, heavy, and often tedious.

3

Bush work, 1900–1945

Kalle Koski's Last Testament

It happened on a job like this:

A gang was hauling logs.
The chain broke with a clang.
We came down the hill at breakneck speed;
The load burst apart with a crash.

Others fled.
Kalle Koski tripped on a chunk of snow:
The luckless fellow was pinned beneath the logs.
They rushed to his side
And took away the log
That had felled the frightened Kalle.

Johnson – the boss – examined the wounds.
'Men, this is death.
His spine has been badly injured.'

'Let me rest in peace,' uttered a deathly pale Kalle Koski.
The expression on his face is earnest; he is speechless.
He was very fond of the dying man.
'You were my best friend,' said Kalle Koski.
'Our roads part:
I remain here.'

'This is my last request:

Look for my picture – You remember the one –
Somewhere . . . it might be in my wallet.
Take it, along with my love, to my fiancé in Toronto.
My gold watch – that is your's.
Tear open my shirt:
I hid my dollars in a pocket.
Send them to my old mother in Perho.
Write to her saying
I remembered her, and my childhood.'

Then his head suddenly jerked:
He had passed through the gates of the House of Death.

So ended the journey of one wanderer – Kalle Koski.
Born in Perho, Died Now.
In the forest, beneath the skies of Canada.[1]

Anon., Montreal 1932

This poem, penned by a Finnish immigrant who cut pulpwood in the
Shield country, is a poignant reminder of the dangers of logging. A bushworker's job changed with the seasons and varied according to the specific
tasks assigned each man. The professional bushworker, who tried to make
logging a year-round occupation, might have begun felling in September,
gone on to haul wood by horse and sleigh in the heart of winter, and then
taken up river driving in the spring. Yet most of the tasks shared certain
characteristics. Danger was one. Another was the tremendous amount of
heavy, backbreaking bullwork that taxed even the hardiest man. It would
be wrong, however, to perceive logging as merely a pick-and-shovel occupation, because bushworkers needed specialized skills and had to exercise
considerable judgment in order to adjust to the varied and ever-changing
conditions they encountered. Moreover, because bosses could not directly
supervise such a scattered work force, woodsworkers enjoyed considerable discretion in completing their tasks.

PREPARING FOR THE HARVEST

Before bushworkers could begin felling timber, specialized personnel had
to make various essential preparations. First of all, the area had to be
cruised so that operators could plan their logging campaign with a fairly

clear idea of the local geography and the amount, quality, and types of timber growing on the limit. In most operations before 1920, and in many others long afterwards, the job of cruising fell to unschooled men known for their abilities in sizing up logging prospects. In preparation for winter logging operations in 1908–9, the camp foreman of Rat Portage Lumber Company spent the summer of 1908 cruising the firm's timber limits near Lake-of-the-Woods. One of these foremen, who was known to be a good woodsman with much local experience, spent about two weeks estimating the timber in the vicinity of his camp. Apparently he had 'no particular method of cruising,' but simply travelled through the area and then 'estimated "in lump." ' Like experienced cruisers everywhere, these men were comparatively well paid. in 1908–9 Rat Portage Lumber Company paid its cruisers $10 a day and its lumberjacks about $1.[2]

After World War I, as young, university-trained foresters entered the job market, cruising became a more exact science, at least in the bigger companies that hired the foresters. In order to facilitate advanced planning, the forestry divisions made detailed maps of the vast pulpwood concessions using data compiled from ground and aerial cruises.[3]

Before felling could begin another preparatory step had to be made: road-making. The actual work of constructing logging roads involved heavy labour and little skill. A forestry student described how the crews of the Hope Lumber Company made roads at a logging camp near Ruel, Ont. in 1925: 'No teams were used for the construction of haul roads. Trees were grubbed around and cut out by the roots, the weight of their tops helping to pull them over. They are sawn up into logs and rolled off the road or if of suitable size used to fill in hollows. Some of the larger trees required a few sticks of stumping powder [dynamite] set off below their roots before they would fall.' Where routes crossed or followed a creek, men would corduroy the road. Surfaces did not have to be very smooth, for as one observer put it, 'frost is ... the great road builder.' Labour amounted to 83 per cent of the total cost of Hope Lumber's road at Ruel.[4]

The men who made roads were called beavers. Joe Mason, who at sixteen years of age worked in logging camps on the French River, explains that the name 'originated because roads were usually cut by greenhorns, and a greenhorn chops all around a tree, as does a beaver.' Crews worked under the direction of the buck beaver, usually an old bushworker well past his prime. 'At thirteen years old I started to cut trails in the bush,' says Jack Campbell of McKellar, Ont., recalling his turn-of-the-century boyhood, 'that's the job they put a fellow on when he's a boy.' In other instances, road makers were greenhorns recently out from Europe. In 1908 the Victoria Hart Lumber Company, operating on the Whitefish River, experimented with hiring Italian navvies. Departing from the common practice in railway construction where foreign-speaking workers were given separate, inferior accommodation, these men slept in the main bunkhouse and ate 'sumptuously' at the camp table. According to an observer, the experiment had proven a success; the Italians worked 'with a heartiness that would astonish many a contractor.' Joe Sarazin, a veteran lumberjack at Blind River recalls that in the late 1920s and the 1930s, 'Slavic immigrants – we called them "Balkans" – did the manual labour on the main roads.' In his district, only the outstanding Slav who spoke English was ever promoted to a more prestigious job. But not all beavers were greenhorns. In some operations skilled bushmen who arrived at camp early in the fall would make roads before beginning their felling jobs. Road builders hired on as 'general hands' and, as Appendix 6 shows, were paid a little less than teamsters and choppers.[5]

In contrast to the work of the road-makers, the job of planning and laying out the road network required a great deal of experience and knowledge. The success of the entire logging campaign depended heavily on how well the routes had been cleared. Ideally, logs were transported from the stump downhill to level roads that ran along flat valley bottoms. Low, swampy ground was not a handicap since roads were used only when the ground was frozen. However, the Shield country did not lend itself frequently to this neat formula. Keen judgment was needed to select the shortest routes that avoided steep slopes, rocky outcroppings, and sharp turns. Poorly laid-out roads might result in wasted time during the short hauling season when ice conditions were ideal for sleighs carrying logs.

Since so much depended on the selection of routes, in some larger firms specialized personnel assumed this responsibility. In 1927 Abitibi had a Logging Engineering and Control Branch in its Engineering Division. Under the direction of the forest engineer, an experienced professional, branch staff planned all road and other construction projects. These plans were then executed by the woods department or Logging Division as it was then called.[6] Such specialized departments appeared only in companies where the scale of operations necessitated more complex management structures, and where it was cost-effective to hire professionals. (Figure 2 illustrates Abitibi's complex management structure of the late 1920s.)

In some pulpwood operations and in nearly all lumbering campaigns, the job of choosing camp sites and road routes fell to the camp foreman.

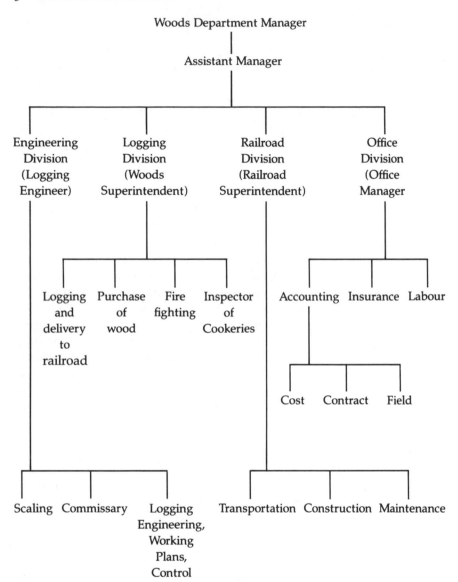

FIGURE 2 Organizational chart Abitibi Power and Paper Company Ltd Woods Department 1926. SOURCE: University of Toronto Archives, Faculty of Forestry Collection, Logging Report no. 57, J.W. Johnson and L.R. Seheult, Abitibi Power and Paper Company Ltd 1926

This task was probably his most vital one, although he might also perform others, such as cruising, hiring and firing employees and maintaining overall discipline in the camps. These responsibilities were carried out without much interference from more senior supervisors or managers. In lumber companies a walking boss, or walker, would visit from time to time and report back to the owner. In the bigger lumber companies, the management hierarchy was more complex (see Figure 3), but even then the camp boss was expected to conduct operations with little outside interference. 'The foreman may be likened to the lieutenant of the army,' observed a Forestry student in 1909, 'because he provides the personal link between the men and the officers and within certain limitations has a free hand in directing the operations in the field.'[7]

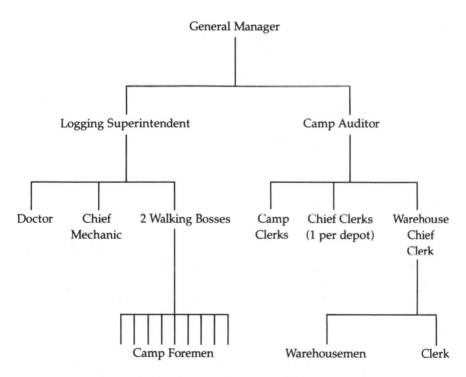

FIGURE 3   Organizational chart Carpenter-Hixon Company Ltd Woods Department 1928. SOURCE: University of Toronto Archives, Faculty of Forestry Collection, Logging Report, W.O. Faber, A.P. Maclean, A.B. Wheatley, Carpenter-Hixon Company Ltd, Blind River 1928

Since the camp foreman had the power to hire and fire and was on the scene daily, he was the boss as far as the bushworkers were concerned. Before 1945 Ontario logging camps lacked an elaborate supervisory hierarchy; most men came more or less directly under the authority of the camp foreman. Though there were some gradations of pay among jobs (see Appendix 6), once the greenhorn had passed through the junior jobs, such as clearing trails or road-making, then he found his place. There were also few promotional opportunities. The highest position to which a professional lumberjack might aspire was camp foreman.

Recognizing the vital importance of having talented foremen, company officials kept an eye out for woods employees with outstanding abilities. Foremen needed no special training or education; indeed, many were illiterate. What counted was woods experience and demonstrated abilities 'both in handling men and handling logs.'[8] Naturally, the foreman had to understand every step of the work process and be flexible enough to adapt to local topological and forest conditions. Moreover, in order to motivate his men and win their respect, the foreman had to demonstrate that he knew his business fully and could stand up to any challenge to his authority.

Generally, the bush foreman liked to portray a tough image. If tempers flared in the bunkhouse, or a rebellion broke out on the job, then it was the boss's responsibility to re-establish peace. During the last months of World War I, a time when bushworkers were unusually restless, lumberman D.A. Gillies noted that it required 'a particularly resourceful and cool-headed [individual] to handle a gang of men and get any work out of them.' And he added, this was especially true when a foreman was 'isolated, being many miles from headquarters and ... entirely on his own responsibility when an emergency arises.'[9]

Since most foremen were promoted from the ranks, they usually began their duties with established reputations. However, college-trained Alton Morse was an outsider when he became boss of a Chapleau area lumber camp in 1914. To establish his authority, Morse set up a boxing ring in the camp and offered to fight anyone. Thanks to his skills as a pugilist, he quickly gained the respect of men long accustomed to far less educated bosses – men with nick-names like Dirty Face, Iron Head, or Tin Can.[10]

Not all foremen had the required skills in handling men. Writing in the 1920s, Edmund Bradwin, a Frontier College educator, criticized foremen who easily lost patience with, and mistreated, their foreign-born workers. 'A breach of some detail early displeases and leads to prompt dismissal,' noted Bradwin, 'for if there is a wrong way in which to hold an axe or to cut a trail the newcomer is sure to follow it.' Woods managers were slow in coming to grips with this kind of problem. In his 1939 report *Woods Labour*, L.A. Nix insisted that his fellow woods managers should make a start at training foremen in human relations, but few steps were taken until after World War II.[11]

TIMBER-R-R!

Logging operations began in earnest with the start of felling activities. Throughout the early autumn, as the first frosts set in and the hardwoods began to turn colour, increasing numbers of choppers or pulp cutters would arrive at the camps until, by late November, the camp reached its full complement of men. Cutting represented the most labour-intensive operation in the annual logging cycle. A 1937 report suggested the following breakdown:

Cutting	96,000 man-days	
Hauling	40,000	" "
Driving	13,000	" "
Improvements (roads and stream)	31,000	" "
Total	180,000	" "

The Woodlands Section of the Canadian Pulp and Paper Association (CPPA) estimated that the cost of cutting usually represented at least 20 per cent of the cost of prepared pulpwood at the mill. Nearly all a company's expenditures on cutting were in the form of wage payments or boarding costs.[12]

In sawlog operations at the turn of the century, felling gangs generally had three members: an axeman and two sawyers. The axeman served as the chief log maker or head chopper, a position with some prestige. Although sometimes foremen blazed the trees to be felled, in most operations it was the axeman's responsibility to select appropriate trees and to plan the order and direction in which they should fall. Using his axe, the head chopper notched the tree on the side he wanted it to fall. Then he stood back and let the sawyers make the backcut with their long, two-man crosscut saw. It was now the sawyers' turn to rest while the chopper marked off the log lengths and cleared away branches to provide room for the sawyers. They sawed or bucked the tree into lengths of sixteen feet (plus six inches to allow for possible damage in transit). Removing the remaining branches from the logs was generally left to the swampers – less experienced men who also cleared the trails in preparation for the later steps. The daily output of sawyers depended on the size of the trees, the density of the timber, and ground conditions. In 1912 cutting gangs for Graves, Bigwood and Company working near Nairn averaged 176 logs daily per gang, though days when 250 logs were cut were not uncommon. At the end of the shift the head chopper reported to the camp clerk.[13]

When the pulp and paper firms began conducting logging operations they adopted the same felling system used in the sawlog sector. University of Toronto Forestry students who in 1928 visited the pulpwood logging camps of the Spanish River Pulp and Paper Company described felling gangs organized in precisely the same manner as three-man sawlog crews.[14] Perhaps the system made sense where spruce pulpwood logs had diameters as large as many sawlogs: it took two men to saw through such big timber. Highly experienced head choppers selected only the most suitable trees and measured out sixteen-foot logs. However, as the Ontario pulp and paper operators became more experienced, and as the industry grew more competitive with the soaring mill capacities of the 1920s, companies developed cheaper techniques better tailored to the needs of the pulpwood sector.

Some woods managers, such as those at Spruce Falls Power and Paper, began streamlining their operations: they eliminated the head chopper and had the sawyers notch the trees and measure the log lengths.[15] As a result, fewer rest breaks were built in to the rhythm of felling and sawyers could work more continuously. With the two-man crew, however, one sawyer still stood idle while the other notched and branched. Consequently, some managers introduced the one-man crew, which eliminated this waiting time as well.[16] Supervisors found that the one-man crew system increased the productivity of the whole operation. In 1929 Abitibi reported that in its Iroquois Falls division, two-man crews produced an average of 125 logs per day, but individuals working alone could each cut 80 to 150 daily.[17]

In the one-man system, each cutter was assigned a timber strip about sixty-six feet, or one chain wide, and ten to fifteen chains deep. He cleared a trail down the centre of his strip along which logs could be drawn. He felled trees by using either a crosscut saw with one handle or a bucksaw, a saw with a narrow blade set in a wooden frame. (By the late 1920s steel-frame saws, usually called Swede saws, had become increasingly popular.) Felling was back-breaking work because the cutter had to bend double from the waist, hook his torso around the tree, and fell it by sawing towards himself. After he had cut a few trees he would remove the top and branches from each and then buck it into logs.

Instead of making sixteen-foot logs, pulp cutters working alone usually bucked trees into bolts of four or eight feet. They then assembled the wood in piles of about half a cord each along the strip trail. Many operators turned to the short-wood system partly because it was easier to drive short lengths down the narrower streams encountered as they went farther and farther up country. Furthermore, long lengths, which fetched higher prices in lumber markets, had no advantage as pulpwood because it was cut into short pieces before being milled. Some operators also thought output increased because bushworkers could handle short bolts more easily. 'With the increased demand for bush labour by reason of more and longer operations,' declared Quebec woods manager, J.D. Gilmour, in 1927, 'one has to deal with less experienced bushmen than were formerly available. It is found that there is not the same decrease in efficiency where such labour is employed on short wood operations. This applies to logging and driving.'[18]

It was also back-breaking and exhausting to handle and pile eight-foot bolts. Arvi Tuuamen, a Finnish-Canadian who has many fond memories of his days in the 1930s when he cut pulpwood in Algoma, admits his work was often tantamount to torture. 'I nearly killed myself making eight-foot piles,' he says. 'Many of those logs had ten-inch diameter tops, I found myself crying, it was such strenuous work. Once I was off work for two weeks, I had strained myself so badly.' The 1947 *Report* of the Ontario Royal Commission on Forestry based its recommendation that operators abandon the eight-foot system partly on 'humanitarian grounds.'[19]

Whether cutters worked alone or in gangs, felling timber required a considerable amount of skill, in addition to brute strength. In selective cutting operations, the head chopper had to exercise judgment in choosing the trees to be felled. He had to assess whether they were sufficiently large, straight, and sound to allow for making sixteen-foot logs of at least the minimum diameter required by the firm. In determining the direction a tree was to fall, gangs had to take into account several factors: crucial was the lean of the tree and the shape of the crown. Few crowns are symmetrical, one side usually being heavier because of better light conditions. This preponderance of weight on one side acted as a powerful lever and had to be considered. It was important to avoid lodging the tree in other trees and to select a spot to place the tree so that the trunk would not be broken by stumps or rocks. 'Woe betide the sawyers who had one of their trees "hang up," or lodge in a tree, as it was felled,' writes Joe Mason. 'This was immediately greeted with a loud, raucous cawing, like a crow, by any man who happened to see it.' Skilled cutting crews also ensured that trees fell in a pattern that would facilitate log making and skidding. Valuable timber could be wasted by head choppers who failed to recognize the extent of rot or who measured off short lengths where longer ones could have been made. As three Forestry students found when they visited the Carpenter and Hixon Lumber Company camps near Blind River in 1928, 'good judgement is required by the notcher in dividing the bole. It pays to have a man who is capable of sizing up the situation and who can make the most of a tree.'[20]

Productive pulp cutters also needed to be skilled. Axe blows had to be accurately directed and saw strokes long and even. Fellers had to plan ahead so that trees would fall in a pattern that would maximize output during subsequent bucking and piling operations. Arthur Cole, a journalist for the *Globe and Mail*, described the skills of cutters he saw at an Abitibi camp northeast of Iroquois Falls in 1942: 'A real artist minimizes the heavy labour for himself by dropping the trees within inches of where he wants them. And that is no mean trick, any novice of the game will find. By dropping the tree mid-way across his skid-pile, the real artist can cut into lengths, strip the branches and pile neatly with little more than a twist of the wrists or the leverage afforded by a handy pike pole.' Another observer, John Currie of the Fort William Trades and Labour Council, summed up what he called the craft of woods work by saying: 'When you see how a pulp cutter saws, it is a beauty to behold.'[21]

Until World War II, employers could generally find a ready supply of experienced cutters who could not only get out the bulk of the harvest but also train greenhorns in a kind of informal apprenticeship system. Frequently fathers trained their sons, either at the camps or back home on the farm woodlot. 'More often than not the young fellow would start by piling with the pulpwood the wood cut by his parent,' a woods manager later recalled. 'Once this was mastered, he would progress to the axe and bucksaw.'[22]

As experienced woodsworkers were lured to other occupations during World War II, woods managers grew increasingly aware that cutting pulpwood was a skilled occupation and that newcomers to the bush needed training. In 1942 the Woodlands Section issued a booklet based on the results of years of research in the field. *The Woodcutter's Handbook* began with the assertion that the best cutters 'cut much more wood,' made 'much more money,' and were 'more highly respected.' According to the booklet, their success derived from the fact that they knew 'how to plan the work, how to do it best, and how to keep their tools in the best condition.' The authors outlined in great detail the various methods that would permit employees to improve their productivity. They insisted that good judgment was required to ensure that falling trees did not lodge in other trees or snags; but if this did occur, they warned: 'Don't get angry or excited when the tree is lodged ... You need a cool head to decide best how to bring it down with ease and safety.' Much of the *Woodcutters' Handbook* was devoted to explaining the intricacies of filing and setting up a bucksaw. Taken as a whole, the publication is a vivid description of the pulp cutter's skills.[23]

The skills of the cutter, the amount of effort he was willing and able to expend, and the bush conditions, greatly affected his productivity. Appendix 7 shows the output of cutters in a 165,000 cord operation during the 1935–6 season. While the average per man-day was 2.14 cords, nearly one quarter or 23.4 per cent of the work force averaged 2.67 cords or 37.7 per cent of the total cut. On the other hand, 22.6 per cent of the work force produced at a rate well below average, for only 7.1 per cent of the total. Because of their low productivity, poor producers were soon fired or quit their jobs. Of course, even some of the cutters who were satisfied with their comparatively high earnings abandoned the bush at Christmas; others hoped to make even bigger stakes by working on other phases of the harvest.

ALONG SKIDDING TRAILS

When logs were cut in long lengths, the next step in the annual logging cycle was skidding – dragging the logs by horse from the stump to the roadside. (In short-wood operations, men simply carried the bolts to the strip road, where they piled them in readiness for the sleigh haul.) Skidding methods varied, depending on geographical conditions and local customs, as well as on the preference of woods managers. Logs were usually skidded by one of two methods. In chain skidding, the teamster fastened a chain around one end of a big-diameter log (or several smaller ones) and then his horse dragged the load with the leading end raised off the ground. In the less common bobbing operations, the front end of the load rested on a bob or a small sled with runners which was drawn by a team.[24]

Generally, skidding began at least a few weeks after the fellers had started work, so that there was a substantial backlog of timber to be transported. The optimum skidding season came in late fall and early winter, when the snow reduced friction. At that time, men with expertise in handling horses would arrive in camp to conduct skidding operations. They would be joined by fellers who had completed their assignments. In this way, all the timber would reach the roadside by New Year's Day, when ice conditions made it possible to begin the sleigh haul.

Traditionally in the Ottawa Valley many experienced teamsters came from nearby farms and brought their own horses with them. This practice was continued into the 1950s in the Iroquois Falls area, where Abitibi hired farmers and teams from neighbouring Quebec.[25] More commonly in twentieth-century operations, logging firms purchased their horses from major dealers like the Union Stock Yards Horse Exchange in Toronto or from a big western Canadian outfit. Some operators rented their teams on a seasonal basis; others purchased them and each spring shipped them by rail to pasture lands in eastern Ontario. The most popular breeds were Clydesdales and Percherons. Experts recommended that the horses weigh between 1,500 and 1,600 pounds and be from six to ten years old. However, surveys show that the industry often relied on much lighter and older horses – with adverse effects.[26]

The effectiveness of skidding operations also depended on matching crew set-ups to local circumstances. Generally, in the sawlog sector skidding crews consisted of three or four swampers, two teamsters, and two rollers or deckers. Swampers cleared trails suitable for a single horse to snake-out logs, and they prepared the skidways where the logs were piled. This latter step involved clearing an appropriate site and building a crude, log platform to serve as a base. Swampers also assisted in removing branches from the logs if the cutting crew had not completed the job. The teamsters spaced themselves, so that when each arrived at the skidway, no waiting was required. Rollers took the load and piled or decked it, while the teamster headed back to pick up another one. In spare moments, one of the rollers would stamp the logs with the company's mark so they could be identified in log drives. Ideally, there was a continuous flow of logs reaching the skidways. It was the head rollwayman's job to co-ordinate the crew and keep the operation going like clockwork. Each night he reported to the foreman the day's tally of logs skidded and decked.

Pulpwood skidding crews before the 1920s resembled their sawlog counterparts, but in later years operators introduced a simplified, and apparently less costly, system of one- or two-man crews. Sometimes a teamster worked on his own, snaking-out the logs along the strip trails and piling his loads at the roadside. Other times piling was performed by strong young men hired specifically for that purpose.

Skidding crews required various skills. Swampers had to have a keen eye to determine the best route for trails so that up-grades and obstructions were avoided and the wood reached the skidway in a direct and smooth-flowing manner. It was also important that they choose locations that took advantage of the topography. Even rollers had skills. 'Rolling was a job which I liked very much, but which I had some difficulty in mastering,' says Joe Mason. 'There is quite an art to guiding the logs evenly up the short skids onto the top of the skidway.' The experts on the staff of the Woodlands Section agreed that efficient rolling required a proper knowledge of technique, and they listed nine steps to more efficient decking.[27]

The teamster had the most demanding skills. He had to know how to make up loads so that logs would not fall out of the chains *en route*, and he needed to watch out for his own safety as well. 'The teamster,' remembers Mason, 'had to walk along beside the logs as they slithered and slid through the snow. If he was not very careful, he could easily have a foot or leg jammed between the logs and a stump or a tree.'[28] A good teamster developed an understanding with his horse and avoided using his whip. His job also required that he provide good care for his horse, a responsibility he shared with the barn boss and blacksmith. In an attempt to improve horse care, the Woodlands Section published in 1934, the recommendations of equestrian expert J.W. Sutherland. He suggested that teamsters grease the hooves of horses and carry a balling hammer to ensure that 'a horse's feet do not "ball up" in snow, as walking on such balls is very hard on tendons, shoulders.' He also gave advice to blacksmiths, warning them to 'avoid excessive trimming of the frog, whittling at the sides of the cleft, and using the rasp too much on the outer wall of the shoe.'[29]

Obviously, Sutherland's instructions to blacksmiths were intended for men with specialized knowledge. That the blacksmith had such knowledge was also reflected in his comparatively high pay (see Appendix 6) and in the testimonies of old-timers. Lumberman Alton Morse recalls that the talents of blacksmiths were clearly demonstrated when they shod horses brought in from the Prairies, because these horses had never worn shoes. 'Now, to shoe a horse that has never been shod is no picnic. But those blacksmiths were experts!'[30]

SLEIGH BELLS AND BRAG LOADS

A spirit of competitiveness prevailed on the sleigh haul, for workers knew that the success of a logging campaign depended on getting the entire cut hauled out of the bush during the short mid-winter season when sleighs moved most easily along the iced logging roads. Gangs of men and teams of horses scrambled to beat the spring thaw. In order to extend the working day, hauling crews worked by torchlight.

It appears that the practice of carefully grading and icing logging roads was introduced in Ontario by American operators who logged the Georgian Bay country in the 1880s. A Canadian lumberman who visited American operations in the Wahnapitae River valley in 1888 observed, 'They spare no expense in grading their roads and using sprinklers, making a solid ice road in a very short time.' A half century later, American-born, veteran lumberman D.L. White recalled how he had astonished local Georgian Bay lumbermen in the 1880s by paying 'the closest attention to grades, snow plows and sleigh runners.' He had even made sure that manure was cleared off the roads to prevent the runways from melting. That was something the Canadians 'regarded as carrying efficiency too far.' By the turn of the century these techniques had become the norm and they changed little in ensuing decades.[31]

On the haul, the daily round of chores began in the middle of the night, when tanking crews prepared the ice roads. Throughout the cold nights, a teamster would drive along the ice roads with a sleigh specially fitted with a large wooden tank. His conductor filled the tank using a barrel or pump. The crew sat atop the sleigh as it sprayed water onto the ruts that would guide the runners of the hauling sleighs. 'You had to be quick,' recalls an old-timer. 'If your tank leaked you'd freeze, sleigh and all, right to the blasted ground and you'd have to hammer the runners loose.'[52]

The lead teamster rose long before dawn, and the rest followed, one after the other, until the last sleigh departed. It must have been agony to rise early and head out into the sub-zero dark, and yet the old-time lumberjacks cheerfully sang about their experiences:

At four o'clock each morning,
the boss begins to shout,
'Heave out, my jolly teamsters,
It's time to start the route.'

The teamsters they all jump up,

in a most fretful way,
'Where is me boots? Where is me pants?
'Me socks is gone astray.'[33]

In sawlog camps, the loading crew usually consisted of a top loader, who acted as crew boss, two senders, two rollers, and a teamster. Young men served their apprenticeship in the position of roller. With the aid of a canthook, a tool resembling one half of a pair of ice tongs, the roller shoved the logs off the skidway, passing them to the senders. At the turn of the century, loading was done by means of a chain or decking line. The chain ran from the horse's harness, through a block rigged to a convenient tree or a pole. It was looped around the log and then brought back to the sleigh, where it was anchored with a hook. The senders, also armed with canthooks, positioned the log so the decking line could be looped around it, and then guided the log upwards, as the horse drew on the line. The top loader then brought the log aboard and positioned it on the sleigh. At the same time he freed the decking line.[34]

According to local lore, shortly before World War I Peter Wallis, a Blind River lumberjack, patented the jammer, a device that soon replaced the decking-line throughout the north.[35] His invention was a primitive crane mounted on a sled that could be moved from skidway to skidway, as required. A horse pulled on a cable that ran through a block at the top of the jammer and down to the loading area. Attached to the end of the cable was a device with two hooks which were fastened to each end of the log.

As the loads were built up, the crew fastened chains around them. When the load was complete, a final chain, the wrapper, was put round the entire load. It was a matter of pride for lumberjacks to build large, solid loads. Men occasionally spent Sundays – their day off – building giant loads, called brag loads, that would surpass the records set by their rivals in nearby camps. Enterprising professional photographers took shots of such loads and sold the prints to proud participants.[36]

Senders and top-loaders were among the most highly skilled men in the camp. Taking into account the size and shape of the logs, the top-loader selected the logs in an order that would enable him to build a compact load. His life was constantly in danger. If he slipped on the icy logs, mishandled a big one, or built an imbalanced pile, he could easily be crushed. 'I mind one day,' says Marshall Dobson, recalling his logging days before World War I, 'I was foolish enough to be up there – I was top loadin' – and the log hit, and the line flew and went round my neck. It hooked round my neck. I grabbed a hold of her and unhooked her, jumped straight for the block, had to have slack ... Oh did them fellers laugh?'[37] Senders also had to be adept with their canthook or the logs they were loading might fall on them.

The safety of the teamster depended on the loading skills of the cant-hookmen because he stood atop the towering load. He had to rely on his own skills as a driver as well. Since the valuable loads and sleighs might easily be upset or damaged and the tight schedule disrupted, only the most experienced men, the aristocrats of the camp, were allowed to drive the sleighs. Teamsters were assisted by road crews who helped brake the sleighs as they descended hills. Because there was a great danger that the load might travel faster than the horse could run, it was the job of road crews or road monkeys to pour hot sand on the slopes, thus slowing the runners. On steeper hills sleighs were braked by means of a loop of cable hitched to the rear of the sleighs and fed through the giant pulleys of a Bareinger brake or Crazy Wheel. By heaving on the lever of this patented braking device, the brakeman could slow down the sleigh.[38]

Despite the best efforts of loaders, teamsters, and road crews, some-times a sleigh would topple over as it rounded a bend in the road or descended a hill. When a teamster sensed a load was about to topple, he would scramble to the back of the load: it was safer to jump onto the road than to leap to the side where stumps or other sharp objects could spell disaster.

Many features of pulpwood hauling closely resembled operations in lumbering. When loading long lengths, pulpwood crews also used a jammer. However, in short-wood operations, crews could be reduced in size to one or two members, and they loaded by hand. Because shorter lengths could not be piled as high, loads tended to be longer and lower. Crews piled the bolts crosswise on sleighs that horses pulled into the skidding areas. At the haul road, crews would couple the sleighs together to form a train, which was pulled by two teams or some kind of mechani-cal hauling vehicle, such as a tractor. The job of loading bolts required less expertise and was less dangerous than loading logs. But it was exhausting work, stooping and bending to manoeuvre thousands of bolts a day. In spite of the relative simplicity of pulpwood hauling, the Woodlands Sec-tion stressed that dozens of factors needed to be taken into account in order to haul pulpwood efficiently.[39]

At the end of the main haul road lay the dump site or landing, where the sleighs were unloaded. Sometimes crews dumped their loads at a railway siding, but usually they unloaded them beside a river or onto the frozen surface of a lake in readiness for the spring river drive. Generally, the cheapest method was to place as much wood as possible on the surface of a lake or stream. Where there were small creeks, however, operators put the wood in rollways on the bank so that the drivers could later control the amount of wood entering the water at any one time during the drive. Unloading crews frequently used a jammer, although in some instances they were able to let gravity do much of the work. 'They'd let go the chains around the logs and the whole pile would fly out and come down those skids and start bouncing onto the ice,' recalls Frank Moran of Thunder Bay. 'The guys with the canthook would grab any log bouncing off the skids and just give it a flick with their wrist to get it straight again.'[40]

From New Year's Day to mid-March, the woods resounded with the thunder of rolling logs. But as the days began to grow warmer, bushworkers knew that the job was almost finished. Soon they would be heading back home or to town for the annual spring binge.

DARE-DEVILS ON THE DRIVE

After a few weeks some members of the crew would return to the bush for the river drive. When the spring run-off was at its height, drivers rolled the logs into the water and allowed them to float freely downstream, the current supplemented by water released at dams. When lakes were encountered, the drivers corralled the free-floating logs into a boom, which was then towed or winched across the lake. Northern Ontario operators used driving and booming operations to transport wood over distances anywhere from a few miles to more than 100. Some of the pulpwood that fed the mills at the Lakehead was driven down the tributaries to Lake Nipigon, and boomed across the lake, down the Nipigon River, and along the north shore of Lake Superior to the holding areas at the Lakehead, a distance of more than 150 miles.[41]

In 1946 the Woodlands Section summarized the factors which favoured river driving in the Shield country. The natural advantages included the buoyancy of softwood logs, the great number of suitable rivers, and abundant winter snowfall, and the spring rains. In rough, remote areas, it was agreed that water transportation was usually the only possible method. The low density of timber stands meant that mechanized transportation costs were usually prohibitively high. Yet river improvements such as dams and chutes, as well as tools and equipment, were comparatively inexpensive. In short, river driving was 'generally cheapest, most convenient and often the only major transportation method in this region.'[42]

River driving was also cost-effective in northern Ontario because cheap, experienced labour was readily available. Driving and floating operations required fewer men than winter logging activities, and so the professional bushworkers filled most of the positions. Forestry students visiting northern Ontario found 'the excitement and sport of the drives always attracts the younger men.'[43] Another student report declared:

The work is extremely hard and trying, as well as dangerous, but there is no difficulty in obtaining men for the drive. The best men from the winter crews are chosen for the drive, and they are generally proud of the fact. The hustling and excitement and constant moving from one place to another is a welcome change to the more or less monotonous winter work. Moreover, the pay is better than the winter wage. The fact what tells more than anything else in making the game popular, is probably that a lumberjack's prestige amongst his fellow men is raised when he becomes a river-driver, and no-one desires to be regarded as a dare-devil more than a red-blooded lumberjack.[44]

In recognition of the job's risks, river drivers were paid a little more than choppers (see Appendix 6).

The work of river driving had two distinct phases: constructing stream improvements and flushing the logs downstream during the drive itself. Naturally, the improvements had to be made before the drive began – usually the preceding summer. Improvement crews removed rocks and smoothed or reinforced jagged banks that might obstruct the path of the logs. Operators undertook substantial construction projects if the volume of wood warranted the expense. They built splash dams at appropriate points along the streams so that an increased volume of water could be released when needed. When there were major obstacles, the crews built either crude chutes or water-tight flumes to slide the logs down. Lumber companies sharing a stream usually pooled their resources, and improvements were made by an improvement company in which the firms held shares.[45] As in the case of road making, the engineering departments of the big pulp and paper companies took responsibility for design and construction, while in the lumber sector, dams and flumes were usually built by men whose knowledge had been acquired after years of practical experience.

The first task on the drive itself was to co-ordinate the release of water and logs. Lumberjacks spilled the big logs from the rollways; pulpwood drivers heaved each bolt into the stream. Once the wood reached the stream, the driver spent most of the day prodding the logs with his peavey, a six-foot long pole with a metal point and hook at the tip. Some men worked from long, narrow-beamed boats known as pointers; others waded into the water. When large sawlogs were being driven, the more experienced men rode the logs. To be able to dash out along the rolling, bobbing logs, men needed agility and steady nerves, although a pair of sturdy caulked boots helped as well. Drivers took special care at narrows and bridges to ensure that logs moved freely along, but now and again timber would become lodged on some obstacle resulting in a jam. 'Given a start, jams built up with incredible speed,' writes a witness of some of the big drives on the north shore. 'Urged on by the tremendous force of the current, they soon choked the river to the bottom and piled up like giant matchsticks from shore to shore.'[46]

The most dangerous and skill-testing job on the river drive was jam breaking. River drivers would clamber out to the front of the jam and pry away at the lead logs, trying to find the kingpin which would release the jam. As the kingpin was pried loose, the jam might burst apart, leaving barely enough time to jump clear. However, escapes were not always successful. Describing a tragic jam-breaking incident near Byng Inlet, Jack Campbell says: 'You see he stood on a stick of timber, and when it broke, instead of fallin' behind it, why he fell in front of it, and there wasn't any water where it was fastened. It rubbed him over the rocks like that and pulled his legs off.' Many of the traditional songs of woodsworkers are at once sad laments for jam breakers, and lusty, boasting ballads that celebrate the river drivers' courage and daring.[47]

Dynamiting log jams made the work more dangerous. Bosses turned to blasting powder as a last resort, mainly because it damaged the logs and held up the work of nearby drivers. 'It is good practice for two men to work together when blasting on a stream,' the Woodlands Section recommended. 'After igniting the fuse they should run in opposite directions to warn men working up and down stream.' Although most logging accidents involved one or two individuals, disasters did occur. On a Quebec river drive in 1933 a boat carrying dynamite to a jam site exploded. Seven men were killed and six injured.[48]

After the bulk of the logs had passed downstream, it was the sweepers' job to push along any logs that had been left behind and could still be salvaged. The Woodlands Section held that anywhere from 3 to 10 per cent of logs were lost through sinkage – one of the major disadvantages of transporting wood by means of the river drive. An even greater disadvantage was the danger of wood becoming hung up because of an inadequate or poorly marshalled supply of water. The ultimate result was an acute shortage of wood at the mill and perhaps even the disruption of mill production. Most seasons, however, the annual winter's harvest reached the mill – thanks to the co-operation of nature and the hard work of skilful river drivers.[49]

INJURIES AND FATALITIES

At the end of the year's logging cycle, woodsmen could stand back and assess the carnage. In 1929 the Lumbermen's Safety Association of Ottawa noted that 2,103 serious accidents had been reported in Ontario. Of these, 17 per cent involved accidents with axes; an equal proportion from falls; 13 per cent from felling or rolling logs; 8 per cent from falling trees; 7 per cent from jammed logs; 3 per cent from horses; and 3 per cent from muscular strains. The incomplete lists of serious logging accidents published monthly in the federal Labour Gazette indicate that the vast majority of reported fatalities were caused by falling timber or drownings, though there were some exceptional cases. In December 1903 a Mattawa lumberjack disappeared and was 'believed to have been devoured by wolves.' A few months later at Port Arthur a shanty cook was killed 'by an explosion of dynamite while thawing some by the stove.' And in 1906 the body of a Rainy River woodsman who had been lost in a storm was later 'found frozen in ice.'[50]

Various woods managers expressed concern about the industry's bad accident record. Comparing logging with other occupations, a pulp and paper company official emphasized in 1933: 'the northern woodsman is more likely to be injured in his occupation than is the navigator, railroad man or the fellow engaged in loading artillery shells.' What made matters appear so much worse to employers was that under the Workmen's Compensation Act introduced in 1914, they had to foot the bill for accidents, paying the rate set for their industry. The Canadian Lumbermen's Association called the statute 'socialism of the worst kind.' And no wonder they were critical. For many years, lumbermen paid the highest rate because of the dreadful accident record as well as the seriousness of the injuries. In addition to these charges was the expense of bringing doctors to emergencies in remote locations and transporting the victims to hospital. One study estimated that accidents added as much as 15 per cent to the total cost of wood delivered to the mill.[51]

Although pulp and paper companies had introduced safety campaigns for inside employees by the early 1920s, equivalent programs were not introduced into woods operations until after World War II. In 1927 Abitibi officials held that 'any definite accident prevention campaign' was 'in woods work, practically impossible.'[52] There seems to have been a consensus, although companies never spelled out their reasons for considering woods safety programs impractical. Alexander White, Ontario's chief sanitary inspector, speaking in 1926 at the American Safety Congress, Pulp and Paper Section, insisted that companies could do more. He demanded that first-aid facilities be established in every camp irrespective of size; instruction in first-aid be given to every camp clerk; foremen take responsibility for directing the injured to the first-aid officer; woods management oversee and discipline first-aid efforts of foremen; and visiting camp physicians take an interest in accident prevention.[53] Yet in subsequent years, implementation of this kind of suggestion proved haphazard at best.

THE PUZZLE OF SKILL

In attempting to draw conclusions about the nature of bush work, one is confronted with the puzzling problem of defining skill. What is really meant by the phrase a job requires skill, or the term skilled worker? When the word skill is used in common parlance, it usually refers to the possession of what historian Charles More refers to as 'the two useful qualities of manual skill and knowledge.' More points to the carpenter, who combines manual skill, such as sawing or planing, with a knowledge of types of wood, different joints, and the like.[54] Acquiring this kind of genuine skill usually takes a considerable amount of time – perhaps a few years. Having mastered the wide-range of tasks, the genuinely skilled worker enjoys a good deal of discretion in determining how to carry them out.

In the course of a year's logging campaign, the range of tasks performed by the bushworker was enormous – from felling and piling timber, to hauling by team and sleigh, to driving logs down swollen streams. Each phase demanded considerable physical co-ordination of perceptual and motor abilities, whether sawing and piling, loading by decking line, or jumping from one bobbing log to another. Knowledge of natural conditions was essential in selecting suitable rot-free trees to fell or judging the water volumes needed to flush down timber. Furthermore, bushworkers exercised discretion. As a dispersed work force, they could not be closely supervised, and the ever-changing natural conditions defied the creation of routine tasks. Nearly always the feller, top-loader, or river driver had to rely on his own knowledge and abilities, shaped through years of experience, to avoid costly and dangerous errors. If the tasks sometimes seemed boring and repetitive, it was not because bosses had imposed rigid routines; rather it was the result of the repeated application of thoroughly familiar activities. Certain tasks required little job-learning time, yet it took at least a few seasons before men became well-rounded bushworkers, proficient in the main jobs associated with felling, skidding, hauling, and river driving.

Despite the fact that bush work required quite high levels of genuine skill and specialized knowledge, bushworkers received little recognition for their talents. With the exception of the foreman and a handful of better-paid service personnel, the great majority of woodsworkers were paid very little. Gradations of skill that meant much among bushmen were scarcely recognized on the payrolls – the camp labour force resembled a broad-based pyramid. And monthly pay rates in the logging industry were low in comparison with most Ontario industries. Perceptions of the lumberjack reinforced his low status. Canadians usually referred to eastern Canadian woodsmen as unskilled workers, lumping lumberjacks and pulp cutters with construction labourers, railway extra-gang members, and muckers in mines. Even bushworkers themselves tended to see their work as unskilled.[55]

In order to understand the unskilled label usually attached to bush work, it is necessary to recognize that skill designations are at least in part socially constructed. When people call certain groups of workers skilled, semi-skilled, or unskilled, these designations may or may not bear a close relationship to the actual requirements of the job or to levels of genuine skill and knowledge. The label skilled has been assigned to some jobs partly because of convention and traditions in the trade, or because management and/or unions have effectively defended the high social status and wages accompanying the label.[56]

The gulf between the high levels of genuine skill and knowledge of the bushworker and the label unskilled indicates that the woodsworker's skill has been socially constructed. It appears bushworkers were labelled as unskilled labourers as a result of at least two key factors. First, general perceptions were shaped by the outdoor and seasonal nature of logging, as well as the enormous amounts of heavy lifting that bushworkers had to do. These characteristics were shared with the non-unionized pick-and-shovel work of other so-called unskilled workers, many of whom did in fact have low levels of genuine skill and job-related knowledge. Hence, observers mistook the true requirements of woods work. Secondly, the logging labour market played a key role in shaping assessments of the bushman's calling. In the pre-World War II period many men had learned the basic requirements of logging – as a result of farm woodlot experience or because they had to in order to get winter work. Employers and others, therefore, took the bushworker's skills for granted. Labour abundance gave woods operators a powerful advantage and enabled them to avoid recognizing woodsworker's unions, to designate their employees as unskilled labourers, and to pay them the low wages commensurate with work so defined. Society as a whole, and bushworkers themselves, accepted the dominant view which served employers so well.

Perhaps because bushworkers were deprived of the kind of respect and rewards artisans and mechanics enjoyed, they took such pleasure in presenting themselves as dare-devils and he-men who, in the style of Joe Monteferrand took on any dangerous or heavy task and carried it out with aplomb. Given the realities of their work, it was also not so far from the truth.

4

Cutting costs

During the first half of the twentieth century not all Ontario woods managers were satisfied with conventional logging techniques and the slow pace of innovation in the industry. Some lumbermen, and an even greater proportion of pulpwood officials, insisted that if harvesting costs were to be kept down, bold initiatives were needed. 'In our woods operations,' declared Ellwood Wilson, woods manager for the Laurentide Company, in 1920, 'we [in eastern Canada] are faced with rising costs all along the line and we have made absolutely no progress so far as I know since we first began logging in the old days.' The woods end of the pulp and paper business needed to catch up with developments in the mills. 'Nobody,' Wilson continued, 'would think today of running a big paper mill without trained chemists, without trained engineers, without trained cost accountants, etc., but up to this time we have not had this class of men in the woods.' According to Wilson, and others who shared his viewpoint, the industry urgently required 'men who will think out new mechanical methods for getting out the small amount of timber per acre which stands in our Eastern forests and men who will develop these methods and put them into practice.'[1]

Wilson's outlook was in tune with that of other progressive-era businessmen who placed enormous faith in the power of trained experts to solve social and business problems through the application of scientific principles. As a university-trained forester in the employ of a large paper company, Wilson spoke for one wing of the conservation movement which, for a few years in the early twentieth century, brought together civil servants, hard-headed industrialists, and idealistic nature lovers in a campaign to conserve Canada's forests. Though the movement's successes were few, it did spur large forest companies to make gestures towards forest management and to hire foresters for their woodlands departments.

Industrial foresters such as Wilson had a tough time, however, for their employers made conflicting demands of them. Foresters were charged with ensuring a permanent supply of wood for company mills while reducing wood costs. Reforestation and sustained-yield operations required large capital outlays, but short-sighted executives provided only meagre funding for such work. Experimenting with new logging methods also cost money, and here, too, executives looking at the year-end balance sheet proved tight-fisted. Isolated and often frustrated within their own firms, woods managers with forestry training sought the solace and support of their peers.[2]

In 1917 Carl Riordan, chairman of the Canadian Pulp and Paper Association, won his Executive Board's support for forming a new section of the association that would deal with the 'imperative problem' of providing 'a permanent wood supply at minimum cost.' As the pulp and paper industry expanded rapidly, executives were becoming increasingly uneasy about rising costs as a result of competition for woods labour and convenient supplies of trees. Moreover, the CPPA had a precedent in its Technical Section, formed in 1915 as a means to promote research into the science of pulp and paper making. The membership of the new Woodlands Section, which began meeting in 1918, was composed of foresters, engineers, and accountants from the woodlands departments of member companies. The new section announced that it had three objectives: first, to protect wood supplies; secondly, to disseminate technical information; and thirdly, to develop more efficient logging techniques. As it turned out, members gave scant attention to the protection of wood supplies. From the outset, however, they pursued the second objective, meeting each summer to examine the latest logging equipment and again each winter to present papers, some of which the section published. Despite the keen interest of many members, the third objective – equipment development – proved elusive, especially when the CPPA refused to grant funds for that purpose. In the mechanization field, the section itself made virtually no headway until 1926, when the CPPA executive allotted some money for research and to pay the salary of a professional logging engineer who would become secretary of the section and the co-ordinator of research. The section chose as its secretary Alexander Koroleff, a former White Russian cavalry officer with a striking, aristocratic bearing. With his extensive European and American training in forestry and engineering, he provided strong leadership for the section's practical-minded members.[3]

Under Koroleff's direction the Woodlands Section undertook a host of studies and gave vital encouragement and support to the work of innovators in forest companies and equipment-manufacturing firms. In the inter-war years woods officials made significant advances in two areas: piece-rate incentives brought significant changes to the work of cutters and fellers, while gasoline haulers lengthened hauling distances and made new demands on work crews. Nevertheless, enthusiasts for mechanization remained discouraged by their failure to devise far more sweeping alternatives to conventional logging practices.

INVISIBLE FOREMEN

How best to motivate employees and obtain the most work from them was a topic hotly debated by woods managers during the early decades of this century. It became even more topical at the end of World War I, a time of industrial expansion, labour shortages, spiralling wages, and reduced efficiency among bushworkers. Managers resolved to find ways to stabilize the labour force and increase productivity. In 1918 one woods manager had complained: 'While in the mill the men were bound to keep pace with the machinery, there was no such obligation on the part of the men in the camp. In the woods there was no means of putting a driving force into the men.'[4] This woods official was envying the reliance of his mill counterpart on what labour sociologist Richard Edwards has recently dubbed 'technical control.' Edwards defines it as a structural form of control that 'emerges ... when the entire production process of the plant or large segments of it are based on a technology that paces and directs the labour process.'[5] In 1918 Ontario's new paper mills were excellent examples of this kind of development. In the forest, however, there was little machinery at all, let alone a production process based on pace-setting technology. Moreover, managers found that even far more conventional methods for motivating workers were ill-suited to the forest. In early twentieth-century factories, the so-called drive method of supervision combined 'authoritarian rule and physical compulsion.'[6] When production depended on the pace at which workers toiled, drive foremen maintained a vigilant watch over labourers and semi-skilled machine operators, goading them with verbal abuse, threatening them physically, and instilling deep fears of dismissal. The forest environment presented structural impediments to this system because it was impossible to maintain close, direct supervision over such a scattered work force.

Yet even as early as 1918 some woods operators had already begun to experiment with piece-rate systems as a means of 'putting a driving force into men.' Paying employees on the basis of output, rather than time, had been the common practice in many industries for decades. In the late nineteenth and early twentieth centuries, factory managers throughout North America were preoccupied with solving their labour problem by introducing some kind of piece rate or bonus system. In this regard, the North American logging industry did not lag behind. In the 1923 edition of the textbook *Logging*, Professor R.C. Bryant reported that piece work had been extensively introduced throughout North American logging regions. Ontario operators began to experiment with it about 1914, and they had come to rely on it widely by the end of World War I. Sawlog operators proved more hesitant to introduce piece work. Some began experimenting with piece-rate systems in the 1920s, and by 1945 most of them were probably using such systems.[7]

The operators' rationale for introducing piece work was quite straightforward. It appeared to make good sense in the forest, where supervising a dispersed work force was difficult and operating costly machinery at optimal levels was not a consideration. Pulp cutters, for example, could be left to set their own pace, because the employer only paid for what was actually produced. In addition, as time went on and woods operations increased in scale, piece rates made even more sense because managers could no longer rely on the personal ties between foremen and woodsworkers to maximize productivity. The ethnic diversity of the woods work force also encouraged the spread of piece rates. Canadian-born managers and foremen had difficulty motivating people they did not understand; piece rates or bonus systems offered an apparent solution.[8]

For woods managers, another attraction of piece work was that it could be easily grafted onto the existing production system and required no major expansion of clerical or supervisory functions. Among the various activities in the annual logging cycle, the cutting phase was the easiest in which to measure an individual's output. Since operators were accustomed to having their logs scaled for inventory control and to determine the amount of dues owing the government, it was a simple matter to have scalers measure the output of each felling crew or cutter. In the case of log-lengths, the pieces were simply counted, while with bolts, scalers measured the number of cords, or cordage. At the beginning of each operating season companies set prices for cords of various kinds of timber. In 1936 Spruce Falls paid its cutters five cents per sixteen-foot log and $1.75 per cord of eight-foot bolts of spruce.[9]

Bushworkers performing other jobs also sometimes worked on an incentive basis. Road-building crews were often paid according to the number of feet cleared and prepared. Some hauling gangs received so much for every sleigh hauled, gang members dividing up the total on the basis of an agreed formula. Much more frequently, however, managers offered an incentive bonus for men who completed the haul before a specified date.

When operators assessed the results of piece-rate systems, they generally agreed that piece workers toiled harder and produced more per day than equally experienced men who were paid a monthly wage. In his 1939 study, *Woods Labour*, L.A. Nix maintained that operators favoured piece work 'as a means of correcting inefficiency and waste in wage systems.' It accomplished this by bringing 'out the incentive in the average worker to make more.' In 1941–2, the Woodlands Section conducted a thorough time-motion analysis of the skidding operations of seven companies. The study showed: 'Wage earners take more time than pieceworkers for nearly every phase of the operation. Assembling [logs] is the only main item where piece-workers take longer. This is probably because of their desire to build more compact bundles of logs [in order] to avoid delays in transit. Variable delays are 97% lower with piece-workers.' The same investigation found that the productivity of wage-workers was 26 per cent lower than that of piece workers. The stop-watch men discovered that in comparison with piece workers, employees on monthly rates spent more than two-and-a-half times resting than did piece workers. 'Obviously,' concluded the engineers, 'the piece-worker is reluctant to waste his time, while the wage-worker often fails to spend his profitably.'[10]

Woods employers also derived other benefits from piece work. For one thing, supervision costs remained low because few front-line supervisors were required. The piece rate became a cheap and invisible foreman, goading workers to produce more. Some managers also believed that efficient, hard-working men were more strongly attracted to operations run on an incentive scheme. 'Good men prefer, and often request, the piece-work basis of remuneration, while the poor men are content to work for wages,' maintained Koroleff.[11] If steady, big producers could be attracted and retained, woods managers reasoned, then the annual cut might be made with a smaller work force. This meant fewer mouths to feed and fewer men to house.

Piece work was indeed preferred by many bushworkers who were convinced that it enabled them to earn higher incomes or make their stakes sooner. In 1920, for instance, woods union officials griped again and again about the growing popularity of piece rates among Ontario bushworkers. Much later, a union organizer who successfully signed up thousands of Ontario bushworkers, says that if he had told the men that the union planned to take them off piece work and put them on a good hourly wage, 'they'd have killed me!' Pulp cutters from Finland were especially keen on piece work because they believed their excellent woods skills were more justly rewarded under such a system. Finnish piecework cutters, who were anxious to improve their productivity, popularized the bucksaw or Swede saw as a felling tool in Ontario logging camps during the 1920s. 'We brought the Swede saw, a Finnish invention, manufactured by a Finn,' recalls retired pulp cutter Felix Lukkarila. 'We carried the blade in our packsack and then made the crossbar in the forest. The Frenchmen used to laugh at us, but not after they saw us work!'[12]

Some men also enjoyed the increased freedom from supervision that accompanied piece rates. A piece worker could set his own pace, either working frantically during a short spell in the bush or more steadily for longer periods. Particularly where men cut pulpwood on their own strips, piece rates and the organization of work combined to foster a strong sense of independence. Each morning a piece worker would set out for his assigned timber strip where he worked throughout the day rarely, if ever, seeing a supervisor.

By introducing piece work, operators also fostered the development of a competitive spirit among their employees. Lumberman and pulpwood contractor Bill Plaunt recalls the tense rivalry among his cutters when, at the end of the day, they would line up at the camp office to report the size of their day's cut. Each hoped to report a high total; not only did this mean a big pay packet, it was also a sign of skill and strength. In some industries, big producers were regarded by other piece workers as rate busters. But in logging, it would appear that those cutters who could maintain a pace of two-and-a-half cords a day gained the admiration of fellow workers. (Since companies established rates at the commencement of the season, it was difficult to perceive any relationship between big producers and rate busting.) Canadian painter William Kurelek, recalling his pulp-cutting days, writes: 'At all the camps there was the same yarn-telling, backslapping humour ... the same admiration for physical prowess and productivity.' A bushworker's pride, his status among his peers, and even his manliness were tied up with his ability to turn in a respectable count. Not surprisingly, management tried to take advantage of the workers' sense of pride in their output.[13]

Yet not all employers saw advantages in piece rates. Rather than attracting good producers and stabilizing a camp's work force, some managers believed that piece work had the opposite effect. 'The turnover is certainly not remedied by the piece worker,' declared an Abitibi woods manager in 1930. 'He is always striving to find the type of timber in which he can make the best wages.'[14] Furthermore, some pulp cutters succeeded in tricking the scalers by such stunts as piling wood on top of a boulder so that it was hollow. Operators also complained that cutters on piece rates tended to waste timber and hinder the carrying out of the subsequent logging steps. Some men refused to take the time to pile exceptionally heavy logs with the result that big logs got left behind in the bush. The waste that piece work encouraged, as well as its adverse effects of the future forest crop, were points stressed by the Kennedy Commission on Forestry in 1947. Howard Kennedy repeatedly complained about the pervasiveness of the piece worker's practice of high-grading, or taking out only the timber that could be quickly felled and made into logs. These kinds of problems partially explain why sawlog operators were slower to introduce piece work: the comparatively high value of sawlogs made waste especially costly.[15]

Piece work also had a number of disadvantages for workers. The lure of higher incomes drove men to work hard and fast with few breaks. Given the nature of the work, this put a severe strain on their physical well-being. Appalled by the human costs of piece work, one woods manager insisted that ways should be found to eliminate the practice of men 'working too long hours intensively and continuously.' Veteran lumberjack Joe Sarazin says that he chose not to work under the piece-rate system. 'I didn't have that much ambition, I guess. The work was too hard as it was. Besides, I was single and didn't need the extra money.' Gerry Fortin, who tried piece work cutting for the first time in 1939, recalls: 'I went at it like a maniac, anxious to show I could hold my own with the old-timers. But I soon started to slow up, until I couldn't even move my arms. Each morning it took me longer before I could really get going. Then I became swollen all over.' After three months, Fortin was so ill he had to quit. As he explains: 'Though I'd cut more wood than anyone else, I was *completement brulé*, totally burned out.'[16]

Bushworkers found that piece work had other disadvantages as well. It increased the chances that they would suffer from the unfair practices of a foreman, and it encouraged them to co-operate with, or even bribe, their strip bosses. Since forest conditions are never uniform, bosses could assign strips with the best timber to their favourites. C.B. Davis, Abitibi's woods manager, acknowledged to his fellow woods managers the difficulties of determining fair rates for various conditions. 'Possibly some of us think we can judge the logging operations closely enough to know what we are doing about the piece wage rates,' he commented. 'If the trees were all the same size we could do this, but that is not the case and the first thing we know we are getting into a difficult situation.' Piece workers were also at the mercy of company scalers who underestimated the volume of the wood piles and marked good logs as culls for which bushworkers were not paid. Describing one such scaler near Port Arthur, a bushworker wrote: 'The boys claim these Xs were as sore for men's eyesight as twisted stocking seams on some dames' legs!' It was not until the 1950s that woodsworkers and their union made any progress towards eliminating such inequities. In the mean time, employers could look back with pleasure on the introduction of piece work as a successful innovation that had reduced production costs.[17]

Recently, students of the labour process have argued that piece work had broad consequences. In *Segmented Work, Divided Workers*, economists David Gordon, Richard Edwards, and Michael Reich maintained that the turn-of-the-century expansion of piece work systems in u.s. industry was not solely intended to influence the output of individual workers. They contend, 'the systems were aimed at dividing workers and minimizing collective action.' Industrial sociologist Michael Burawoy, in *Manufacturing Consent*, suggests that by becoming caught up in the 'game of piecework,' employees come to defend its rules and thus consent to their own exploitation.[18]

It seems unlikely that practical-minded logging operators in Ontario foresaw these wider implications when they turned to piece work. Certainly, in the management literature, forest operators did not mention these broader motives, but stressed instead that piece rates offered a way to cut production costs by encouraging workers to intensify their efforts. Nevertheless, whatever their intentions, employers who introduced piece work had, however unwittingly, served the wider purposes of corporate capitalism. The results-oriented piece worker was likely to work hard for himself – and hence for his boss. And since he was paid according to his own, individual record, an important basis for solidarity and collective action was lacking.

STEAM IN THE BUSH

At the same time as woods managers were experimenting with piece-rate systems, some were also attempting to cut costs by introducing more effective logging machinery. In fact, the mechanization of Ontario's woods industry had begun in the late nineteenth century, when inventory began applying steam power to various logging tasks.

One of the first labour-saving pieces of steam equipment to hit the woods industry was the warping tug. Designed in 1889 by John West of Simcoe, Ont., the warping tug was a square-built scow with a powerful steam boiler that drove a winch and the paddle wheels (later, a propeller). The winch, located in the bow, carried up to a mile of steel cable and had a large anchor. Towing crews would board a row-boat and carry the anchor out a few hundred yards and drop it. The flukes of the anchor would catch on the lake bottom, and then, using the steam winch, the tug would be drawn to the anchor. At the same time the tug was towing an immense log raft. Eventually the tug and raft would cross the lake. This kind of tug was usually called an alligator because it could also be winched across portages.[19]

As operators introduced alligators to dozens of operations in the ensuing decades, men were relieved of a great deal of back-breaking toil. Lumberman Bill Plaunt recalls being deeply moved by the sight of oarsmen in a pointer trying to haul a huge boom across a remote lake. As they heaved away for hours on end, sweat and blood from fly bites dripped from their chins. Determined to end his men's agony, Plaunt had an alligator disassembled and transported up country piece by piece, despite claims that it could not be done. Ultimately, the alligator replaced several jobs, but no one mourned their loss.[20]

Early in the twentieth century, innovators introduced various other pieces of steam equipment. Many operators purchased devices such as the Barnhart Steam Log Loader, a bulky, but powerful piece of equipment that resembled a steam shovel to load logs onto railway cars. In 1909 the Hope Lumber Company bought a steam hoist to lift sleighs over ridges that were too steep for horses. Companies also experimented with cable skidding – logs attached by long cables to a steam winch were moved up and down the haul roads. In 1908, Asa Williams, forest engineer for Lidgerwood Manufacturing Company, a major supplier of new logging devices, justified the adoption of such a system: 'Common logging is cheap, easy and efficient. *Then why the skidder?* Because it is inanimate, does not die, eats nothing when it does not work, is unaffected by the weather, disease or insects, is constant or tireless and gets cheap logs: in other words there is money in it.' Although Williams was reputed to have had 'considerable success in placing logging machinery in Ontario,' cable skidding did not catch on in the province until after World War II, when mobile diesel engines replaced steam.[21]

Hauling presented the best opportunities for engineers bent on mechanization, because hauling roads provided smoother and flatter surfaces than those encountered at the stump. Steam railways were an obvious alternative to traditional methods of hauling logs. Where the ground was level and the timber sufficiently dense to warrant the high costs, steel rails were laid through the bush, and small but powerful locomotives pulled cars loaded with logs. In British Columbia, where such conditions frequently prevailed, steam logging railways really caught on.[22] Except for the Cleveland-Sarnia Lumber Company at Diver, the Trout Creek Logging Company on the north shore of Lake Huron, the White Pine Lumber Company near Blind River, and the Shevlin-Clark Lumber Company near Fort Frances, few Ontario operators could justify such an investment. All these companies logged valuable pine limits on flat terrain. Companies logging hardwood also used railways, partly because hardwood logs were not buoyant enough for river drives.

One of the most ambitious northern Ontario logging railways was built by Abitibi through their Iroquois Falls limits. The Abitibi River flowed in the wrong direction for driving wood to the mill, but the flat terrain of the clay belt was ideally suited for a railway. Moreover, the nature of Abitibi's operations enabled the company to benefit from the line for many years and to write off its costs over a long period. The first sixteen miles of the line were built in 1922, and it was extended periodically thereafter. The company's two locomotives could individually pull twenty-eight flat cars containing sixteen cords of wood in each one.[23]

While Abitibi's line was designed by professional engineers, the railway built by the Cleveland-Sarnia Lumber Company was a more makeshift operation. The route was laid out by the walking boss who, according to a Forestry student report, 'applied common sense as a substitute for engineering knowledge and his success has been remarkable.' No survey of the area had ever been made, and when questioned about the degree of the curves, 'the foreman did not know.' The actual construction of the road was done by a gang of thirty to thirty-five Italians, about twelve of whom stayed on during the winter to maintain the track. The railway staff consisted of two crews of three men (engineer, fireman, and brakeman) plus a night watchman who kept up the fires in case of frost. The company also employed a master mechanic and a machinist to maintain its three locomotives.[24] Railway crews were much better paid than most camp workers, a reflection of the bargaining power of skilled railwaymen (see Appendix 1, Chart 2).

Even when companies relied on makeshift methods, railways were costly propositions. Early in the twentieth century, however, alternatives became available. In 1889 the Ottawa firm of Perley and Pattee had purchased the first steam-powered traction engine to pull sleighs on their

Petawawa limits. Their Glover Steam Logger, which weighed twelve tons and was twenty-eight feet long, had been designed shortly before by a Chicago firm and tested in a Wisconsin lumber camp. It was operated by a crew of two men – a steersman who sat at the front, and an engineer, who controlled the steam valves and doubled as fireman. In fact, the crew rarely worked, because the Glover broke down continually. It was soon scrapped.[25]

During the first decade of this century, a few other American firms began manufacturing similar, though somewhat more reliable steam haulers. The most successful was the Lombard Log Hauler designed in 1901 by two mechanical engineers from Maine. A few firms operating in northern Ontario purchased these gargantuan machines which resembled railway locomotives mounted on heavy treads at the rear and skis at the front. The Lombard proved most suitable where uphill slopes made it difficult to haul by team. On the north shore limits of the Wolverine Cedar and Lumber Company in 1911, a crew of five made three trips daily pulling a train of nine to twelve sleighs. Company officials were optimistic that the high cost of crew salaries, which were triple the rate for regular lumberjacks, would be offset by savings in the off-season when, unlike horses who needed to be fed, machine costs would be close to nil. However, Ontario operators soon abandoned steam haulers because of high costs, frequent mechanical breakdowns – a crucial consideration given the shortness of the hauling season – and the heavy hauler's difficulties on downhill slopes where ice conditions were poor.[26]

MOTORIZED LOGGING

In the search for a more flexible and cheaper alternative to railways and cumbersome steam haulers, logging operators next turned to tractors powered by gasoline-fuelled, internal combustion engines. Gasoline tractors had been built for agricultural purposes in the 1890s, although Canadian farmers did not purchase many until World War I.[27] Such tractors arrived even later to the eastern Canadian forest industry. In August 1917 the *Canada Lumberman* reported that for two years the River Ouelle Lumber Company in Quebec had used them to haul sleighs. Alton Morse, who was managing director of the Devon Lumber Company and operating manager of Austin and Nicholson in 1920, claims he was the first person to introduce and to popularize the gasoline tractor in Ontario woods operations. He recalls:

It happened that my wife and I were on a holiday in my old home town of Waterville, Maine. I saw a house moving down the street! I went over to where it was, and here was a tractor with a caterpillar tread and with wheels in front; it was walking along with the house on skids without any trouble. And I said to my wife: 'That's what we've got to have!'

So when I came back to Canada I began to look for such a tractor . . . I heard that Mussens Ltd. in Montreal had a similar tractor called a Linn. In those days it was pretty expensive. But I bought one anyway.

With that tractor, instead of a team of horses hauling only five miles with one sleigh, this gasoline tractor hauled ten sleighs of the same size, twenty-four hours a day. That made it possible for us to haul longer distances, because it was faster.[28]

Gasoline tractors began to appear in numerous operations in the early 1920s, soon after Morse's experiment. Initially the favoured make was the Linn, developed by H.H. Linn of Maine and manufactured in Morris, NY.[29] Major U.S. heavy equipment manufacturers, such as Ford and Caterpillar, soon began producing popular models, most of them smaller and lighter than the heavy but powerful Linn.

A *Canada Lumberman* article of 1923 provides some details regarding the successful operation of Morse's Linn tractor on the pine timber limits of the Austin and Nicholson company. The Linn had a four-cylinder, ninety-horsepower engine and weighed over five tons. The company relied on its own sleighs, with special patented couplings, and the usual type of iced logging road. The maximum load was ten sleighs weighing a total of 150 tons. Altogether, daily operating costs amounted to sixty-five dollars, a savings of seventy-five dollars over conventional methods which required fifteen teams. Obviously, cost reduction was the motivation for introducing the Linn.[30] Despite this kind of success, the horse did not disappear. Some operators were tradition-bound. Others lacked the capital for heavy equipment. And it was generally agreed that horses were cheaper where hauling distances were short.

The introduction of tractors put new demands on the work force. At least initially, experienced tractor chauffeurs were in short supply. 'I don't know whether our chauffeur understood his business, but he claims it [a light Fordson tractor] up-ended going up the steep hills,' reported Duncan Lunam, woods manager for the Hawkesbury Lumber Company in 1928. When Gillies Brothers purchased a used tractor from the Fassett Lumber Company, D.A. Gillies made a special effort to recruit an experienced driver along with the tractor. Gillies promised Hugh White of Callender steady work as a handyman before the freeze-up and eighty dollars a month, a wage nearly double that paid to the teamsters who worked with horses. By 1930 tractor manufacturers provided instructors to train drivers and mechanics. It did not solve all the operators' problems, however, for in the late 1930s, woods managers were calling for more thorough training courses.[31]

In his memoirs Ken Collins gives us a sense of what work was like in a mechanized operation in the 1920s. In 1926 he worked on the sleigh train belonging to the Indian Lake Lumber Company. Three crews were assigned to the one Linn tractor so that it could be kept operating round-the-clock during the short hauling season. A return trip was supposed to take seven or eight hours, but in practice, 'Something always seemed to go wrong and most ... trips were from ten to twelve hours' duration.' As conductor, Collins had to start each sleigh, travel back and forth along the length of the train while it was under way, and sand the downhill slopes. 'It was by no means the safest job in the world,' says Collins, 'one had to be alert every minute especially after dark. Travelling over the tops of the loads of logs which were often very slippery with snow and ice adhering to them was dangerous and at night one only had the small trainman's lantern to see by.' When sand was needed to brake 'the conductor would grab the haversack full of sand and run on ahead of the train, awaiting signs from the engineer.' Collins vividly describes the considerable amount of co-ordination and skill demanded of even an apparently simple job like sanding roads:

These experienced drivers could tell when the weight of the train was overcoming the weight of the geared down tractor and before it could get out of control they would signal for some sand to be thrown into the tracks. One blast of the horn meant, 'Give me a *little* sand.' Two blasts meant 'give me more sand' and three or more blasts meant, quite literally, 'What the hell are you doing, gone to sleep or something? Give me sand damned quick!'

But the conductor had to be very careful with the use of sand at that. If he panicked and dumped too much in the sleigh track the whole train would grind to a halt and you could bet that if this occurred the conductor would get all the blame.

Mechanized hauling operations may have reduced the number of workers employed, but the dangers and the need for skills persisted. Skill requirements and the seriousness of hazards probably increased with the use of the new equipment.[32]

During World War I, Ontario logging operators also began to experiment with motorized trucks, first for toting supplies and later for hauling timber. The *Canada Lumberman* kept a close watch on u.s. experiments with trucks. 'Having revolutionized retail deliveries by building motor trucks to meet the special requirements of the lumber trade, motor truck manufacturers are giving greater attention to other fields of work in this industry,' noted the journal in 1913. By the fall of 1914, the Hope Lumber Company was using a Packard truck to tote supplies to its camps fifty miles north of Thessalon. Travelling at four or five miles an hour and carrying four-ton loads, it was reported to be doing the work of fifteen teams. It was also said to increase the value of timber where tote distances were long. Other companies followed this lead, whenever distances warranted it and road construction costs were not prohibitively high.[33]

Hauling timber by truck still had to await advances in automotive engineering. It was not until the late 1920s that Ontario operators found trucks to be powerful enough to haul heavy loads efficiently. The first to introduce them were settler-cutters who hauled small loads by means of farm trucks on provincial roads. About 1930 operators began using trucks to haul sleighs and sleigh-trains on iced logging roads. Among the first was the Newaygo Timber Company of Hearst, which used five trucks on its nine-mile iced logging road.

The number of trucks and tractors used in Ontario hauling operations increased dramatically in the 1930s with the arrival of powerful and cheap-to-operate diesel engines. By the late 1930s, diesel trucks and tractors were as common on the sleigh haul as horses. When road-building costs were not too high, operators came to rely on diesel-powered Mack trucks for hauling logs from the bush to the mill, eliminating the need for river-driving their wood. They also began deploying diesel bulldozers for such varied purposes as swamping skid trails, plowing snow, and shoving logs into streams during the drive.[34]

Despite these innovations, operators found little new technology that could be introduced in the cutting and skidding phases of the logging operation. 'Is it possible for the old cross-cut saw to form an armour that cannot be pierced by the scientific brains of the age?' a mechanization advocate inquired incredulously in 1917.[35] For many years it seemed that this was the case. The *Canada Lumberman* and the *Woodlands Review* reported on various experimental felling devices such as an electrically heated wire and portable circular saws, but all proved impractical.[36] During the 1920s, northern Ontario operators introduced a few gasoline-powered chainsaws, a tool that Alexander Koroleff called in 1930 the 'most promising for eastern Canadian pulpwood cutting.'[37] Various experiments showed that such saws had severe limitations – they broke down frequently and were difficult to repair. Because the saws weighed sixty to seventy-five pounds, two strong men were needed to operate them, and even then the work was fatiguing and dangerous.

Koroleff maintained that the introduction of power saws had been retarded by 'the inertia of loggers and by the difficulty of arranging between them and the manufacturers an effective co-operation to adapt foreign saws to Canadian requirements.'[38] To some extent this inertia was overcome during World War II, when supplies of German power saws were cut off and Vancouver firms began producing them. Ontario operators then showed a keen interest in developing chainsaws suitable for boreal forest conditions. 'A machine must be developed which can be handled by one man for reasonable periods without fatigue,' declared a hopeful Gordon Godwin of Ontario Paper Company.[39] Yet no significant advances were made until the post-war period.

Thus, during the first half of the twentieth century, operators had their best success in mechanizing the sleigh haul. Felling and skidding wood under off-road conditions still defied the innovators. Even on the haul, however, the new methods did not sweep aside the traditional ones. In any year before the end of World War II, more wood was probably moved by horses than by mechanical means.[40]

IMPEDIMENTS TO INNOVATION

Though productivity-conscious woods managers were somewhat heartened by advances such as piece work and tractor-haulers, throughout the 1920s, 1930s, and 1940s spokesmen within the industry continually griped about the failure of the eastern Canadian logging industry to find far more drastic cost-cutting methods. Even as late as 1949 two officials from the Woodlands Section stated: 'Few companies have looked at the fundamental methods of pulpwood production with a questioning eye, and we must admit that our policy has not been toward long-range development of new methods.'[41] Woods managers offered several explanations for their limited achievements; some chose to focus on natural constraints imposed by the eastern Canadian forest environment, while others stressed the shortcomings of the industry itself.

Observers placed much of the blame for what they perceived to be technical stagnation on the Shield country. Many logging areas in the eastern and southern United States had gentler slopes, more stable and even ground, and denser forests. Consequently, large firms there had had greater success mechanizing skidding and hauling by steam and later gasoline tractors. When an American manufacturer of steam haulers tried to clinch a sale to Gillies Brothers, D.A. Gillies pointed out the problem of deploying such a machine in Ontario: 'The weight of twelve tons would be difficult to handle taking the machine in long distances over hilly roads. . . . The country in which we operate is much cut up with lakes and marshes which would be difficult in many cases to get around and we are under the impression that it would be impossible to use this engine on ice without considerable risk.' Gasoline and diesel tractors were also ineffective as skidding machines in the boulder-strewn, muskeg-pocked Shield country, though they worked well in the southern United States. Similarly, the mountainous topography and far denser forests of coastal British Columbia had made it necessary – and economically feasible – for firms there to introduce mechanical logging equipment virtually from the industry's birth. But in eastern Canada's comparatively sparse forests, it rarely paid to set up steam skidders and hauling railways.[42]

Men such as Koroleff insisted that eastern Canada's forest conditions simply presented an inviting challenge to engineers. In 1930 he explained that the real problems lay in the unhelpful attitudes of nearly everyone involved in the industry: bushworkers and jobbers resisted change, preferring familiar methods; machinery manufacturers were not interested in improving their equipment and providing adequate service and instruction to operators; and top industry executives refused to allocate sufficient funds for the research and development of equipment.[43] Years before, at the first meeting of the Woodlands Section, J.M. Dalton, a woods manager for the St Maurice Paper Company, said: 'I don't think the heads of the paper mills go out of their road sufficiently to learn the problems we are up against. If it was not for the woods they would not be running paper mills.' More than two decades later Koroleff was still chastising top executives for granting 'liberal appropriations for research in manufacturing pulp and paper,' while 'woods departments have in many cases miserably small appropriations for research.'[44]

Koroleff's analysis really only begs the question, why did these various people have such unhelpful attitudes? Structural factors largely explain their points of view. Because bushworkers and jobbers were often paid on an incentive basis, they refused to experiment with new equipment that might limit output even temporarily. Moreover, woodsworkers who were paid on a piece-rate system insisted on the right to choose their own tools and methods. As one woods supervisor pointed out it was difficult to implement the recommendations of a Woodlands Section study on bucksaws: 'As long as a man is working on his own piece work ... he certainly will retain the right to use the type of saw he wants to use.'[45]

Senior level executives refused to allocate large sums for research and development in the woodlands because they doubted whether such investments would pay off as handsomely as capital allocations for mill research. These men almost invariably had gained their training in pulp and paper mills and continued to be more interested in the manufacturing end of the business. To such individuals, mills made profits but woods operations ran up expenses. The outdoor men had to plead their case for more funding before superiors who seemed to view woodlands departments as mere adjuncts, headed by men with practical experience and training in forestry but limited financial or technical expertise.[46] This amounted to an internal structural constraint imposed on advocates of mechanization. And since companies seemed to lack the capital to invest in woodlands equipment, manufacturers and their sales representatives paid less attention to the industry than they might have done.

The meagre funding executives provided for woodlands departments had a snowballing effect. Without such funding, basic scientific and engineering research was minimal. And until woodlands departments, the Woodlands Section, or equipment manufacturers had built up a body of research, operators could expect to see few mechanical breakthroughs. As a logging engineer of the post-war period has put it, 'the infrastructure that a science-based technology needed was missing and had yet to be created.'[47]

In the inter-war period Ontario logging engineers and the Woodlands Section began to conduct scientific research. In 1928 Abitibi conducted a scientific study to solve a problem encountered in the holding pond outside their mill at Iroquois Falls. Because the company had incurred heavy losses when its booms broke, engineer Herb Soderston, a graduate of the Sheffield School of Engineering at Yale, applied engineering principles to the problem. He was unable to make a start – measuring the tension on booms and monitoring potential crises. One of Koroleff's first projects at the Woodlands Section was to test the efficiency of bucksaws. Because bush trials of different saws failed to give conclusive results, the section funded the construction of laboratory testing equipment. In 1933 tests were conducted under the supervision of W.E. Wakefield of the Forest Products Laboratories, a branch of the federal Department of Interior's Forest Service and in co-operation with saw manufacturers. The investigators studied the changing energy consumption levels of different bucksaws when cutting various woods at several temperatures. The findings helped Koroleff write exact instructions for filing and setting the saws.[48]

Despite such experiments, by mid-century the industry had only started to lay the foundations for a science-based industry. Crude, traditional logging methods would prevail until executives agreed to provide more funding for research and engineers had a legitimate chance to work on the problem of mechanizing logging operations in northern Ontario. Contributing to these problems was one central factor: labour abundance. Until large numbers of men stopped offering their labour in the bush camps, the executives lacked an incentive to spend money to develop new, more capital-intensive work methods. As Koroleff admitted, as long as labour was 'plentiful and cheap, if production at a logging camp was low, the order "Get more men" could more or less counteract the inefficient work.' To the frustration of Koroleff and his colleagues, the views of powerful forest company executives, such as Senator W.C. Edwards, prevailed for decades. At the first meeting of the Woodlands Section in 1918 the senator had dismissed new cutting equipment with the quip: 'Give me two French Canadians in preference to any machine you can introduce.'[49]

5

In the camps

When old-timers reminisce about their logging days, not only do they enjoy recounting how hard they worked, they also delight in describing the rugged camp conditions. Indelibly etched in their memories are the obnoxious odours of the bunkhouse, the maddening itch of bedbugs, the stifling heat of nights spent in the top bunk, and the bitter morning cold that froze hair to the camp walls. Such subjects form a vital part of their tales because they were part of the bushworker's physically demanding calling. Unlike most workers who returned to their homes and families at the end of a shift, woodsmen lived with their workmates – no sharp line was drawn between work and leisure. The camp was an all-encompassing experience, a fact which would have important consequences for woods unionization.

THE CAMP LAYOUT

On a sunny day in late September 1923, Magne Stortroen and his friend Karl Brandvold, two recent Norwegian immigrants, arrived at Abitibi's office in Iroquois Falls. They were hired on as bushworkers, given employment slips, and told to wait for the afternoon mail-car which would take them to camp. After a fifteen-mile ride along the company's crude logging railway, the pair found themselves in their first bush camp. As soon as they had disembarked they began to take in their new surroundings. 'It was a rough looking yard, if it could be called a yard, with many stumps between the buildings,' recalls Stortroen. 'A grindstone with a hand crank was sitting on an iron rod between two poles ... and two washtubs rested upside down against a stump.' The scene was dominated by two long, log buildings. They could tell that one was a sleep camp, for through the doorway they could see rows of bunks; the other proved to be a dining hall with a kitchen, or cookery, at one end. Behind the bunkhouse stood what was apparently the stable because hay bales were piled beside it.[1]

Magne and Karl's first camp was typical of the logging camps built in Ontario throughout the first half of the twentieth century. Almost invariably camps consisted of just such a cluster of log buildings. By about 1904 woodsmen had seen the last of the old camboose shanties in which they ate and slept around an open fire pit.[2] But it was not until the late 1940s that some operators began to abandon log camps and build frame structures that could be moved to a new site at the end of a season. Overwhelmingly, in the period before 1950, Ontario bushworkers ate, slept, and spent their leisure hours in crude log dining halls and bunkhouses.

Camps resembled one another because common guidelines were followed in laying them out. In choosing a site the foreman looked for a level, well-drained spot with convenient access to the cutting areas, supply routes, drinking water, and the waterways used for the floating and driving operations. Ideally the surrounding forest provided suitable timber for construction of the buildings. However, it was seldom possible to find the perfect site. When the Rat Portage Lumber Company built a camp in northwestern Ontario in 1913, the boss opted for a site at the tip of a peninsula. Although not at the centre of the harvest area, the location was sheltered from the north winds, offered even ground and excellent drainage, and faced onto a bay which had a good landing area for the tote scows. Furthermore, the nearby forest of poplar and birch trees, was ideal for building camps although these trees were not easily floated to the mill.[3]

THE CAMP CLERK

The first person every bushworker met when he arrived at a camp was the clerk. He worked in a small building that served as an office, a storehouse, and a van where employees could purchase goods, such as patent medicines, tobacco, candy, clothing, and boots. The clerk would usher the newcomers inside and take their employment slips. 'After writing down our names, he gave us each two gray blankets and walked to the sleeping camp with us,' writes Magne. 'There he showed us two empty bunks, one top and one bottom, then left us standing there.' None too welcoming, but as one woods manager admitted, clerks were notorious for giving the newcomer a 'too rigid, uninterested induction.'[4]

The clerk performed several important tasks in addition to signing on new arrivals. He did all the paper work: he ordered the food supplies requested by the cook, oats and hay by the barn boss, and the tools and equipment by the foreman. The clerk kept the camp accounts in which he recorded the amount of wood cut and hauled by each crew or piece worker, the wages owed them, and the cost of supplies and equipment. In addition, he operated the van, selling goods supplied by the company at prices that usually provided for a small profit which could then be used to pay part of the clerk's wages. Unlike the infamous company store of early frontier towns, prices in twentieth-century logging camps were rarely exorbitant, thanks perhaps to the competition of such operations as Eaton's mail-order service.

The clerk might also pen letters to head office, to institutions such as the Workmen's Compensation Board, or even to the family and sweethearts of illiterate bushworkers. 'It was an unusual experience to write a personal letter to someone you did not know or had ever seen,' writes Ralph Thomson, who was a clerk at a camp near Lake Abitibi in 1916. 'First I would get some knowledge about the person. How old was she? What is the relationship, if any? With such knowledge I could then write and when partly through would read back what was written ... Then I would go on some more and do as before till the letter was finished.'[5]

Industry publications occasionally commented on the skills clerks needed. A 1911 *Canada Lumberman* article emphasized that too often clerks were sloppy and failed to keep records up to date. 'Accuracy and simplicity saves money and avoids conflicts when men demand their pay slips,' noted the author. A similar article, by Camp Clerk, listed a number of necessary qualifications, from a knowledge of first aid to a willingness to cut firewood. 'Above all else he should not be a poker player,' the writer stressed. 'No man can handle books and cash and play poker at the same time.' The author even suggested that a good camp clerk could provide moral guidance to camp employees, citing the advice he gave to a bushworker who was planning to skip out on a girl he had 'got into trouble.' This clerk said he had a close rapport with the men. According to another observer, however, the 'book education' of the clerk often caused him 'to adopt a superior attitude' that made it difficult for him 'to become accepted in the camp as one of the gang.'[6]

The structure of the situation accounts for the aloofness of many camp clerks. Because he slept in the office and spent his evenings operating the van, the clerk was physically cut off from the men. Moreover, he occupied a peculiar position in the camp hierarchy. The clerk was an employee who received wages roughly comparable to the bushworkers. But he was a member of the management team as well and as such was expected to interpret company policy to the employees. In a jobber's camp he was also supposed to check up on the dealings of the jobber. One clerk, who identified with management, believed that it was 'good if the clerk can keep an eye on camp,' reporting to the management incidents such as teamsters 'sneaking home early.'[7]

Clerking had several drawbacks in addition to the risk of being shunned by bushworkers. The working day was long, usually extending from eight in the morning until 8:30 PM. Clerks, who got little exercise, complained that the rich food of the bush camp sat heavily in their stomachs. And Arvi Tuuamen, who worked in the Algoma district, remembers how frustrating it was to be continually interrupted by men wanting van goods when he was in the middle of mentally adding a long column of figures. Nevertheless, as another clerk noted, in comparison with most office jobs, camp clerking had its advantages: 'You are not ruled by a time clock; no office supervisor is watching over you to see that you do not lose a minute.'[8]

IN THE SLEEP CAMP

Many newcomers were appalled by the primitiveness of the bunkhouse that was to serve as their new home. In the dim light that filtered through two small windows, Karl and Magne saw the bathing facilities – a shallow wooden trough in which sat two up-turned wash basins: 'rather limited facilities to allow fifty or sixty men to keep clean.' But they were even more surprised by the sleeping arrangements. Along each side of the sixty-foot-long building ran one double-tiered 'solid bunk . . . with a piece of board as the only division between each man.' These were called muzzle-loaders – each man shoved himself into his bunk at the foot and then slept with his head to the outside wall. In the middle of the seven-foot space between the two sets of bunks stood a stove that resembled an oil drum turned on its side. 'For a final touch,' adds Magne, 'there was haywire strung from one end of the camp to the other so the men could hang their wet socks and shirts when they came in from the bush.'

Nearly all Ontario sleep camps in the pre-World War II period were just as rough in appearance and as primitively fitted up. Most operators avoided capital outlays for lumber and factory-made furnishings, preferring to rely on materials already at hand. A report written by a University of Toronto Forestry student vividly describes the home-made bunks of a camp in 1913:

The bunks were arranged as usual, two tiers high on each side of the building. The frame work of the bunks was made of round timbers, the upright supports being of saplings 3 inches in diameter at the upper end to fit into auger holes which had been bored in the long timber which formed the front of the upper bunk. The lower bunk rested directly on the floor; the upper one on cross pieces which were let into holes bored into the wall and at the other end passed through holes in the timber at the front of the upper tier of bunks. On top of these cross pieces a row of small poles were laid lengthwise forming the floor of the upper, and the roof of the lower tier of bunks. The men used whatever they wished in making their beds, some using hay, others moss or brush.

Bunks like these remained common into the 1940s, although as early as 1916 some operators opted for collapsible steel bunks with army-type mattresses. Perhaps they had been persuaded to purchase them by *Canada Lumberman* advertisements which stated: 'If your men sleep on old fashioned, vermin-infested, hard, wooden bunks, you cannot expect them to go to work with energy.'9

Virtually all camps were dingy and lacked convenient bathing, toilet, and laundry facilities. As early as 1912 logging operators began to install electric lighting in some of the camps, but the great majority built before 1950 used candles and kerosene lanterns. Running water was a luxury rarely found. At best, bushworkers could expect to find six-seater outhouses; at worst, they squatted on the ground outside the sleep camp. In the first years of this century, operators who were concerned about sanitary conditions began providing laundry services, the cost of which were covered by deducting twenty-five cents a month from each man's pay. Sometimes a foreman's wife living in a cabin at the camp site would do the laundry or homesteaders or Indians living nearby did the job. By the 1920s wash houses with pails and basins had become a common feature of the larger camps, but very few had hot showers until well after World War II. When confronted with bathing facilities that turned men blue with the cold, many chose to remain dirty.

Only in the camps where Finns worked was it easy to bathe. Whenever a few Finns moved into a camp, they would build a sauna; Lakehead logging contractors provided steam baths as a matter of course. 'I wouldn't have a camp without one,' recalled Oscar Styffe, a Port Arthur pulpwood operator. It was a simple matter to throw up a rough log cabin, add a barrel stove, and call it a sauna. Siami Hormavirta, the widow of Hans, an Algoma jobber, remembers how every evening in winter and twice a week in warm weather, the chore boy would light the sauna fire and set a great cauldron of water to boil. Some sixty men enjoyed taking a hot bath every evening. Not surprisingly, Finnish bushworkers gained a reputation for their cleanliness.[10]

Conditions varied greatly. Because jobbers often had their own following, they had less need to provide attractive camps; moreover, every penny a jobber saved on construction and maintenance went straight into his pocket. Consequently, sanitary inspectors found it 'almost impossible to educate these people in matters pertaining to sanitation.' Small lumber companies frequently had lower standards than the larger pulpwood operators. A Forestry student reporting on Temagami area lumber camps in 1942 noted: 'None of the camps visited compare with the pulp camps the writer has visited either in general layout or conveniences.'[11]

Foremen provided themselves and a few privileged employees with superior living quarters. One observer remarked on the 'strong contrast between the bright, clean office for the boss and the dungeon-like bunkhouse for the men.' There was a distinct hierarchy in the camps of the Indian Lake Lumber Company in the 1920s. Ken Collins notes that at the main site, 'the superintendent lived with his wife and one small child in a nice log house on the outskirts of the camp.' The buck beavers, camp clerk, and Linn-tractor crew stayed in 'a separate log building, clean and comfortable and equipped with steel cots, washing facilities, tables and chairs for off-duty use.' By contrast, 'the men who did the actual logging were housed in what can only be described as deplorable conditions.' This kind of arrangement was typical of the bigger operations, but even in the smaller ones the foreman, clerk, blacksmith, mechanic, and cooking staff often lived in separate quarters.[12]

EVENINGS AND SUNDAYS

During the evenings and on Sundays some of the men played poker, using wooden matches as chips. In the dim light of a single coal-oil lantern, others mended socks or patched pants and shirts. What caught the attention of Karl and Magne on their first night in camp were two men at the far end of the building who had taken off their shirts and were picking lice from their underwear and their armpits and throwing them on the floor. About 9:30 pm the bullcook came to stoke the fire. On leaving, he doused the lights.

Bushworkers spent most of their Sundays and short hours of evening leisure in quiet pursuits. Exhausted from their strenuous work, they rarely had the energy to do much else. The industrious mended clothes or sharpened their axes and saws. Many played cards or talked, while others stuck to themselves, reading or simply enjoying a smoke. Their right to privacy was respected, as it had to be in order for peace to prevail in such close quarters. Nearly every camp had its musician who played the mouth organ, accordion, or fiddle. 'There was always a Finn playing his own accordion,' says Alva Korri. 'He'd play real nice old Finnish songs.' Jim MacDonald describes the enjoyment and relaxation men found in listening to 'the plaintive strains of "Annie Laurie" or some other old, familiar melody flow[ing] softly through the camp.'13

In the odd logging camp, some of the men would gather together in the cookhouse or a corner of the bunkhouse to study English, arithmetic, or citizenship under the direction of a labourer-teacher sent out by Frontier College. There were few such instructors available because most of the college's tutors were university students and hence unavailable in the winter.14

Occasionally the routine was interrupted by the arrival of a visitor. In the less remote camps, pedlars selling jewellery and watches made frequent appearances wherever foremen allowed them. Photographers also toured the camps, taking group shots of crews standing in front of their bunkhouse or showing off with a brag load of timber. During World War I, union organizers began visiting Ontario logging camps, bringing news of labour struggles, signing up new members, and collecting dues. Priests from northeastern Ontario sometimes said mass in the cookhouse or heard confession behind a gray blanket suspended in a corner of the camp office. And a handful of Protestant missionaries annually tramped the bush, distributing Bibles and tracts, preaching, and leading hymn-sings.15

Although Canada's major denominations sent a few missionaries to the logging camps, the best-known preachers came under the auspices of the Shantymen's Christian Association, an organization that propagated a robust gospel its supporters called 'the lumberjack's religion.'16 The association was formed in 1908 by William Henderson, a Presbyterian Scot and former superintendent of a Hespeler, Ont., woollen mill. By the time of Henderson's death in 1925, the Shantymen's Christian Association had missionaries in logging districts from Newfoundland to British Columbia and across the United States. Each year its preachers hiked thousands of miles through the bush, carrying heavy packs filled with tracts, because, as they put it: 'We believe the lumberjacks' greatest need is the gospel of Jesus Christ our Lord, straight from the shoulder.'17 The influence of these fundamentalists was probably quite limited. 'Everybody was very polite to them, but nobody reformed,' recalls one New Brunswick lumberjack.

'We used to like the music. That was the thing.' A Forestry student at a McNamara Lumber Company camp watched one travelling preacher who spoke 'to the men at night and exhort[ed] them to follow the straight and narrow path.' However, since the preacher spoke in English, which most of the French-Canadian lumberjacks did not understand, 'the games of checkers and cards progress[ed] at the same time as his speech.'[18]

Missionaries rarely missed an opportunity to fulminate about the evils of alcohol. Yet drink played little part in camp life. By the mid-nineteenth century temperance crusaders and employers had largely eliminated alcohol from the camps, and it would not reappear for a century.[19] As A.R.M. Lower recalls working in a frontier camp in 1910, 'the only law that seemed to be taken seriously was that of forbidding alcohol. Alcohol led to fights and idleness, so it was carefully watched.' Visiting a prostitute was similarly a pleasure sought in town and not in the camps.[20] Of course there are plenty of tales about how some clever chap succeeded in sneaking a bottle past a vigilant camp foremen. And those who remained behind at Christmas usually found some alcohol. Generally, when men wanted to drink they had to settle up at the office and head for town.

Even without alcohol, evenings in the logging camp might occasionally get quite lively. As late as the 1930s, some lumberjacks still occasionally engaged in a Saturday night stag dance. Joe Mason, who logged the French River country during the depression, remembers what it was like 'to draw as a partner a teamster who ... smelled not only of dirt and sweat, but also very strongly of the horses with which he worked ten and twelve hours a day!' However, in most areas buck dances, along with the custom of telling tales, had already begun to die out by World War I. Quite different preoccupations then developed. 'At the camp our entertainment was to argue over politics,' recalls Toivo Tienhaara. 'If there were Finns, there were Reds and Whites. I was a White. Even though I was indisputably in the minority, I always spoke my mind. Sometimes there were men all around my bunk trying to convert me.'[21]

In 1931 the *Pulp and Paper Magazine of Canada* published an amusing article in which the author pretended to report the results of his quantitative study of the social habits of lumberjacks. Alleging to have timed their conversations with a stop-watch, the writer listed the amounts of time lumberjacks spent discussing various subjects: 'Pornographic stories, experiences and theories, 23 per cent; Personal adventures in which the narrator is hero, 11 per cent; Outrages of capitalism, 8 per cent; Prohibition, bootlegging and jags, 6 per cent; logging techniques and lore, 5 per cent.' He also reported that the lumberjacks uttered an average 136 words 'unmentionable at church socials' every quarter hour, '31 per cent of which were of sexual import, and nine per cent were excretory in nature.'[22]

Certainly the games and practical jokes woodsworkers sometimes played are illustrative of a masculine culture. Hot Hand, the favourite game in the old pine camps, was aptly named. The object was to slap a blind-folded man as hard as you could without having him guess who you were. Tests of strength like arm wrestling and wrist twisting were also popular. When a Forestry student visited an Acme Timber Company camp in the Sudbury district in 1931, he was surprised to find the crew had cleared a space on the lake where they played hockey, using shovels, broom handles, and six-inch boards as sticks. 'This pastime,' concluded the student, 'provided fun and amusement for the men who seemed to take a great deal of pleasure from the punishment they received.' Although it was unusual for bushworkers to play group sports at camp, their machismo was definitely characteristic.[23]

AT THE SOUND OF THE DINNER BELL

If bushworkers usually had little to look forward to in the way of lively entertainment, they could count on eating whopping big meals. 'When the bell sounded,' recalls Magne, 'it was like the signal for a race and not just a meal. Half the fellows were running, dodging or jumping over stumps . . . on the way to the cookery.' Karl and Magne were impressed by the abundance and variety of the grub, and by the way in which the hefty cook enforced the no-talking rule as he patrolled the length of the dining hall brandishing a big butcher knife. At one point, when two men started to talk, the cook raised his weapon high in the air and shouted 'Shut up!' in a voice that boomed above the noise of sixty men spooning food from tinware bowls and plates. The room suddenly became quieter, and in remarkably short order the woodsmen had polished off the evening meal.

Newcomers and visitors to Ontario bush camps in the period 1900–45 were inevitably amazed by the enormous amounts of food served, the business-like way in which the men wordlessly consumed it, and the short time it took them to complete the job. These long-standing camp traditions seemed all the more astonishing because the abundance and discipline in the cookhouse contrasted so sharply with the sparseness and disarray of the bunkhouse. The tables and benches might have been roughly hewn, the tinware battered, and the cook-stove rusty, but bushworkers insisted that the cook provide hearty meals. In return, the cooks demanded the men refrain from talking and eat with dispatch so that preparations could soon get under way for the next meal.

Each day the cook had to prepare two sit-down meals, breakfast and dinner, and make arrangements for the noon meal. During the autumn felling operations, after every breakfast the men would pack their own lunches from a selection of cold meats, bread, and pies spread out on tables. At noon they would eat alone or in small groups in the cutting area. During the cold winter haul, however, the men worked in larger groups, and so the cook make a hot meal which was brought to them in the gut wagon, a small sled. Ken Collins recalls that every morning the cook would prepare the same meal: 'a huge cauldron of rich hot soup of his own making and another large cauldron of beans cooked with molasses and liberally loaded with big chunks of salt pork.'[24] For dessert, there was always plenty of pie.

'Complaints about the quantity of food served in the camps do not exist,' writes historian Joseph R. Conlin, an authority on the social history of food in North American logging camps. Certainly the Ontario experience was no exception. During a labour dispute in 1934 in the Chapleau area, a strike leader wrote to his local member of parliament complaining about the dreadful camp conditions. Yet he had to admit that the food was 'comparatively abundant' – a fact he attributed to 'the simple reason that even a steam boiler must be stoked with sufficient fuel to give pressure enough to do the job.'[25]

Everything to do with meals was done on a grand scale. From wholesale grocers such as H.P. Eckardt and Company of Toronto or T. Long and Brothers of Collingwood, logging operators ordered staples in enormous quantities. In the 1923-4 season, the Shevlin-Clark Lumber Company of Fort Frances ordered 1,445,000 pounds of food: including 250,000 pounds of beef, 14,000 of bacon, 325,000 of potatoes, and 22,000 of beans. The *Canada Lumberman* reported that during the 1914–15 seven-month season 100 men in one camp ate 91,534 pounds of bacon, 32,108 of beef, 14,525 of butter, and 173,222 of potatoes. A study undertaken by Alexander Koroleff and the Woodlands Section in 1931 showed that the eastern Canadian bushworker consumed an average of five-and-a-half pounds of food per day, or 7,250 calories. Yet as old photographs clearly show, few men had pot bellies. Their work was so strenuous that they needed large amounts of calories. According to one source, workers carrying or dragging logs burn 12.1 calories per minute, nearly twice the rate of men drilling coal and three times that of men laying bricks. Moreover, Ontario bushmen may have burned calories at an even faster rate, because cold weather increases caloric consumption, as does the resistance to movement caused by heavy clothing and deep snow.[26]

Certainly the meals were big, but were they appetizing. 'The food ranged from very good to god awful,' remembers Buzz Lein who began working in northern camps during the 1930s. The standard of fare depended on the raw ingredients provided by the boss and on the skills of the cook. Before World War I, lumberjacks employed by the Eddy Brothers Lumber Company and the Georgian Bay Lumber Company at Blind River had objected to the monotony of their diet by chanting:

Who feeds us beans until we're blue?
Eddy Brothers and the Georgian Bay.
Who thinks that nothing else will do?
Eddy Brothers and the Georgian Bay.

By the turn of this century, improvements in canning techniques and in grocery wholesaling enabled logging operators to furnish their cooking staff with a much wider range of supplies than had been possible. Previously cooks had been given little more than salt pork, molasses, and dried peas, beans, and apples. Some companies contracted catering companies, such as Crawley and McCracken, whose representatives maintained they provided foods specially tailored to the tastes of different nationalities in the work force: pea soup for French Canadians, macaroni with parmesan cheese for Italians, roast mutton and tripe for Englishmen, carroway-seed bread for Finns, and so forth.[27]

In the Shield country, where farms were few and toting could be difficult, logging companies often found it physically impossible or prohibitively expensive to bring in fresh supplies. As operators reached ever deeper into the woods, it became even more difficult, especially before the freeze-up. There was no excuse for penny-pinching contractors like O. Lamer who was convicted at the Sault for serving his bushmen horseflesh unfit for human consumption.[28] Despite such problems, the editor of *Canada Lumberman* was probably correct when he declared in 1914: 'In no other thing is the tendency towards improvement more noticeable today than in regard to the class of food which is put before the men in the bush.'[29]

Certainly, variety and quality improved towards the end of World War I. Because of labour shortages, woodsworkers demanded, and got, the best in camp fare. Many men travelled from camp to camp in search of superior meals. As operators competed to provide the most sumptuous tables, their cooking costs spiralled – dramatically so in this period of high inflation. Alarmed by this trend, lumbermen from the Ottawa and Georgian Bay areas met in April 1918. They resolved to ask the federal food controller to approve a set of rations for lumberjacks and establish a licensing system backed up by 'heavy penalties.' Drawing on wartime rhetoric, the *Canada Lumberman* insisted: 'The truth must be driven home to the lumberjack: that waste is a crime, gluttony treason, and sane rationing the supreme need of the hour.'[30] Notwithstanding the lumbermen's efforts, food costs continued to rise until the recession of 1920–1 when wholesale prices fell and a flooded labour pool reduced the bushworkers' power, and their gluttony.

During the depression, when balance sheets showed red and good bushworkers were a dime a dozen, woods managers took a keen interest in reducing the costs of camp food. 'I don't know of any field that we have in our woods operations where it is easier to save a very marked sum of money than in handling the feeding of men,' said C.B. Davis, Abitibi woods manager in 1932. Eliminating waste was one target. Company officials checked up on their cooks and urged them to make better use of leftovers. Woods managers also hoped to persuade bushworkers to eat less meat and larger quantities of cheaper food such as pie and canned vegetables. As one commentator explained: 'pie does not cost much when it comes to a choice between that and beef, and it fills up mighty gaps with hurriedness.' Another woods manager preached to his cooks, 'Shove the vegetables to them, . . . your vegetables cost 1 and 1/2 cents a pound, your meats from 15 to 25.'[31]

As early as 1931 Alexander Koroleff reminded woods managers that, 'lumberjacks are rather tough, but they are not ostriches.' It was not until World War II, with its labour shortages, that operators began to improve camp meals. In 1943 the Canadian Pulp and Paper Association formed a Committee on Balanced Camp Diet, and the next year the Pulp and Paper Research Institute of Canada sponsored a survey and study of camp kitchens, cooks, diets, and food values.[32]

THE CAMP COOK

Good cooks who worked hard and served first-rate meals were greatly appreciated by bushworkers and their bosses; and their comparatively high pay reflected their importance (see Appendices 6 and 8). It was not an easy job to feed sixty or more hungry woodsmen, especially when the camp lacked electrical appliances. The cooks usually did the butchering, and they baked bread from scratch in the big Adam Hall wood-fired camp-ranges. Sometimes they were assisted by a bullcook – usually an older man or a young lad – who hauled water and stoked the fires. The cookees set tables, washed dishes, cleaned the cookhouse, peeled potatoes, and served the food. Despite such help, a cook could expect to work sixteen hours a day every day during the seven-month season. Helvi Syrjä, who cooked for A.E. Wicks of Cochrane for many years, recalls starting work every morning at four and finishing in the evenings at nine, with an hour-and-a-half off in the afternoons. And the pace could be gruelling. After preparing a breakfast of pancakes and steaks for 200 men, Len Shewfelt of Thessalon says he would then 'start on my pies, 60 every morning, a pie a minute ... By the time I got my pies made I'd swing into the cookies and cupcakes and by then the bread would be ready to pan and you'd make big loaves, five in each long sheet-iron pan, 40 or 50 loaves at a time.' With such a demanding routine, no wonder so many cooks were notorious for flying off the handle at the slightest provocation.[33]

It was not enough, however, for cooks to be skilled in the kitchen, they also had to earn at least the grudging respect and co-operation of the men they fed. 'Quite apart from any question of good food and lots of it, there is a peculiar psychological aspect to the problem of boarding a bunch of lumberjacks,' explained one exasperated official in the *Pulp and Paper Magazine of Canada*. 'There are bad cooks whose "grub spoiling" will never raise a kick from the men. There are good cooks who are forever moving on because they can never please. Again, there are lumberjacks who will be quiet and contented for weeks on end, and will then, suddenly, apparently become possessed of a devil, and will find all manner of fault with the food, and the serving, and who simply cannot be satisfied.' Respected cooks were strict and maintained an iron discipline in the cookhouse. 'Little Buster Gower of Thessalon was cantankerous, but he could really cook,' recalls Buzz Lein. 'He'd walk up and down with a meat cleaver. He never intended to use it – but he had a reputation to keep up.'[34]

Like the men, bosses also found 'the cook a hard fellow to fool with.' As woods manager L.A. Nix explained in 1932, if a company official suggested any changes to the cook, he was apt to reply: 'Well boss, if you [don't] like the way I put up the meals, you step in here and cook. I'm going down.' Abitibi's C.B. Davis agreed: 'You get about as far laying down the law to the cook as with turning up your nose at what the wife lays on the table.' Nevertheless, bosses recognized the key position of the camp cook and did not begrudge paying comparatively high wages. As operators never tired of saying, a poor cook might waste the equivalent of ten times his monthly wage. Moreover, the operators knew that good meals were essential to attract and retain efficient workers. As a Toronto Forestry student succinctly put it: 'Men may grumble at early hours, hard work, unpleasant tasks and heartily curse the boss, but when it comes to poor grub they don't kick very much, they quit.'[35]

Perhaps the most celebrated cooks in northern Ontario were the Finnish women whose delicious meals and spotlessly clean cookhouses earned them wide acclaim. According to Buzz Lein, 'Northern Ontario was one of the few areas in North America where there were female cooks in the logging camps. But not a man could stand half up to the Finnish women. God, they even used to scrub the benches that guys sat on.' Helvi Syrjä, who learned to cook in a shacker camp and worked her way up to operations where she fed 300, boasts that men liked her cooking so much they followed her seasonal moves to new camps. Finnish bushmen especially appreciated it when these women served favourite national dishes such as *liha* and *kala mojakka* (meat and fish soup) and *vispipuuroa* (cranberry pudding).

It is puzzling why Finnish women gained access to cooking jobs at a time when so few other women entered the traditionally male domain of the camp cookhouse. Elsa Silanpää's story is probably typical. Fifteen-year-old Elsa arrived in northern Ontario in 1926 and through her Finnish contacts she immediately found a job as a cookee in a big logging camp. The next year she took a position in a twelve-man camp, where she learned to cook. After that she cooked in increasingly bigger camps, because the bigger the operation, the higher the pay. Before long, she had married a bushworker and took her young children with her even though she worried about being so far from a doctor. When her children reached school age, she either sent them to town to stay with relatives or she cooked in the boarding house of a sawmill town. She was eager to continue cooking because the pay was far better than that given a maid, the only other job for which she considered herself qualified. There was also little chance to spend money in the camps and she found cooking to be 'clean, nice work.'[36]

It was a strange life for these women who lived and worked in a nearly all-male environment. Female camp workers stuck together. They were provided with separate sleeping quarters, usually located just off the kitchen. Old snapshots in Elsa's photograph album show her, along with two other female cookees about her own age, cavorting in the snow at the first logging camp in which she worked. She remembers enjoying precious afternoon breaks when the young women would toboggan or read Finnish newspapers and magazines. Women who worked in the camps emphasize that there was no fooling around with the bushworkers. Buzz Lein, who agrees there were 'never any shenanigans,' explains that 'the girls were treated with respect because they demanded it.' And he adds that their 'brothers, cousins etc. might be in camp; you didn't know.'

Bushworkers probably found it easy to accept women in the cookhouse, partly because female camp workers were doing jobs that, outside the camps, had traditionally been women's work. And female cooks and cookees were not a threat to the jobs performed by the great majority of men in the logging industry. Nor did the women challenge the bushworker's manliness. The men appreciated the skills of competent female cooks who, like their male counterparts, made the hard work and rugged conditions of the bush seem a great deal more tolerable.

REFORMERS AND THE CAMPS

On the second day in the bush camp, Magne and Karl, the two Norwegian greenhorns, began to believe that they would be better off seeking their fortunes elsewhere. That evening, as they played cards, the two looked around the bunkhouse at 'those men who had worked so hard and lived in ... miserable conditions'; they could hardly believe the contrast with the stories of America they had heard back home in Norway. The next morning they checked out at the camp office, where the clerk deducted from their earnings the cost of their meals, tools, and van purchases. The disillusioned pair tramped the fifteen miles to Iroquois Falls to resume their quest for fortune, though never again did they seek it in a logging camp.

Countless young men followed the same path as Magne and Karl. They rejected the primitive camp conditions and the hard, low-paying jobs. Yet there were others – both inside and outside the industry – who sought to improve camp conditions and the bushworkers' lot.

From the turn of the century, spokesmen for Frontier College campaigned to awaken Canadians to the problems and needs of the country's long-neglected frontier workers. In 1901 Alfred Fitzpatrick, a Presbyterian born in Nova Scotia who was influenced by the Social Gospel, formed the Reading Camp Association to provide reading materials for lumberjacks working in the isolated logging camps of northern Ontario. Before long Fitzpatrick, through his Frontier College, was attempting to provide a wider range of educational opportunities to as many frontier workers as possible. The college's main approach was to send university students into Canada's remote camps where they served as labourer-teachers, working alongside the men during the day and leading classes in the evening. Fitzpatrick believed his teachers could only gain the respect of the men if they worked at the same tasks. 'The river-driver's standard of character is ability to handle the peavy, ride a log and break a jam.'[37]

Yet neither Principal Fitzpatrick nor his long-time associate and eventual successor, Edmund Bradwin, felt that directing the college's camp work was his only role. Both men were eloquent and insistent propagandists, eager to rally the universities, governments, employers, trade unions, and all concerned people to the cause of improving the lot of the bunkhouse man. In *The University in Overalls*, published in 1923, Fitzpatrick criticized Canada's frontier camps where 'men suffer not only the physical discomforts of the bunkhouse, but also from the deadening monotony of camp life, the absence of culture, or of any refining and elevating influences.' He saw 'no excuse for confining them in the physically wretched quarters, which [had] too long prevailed.' Five years later Bradwin's *The Bunkhouse Man*, exposed the dreadful frontier working conditions and called for reforms. Both educators insisted that by providing better conditions and programs, foreign-born camp workers could be Canadianized and radicalism would be suppressed. According to Fitzpatrick, 'for years back ... all kinds of loose talk had gone unchecked among the masses of workers.' The result was the men in the camps, and particularly the foreign-born, had come to accept the agitator's viewpoint, 'lurid and grotesque as it sometimes is.'[38]

While it is clear that only a tiny minority of logging camp workers ever came into contract with Frontier College instructors, it is harder to assess the impact of the wider public campaign. Lumbermen generally supported its educational efforts. They provided the college with funds and prominent lumbermen sat on its board of directors. Yet when Fitzpatrick made specific proposals about improving camp life, they were firmly rejected. In March 1918 he called for an end to the all-male bunkhouse because it was a breeding ground for immorality. Later he suggested that operators might increase labour stability by building cottages (with private rooms, showers, and central heating), where bushmen could live with their families.[39] Lumbermen scoffed at these unrealistic proposals and contended that not only would cottages be too costly, but restlessness would not be reduced. One operator replied: 'I think there is no doubt the lumberjack would choose a camp to suit his stomach rather than his idle time and sleep time; and if he were compelled to take a daily or even a weekly bath in wintertime, he would vamoose without warning.'[40]

A second group of reformers, known as sanitarians, came from the public health sector. These individuals also criticized camp conditions, but they sought to improve them through the government's regulatory power. In 1900 these reformers began to take a keen interest in the sanitary conditions of the camps when a smallpox epidemic rapidly spread from Ontario lumber camps to the general population.[41]

Dr Peter Bryce, secretary of the Provincial Board of Health, and his small but influential band of public health reformers, called for bold and sustained government initiatives to protect the health of camp workers and the public at large.[42] In 1901 the legislature passed An Act respecting Sanitary Regulations in Unorganized Territories. The statute and its accompanying regulations required logging operators to make provisions for the ongoing medical care of woods employees and to maintain sanitary camps so that diseases such as typhoid would not spread.

On the surface the regulations marked a significant departure from previous *ad hoc* medical provisions in the camps where patent medicines and the cook's mysterious concoctions had long prevailed. The new regulations called for the construction of a hospital in every camp. A doctor on contract with the lumber company was to make regular visits and provide free medical supplies. The doctor's fees were to be paid by the workers – fifty cents to a dollar were to be deducted from the monthly pay. In fact actual conditions fell far short of the reformers' goals, because the regulations were impossible to enforce. Employers refused to build hospitals – the penalties were too light to have any effect. Many operators did not trouble to contract physicians, and some who did found ways to profit from the scheme at the expense of their men. By 1907 the politically influential lumbermen had brought about a relaxation of the regulations. In subsequent years the overworked health inspectors would find it difficult to enforce even these standards.[43]

The 1901 regulations concerning sanitary standards also established strict requirements: stables could be located no closer than 125 feet from a kitchen or dwelling; sleep camps had to have at least 300 cubic feet of air space per occupant; bunks had to run parallel to the side walls; and separate cooking facilities, laundries, bath houses, and privies were required. But once again inadequate inspection and enforcement provisions prevented the reformers from imposing the standards. It did not, however, stop the inspectors from the Board of Health in their attempts to shame even large employers. In 1916 Egerton George, district health officer, chastised Abitibi for its willingness to 'hazard the vigour of the men negligently, inadvisedly, if not selfishly.'[44]

During the 1920s camp sanitary standards and medical provisions improved, at least in the larger camps.[45] These improvements came about because of the labour conditions in the immediate post-World War I period. Amid acute labour shortages, bushworkers jumped in unprecedented numbers, causing the companies considerable production losses, as well as increased costs. At the same time, the bushworkers began to join radical industrial unions that demanded improvements. As a result increasing numbers of logging operators took a keener interest in improving their camps to attract a stable labour force and to undercut the unions.[46] Public health reformers quickly took advantage of the new mood in the industry, as did the new and sympathetic provincial Farm-Labour government. In consultation with lumbermen and union leaders in 1920, the Ontario health authorities drafted far more stringent regulations and won cabinet approval for more effective inspection and enforcement.[47] According to the Board of Health reports in the 1920s, conditions and medical care did improve – though never in the small camps run by jobbers who resisted spending the necessary money.[48]

Much of the momentum behind the movement for improving the camps was lost during the depression. Cost cutting became the order of the day in all logging operations. A flooded labour market brought stability and made it unnecessary to spend funds on camp improvements. The Health Department also suffered a reduction in staff that made inspection virtually impossible. Improvements were few until after World War II. In the early 1940s, forestry students visiting contractor camps described deplorable conditions and 'dungeon-like bunkhouses.' Even as late as 1946, the field staff of the Royal Commission on Forestry discovered many substandard sites. Perhaps the most telling evidence comes when prisoners of war were being considered as a source of labour. The Ontario Forest Industries Association was compelled to consider building 'better housing facilities' than 'present logging camps ... built and operated according to Provincial Department of Health specifications.'

It was clear that significant changes in camp standards would take more than the exhortations of reformers such as Fitzpatrick and Bradwin and the influence of public health reformers whose regulatory powers were limited in an industry where politically powerful employers had long enjoyed considerable success in dealing with the Department of Lands and Forests. Notwithstanding these attempts, camp conditions remained poor throughout the period before 1945. The rhythms of camp life, and the living conditions endured by the industry's seasonal wage earners, changed little, just as the work itself went largely unaltered. Yet during the 1920s, 1930s, and 1940s, significant numbers of Ontario bushworkers joined the union movement and went on strike for increased wages and improved living conditions. The union movement challenged the long-standing relations between bushworkers and their bosses. Eventually the protests and demands helped bring about a major transformation in camp conditions and in the very nature of bush work itself.

6

Bushworkers in struggle, 1919–1935

Draughty bunkhouses, bedbugs, low pay, dangerous work, sparse timber, unfair foremen – bushworkers had plenty to complain about in Ontario's woodlands. Certainly as individuals they frequently protested by jumping from camp to camp or by going on a binge in town. Yet the unionization of the province's woodsworkers came about slowly, after many years of apparent inactivity followed by two decades of struggle. Not until the immediate post-War II period did the province's bushworkers win contracts from the major employers.

Labour abundance was a significant obstacle blocking successful unionization in the woods. As in most North American industries before the mid-1930s, workers with hard-to-replace skills took the lead in building unions in the forest industry. The first enduring labour organizations were formed during the early 1900s, by highly skilled papermakers. They joined the International Brotherhood of Papermakers, an affiliate of the American Federation of Labor (AFL) based in Washington and the Trades and Labour Congress of Canada (TLC) headquartered in Ottawa. Shortly after, mill managers also recognized the International Brotherhood of Pulp, Sulphite and Paper Mill Workers (AFL-TLC), its semi-skilled members benefiting from the manager's eagerness to attract to isolated mill towns a stable work force that would maintain the continuous operation of costly pulping and papermaking equipment. In the seasonally run sawmills, workmen lacked these advantages, and paternalistic owner-managers stifled union activity.[1]

Logging presented its own peculiar barriers to unionization. Because in most years before World War II it was a buyer's market for labour, bushmen lacked bargaining power and employers could easily replace 'agitators and malcontents.' Bushworkers also spent much of their time on the job working alone or in pairs, isolated from others – a situation hardly conducive to solidarity. Merely reaching the many, scattered and remote sites was a challenge for organizers, especially when ever-vigilant bosses blocked entry to the camps. The seasonality of logging also made unionization difficult, because every spring the workers scattered. The next year the union organizers might have to begin from scratch with an entirely new crew. Even during the course of a single season, the practice of jumping made it hard to hold together workers who had signed membership cards. And furthermore, jumping acted as a safety valve, providing angry or restless bushmen with an outlet for frustration that might have found expression through collective activity. On top of all these structural hurdles was the challenge of organizing men who saw themselves as temporary sojourners in the Canadian bush, or as independent farmers rather than wage earners. The ethnic diversity of the labour force caused communications problems as well among workers and encouraged social divisions within the camps.

However, certain aspects of the job provided a basis for solidarity. In the camp system workers shared similar experiences. Rotten food, poor cutting chances, or a driving foreman were topics griped about around the stove. Even the practice of jumping could alert the workers to the need for unionization because they might become aware that their problems were not confined to a single cheap boss or crooked scaler and thus had to be fought on an industry-wide basis. Ideas regarding the possibility of unionizing might also spread rapidly among such a mobile labour force. Of course, the seeds for such thoughts had to come from somewhere.

In the Ontario woods, the union idea came, in part, from British Columbia. Coastal loggers and union organizers provided the example of militant industrial union drives and inspired Ontario bushworkers to take up the same cause in 1919 and 1920. Yet this post-World War I upsurge would have been far weaker and of little lasting significance had it not been for the contribution of the radical Finnish immigrants.

Although the Finnish immigrants dominated the work force in the pulpwood camps near the Lakehead, up the Algoma Central Railway, and along the Canadian Northern Railway west of Sudbury, their participation in early unionization drives was far higher than their numbers in the industry as a whole. Their activism grew out of the radical, Finnish-immigrant culture that thrived so vigorously in the north.

A substantial minority of the Finns who settled in northern Ontario had already been radicalized in the old country. They did not arrive in large numbers until the early twentieth century, at the very moment when radicalism was rapidly spreading in a Finland gripped by problems arising from industrialization and the czar's Russification program. Many of those who came to Canada had earlier been forced from their farms by population pressures and the commercialization of agriculture. When they sought relief by turning to wage labour in Finland's growing industrial centres, they found erratic employment, overcrowded housing, and poor wages and working conditions. The burgeoning Social Democratic Party, which sought redress of these problems and successfully marshalled widespread anti-Russian sentiments, recruited enormous numbers of these people. But when relief did not come quickly, thousands of the new socialists emigrated.[2]

Many of these people came to northern Ontario, a region that looked like home and that offered the possibility of combining farm ownership with wage labour in mining or logging. Like immigrants of every background, the Finns sought the company of their compatriots and established networks and institutions that provided practical benefits, as well as cultural continuity. For the radical Finns, that meant building socialist halls for mutual help, recreation, education, and political action. Leadership frequently came from highly motivated Finnish leftists. Especially during the 1920s, in the wake of Finland's civil war which saw the Whites triumph, Ontario's Finnish community attracted numerous Red activists. Even Oskari Tokoi, the prime minister of Finland's short-lived socialist government, and some members of his cabinet found temporary refuge in a logging camp near New Liskeard.[3]

Yet it is likely that a majority of the Finns who arrived in Ontario during the first three decades of this century were either untouched by radicalism or active anti-socialists.[4] Most settlers came from rural areas remote from the Social Democratic Party's strongholds in and around Helsinki. The more politically active from these areas were apt to have backed the Whites or served in the White Guard; in North America many of them continued to hate the Reds and played an active part in church activities or in anti-communist organizations such as the Loyal Finns of Canada. More surprisingly, a significant proportion of the apolitical immigrants were radicalized in the northern Ontario communities where their social life was dominated by highly motivated leftists.[5]

In large part it was the combination of a weak Lutheran Church and strong socialist halls that enabled leftists to recruit substantial numbers of Finns who had not been radicalized at home. Since the powerful state church in Finland condemned emigration, it gave little support to the struggling congregations in Canada.[6] The few pastors who ministered to the Finns in Ontario preached an other-worldly theology and a strict moral code that had little appeal for many of the young people who had been bold enough to venture to Canada. When freed from the disciplines and restraints of the old country, the habit of church attendance could be easily thrown off. On the other hand, the busy round of activities at the socialist halls served to attract new members and to keep Finnish culture alive, while presenting radicals with plenty of opportunities to educate participants. Theatre groups presented plays that combined romance and radicalism. For example, Alf Hautamäki, a bushworker organizer, wrote a musical entitled *Erämaiden Orjat* or *Slaves of the Wilderness* which combined a call for solidarity with dramatic material about logging camp life, strikes, a theft, love affairs, alcoholism, and a lost husband. Sporting events and weekly dances attracted new members and served to raise funds. Closely linked to the halls were Finnish co-operative restaurants and stores, which provided much appreciated services, opportunities for social interaction with comrades, and concrete examples of alternatives to capitalist competition. Also associated with the halls were the Finnish-language socialist newspapers and magazines. The Finns who were unusually literate in comparison with other European immigrant groups, avidly read such publications for news of the old country and for information about popular local events. At the same time they were exposed to a left-wing political analysis.[7]

Through their many activities, Finnish radicals succeeded remarkably well in taking the immigrants' sense of ethnic separateness and directing it towards leftist politics. But the vitality of this radicalism was also rooted in the tough working conditions the Finns encountered in the frontier industries of the Canadian Shield and it drew strength from the ongoing struggles in the workplaces of such industries as mining and logging. Since so many Finns had found jobs in the woods industry, organizing bushworkers became a primary target for these leftists. Their pre-1935 activities divide conveniently into three periods: the syndicalist phase before 1921, the years of regrouping and rebuilding in the 1920s, and the depression-era collapse and resurgence that climaxed in the class warfare of 1933-5.

FIRST UNION DRIVE

At the turn of the century, Ontario's bushworkers lacked a tradition of collective action. In the past lumberjacks had occasionally drawn together to fight for scarce jobs, as had happened during the Shiners' war on the Ottawa River during the 1830s, or to resist wage cuts as George Thompson's men had done in Haliburton during the 1870s. But such instances were rare. Rarer still were attempts by lumberjacks to form lasting labour organizations. Even the most likely nineteenth-century organizer of lumberjacks, the Knights of Labor, had little effect in the Ontario woods, though Muskoka and Ottawa sawmill workers had been caught up in the movement in the 1880s and 1890s. When radical workers from the Finnish community began to organize woodsworkers during the second decade of the twentieth century, they were breaking new ground.[8]

Finnish radicals in Ontario appear to have made their first attempt at building a woodsworkers' union in 1911 at Port Arthur, when they formed the Ontario Lumber and Railroad Workers Ring, or the *Ontarion Metsä- ja Rautatietyöläisten Rengas*. From its name it is apparent that the Finns hoped to organize into one unit workers in two seasonal industries where labour demands dovetailed and where many immigrants found jobs. The dearth of information about the union indicates that its impact was probably quite limited. Similarly in 1913 the Port Arthur Finnish socialist newspaper *Työkansa*, or *Working People*, published an editorial calling for the unionization of lumber workers. But little headway can have been made because the paper regularly published reports of strikes and union activities and yet it apparently printed none concerning Ontario bushworkers.[9]

Evidence for actual accomplishments by early organizers can be found in the memoirs of Amos Tobias (Tom) Hill, a Finnish leftist who for more than thirty years worked to build an Ontario bushworkers' union.[10] Hill came to Canada as a young man shortly before World War I. Since he and his family were socialists in the old country, it was only natural for him to take part in the activities at the socialist hall near his new home in northwestern Ontario. In the summer of 1915 he worked as a harvester in the United States, where he was recruited by the Lumber Workers Industrial Union no. 120, part of the Industrial Workers of the World (IWW). Back in Canada during the winter of 1916–17, Hill found a job in a logging site near Ignace, where he claims to have organized a union among his camp mates. During the next two or three years, he and a few comrades apparently organized several camps northwest of the Lakehead. Their work was undoubtedly made easier by the arrival of many socialists and IWW members who had come to Canada to avoid both the draft and the severe repression they were then encountering in the United States.[11] Although Hill's accounts are not clear, it appears that some, or all, of these unionists became members of the IWW no. 120.

The IWW had an obvious appeal for Ontario's Finnish bushworkers: its strength had always been among highly mobile unskilled workers of the frontier. Formed in 1905, the radical industrial union had its roots in the bitter workplace struggles of hardrock miners in the Rocky Mountains. Soon after 1905 the organization had swept through the mines, railway construction sites, and sawmill towns of the American west and British Columbia. Though many individual members were socialists, the IWW as an organization shunned political action and stressed direct action at the workplace. Like European syndicalists, the Wobblies, as they were called, combined a commitment to achieving immediate improvements in wages and working conditions with a long-range goal of overthrowing capitalism. Wobblies believed that by joining together in a fiercely democratic 'one big union,' and by fighting for immediate demands, a solidarity would develop that would one day prove powerful enough to emancipate capitalism's 'wage slaves.' Eschewing collective agreements, high union dues, craft exclusiveness, as well as the ballot box, the Wobblies' methods had a particularly strong appeal for immigrant and migratory workers. They gained from the movement a sense of self-worth, a purpose, and sometimes immediate improvements in their pay and conditions.[12]

The IWW advanced rapidly in certain logging regions, particularly the Pacific northwest, Louisiana, and Texas.[13] Direct action aimed at improving on-the-job conditions and a system of camp delegates who worked as loggers and signed up men at the same time, proved effective for organizing in the woods. According to one historian, in the Pacific northwest, the Wobblies successfully seized 'upon the loggers' desire to be treated with dignity, which in the lumber industry meant largely the eight-hour day, decent bedding and wholesome board.'[14] The organization had also spread widely among Finnish immigrants working in the mines and lumber camps of the Midwest, where many Finnish socialists had abandoned the ballot box after employers used the coercive power of the state to break strikes. Historian Douglas Ollila explains that the Finnish worker had come to believe 'that the raw power of the worker organized along economic lines in one gigantic union was the only possible way by which his condition and position could be ameliorated. The Finnish worker also dared to dream vaguely with Big Bill Haywood and Leo Laukki that a future general strike of all workers would usher in a new commonwealth, an industrially-managed society where justice for the worker would prevail.'[15]

In the logging camps of Ontario, where conditions were just as bad, some Finnish immigrants who read the newspapers and leaflets issued by Finnish Wobblies in the midwest came to similar conclusions and joined this North American movement. Though harassed by police and immigration authorities, Finns travelling back and forth across border points at Fort Frances and the Sault brought ideas, news and iww propaganda from radical strongholds in Wisconsin and Minnesota.[16] At one point, an Ontario Provincial Police (opp) constable at Port Arthur wrote with exasperation to his superior: 'Now the Finns are the worst foreigners we will have to deal with regarding this bolseviki plague. They are very cunning and hard to catch.' The constable had recently discovered that local Finnish Wobblies had received through the mail banned literature wrapped 'in Chinese paper and [with] Chinese writing in order to fool the po [Authorities].'[17]

At about the same time as Hill and his comrades began their union drive in Northwestern Ontario, Finns working in pulpwood and tie camps up the Algoma Central Railway were also busy organizing. A decade later Finnish union activists recalled how in 1917 and 1918 Algoma bushworkers had Marxist study groups, as well as a fist press, hand-written newspapers informing others about their activities and ideas.[18] Confirmation of these activities is provided by the records of the opp, which co-operated with the federal government's dominion police in maintaining a surveillance of radical activists in the north. A police translation of Finnish union minutes dated 25 March 1918 shows that organizers were attempting to co-ordinate the tactics of river drivers who were planning to demand improved wages and conditions along the Algoma Central. The meeting also decided that 'the fight' would be carried out 'in the name of [no] known organization' but simply in the name of 'the working class.' This preference for autonomy may have been the result of political differences among activists, or it may have been a pragmatic move aimed at winning the widest support and minimizing the likelihood of police repression. The commissioner of the opp, nevertheless, believed that this development was 'part and parcel of the i.w.w. business.'[19]

What ultimately came of this meeting is not recorded in police files. For the most part these Algoma Finns must have maintained a low profile. There does not appear to have been any mention of them in the *Canada Lumberman*, which took a keen interest in Wobbly developments in the distant Pacific northwest. Of course, amid the tense wartime atmosphere foreign-born socialists in Canada had to tread cautiously. A.T. Hill explains that 'the Lumber Workers 120 groups functioned as small underground groups, supported by the Finnish Federation of the Social Democratic Party of Canada.' Despite their low-key activities, these Finns at least had laid a foundation on which organizers might build in more favourable times.[20]

Once the war was over the prospects of the labour movement in Canada improved enormously. Eager to see incomes catch up with the spiralling cost of living, fired by rhetoric about 'a world fit for heroes,' and released from wartime restraints, workers throughout Canada surged into unions in unprecedented numbers. In 1919 westerners appeared especially restless as evidenced by Winnipeg's giant, six-week general strike and by their strong support for the creation of a new Canadian-based industrial union – the One Big Union (OBU).[21]

The logging industry did not remain untouched by these developments. On the west coast in January 1919 lumber workers had formed an independent industrial union, the BC Loggers' Union. Under the direction of socialist Ernie Winch, an immigrant from England, the union spread 'like a forest fire.'[22] Almost as soon as the OBU had been formed in the summer of 1919, the BC Loggers voted to join the new union and their organization was renamed the Lumber and Camp Workers Industrial Union of the OBU (LWIU). Unlike most who joined the OBU, the loggers did not enter as individuals. Rather, they affiliated with OBU headquarters in Winnipeg through their industrial union, which retained its newspaper, executive board, and Vancouver offices.[23]

Neither the Lumber Workers nor the OBU itself was content to recruit among western Canadian workers. Both sent activists east to Ontario. From Edmonton came OBU organizers Joe and Sarah Knight, who made 'Ontario their special domain,' and from Vancouver came Ernie Winch himself and British-born socialist, Walter Cowan. The latter became district organizer for the Lumber Workers in northern Ontario. Ties between Finnish socialist leaders and Cowan were close, and in this early organizing drive, Sudbury's Finnish newspaper *Vapaus*, or *Freedom*, gave hearty support and much coverage to the Lumber Workers of the OBU.[24] Initial support within the province came from a number of Finnish camp organizations which joined the Lumber Workers as going concerns. Only a few of the IWW affiliates resisted the move.[25]

The success the LWIU and OBU enjoyed in western Canada provided organizers in northern Ontario with a powerful propaganda weapon. Leaflets tantalized eastern bushmen with descriptions of west coast conditions: the five dollar, eight-hour day; semi-monthly pay days; sheets, pillows, and pillowslips; wash-houses; and dry rooms. 'Are you willing to assist in winning these conditions,' asked a leaflet. 'Or are you willing to drift along in the same old rut that your grandfather did, ignorant of the fact that the world has changed? ... Prove your manhood! Think for yourself!'[26]

Because surviving evidence is spotty, it is difficult to establish how large the OBU grew in the Ontario bush during its heyday in 1919–20. It is clear that most Finnish radicals joined up, as did large numbers of other Europeans and English Canadians. Perhaps 3,000 to 4,000 signed union cards, but only a few hundred paid regular dues. The highly mobile woodsworkers easily flowed into – and out of – the union.

The most useful source for reconstructing the history of the Lumber Workers in Ontario is the union's fortnightly newspaper, *Le Travailleur/The Worker*. Apparently funded in part by westerners, it was meant to serve as a major vehicle for the union drive in northern Ontario. Its bilingual title and the occasional French-language article indicate the organizers' interest in reaching French-Canadian bushworkers. Nevertheless, it was essentially an English-language paper that carried a large number of camp and district-level reports translated from Finnish. From its pages it is possible to perceive the concerns of bushworkers and union activists, as well as their organizing techniques.

Reports of resolutions passed at meetings of the Lumber Workers make clear the priorities of Ontario's organized bushworkers. Concrete demands for better pay and camp conditions came first. At the top of the list stood the call for a five-dollar, eight-hour day. This amounted to a significant increase in wages and a substantial decrease in the work day, especially on the river drive where days of sixteen hours were not unusual. At the district level, bushworkers called for an end to piece work and end-of-contract bonuses. But the paper acknowledged that members were actually doing little to fight piece work; in fact, more and more bushmen were agreeing to work on an incentive pay system. Reports of camp meetings show that union members demanded not an end to piece rates, but higher rates. As presented, these demands were greater than simply a cry for 'more!'; the editors explicitly portrayed the fight for such goals as an initial step towards the achievement of self-respect and dignity and ultimately the workers' triumph over the power of capital.[27]

In relating the day-to-day battles in the struggle to organize the woods work force, *The Worker* complained about the restrictions placed upon organizers by tyrannical bosses and about the very structure of work which they believed was also impeding the drive. Organizers lashed out at bosses who ruled their isolated camps like personal fiefdoms, restricting access and censoring mail. After describing the bedbugs at his camp one correspondent wrote: 'Another kind of vermin here is the scissor-billed clerk who runs the depot, he having stated that any men working for the OBU should not be fed or kept anywhere.' Organizers noted that because of the camp system, woodsworkers were isolated and lacked 'the opportunity to hear any speakers and lecturers who explain affairs that are of common interest to the working class.' Unionization was also confounded by the easy way in which pulpwood operators shifted their cutters to piece work. When woods employees of Continental Wood Products demanded the eight-hour day the boss responded by switching to piecework and 'telling the workers: now you are working for yourselves and the longer you work the more money you will make.'[28]

The biggest problem organizers faced was the intense opposition of employers who rejected unionization and drew on current red-scare rhetoric to combat unionists. In March 1920 a lumberman reported that throughout the north the discontent was 'simply awful,' a state of affairs he blamed on the 'Bolsheviks, the One Big Union, the Reds, the IWW and other cults.' Only the French Canadians appeared relatively immune to the radical upsurge. As the editor of the *Canada Lumberman* fumed, the radicals were sweeping all before them:

Like a pestilence, Bolshevism, this disease on the body politic is hard to suppress. The methods of the IWW, Reds and OBU are insidious and clandestine, playing on the cupidity of the ignorant, and restless and foreign. In the eastern lumber camps, the 'come on' literature scattered by the Bolsheviki and the IWW is as alluring in tone and deft in touch as any that was ever put up by a wild-cat mining concern or a smooth, oil-well promoter ... Law and order must prevail! From the top to the bottom, Bolshevism is composed chiefly of featherless buzzards and moral hyenas. Its instincts are a cross between those of Jack-the-Ripper and Lucretia Borgia. Its idealism is that of the foul Harpees who consorted with Medusa. Its sensibilities rival those of the Yahoos whom Gulliver met. Its idea of Heaven is a defenseless woman. Its chief God is a rape fiend. Its coat-of-arms a vulture with outstretched wings. It was bred in darkness, conceived in iniquity, and born in the lower left-hand corner of Hell. Its final resting place will be its shameless birthplace. Let's speed the funeral![29]

Despite the impassioned determination of employers and all the barriers that organizers had to confront, the union nevertheless enjoyed some success in its major Ontario campaign – the drive to improve camp conditions and medical services for bushworkers. Developments can be traced in *The Worker*, which publicized poor conditions, provided an analysis of the reasons for this state of affairs, and proposed remedies. In order to expose bad camp conditions, the editor of the newspaper urged readers to submit reports containing specific information about their camps. Dozens responded. 'The pigs are the only animals that are satisfied with the conditions,' wrote J.M. from a Manley Chew camp near Milnet. 'Frequently they can be found in the kitchen, the cook feeding them out of his hand until there are too many. He then persuades them to get out by giving them a bath with hot water. Lucky pigs, the men can get a bath [only] when they go to town.'[30]

The Worker also provided a radical analysis of the bushworkers' problems. Under the heading 'Are You Satisfied?' one writer argued that 'to extract all the profits possible out of the workers, they house you under the most unsanitary conditions possible.' Other articles held that workers produced the wealth that the capitalist parasites enjoyed. In an article, 'The Robbery,' it was noted that the Spanish River Pulp and Paper Company had reported profits of $3,000,000, a sum which was divided among shareholders, most of whom 'would not know spruce from Jack Pine,' and whose hardest work was 'to draw their dividends.' Cartoons vividly conveyed this message. One had a heading 'Bossism' which showed a fat capitalist clutching his money bags while he looked contentedly at a run-down logging camp; in the accompanying drawing, labelled 'Unionism,' a proud, strong lumberjack stood beside his neat, well-built camp.[31]

In the tradition of the IWW, the Lumber Workers saw the fight for immediate improvements in pay and conditions as a means to build solidarity, educate participants, and prepare 'for the day when production for use shall replace production for profit.'[32] But as an OBU affiliate, the union sought to muster what limited political clout it could in order to gain favourable government policies. Consequently the leaders agitated for reforms in standards of camp sanitation and medical care, and for stricter enforcement of the regulations. Throughout 1920 Lumber Worker officials flooded the Health Department with letters describing substandard conditions and demanding inspections and enforcement of the Health Act. Walter Cowan wrote from Sudbury regarding a Poupore Lumber Company camp at mile 101 of the Canadian Northern Railway. 'The floors,' he said, 'are made of poles and vermin are crawling all over the place. The men eat and sleep in the same room in which the cooking takes place.' Another union official reported that in camp 9 of the Hope Lumber Company the beds were 'so close the same blanket could cover two men,' and 'an army of pigs' was 'running around loose, making the lake a playground.' Such reports sent the north's few sanitary inspectors scrambling into the backwoods.[33]

The Worker also blasted the Ontario Farm-Labour government for the inadequate regulations. In the spring of 1920 readers were told that health regulations had not been adequately enforced 'because the Government and the men are completely at the mercy of profiteering Employers.' That summer, in consultation with Cowan, provincial authorities drew up stricter regulations. But soon *The Worker* complained that these were poorly enforced because the men lacked the vote. In October a banner headline read: 'What Use is a Labour Government? – Ontario has best health laws and worst Camps in Canada.' Gradually, stricter enforcement of the new regulations did lead to improvements at least in the bigger camps. Yet the Lumber Workers as an organization did not survive to see the improvements. During the 1920–1 winter season, union organizing ground to a halt.[34]

The collapse of the Lumber Workers's drive in Ontario was due in part to conflicts among unionists regarding the most effective form of organization. Some Lumber Workers in British Columbia and Ontario called for the dismantling of the Lumber Workers' structure and for direct affiliation with the OBU. They supported the plan of organizing geographical units that would bring together workers from all industries in a district. Disputes at the Port Arthur district convention in February 1920 led to a referendum on the issue and in May to the district's break from the Vancouver headquarters of the Lumber Workers. Further splits developed at the national OBU convention held at Port Arthur in September. OBU leaders refused to seat key British Columbia and Ontario Lumber Worker delegates, ostensibly because the union had been delinquent in forwarding dues. At the Lumber Worker convention, which met at Vancouver in January 1921, the union resolved to withdraw formally from the OBU, 'until such time as the One Big Union conforms to the principles of democratic industrial unionism.' The union was split in Ontario as well; some bushworkers stayed with the Lumber Workers and others with the OBU.[35]

From the time of the split neither faction flourished. Throughout the winter of 1920–1 the OBU and Lumber Workers in Ontario and the west watched members abandon ship in droves. The reasons were obvious. In December 1920 the *Canada Lumberman* reported: 'Several operators have written ... saying that the present wave of unemployment is making the men, who are already engaged in logging operations, more efficient, contented and progressive.' A little later, University of Toronto Forestry students visiting the operations of J.R. Booth near Kiosk highlighted the transition: 'It is the foreman's day, and, being human, he has not forgotten his trials of the last two years, and may be excused for exercising considerable severity in dealing with the labourers. They, on their part, are very subdued, work well, and know too well that a complaint means discharge, and discharge, no job, and very little prospect of another.' Labour conditions throughout Canada had suddenly changed and everywhere it was 'the foreman's day.' From late 1920 to at least the end of 1922, unemployment levels rose sharply, undercutting the recently gained leverage of Canadian workers, and talk of democracy in industry gave way to the much more familiar pattern of employer dominance in over-stocked labour markets. The owners beat the unions not only in northern Ontario but in virtually every craft and industry of North America. The euphoria of 1919–20 had passed. Labour was on the run.[36]

REGROUPING AND REBUILDING

The task of rebuilding the labour movement in the Ontario bush was taken up during the 1920s almost entirely by Finnish immigrants who provided the leadership and the vast majority of union members. Following the 1920 split in the OBU, rival groups within the Finnish-Canadian left developed two competing bushworkers' unions.

One of the unions evolved from work done by some of the members who had stayed with the OBU in the months after the split. These men enjoyed some financial support from the thriving social clubs at Port Arthur, Nipigon, the Sault, Timmins, and Sudbury, which called themselves *OBU:n Kannatusrengas* or OBU Support Circles.[37] But the OBU was weak in the north, and it was further undermined by the activities of the IWW. In the mid-1920s, even after the IWW had been smashed in the United States, the remarkably tenacious Finnish-American Wobblies gained considerable influence in northern Ontario. Their success would be attributed in part to their publication *Industrialisti*, which had a wide circulation in the north and in part to the presence of several Finnish-speaking Wobbly leaders who had fled the United States and had come to the Sudbury district.[38] In December 1923 a referendum was passed in the Sudbury area which brought local OBU bushworkers into the IWW's Lumber Workers Industrial Union no. 120. Other woodsworkers were to take the same course, including the followers of O. Freeman who in 1925 would leave his position on the OBU General Executive Board and join no. 120. Shortly before he had helped launch a new organization known as the CTKL or *Canadan Teollisuusunianistien Kannatusliitto* (Support League of Canadian Industrial Unionists). Close to the IWW, it was mainly a cultural organization that would eventually grow to include twenty-three halls in Ontario,

Alberta, and British Columbia. These halls helped support the bush-workers in the IWW no. 120 during strikes, and they provided a useful recruiting ground for new members.[39] In the period 1923-5, 1,200 to 1,500 Ontario OBU members abandoned their organization and joined the IWW no. 120.[40] The OBU was left with a rump, its older rival having won the day.

The second bushworkers' union in Ontario emerged from the ashes of the Ontario wing of the Vancouver-based Lumber Workers Industrial Union. Finns who supported the recently formed Communist International began to build an organization independent of that run by their rivals associated with the OBU and IWW. Although the members of the Lumber Workers' in Ontario had dispersed in winter of 1920-1, some of the Finnish socialists in the north tried to keep the organization alive. A key supporter was A.T. Hill. By 1921 Hill had become the leader of the large Finnish-speaking group within the newly formed Workers' Party of Canada later known as the Communist Party of Canada (CPC). In the early 1920s, Hill and his comrades attempted to follow Lenin's teachings and, whenever possible, work as a left caucus within the mainstream of the Canadian labour movement. In most Canadian industries that meant opposing the OBU, staying in the AFL craft unions, and pushing them toward industrial unionism.[41] In the Ontario logging industry where there was no AFL union, the Communists' opposed the OBU and IWW organizations and tried to build a strong industrial-union alternative. In early 1924 Communists Kalle Salo and Alf Hautamäki undertook organizing drives among the northern bushworkers. That spring, under the auspices of the Finnish section of the CPC, a meeting of woodsworkers at Sault Ste Marie launched the new Lumber Workers Industrial Union of Canada (LWIUC).[42]

During the 1925-6 logging season, the LWIUC began to recruit significant numbers of Finnish pulpcutters in the Algoma and Lakehead districts. December 1925 saw the appearance of *Metsätyöläinen (The Lumber Worker)*, the organization's Finnish-language monthly magazine which was edited at LWIUC headquarters in Toronto by Alf Hautamäki. In addition to serving as editor, Hautamäki was the secretary of the Finnish Organization of Canada (FOC), a vital cultural organization closely connected to the CPC. The FOC would recruit union members in its many halls throughout the north and provide essential support for the LWIUC union drive.[43]

From the pages of *Metsätyöläinen* it is possible to reconstruct the organizational methods of left-wing Finns. When the LWIUC began to plan an organizing drive among bushworkers in 1926, strategists decided to begin the drive in Ontario's pulpwood sector; later they would unionize lumberjacks and then 'use the strength built in Ontario to launch a campaign in Quebec.' The planners believed that the chances for a successful campaign were best in Ontario's pulp camps where there were 'fewer nationalities involved and the Finns [made up] the largest group.' As the paper explained, the Finns were 'more knowledgeable about unions,' and had 'other strong organizations.' In February 1926 union leaders estimated that they might organize at least 2,000 Finnish pulp cutters, 600 Swedes, and about 300 others.[44]

In order to carry out its plans, the LWIUC sought to make *Metsätyöläinen* a publication that would draw readers into the union by articulating the complaints of bushworkers and in turn making the workers conscious of their exploitation. The paper stressed that bosses bullied bushworkers, treating them like 'feudal slaves.' It alleged that there was one camp in which the boss wielded a revolver to chase his men to work at 4:30 each morning. The publication regularly pointed out the various ways in which bushworkers were cheated by bosses who broke oral agreements, refused to itemize deductions, or failed to provide promised medical services. It also maintained that the woodsworker's lot had been declining steadily, as had his status: 'Now even the lowliest female dishwasher won't speak to lumberjacks, and so they must go to the saloons and brothels for amusement.'[45]

Monthly issues included entertaining and inspirational stories and poems as well. One short story recounted how an irresponsible, drunken lumberjack who had been injured went to a hospital where he began reading left-wing literature. Eventually he became a fine unionist. There can also be found several poem's by Aku Päiviö, a poet renowned in the left-wing Finnish-Canadian community. One of his verses provided a caption on the cover of a 1929 issue; it powerfully expressed the union's central message:

Rise you sinuous men against those who would steal your strength!
Rise by the thousands, like the forest itself!
That will be your only salvation.[46]

When it came to practical organizing, the LWIUC depended heavily on techniques pioneered by the IWW camp delegates during World War I. *Metsätyöläinen* explained that union delegates 'must work in secret, pretending to be ordinary workers'; in reality they were to use all their free time to recruit members. Organizers were also supposed to go to the towns where bushworkers congregated and 'infiltrate pool halls, restaurants and street-corner organizations.' According to the paper, this system was 'the key to raising membership by the thousands.'[47]

In recent years Edwin Suksi of Sudbury recalled his experiences as a LWIUC organizer in the Thunder Bay district in 1926 and 27: 'It was tough. There's not much friendliness. You have to walk from the railroad 28 to 30 miles in through the bush, and when you get there you get a very cold reception from the came foreman if he happened to be there ... One time, I walked into the camp at one o'clock and had to leave by evening.'[48] Like nearly all the other union delegates, who were men under 30 'in the best of manhood,' Suksi learned the art of organizing as he went along. He soon discovered that 'in the camps when organizing, mainly you talked bread-and-butter issues, not politics.' The men were always interested in pay first, and camp conditions second. With the exception of recalcitrant White Finns, Suksi found his fellow countrymen the easiest to organize because they 'were radical immigrants; they got solid unity.' But he added that the camp system also made organizing easier. 'When people stay six months in lumber camps in close quarters,' he said, 'they come to trust each other. If they decide, they'll be like one. If they decide to organize the union, they will be one.'[49]

The objective of the LWIUC organizers was not merely to sign up members, they also hoped to establish camp committees with chairmen who would maintain communications with the union and serve as spokesmen. Ideally the chairman would be a militant willing to challenge the boss. Finnish socialist Reino Keto was one such committee chairman. When the men at his camp grumbled about their poor lunches, he recalled how he set about to demand improvements:

I called together a meeting at the camp that night. Good. The boss came, and I explained that the men wanted better food. There was silence; no one uttered a word. No one, dammit! And everyone had mourned like old hags; but now they said nothing.

So the boss said, 'Well Reino, I can give you a packsack full of food so you can have enough, since no one else is troubled.' Then I said to the men, 'Listen now, why don't you complain? Who are you afraid of? Are you afraid of that old man sitting there? You have chosen me to represent you and now not one of you will help. Come and take my place then.'

So then one man said slowly and calmly, 'Yes, I am on Reino's side. I have heard men complain at night. Speak up! We can't desert Reino now and get him in trouble.' There started to be some movement; heads started turning, and here and there men spoke up.

And so things slowly got better. We put on pressure, and finally got so organized that we said, 'If the cook doesn't leave, the men will.' We got a new cook![50]

It is possible there were many little victories similar to Keto's, victories that have gone unrecorded. But on the basis of the few reported cases in which bushmen at a single camp went as far as to strike for extra pay or better living conditions, it appears the strikers did not do well. Reports of successes, which the left-wing press would have been eager to publish, are noticeable by their absence.

Far more drastic were the so-called general strikes involving woods employees of many operators in a district (see Appendix 9). The first, and one of the most successful, began in late September 1926 when at least 700 pulp cutters walked off their jobs in the Thunder Bay district. Preparations had begun in the summer, when joint meetings of Wobbly and LWIUC camp delegates met to decide on wage demands. According to LWIUC secretary Alf Hautamäki, first the jobbers and then later the pulp and paper companies had rejected the men's demands for higher piece rates and a monthly wage of at least sixty dollars (about twenty dollars higher than the going rate).[51] A test of strength ensued. For a few weeks the operators refused to negotiate. In the mean time, the inexperienced strikers and the union did amazingly well at cutting off the supply of strike-breakers and providing food and accommodation for all needy supporters. Finns, Slavs, French Canadians, and others enjoyed the aid of the entire left-wing Finnish community as both CTKL and FOC halls rallied to support a strike that had been endorsed by the IWW no. 120, as well as the LWIUC. The latter organization accepted strike donations totalling an impressive $3,292.57. By the end of October some of the operators had agreed to the demands, while others insisted on a compromise and paid $50 per month. Even this amounted to a significant advance which leftists hailed as the start of 'a new chapter in the history of our movement here in Canada.'[52]

In the years immediately following the 1926 breakthrough, no other strike involved as many pulp cutters or brought the unions such favourable results. General strikes fizzled in the Cochrane area in 1927 and in the vicinity of Kapuskasing the following year. LWIUC activists blamed these defeats on their failure to take into account the limited support for strike action among the predominantly non-Finnish bushworkers of these areas.

They also pointed to 'the deceit' of IWW no. 120, which had representatives on the strike committee. This would not be the last time the rival organizations would have difficulty co-operating.[53]

During a strike at Shabaqua in 1929, tensions between the LWIUC and the Wobbly organization reached the breaking point. LWIUC camp representatives meeting at Port Arthur in October 1929 had decided 'because pulpwood production is so active now, the time is ripe for fighting.' But once under way, the strike was a disaster. The IWW no. 120 blamed the failure on the opportunism and deceptions of its rival: 'Booze is as necessary to the officials of the LWIUC as gasoline is to a Ford; for without it they would not have the nerve to face the workers they have been deceiving.' Hautamäki replied: 'Without the underhanded opposition of the IWW this struggle would have become one of the most important struggles of the lumber workers of Canada.'[54]

This inter-union war of invective obscured for a time a far more serious development in the Shabaqua strike. In an attempt to extend the strike to additional camps, two union organizers, John Voutilainen and Viljo Rosvall, volunteered to try to organize about 100 men at the Onion Lake camps of Pigeon Timber contractor Leonard Mäki, or *Pappi* (Reverend) Mäki, as the one-time lay preacher was known.[55] Rosvall and Voutilainen realized it was a dangerous mission, for the vehemently anti-union Mäki employed mostly White Finns. But the two bravely set out on 18 November. They were not heard from again, though Mäki admitted to having talked to them on their first day. Eventually, in mid-April, a union search party found the organizers' bodies in a creek flowing out of Onion Lake. At coroners' inquests in which confusing testimony was heard, jurors quickly returned verdicts of accidental drowning. But LWIUC leaders, and the Finnish-Canadian left in general, rejected this finding. It was impossible for them to believe that two experienced bushworkers – one of them a trapper with a camp on Onion Lake – could have drowned in shallow water, especially as Rosvall had received a blow to the skull and his clothing was torn. The Finnish unionists were convinced that a gang of Whites from Mäki's camp had murdered the organizers.

On 28 April 1930, the day of Rosvall and Voutilainen's funeral, a giant procession of several thousand people followed the pallbearers through the streets of Port Arthur. In the front of the procession, union delegates carried a red ribbon with the union cards of the two organizers pinned to it, followed by the FOC brass band playing Chopin's *Funeral March*. The event was further dramatized by what appeared to be a symbolic eclipse of the sun. Thereafter, the Finnish-Canadian left and the woodworkers' union hailed Rosvall and Voutilainen as martyrs of the bushworkers' organizing struggles and as heroic victims of the class war.

RETREAT AND RESURGENCE

The tragic events involving Rosvall and Voutilainen served as a kind of exclamation point to the bushworkers' union activities of the 1920s. The next three years saw the woodsworkers retreat and regroup. Organizing and strike activity ground to a halt, as thousands of men who had relied on bush jobs found themselves unemployed. By the time of the LWIUC convention in 1930, income from dues was already down 30 per cent and the union had a formidable debt of $3,306.72. Matters did not soon improve. From 15 April 1931 to 31 July 1932 the LWIUC managed to collect in all of Ontario and Quebec a meagre $88.86 in dues and just $4.40 in initiation fees. In such a situation union leaders reported that they could only 'concentrate' efforts on 'education and agitation in unemployed organizations,' and stand by watching the 'vicious wage cuts in the limited number of camps operating.'[56]

During the early 1930s the LWIUC's strength was sapped by other developments as well. The Finnish-Canadian left generally, and the LWIUC in particular, were seriously weakened by the emigration in the early 1930s of more than 2,000 Finnish Canadians to Soviet Karelia. During the winter of 1930–1 Soviet officials requested that Canadian Communists send at least 1,000 skilled bushworkers to teach the art of woods work and to help the Karelians achieve the objectives of the first Five Year Plan. Finnish-Canadian woodsworkers, many of whom were jobless, easily caught Karelian fever. Early in 1930 *Karjalan työkuunta*, or the Karelian Work Unit, under the direction of three of the LWIUC's most active members, Alf Hautamäki, Kalle Salo, and Hannes Sula, devoted much energy to promoting and organizing the emigration. In 1931 the paper *Metsätyöläinen* published many articles extolling Karelia's economic and social opportunities, and the LWIUC convention strongly favoured the movement overseas. Notwithstanding the union's support for the scheme, there can be no doubt that the emigration took away a significant proportion of the most committed followers. In April 1932 the Timmins district LWIUC representatives reported at a meeting: 'We had to change the secretaries of the regional committees three times, because all the secretaries have left for Soviet Karelia, and therefore the membership . . . has fallen significantly; the work of the locals has just about ceased.'[57]

To make matters even worse, the left-wing Finnish community was torn by internecine battles. At the LWIUC convention in 1931 Secretary Hautamäki came under fierce attack from delegates who criticized the way he had been performing his duties and who charged that members had 'shunned the work of the LWIUC because they do not like Hautamäki personally.'[58] Hautamäki was also criticized by top-level leaders of the CPC. During the 1920s CPC leaders had taken a hands-off approach to the LWIUC, thus allowing Finnish members and 'fellow travellers' to run the organization virtually unimpeded. The language differences between English-speaking party leaders and Finnish-speaking activists reinforced this autonomy, as did the remoteness of union activities from party headquarters in Toronto. Towards the end of the decade, however, the Communist International and Canadian party chief Tim Buck had adopted the policy of Bolshevization and moved aggressively against the autonomy of the 'language federations' composed of Jews, Ukrainians, and Finns. One result was the souring of relations between activists in the FOC which was one of these federations and the party leaders.[59]

Tensions increased with the adoption in the winter of 1929–30 of new 'Third Period' policies. The party now abandoned its work within labour parties and AFL unions, declaring such activity 'reactionary.' In preparation for the imminent revolution, Communist strategy called for the creation of separate 'revolutionary industrial unions' under the direction of a new trade-union centre, the Workers Unity League (WUL). The LWIUC had never been a mainstream, AFL union. Therefore the Communists continued to work within it and it eventually became an affiliate of the WUL.[60] Precisely what a revolutionary union meant remains unclear. But at the LWIUC convention in 1931, WUL chief Tom Ewen lashed out at Hautamäki's 'pessimism and defeatism' and his policy of concentrating on educational work among unemployed bushworkers. Urging the union to follow the party line, Ewen declared: 'The main focus must be in the camps, at the work place, organizing them for strikes, rather than serving as a propaganda organization.' The upshot was the convention elected a new secretary, Emil Whalen. However, the union could not realistically follow Ewen's advice as long as the forest industry continued its decline.[61]

It was not until mid-1933 that the industry began to show definite signs of recovery. While bushworkers welcomed the increased job opportunities, they were not impressed by the very low wages and piece rates the companies were offering. Naturally, union leaders saw opportunities in a situation where woodsworkers were not only resentful, but also somewhat more confident that their services were in demand. At the same time the LWIUC was making determined efforts to build beyond its Finnish base. In

December 1932 there had appeared the first issue of the union's short-lived, English-language newspaper, *The Lumber Worker*. At the union's convention in the spring of 1933 J. Gillbanks, an English-speaking Communist Party member from the Lakehead, was elected to assist union secretary Kalle Salo.[62]

Beginning in the summer of 1933 and extending through the next two years, the LWIUC took a leadership role in a series of large, militant strikes that involved not only Finns, but also substantial numbers of French Canadians, English Canadians, Swedes, Slavs, and others – men who worked in every major logging district of northern Ontario (see Appendix 9). At last LWIUC and WUL leaders were able to take advantage of the restlessness and potential for militancy that the Third Period strategists of the Communist International had been insisting was there all along.

The strike wave of 1933–5 began on 5 June 1933 with a walkout of about 700 pulp cutters, most of them working for the Pigeon Timber Company near Onion Lake. The Pigeon Timber strike established some of the themes for subsequent battles. As in most conflicts during the period, the men had worked out their demands at camp meetings and at a district wage conference on 3 June. The LWIUC took credit for calling the conference, although local Wobblies also took part and served on the joint strike committee which emerged. Delegates demanded that piece rates be increased from $2.50 to $3 per cord and that board charges be decreased from 85 cents or $1 a day to 70 cents. Members gave top priority to wage demands, although they also insisted that the operators recognize camp committees and eliminate yellow-dog contracts. As in most disputes led by the WUL, the strike committee gave the employers less than forty-eight hours to meet the demands.[63]

During the ensuing confrontation the strikers gained only a little support from the general public. Alex Gibson, a pro-labour alderman from Port Arthur, registered his 'disgust at such a damnable contract as this ... a "yellow dog contract."' And civic officials and a local MPP objected strenuously to the attempts by the Pigeon Timber Company to bring in strikebreakers from Montreal because they feared the outsiders would end up on the area's relief rolls. However, local newspapers were filled with reports that radical strike leaders were preventing workers from going to work, that militants had threatened to burn down camps, and that 'one camp was seized by strikers who only were ejected when provincial police were called in.' Criticisms increased when the operators insisted that the dispute had been caused by Communists. 'The purpose of this strike activity,' they declared in a public statement, 'is to increase the cost of production of Canadian wood in order that Russia will have the price advantage on their own production.'[64]

In response to such charges, strike leaders neither openly denied nor affirmed the political connections of the strike committee or any of its members. A carefully worded reply stated: 'The Operators deliberately drag in the question of Russia in order to give the strike a "red" complex. If Russia can sell her products at lower rates than Canada it is due to a different organization or methods of production and distribution, and also to the elimination of profit.' True to the Third Period line of the day, WUL leaders also took swipes at the reactionary AFL leaders of the paper makers' unions who had not supported the strike.[65]

For several weeks the operators refused to meet with 'Red agitators' and the strike committee insisted it would only meet them at the Finnish Labour Hall. Eventually, the minister of Lands and Forests, a local MPP, and civic officials proposed a compromise that met with the approval of operators who were anxious to get their wood peeled before the sap stopped running and with strikers who were eager to return to camp meals and their pay. The two parties agreed to a rate of $2.75 per cord and board charges of 75 cents. Though the strikers had wanted more and their leaders disapproved of compromises, the LWIUC hailed it as a major victory.[66]

Encouraged, the LWIUC worked hard to prepare for the resumption of cutting operations. A joint IWW-LWIUC committee called a northern Ontario wage conference for mid-August, an event which had a reported attendance of more than 400 bushmen. The conference demanded wage increases of 20 to 25 per cent. Delegates also issued a statement criticizing the declining camp conditions, increased accident rates as a result of speed-ups, and the bosses' unfair statements in the press about the big money piece workers could earn. 'By giving their "friends" the best timber,' a conference statement declared, 'the bosses try to make the public believe all workers can make good wages and those that do not are called no good and lazy.' By November bushworkers were on strike at Thunder Bay, Fort Frances, Hearst, Kapuskasing, Iroquois Falls, and in neighbouring Rouyn, Que. In early January 1934 Chapleau tie makers had also walked out.[67]

Although the committees maintained that strikers had united to demand better pay and conditions, several employers insisted that Red agitators were the real cause of the walkouts. In the House of Commons, George Nicholson, the member for East Algoma, whose own logging operations in the Chapleau area were affected, thundered about Moscow-financed 'Communist agitators.' A spokesman for the strikers dryly replied: 'Nicholson says that our funds are backed from Moscow but we haven't seen any "Moscow gold" as yet, nor do we expect to require it.' The spokesman, Ellard Connolly, made it known that he was 'a Canadian citizen of British pioneer stock, born, reared and schooled in Bromely Township, Renfrew County.' He also insisted that the strikers 'here want only a living wage and civilized living conditions.'[68]

It was Nicholson's charges that captured front-page headlines throughout the province. The press also gave much attention to instances of picket-line violence. It was duly reported when 250 striking employees of the J.A. Mathieu Lumber Company boarded a train in Fort Frances carrying some fifty strike-breakers and coach windows were smashed, two policemen were injured, and Mathieu himself received three broken ribs.[69]

Yet the strikers did gain some public support. The Porcupine *Advance* reported favourably on the strike leaders' insistence on discipline in Kapuskasing. 'In the rough and ready language of the bush,' the leaders had warned the strikers that 'if they got drunk or caused any disturbance, even individually, they would be "grabbed by the neck and thrown out of town." ' The Winnipeg *Tribune* held that the strikers of northern Ontario had '100 per cent public sympathy and support on their side,' because employers had taken advantage 'of the state of the labor market to an almost criminal degree.' Certainly there must have been a good deal of support, because the strike-support committee succeeded in raising $6,453.38 in November and December 1934. In the House of Commons, Joseph Bradette, a Liberal member of the opposition for North Temiskaming, stated: 'I know the strikers in places like Kapuskasing, Cochrane, Iroquois Falls and Smooth Rock Falls were absolutely well behaved and had the wholehearted support of the citizens in those towns and localities.' He also reported that for six or seven weeks Chapleau had maintained the strikers on relief, so great was the town's sympathy. Bradette and another northern Ontario Liberal, Peter Heenan, criticized the Conservative governments in Ottawa and Queen's Park for failing to get a square deal for the strikers.[70]

Federal Labour Minister W.A. Gordon replied to his critics that conciliation efforts had proven impossible where 'certain elements were at work which argued and advised and cajoled and did everything possible to keep employer and employee apart.'[71] Some civic officials in northern Ontario demanded that the Department of Lands and Forests take action – form an independent tribunal to investigate the strikes. It was also suggested that a permanent, central authority was needed to adjust differences between operators and bushmen on a continuing basis.[72] As it turned

out the season's strikes were settled without substantial, third-party intervention. Generally employers offered wage increases which strikers readily accepted and which the unions hailed as major victories.

In response to the bitter confrontations and the apparent growth of
radicalism, the Ontario government introduced the Woodsmen's Employment Inquiry Act in the spring of 1934. It was an attempt to avoid a
repetition of the strike wave and to respond to the criticisms the government had endured. Under the new act, the minister of Lands and Forests
was empowered to appoint an investigator and assistant investigator who
were charged with inquiring into the terms and conditions of employment
in bush operations on crown land. They were to report to the minister
who in turn might make binding recommendations. Although no particular standards were established the provincial authorities were in a general
way acknowledging some responsibility for employment standards in the
crown forests. And the investigators – Thor Ehn and Walter Woodward –
brought to the job specialized knowledge of bush operations, something
Department of Labour officials had lacked.[73]

Another development that grew out of the 1933–4 strikes was a new
woodsworkers' union, the Canadian Bushmen's Union (cbu). This affiliate
of the All-Canadian Congress of Labour was led by a Port Arthur alderman, George Salverson, formerly a member of the Brotherhood of Railway
Telegraphers. Salverson hoped to recruit unorganized bushmen who, he
said, 'have determined that these Bolsheviki side shows shall cease.'
According to the cbu leader, his organization stood for 'peace in industry,
intelligent discussion, goodwill regarding workers' problems and a fair
deal.'[74] Salverson reported that the union had been organized by 'Cana-
dian-minded workers of several nationalities.' He appears to have tried to
unite White ('Canadian minded') Finns with 'Anglo Saxons,' although
much of his appeal was blatantly nativist.[75] An Ontario Department of
Labour correspondent at the Lakehead reported that 'at the time the cbu
was organized, the officers were nearly all . . . foremen, Superintendents or
timekeepers' in the employ of the Pigeon Timber Company.[76] In other
words it was a company union. At the lwiuc convention of 1934 delegates
expressed concern about the cbu; but it never grew large.[77]

There was a third development that grew out of the 1933–4 strike wave.
In the woods operations of the Spruce Falls Power and Paper Company
near Kapuskasing, strikes continued throughout the winter and into the
summer despite the company's offering a 'small bonus to get the work
out,' and its use of provincial police to intimidate woods employees.[78] The
continuing unrest drove Spruce Falls to attempt more lasting solutions to

their labour problems. The firm began to use mechanized equipment in an effort to develop year-round logging and thus build a permanent, loyal work force and undercut the advantage unions enjoyed during the crucial, short period of the ice haul.[79] The company also developed a card system designed in part to weed out uncooperative employees, and it introduced an employee-representation plan. As in other industries, the representation plan was intended to improve communications with employees, creating at least the illusion of consultation and thereby avoid unionization. No longer did the company have to deal with 'unwieldy camp committees of ten or twelve'; instead, one man in each camp provided a liaison and was 'willing to listen with an open mind to the company's views.'[80] Leftists dubbed this a company union and said its chief was 'a former company thug,' who dared not 'show himself after dark.'[81]

Strikes continued through the 1934–5 season. The first one quickly fizzled, due, the union later admitted, to a 'lack of organization' among the Lakehead strikers.[82] A second dispute, which erupted in the Cochrane area, was much stronger and captured a good deal of public attention. Articles in daily newspapers throughout the province reported the charges of operator A.E. Wicks that 150 strikers, who were foreigners, 'armed with spiked clubs, a rifle and several revolvers, swooped down on [a] pulp-cutting camp ... and roughly ordered the 40 [Canadian] workers in the camp to march 22 miles to Cochrane on five minutes notice.'[83] L.A. Dent, a special investigator sent to the scene by the Ontario Department of Labour, believed Wicks had exaggerated the incident and was 'endeavouring to make a racial issue of the matter.' Dent was impressed by the representativeness of the strike committees and felt they 'should not be disturbed in any reasonable activities.' He also believed 'great credit' was due the LWIUC for 'what they had accomplished and that they should be recognized.' For a while, despite considerable public criticism, Attorney General Arthur Roebuck refused to provide extra provincial police. But after Thor Ehn, an investigator from the Department of Lands and Forest failed to bring the parties together, the government sent in police to protect non-striking bushworkers. As a result, the strike was broken. Dent privately reported that he believed the real barrier to a settlement had been Wicks, who had assumed from the start 'a pugnacious attitude towards the strikers.' Dent also criticized the members of the OPP for openly expressing their sympathies with the operators.[84]

Equally controversial was the strike in the fall of 1934 which involved several hundred bushworkers in Algoma. This strike has been examined elsewhere in detail.[85] Once again the Finns were the most active group in enlisting the support of bushworkers, organizing effective pickets, and arranging for food and accommodation for strikers. During the conflict IWW activists issued statements listing contributions from Wobbly branches throughout northern Ontario, the northern Midwest states, and even as far away as California. Altogether they collected $1,405.75. At the same time, the Workers International Relief, a Communist organization, reported collections totalling $853.99, which came mainly from FOC branches, sports clubs, and women's groups.[86] The Finnish halls held dances and women's organizations ran bazaars to raise funds. Finnish halls also served as meeting places for strikers and as boardinghouses where the men could sleep on the floors. At the Finnish co-operative restaurants, women volunteers served pickets cheap or free food, much of it donated by Finnish farmers. Gertie Grönroos recalls that 'If the farmers hadn't supported those strikers heaven knows what would have happened ... Money was hard to come by, but they did have food.' However, little support came from outside the Finnish community. In the end the strike was broken when pickets were outnumbered by what *Vapaus* described as 'a large group of police on horseback, legionnaires and fascist citizens.'[87]

The last of the big strikes in which the LWIUC would play a part began in the Nipigon area in June 1935. About 2,100 men working in the pulp-peeling camps walked off the job demanding higher piece rates, the recognition of camp committees, and improved camp conditions. Once again employers blamed the walkout on Red agitators and said that strike leaders refused to negotiate. Of course the strike committee spokesmen insisted it was the operators who refused to meet with them. They also complained that one of the employers, Charlie Cox, who was also an MPP, had made sure that the Department of Lands and Forests declared the area a fire zone and refused to grant permits to pickets wishing to enter the zone. After a month-long battle, the strikers settled for a small increase in wages and, more important, the recognition of camp committees.[88]

The year 1935 marked the end of an era in the history of the Ontario bushworkers' union movement. Thereafter Finns would play a somewhat less prominent role and, more significantly, its leaders would begin to pursue a less confrontational approach within a different union structure. Later activists would build on the foundations laid by the Finns in the preceding two decades. Whether inspired by the militant industrial unionism of the IWW, or by the Russian Revolution and the promise of Leninism, Finnish organizers had won the support of most of their immigrant community and they had begun to build beyond it. The relations between Ontario's bushworkers and bosses were never more tense than during 1933 and 1934 when radicals succeeded in waging 'class war' in the bush. In the depths of the depression, as employers slashed wages and piece rates, the radical unionists gained a large, if impermanent, following. Despite the enormous unemployment of the period, and the fierce opposition of employers and the police, the unionists sometimes succeeded in making concrete gains. Woods operators did not enjoy uncontested control over their men. For unskilled workers during the depression, this in itself was a considerable achievement.

7

Building the Lumber and Saw

In the fall of 1935 the labour movement in the Ontario bush entered a new phase. The Lumber Workers Industrial Union of Canada was disbanded and its left-wing activists were soon pouring their energies into building the Lumber and Saw Mill Workers Union (LSWU), a branch of an old craft international, the United Brotherhood of Carpenters and Joiners of America.[1] Rather than blasting employers with class-war rhetoric, collective bargaining and signing agreements became the major objectives of the unions. Instead of criticizing the government's latest schemes for deluding workers, key union leaders began to take advantage of Ontario's new Industrial Standards Act (ISA). Before long the Lumber and Saw, as the union was popularly known in the north, had established a kind of rudimentary, collective-bargaining relationship in major parts of the forest industry. A decade later the union would win its first industry-wide collective agreement with the major pulp and paper companies operating in the north. Thereafter, the Lumber and Saw, though rocked by the anti-communist sentiments of the Cold War, made headway in providing much-needed services and better pay and conditions to an ever-increasing proportion of the woods work force.

A NEW APPROACH

The impetus for change in the woods labour movement came from the policies adopted by the seventh congress of the Communist International in the summer of 1935 and announced in November at the ninth plenum of the Communist Party of Canada. The party formally abandoned its revolutionary posturing of the Third Period and, in a bid 'to fight fascism at home and abroad,' its leaders sought alliances with other progressives, including members of the Co-operative Commonwealth Federation (CCF) and some Liberals. The new policy meant abandoning the revolutionary unions of the Workers Unity League, promoting unity within the labour movement, and 'building up' AFL affiliates in Canada.[2] A final convention of the WUL, held immediately after the ninth plenum, resolved that each affiliate 'take up the question of unity in its own industry and on the basis of concrete conditions prevailing in each industry, strive to establish one union of all workers in such industry.'[3]

A key leader among northern Ontario's bushworkers at the time of this so-called Unity Convention and for the next decade and a half was Bruce Magnuson. Significantly, he was a Swedish immigrant who by the mid-1930s spoke English comparatively fluently and was well equipped to reach the ethnically diverse bush work force. As a young man in 1928 Magnuson immigrated to Canada. He spent his first years working as a teamster on farms in Saskatchewan. There he took an interest in local left-wing politics, becoming, he says, 'class conscious.' In the winter of 1933 Magnuson went to Port Arthur in search of a bush job. On his arrival he found that Lakehead woodsworkers were on strike. He immediately supported the strikers, and in his spare time read Marx, Lenin, and William Z. Foster. The young Swede soon became a member of the CPC. When the strike was over, Magnuson found work as a teamster in a logging camp. But his career as a bushworker was short-lived. After a week on the job he was injured when a load of logs crushed him. For the next eight months he remained on compensation and took the opportunity to strengthen his left-wing ties in Port Arthur. In the fall of 1934 he began working as a LWIUC organizer, living on a portion of the dues he collected in the logging camps of northwestern Ontario. Magnuson was soon keeping the books for the Lakehead local and assisting A.T. Hill and other more experienced leaders. In November 1935 he attended the WUL convention in Toronto as a LWIUC delegate, and then he and the others plunged into the task of interpreting party policy to the logging industry.[4]

In the logging industry of Ontario, where there was no active AFL union, it was not at first clear what the party's new policy of unity would entail. Immediately after the WUL convention, the national executive of the LWIUC sent a letter to the Iroquois Falls local of the International Brotherhood of Pulp, Sulphite and Paper Mill Workers, an AFL union, suggesting joint organization of the entire industry. *The Worker* reported, however, that on orders from the International's vice president, the LWIUC's letter had been 'thrown in the waste basket.'[5]

Rebuffed by the Pulp Workers, the LWIUC soon began negotiations with the United Brotherhood of Carpenters and Joiners – in northern Ontario and on the west coast. In early February 1936 Ontario's bushworkers presented a formal request to join the Carpenters *en bloc* under the name of the Lumber and Sawmill Workers Union.[6] (Some months earlier, independent of the Communists and the LWIUC, sawmill workers at Fort Frances had formed a union, applied for an AFL charter, and become Lumber and Saw Mill Workers local 2558.)[7] The United Brotherhood agreed to grant them charters for locals which would be directly affiliated to the International, but known as Lumber and Saw Mill Workers Union locals. In March 1936 the last LWIUC convention held in northern Ontario ratified the move into the Lumber and Saw. A referendum in April backed the move in British Columbia. Soon former LWIUC activists like A.T. Hill, Harry Raketti, Bruce Magnuson, and others were hard at work establishing the union's major logging locals based in Port Arthur (no. 2786), Timmins (no 2995), Sudbury (no. 2537), and Fort Frances (no. 2560).[8]

In many respects the Communist-led woodsworkers were a strange component in the creaky, old United Brotherhood, which had been formed by highly skilled craftsmen in 1881. Before the mid-1930s the Brotherhood had claimed jurisdiction over woodsworkers but had refused to organize them. In 1933, however, the AFL began chartering federal locals in the lumber industry of the Pacific northwest, a development that alarmed the Brotherhood officers who feared the emergence of a rival union. As a result of pressure, in February 1935 the AFL transferred some 7,000 lumber workers to the Brotherhood. Although the transferred workers were given the option of taking out 'beneficial membership,' nearly all preferred to pay lower dues and forgo the benefits. When Ontario's Lumber and Saw locals affiliated, they too chose non-beneficial status. Naturally the Ontario logging locals and their members came under the full authority of the Brotherhood's constitution, and the union expected the locals to co-operate with its regional and general representatives.[9]

It must have been with some apprehension that Communist LWIUC leaders, accustomed to having a free hand in the WUL, accepted the authority of one of North America's most conservative unions. Before long, in British Columbia and the Pacific northwest, there were serious conflicts between left-wing loggers and Brotherhood officials. At the Carpenters' convention in 1936, the General Executive Board denied voting rights to non-beneficial members. This action enraged western loggers and triggered the secession of a great number of the locals. The following year these locals formed the International Woodworkers of America (IWA) and affiliated with the new Congress of Industrial Organizations (CIO) based in the United States.[10] As in most industries the Communists threw their considerable energies into building the rapidly expanding, militant, and progressive CIO union. Not surprisingly, in northern Ontario there were continuing tensions between left-wing Lumber and Saw activists and the Brotherhood's general representative Andy Cooper in Toronto. But unity prevailed. Though the IWA organized Ontario furniture workers, it never made headway in the northern bush. It is hard to understand why the leaders of the Ontario Lumber and Saw locals kept their locals in the conservative Brotherhood. Bruce Magnuson maintains that they did so because, unlike the lumber workers in British Columbia, this province's pulp cutters had to work closely with the AFL pulp mill unions.[11]

At the same time as the leaders of the bush union were regrouping, officials at the Ontario Labour Department tried to secure agreements in the logging industry under the recent Industrial Standards Act (ISA). The act had originated in the election campaign of the Liberal Party in 1934, when Opposition Leader Mitch Hepburn made a bid for the votes of working people. He alluded in part to an Ontario version of labour policies found in President Roosevelt's New Deal that were encouraging collective bargaining south of the border.[12] The impetus for the act also came from employers who hoped to avoid collective bargaining while stabilizing labour costs in their depression-ravaged businesses.[13] In April 1935, nearly a year after the Liberals' victory at the polls, the Hepburn government quickly passed a compromise proposal. According to Hepburn, the new legislation would improve 'the social standards of labor and at the same time ... eliminate unfair and cut-throat competition in industry.'[14] Under the act the minister of Labour was empowered to designate officials who could convene regional meetings at which employers and employees, who represented a preponderant group in an industry, could discuss wage standards and hours of labour in their industry. If with the help of the Labour Department the two parties agreed on a wage schedule then the minister could declare it binding on all employers and employees in the region for a period of one year. Some businessmen thought the act might bring stability by reducing the ruinous price- and wage-cutting most frequently practised by small companies or contractors. Critics said the act lacked sufficient coercive powers, and in many industries it did prove to be a dead letter. However, in the logging industry, where labour relations had been especially tumultuous, the ISA became a vital aspect of labour-management relations.

Provincial officials made their first attempts to establish a wage schedule for the logging industry at meetings held at Port Arthur in early 1936. The very active chairman of the meetings was the chief conciliation officer of the Department of Labour, Louis Fine, who had once been an official of the United Cloth Hat, Cap and Millinery Workers International Union (AFL).[15] On the morning of 6 January Fine met a group of worker representatives who he later reported had been 'chosen supposedly by the employees of the various camps.'[16] The transcripts of the discussions show that these men had great difficulty expressing their views clearly. On the other hand, the operators with whom Fine met in the afternoon were very articulate, suggesting rates for various classes of labour. At five o'clock the official tripartite conference began. From the testimony of the worker representatives it is abundantly clear that several of them had been hand-picked by their bosses, a fact Fine noted privately. Nevertheless, it appears he was willing to go ahead with the agreement the parties reached.[17]

At the last moment LWIUC leaders got wind of what was happening. That evening they met with Fine. They voiced their disapproval not only of his failure to inform them about the conference but also his willingness to recognize what amounted to an embryonic company union. Fine agreed to postpone any final decisions, thus allowing the unionists a chance to rally support. The Lakehead labour councils backed them up, as did dozens of union members who wrote from their camps.[18] In the end Fine approved a few amendments to the schedule and let LWIUC officers sign the revised document. His willingness to recognize the LWIUC – and soon after the Lumber and Saw – amounted to a significant breakthrough for unionists in an industry where most operators had long refused to bargain collectively with their employees. In the years ahead the Lumber and Saw would try to use the forums provided under the ISA as a means of achieving a kind of quasi-collective bargaining relationship with operators throughout the north. In pursuing this objective, the union met with mixed results.

The leftist leaders of the Lumber and Saw eagerly sought to wring every advantage they could from the act. As 1 October approached, the expiry date for the 1936 Thunder Bay agreement, union officials from Fort Frances, Timmins, and Sudbury urged the provincial Labour Department to call a province-wide conference for the logging industry. Presumably they believed that central negotiations and an industry-wide agreement would strengthen the union, especially in the northeast where it had been the weakest. Fine rejected their request on the ground that 'proper representation by employers and employees would not be possible at present on a province-wide basis.' At the same time the Lumber and Saw proposed that the new agreement in Thunder Bay provide for far more than just wages and hours. Port Arthur local 2786 called for a guarantee of free access to union representatives wishing to enter camps, dues check-off, and a clause preventing discrimination against union members.[19] The problem of access to the camps for union officers was particularly acute, since several Lakehead operators had prevented entry during the summer of 1936.[20] The Thunder Bay District Logging Advisory Board, a joint labour-management board established to administer the ISA agreement, recommended that representatives be allowed 'reasonable visits and inspections.' But the operators attending the ISA conference in September 1936 refused to agree to such a clause and no agreement was signed. Despite a vigorous union organizing campaign which coincided with the talks, the Lumber and Saw did not yet have the muscle to compel operators in Thunder Bay to accept the union's proposals.[21]

Shortly after the failure at Port Arthur, Bruce Magnuson, who had organized local 2560 at Fort Frances in the summer of 1936, requested that the Labour Department hold an ISA conference for the Rainy River District. Fine refused this and subsequent requests, maintaining that it would be pointless to hold such a meeting as long as Thunder Bay had not settled.[22] The union was compelled, therefore, to use its own weight to force the district's major employers – Shevlin-Clark Lumber Company and J.A. Mathieu Lumber Company – to the bargaining table. According to Lumber and Saw sources, as soon as the union began circulating petitions requesting bargaining among its camp committees, Shevlin-Clark fired committee members at its Camp 61. These firings triggered an immediate, spontaneous strike at that camp on 6 July 1937, and soon after at some sixteen other Shevlin-Clark and Mathieu camps. Inspired by the celebrated sit-down strikes of the era in the United States, the strikers decided to fight the same way. It proved difficult, however, to sustain a sit-down strike in the bush. While the two forest companies failed to evict the strikers, the firms succeeded in preventing unionists from sending in messages or food supplies. Confusion and food shortages quickly developed. By mid-January attempts at food rationing had failed, and so in bitterly cold weather, the hungry strikers began to trek the forty to sixty miles to the railway that would take them to Fort Frances.[23]

In the mean time, negotiations were underway at Fort Frances. Despite the eagerness of Louis Fine and Andy Cooper to achieve a settlement, an agreement was delayed by the reluctance of the manager of Shevlin Clark to agree to a clause guaranteeing non-discrimination against union activists, and by the militants' demands for higher pay. In the end the strikers had to accept very modest pay increases in exchange for a non-discrimination clause. For Magnuson and the more militant strikers it was a disappointing end to a dispute that had begun so dramatically. However, in the fall of 1937, the terms won by the strikers became the basis for the first ISA agreement in the Rainy River District and hence for the beginning of a form of collective bargaining.[24]

In subsequent years the Lumber and Saw continued to pursue agreements under the ISA. At conferences held in Port Arthur in May 1937 Louis Fine supported the union demands, pushing the operators so hard that Eddie Johnson of the Pigeon Timber Company exclaimed: 'Last year we discussed a 10 per cent increase, this year 15 per cent, making 25 per cent ... It seems to me this is getting entirely out of line. I don't think this is being handled at all properly.' In the end the union got its 15 per cent increase, though board charges were also raised. A year later the demand for wood was down again, and yet the union succeeded in raising the rates about 6 per cent. At the same time the Lumber and Saw won several new provisions in the agreement, the most important one being higher piece rates for scattered timber. In addition, clauses were added requiring free mail service, luggage transportation, and free board for monthly men on all days of the month including Sundays and holidays. Although the union had to remain vigilant in protesting any practices that contravened the standards, it forwarded remarkably few complaints to the Labour Department. It would seem the Lumber and Saw was enjoying some satisfaction under the ISA.[25]

Of course, despite the union's success in negotiations, labour disputes did not vanish. In January 1938 the men in the camps of Lake Sulphite mounted a series of sit-down strikes to demand improvements in wages and living conditions. Thomas Warren, an Ontario Provincial Police officer, who travelled from camp to camp by dogsled, agreed that conditions in some sites were in need of 'much improvement.' He reported that at 'Simon Cote's Camp the toilet was unsanitary and not boarded up – the outhouse was useless and most of the men were lousy – the cookery floor never scrubbed.' The men's protests did result in some small improvements.[26]

Throughout the late 1930s many operators, especially in the lumber sector, remained hostile to the unions. In October 1937 Albert Locking, a Carpenter representative who insisted he was not a radical, but a Liberal, sent a letter to the Ontario deputy minister of Labour in which he explained how J.J. McFadden had tried to prevent access to his camps:

He told me I could not organize his men. At this I arranged a meeting for the men of the various camps for Sunday October 17th to be held on the [Provincial]

Highway which goes through Mr. McFadden's timber limits. On my arrival at the place of meeting I found that Mr. McFadden along with his Vice President, Mr. Fitzgerald, and his Logging Superintendent had held meetings in each of the five camps and had advised the men not to attend my meeting and told them if they did attend my meeting their time would be made out when they arrived back at camp and they could no longer work for him. He also saw fit to travel between camps all day during Sunday and watched the men of the various camps to see who, if any, attended the meeting. I had a very nice turn out from each camp and gathered from the men the information I have mentioned above.[27]

Despite Locking's efforts and complaint, it would be more than a decade before the union could organize McFadden's closely watched camps. In the mean time, the union faced new challenges brought by World War II.

WOODSWORKERS IN WARTIME

Canada's declaration of war on 10 Sept. 1939 heralded the beginnings of profound changes in the nation's labour markets, policies, and movement. Within two years virtually all of the more than 900,000 people registered as unemployed in September 1939 would find jobs or join the service, and manpower shortages would develop in many sectors. During the war the federal government became the pre-eminent power in labour matters. To ensure maximum production, Canada's policy makers hoped to win the co-operation of workers and their unions. However, labour was soon alienated by the government's attempt to halt inflation by imposing a wage freeze and by its refusal of compulsory collective bargaining. But surging union growth in war industries, a major strike wave in 1943, and the growth of support for the left-of-centre CCF did much to persuade the government in 1944 to pass an order in council, PC 1003, that partly answered demands for compulsory collective bargaining.[28]

The war also brought new policies from the CPC. From 1939 to 1941, during the era of the Hitler–Stalin non-aggression pact, Canadian Communists denounced Canada's participation in an 'imperialist war.' In 1940 federal authorities, charging that Communists were impeding the war effort, interned a number of the leaders and drove others into hiding. But when the Nazis began their assault on Russia in June 1941, Canadian Communists suddenly became highly patriotic, urging workers and unions to do their utmost to maximize production and help win the war.[29]

The coming of the war had an immediate effect on the Lumber and Saw. At the same time that war was being declared, the demand for woodsworkers was increasing, as were wages. By late October Lumber and Saw leaders at the Lakehead were demanding a new ISA conference and higher rates, even though the current agreement was not going to expire for several months. 'We must keep our bodies and souls in a healthy condition and high in spirits,' they patriotically maintained, 'to enable us to give the very utmost at this time as Canadians, to help our government and nation at the present crisis.' Louis Fine bluntly refused to open up the agreement, and‚ he was firmly supported by the Carpenters' representative, Andy Cooper. Fine wrote that Cooper 'definitely advised the union officers that neither he, nor his organization, would permit the breaking of any agreements entered into and that he would do everything necessary to see that the ISA schedule remain in force.' The local press commended the Lumber and Saw for 'keeping their agreements,' and cited one local operator who had declared, 'we can always count on them.'[30]

A few months later, however, Eddie Johnson, a prominent timber operator and chairman of the Fort William Industrial Commission, charged that the Communist officers of the Lumber and Saw were 'always fomenting strikes and seeking to sabotage the industry.' Although the party line still opposed the war effort, neither Johnson nor anyone else produced evidence that the Lumber and Saw's Communist leaders were having adverse effects on productivity in the logging industry. Nevertheless, Canadian authorities were taking few chances. In July 1940 they interned the union's key leader, Bruce Magnuson, who remained in custody for the next two years. During that period the union was seriously weakened and in considerable disarray.[31]

For the duration of the war Ontario's logging industry felt the impact of the federal government's manpower and incomes policies. Labour shortages persisted, notwithstanding the propaganda of the National Select Service Commission encouraging farmers to spend their winters logging, and the allocation of conscientious objectors, interned Japanese Canadians, and German prisoners of war by the government to logging operators.[32] As it turned out, federal incomes policies provided an opportunity for the Lumber and Saw. Attempts by the authorities to freeze the wages of woodsworkers in a period of increasing labour shortages raised a number of problems for operators and once again helped to bring the Lumber and Saw into a kind of quasi collective-bargaining relationship with major operators. By a stroke of the pen PC 8253, which became effective on 15 Nov. 1941, made the minimum wages established under the Thunder Bay ISA agreement of 1941, the maximum for the entire Ontario pulpwood industry.[33] Confusion ensued because some firms, such as

Spruce Falls, had been paying much higher rates than the Thunder Bay minimums, and they continued to do so. An official of the Newaygo Timber Company at Port Arthur complained that 'the men are leaving in droves and apparently are taking employment with the Spruce Falls Power and Paper Company.' Operators anxious to obtain woodsworkers were soon circumventing the freeze by devious tactics that violated the order in council.[34]

These problems led to several tripartite conferences held under the auspices of the Regional War Labour Board for Ontario, and eventually, in the fall of 1942, to a new wage schedule. But once again some companies refused to antagonize employees by cutting wages in accordance with government-imposed ceilings. Moreover, nature intervened to defeat the freeze. Unusually deep snow during the 1943 hauling season forced employers to find ways to raise wages again, 'in order to have any work done at all.' In the summer of 1943 another round of negotiations produced a new order from the War Labour Board which imposed higher wages and provided for several non-monetary matters such as free, regular mail service, guarantees that scale slips would be issued within seven days, and no charge for baggage transportation.[35]

During the 1943–4 logging season, the Regional War Labour Board received a barrage of complaints from operators and their associations. Employers reported on competitors who were paying far in excess of the government-approved wage rates, and they griped about recruiters who enticed workers from one district to another.[36] Lumbermen resented the fact that wage rates in the sawlog sector had not risen as fast as those in the pulpwood sector, and that there was thus 'less enthusiasm on the part of the ... sawlog cutters.'[37] By the end of the season operators did not know how to stabilize their industry. What exasperated employers the most was the success the woodsworkers had in forcing up wages without a corresponding rise in productivity. The result was sky-rocketing production costs at a time when lumber and paper prices remained under comparatively tight government control.[38]

Thus wartime developments helped strengthen the bargaining power of woods workers and their union. The availability of opportunities outside the industry had drawn off a large number of job competitors, enabling those who remained in the industry to win higher wages. By jumping to camps where piece rates were high, timber plentiful, and ground conditions optimum, cutters could substantially increase their incomes over pre-war levels. In the meantime, the willingness of officials from the Regional War Labour Board to accept the Lumber and Saw as the mouthpiece of woods labour gave the union legitimacy and enabled its leaders to retain the quasi collective-bargaining relationship initially developed under the ISA. These methods were not substitutes for formal union recognition, full collective bargaining, and collective agreements; they were, however, steps along the way.

POST-WAR VICTORY

Full-blown collective bargaining did not emerge in the Ontario woods industry until the immediate post-war period, when the bushworkers engaged in a decisive battle with their employers. The strike of October 1946 roughly coincided with disputes in a host of North American industries, including a major confrontation in the British Columbia logging industry. Stuart Jamieson, an authority on Canadian industrial conflict, has maintained that 'the larger and more prolonged strikes of the postwar period represented major "tests of strength" between unions and employers in industries in which, for the most part, unions and collective bargaining on a significant scale were relatively new and unfamiliar phenomena.' He argues that the strikes developed on such a huge scale, mainly because of 'stiffened employer resistance to the challenge that this union campaign presented to the traditional authority, prerogatives and procedures of management.'[39]

The determination of Ontario bushworkers and their bosses had been amply demonstrated at an ISA conference held at Port Arthur in July 1946. The operators proposed that the minimum rates established in the agreement should be the maximums set by the most recent order of the War Labour Board. The Lumber and Saw insisted that the minimums should be the going rates, which were in some instances double the approved levels. With the parties so far apart, Chief Conciliation Officer Louis Fine believed only a strike could settle the matter.[40]

During the late summer and early fall, the union issued several press releases that threatened a strike unless operators agreed to demands for 'full union recognition and security,' increased piece rates, a minimum daily wage of five dollars, free hand tools, and the abolition of double-decker bunks. This last item won support from many woodsworkers and members of the public who had little understanding of, or interest in, the trade-union point of view. Toronto-born Buzz Lein, who had begun work in northern Ontario logging camps in 1937, recalls: 'Those first union organizers in the bush must have been brainwashed somewhere. They were new birds to us, a strange species. We'd listen to them and most of what they said didn't make sense – that Marxist philosophy they spouted. Solidarity forever and all that crap! The only thing that did make sense was we'd get rid of those top bunks. *That* made sense!' Even the usually unsympathetic daily press of northern Ontario supported the union's bid for single beds. 'To the uninitiated, such a demand may seem petty,' editorialized the Sault *Star* on the eve of the strike. 'But any ex-serviceman, with the horrors of night-life in double-tiered bunks still fresh in mind, would give it top priority.'[41]

Two days of talks between the Lakehead operators and Lumber and Saw representatives brought the parties no closer. The operators then asked the provincial Labour Department to provide conciliation services. But the minister of Labour, Charles Daley, would only agree to provide such services after the union had called off its threatened strike and applied for certification under the Ontario Collective Bargaining Act – legislation passed in 1943 as a desperate pre-election bid by the Ontario Liberal government to meet the challenges of a rising CCF and a revitalized Conservative Party. Union leaders rejected Daley's appeals because they recognized that the delays resulting from the bureaucratic requirements of certification would make it nearly impossible to win recognition in a seasonal industry which had high turn-over rates. The Lumber and Saw stuck to its strike deadline of 12 October. Later that day, after receiving phone calls from Lakehead employers regarding the strike, the secretary-manager of the Ontario Forest Industries Association recorded in his diary: 'Looks like a pretty fair job has been done by unions.'[42]

Nearly 5,000 bushworkers, most of them from the Thunder Bay district, answered the strike call on the morning of 12 October. In the following few days hundreds more piece workers, who had waited until companies had scaled their wood and issued cheques, began congregating at the main strike centre in Port Arthur, as well as in outlying towns such as Beardmore, Geraldton, and Sioux Lookout. To the east of the Thunder Bay district, the response was spotty, as it was in many remote camps. Once again, Finnish bushworkers proved to be among the most enthusiastic supporters, though the walk-out was not a Finnish event as the battles of the 1930s had been. Union militants of all backgrounds manned picket lines at government employment offices and railway centres throughout the north, while hundreds of the less dedicated strikers simply returned home to await a settlement. A week after the strike had begun, Magnuson claimed that 8,000 bushworkers were out. This number included many female staff whose numbers had increased because of the labour shortages during the war. Clearly this was the biggest walk out in the history of the Ontario logging industry.[43]

During the first weeks of the dispute, each party tested the other's strength. The Thunder Bay Timber Operators Association announced its refusal to negotiate until the union was ready to agree to conciliation and 'call a truce.' With such solid support for the strike among Thunder Bay bushworkers, the union was hardly about to throw in the towel. From the union's perspective, the strike's timing could not have been better. In October the very last of some 8,000 German prisoners of war who had been working in the bush were on their way home. According to data from the National Employment Service, on 19 September there were 8,477 job openings for Ontario bushworkers and a mere 219 unplaced applicants.[44]

After two-and-a-half weeks the minister of Labour summoned representatives from each side to Queen's Park for a meeting on 29 October. The meeting in itself amounted to a partial victory for the union because to that point employers and government officials had refused to begin negotiations with the Lumber and Saw until the union returned to work. At the Toronto meetings, progress was rapid. On 30 October eighteen employers signed a collective agreement. Soon after the strikers ratified it and most had returned to work by 4 November.

According to a spokesman for the employers, C.R. Mills, the manager for the Ontario Forest Industries Association, the entire strike had been unnecessary. Wage rates remained the same as those approved by the Regional War Labour Board in September with the sole exception of the rate for general labour which increased from $5.90 per day to $6.20. Mills wrote, 'I might say ... this rate would have been paid by the employers without any strike.' In the mean time, Bruce Magnuson hailed the agreement as a 'magnificent victory,' that had checked the 'powerful monopolies [which] were seeking revenge and a way back to pre-war conditions.'[45]

There can be no doubt that the strike settlement amounted to a major union advance – its biggest ever, in fact. As in most of the other major strikes of 1946, Ontario's bushworkers won collective-bargaining rights by hitting when their employers' stockpiles were low, product markets keen, and labour in short supply. The contract signed by the logging operators contained the long-sought demand for recognition. Furthermore, the eighteen companies which signed represented all large and mid-size operators in the pulp and paper sector.[46] Even though the strike had been far more solid in the Thunder Bay district, the agreement covered woods employees in the pulp and paper sector across the province. The union could now speak with much greater authority for a work force of more than 15,000. Shortly after the strike, Gordon Godwin, a woodlands official for the Ontario Paper Company, announced to a closed meeting of his counterparts:

The strike was 100% effective. After three weeks an agreement was negotiated and the three main demands were agreed upon. These were:

1) Base net pay of $5.00 (this is $6.20 per day gross, less board at $1.20)
2) Union recognition
3) Single deck beds

The union is strong and its strength will increase.[47]

Whatever face-saving assessments woods employers made publicly, in private they acknowledged total defeat.

Yet as in other industries which established new, collective-bargaining relationships in the immediate post-war period, there were strings attached to the new logging contract. Many labour historians speak of the 'post-war compromise,' which established collective bargaining and often union security, but prohibited strikes and lockouts during the life of an agreement.[48] Thus unions won recognition and increased stability, while employers could be more certain of continuous production. Instead of spontaneous strikes erupting when workers disagreed with a management order, employees had to carry out the order and file a grievance, which might take months to settle if it ever was. The short, simple contract signed in the Ontario logging industry in 1946 contained a no-strike clause, as well as provisions for grievance procedures. And at a meeting in January 1947 of woodlands officials from eastern Canada Ontario managers demonstrated their awareness of some of the advantages of the new industrial relations set-up. One man reported: 'the effect of the union, in the opinion of the operators after the first shock has worn off is (a) the union is not too difficult to get along with (b) the operators in Ontario are exchanging information on common problems.' Another official, noting that corporate industrial relations programs for woods employees were 'poor or non-existent,' hoped that the strike would force operators to pay 'more attention ... to woods labour problems.' And finally, a manager from Newfoundland, where there had been a quasi-company union for a number of years, reassured the Ontario men that one advantage 'of drawing up a year's agreement with a union is that it stabilizes your labour costs and you know where you stand.' He also advised granting the union dues check-off. In his experience, union delegates sent into camps to collect dues 'kept the men stirred up,' while 'union agents with a steady income aren't trouble makers.'[49]

In the immediate post-war period worker solidarity had brought the Lumber and Saw full recognition, an objective that had long eluded it. As in many other industries at that time, labour militancy had pushed industrial relations to a new stage. Immediately after the 1946 strike, however, woods operators began to consider ways to benefit from the new arrangement. Although the strike marked a turning point for the Lumber and Saw, much remained to be done.

FIGHTING THE COLD WAR

Having won a major victory over pulpwood operators in 1946, Ontario's Lumber and Saw officials committed themselves to consolidating their hold over the new recruits and to expanding their base among woodsworkers in the lumber sector. It would be a challenge to ensure the smooth functioning of the new grievance procedures, to negotiate popular contracts that would provide for improved wages, better working conditions, and union security, and to win certification votes in the sawlog sector where most small operators remained fiercely hostile to unions.

Among the tasks awaiting Lumber and Saw leaders in the wake of the 1946 breakthrough were developing a more suitable union structure and improving communications. Before 1947 Lumber and Saw locals in Ontario had no central organization; each was affiliated directly with the Brotherhood. In order to co-ordinate the organizing drive and bargaining strategy, delegates from across the north met at Port Arthur in March 1947 where they elected a new joint council and applied to the Brotherhood for a district charter. This was granted and on 4 July the first issue appeared of the *Ontario Timberworker*, the official organ of the Northern Ontario Joint Council of the Lumber and Saw Mill Workers Union. That fall Lumber and Saw also began producing its own weekly radio program, 'Voice of the Bush,' broadcast by CKGM in Timmins, and the union took part in 'Voice of Labour,' a weekly offering from CKPR in Fort William. Activists at the Lakehead had also established the Woodworkers Welfare Society, with A.T. Hill as full-time secretary. Independent of union dues, the society collected funds which were used for the improvement of the bushworker's cultural and recreational life and his medical care. Using jeeps acquired by the society, Hill and others travelled regularly to camps, taking with them the society's movie projector and electric generator.[50]

It was vital for union leaders to improve their communications because large numbers of the pulpwood employees for whom they spoke were not yet members. The union had no automatic dues check-off; it was up to organizers and camp committees to sign up new recruits and collect their dues. Moreover, thousands of woodsworkers covered by the collective agreement had little understanding of trade unionism or the administration of the agreement. Young recruits to the industry no longer came from Finland, but from regions where radical traditions were far weaker. Members of the ethnically diverse work force had to be reminded that when treated unfairly by a foreman, they could now grieve instead of suffering silently or jumping. At the same time, it was the union's responsibility to warn against spontaneous strikes or wildcats which were now forbidden under the terms of the master agreement, and to encourage members to follow the steps involved in grieving. 'The greatest problem that faces us today, in every camp and mill,' wrote Magnuson in 1947, 'is a proper interpretation of our collective agreement, proper inforcement of its provisions, and an understanding of the proper ways and means of dealing with grievances that arise from day to day.'[51]

Like so many other post-war union leaders, Lumber and Saw officials discovered how costly and frustrating it was to make use of grievance procedures. They also got fed up with the bureaucratic requirements of certification, a problem that was especially acute in a seasonal industry. To be sure, the Ontario Labour Relations Act of 1948 enabled the union to overcome some of the problems previously encountered in recognition battles, but it was no easy matter to achieve certification and bargain successfully for a first contract. On 5 December 1947 the union applied for certification votes for the woods operations of several lumber companies, including that of J.J. McFadden north of Blind River. McFadden appealed to the Ontario Labour Relations Board, contending that the woodsworkers were seasonal employees who did not come under the act. In March 1948 the board dismissed McFadden's argument, but ruled that it was too late in the logging season to hold fair votes. When they were finally held in November, the union won by a landslide. McFadden then challenged the validity of the results, contending that because the men were not employees of the company but rather of the jobbers, separate votes and contracts were needed for each camp. Finally, in February 1949, more than a year after the application had first been made, the board backed the union's position and McFadden was required to begin bargaining in good faith.[52]

Notwithstanding this type of frustration, the Communist, or Labour

Progressive Party (LPP), leaders of the Lumber and Saw worked hard to satisfy the requirements of the law and of the collective agreements. Far from demanding 'the sky,' or being 'strike happy,' these leaders demonstrated moderation and pragmatism in labour negotiations. In early August 1947 the president of the joint council, Jack Quinn, had bluntly denied rumours that the union was preparing for a strike. And after a five-day bargaining session later in the month, the union settled for a modest 5 per cent wage increase and a revocable check-off – on an employee's written request, employers had to deduct dues from the pay packet and forward them to the union. 'Concession on both sides,' declared the *Ontario Timberworker* 'prove that collective bargaining in our industry is both possible and essential. It gives the lie to those sinister forces who oppose our Union with the slanderous propaganda that we are not interested in bargaining in good faith.'[53]

From the limited sources available it appears that the ever-expanding membership supported the bargaining positions and recommendations of their elected officials. Only once did the *Timberworker* publish a criticism of contract provisions. In November 1947 cookhouse staff at some camps complained that the new agreement left them 'practically worse off.' Some of the dissatisfaction came from female cooking staff and was couched in feminist terms. John Cikawski wrote from camp 29 at Auden:

We have some complaints on behalf of the girls in the Union. Why do girl cookees get $5.20 a day? Equal work, equal pay. Do you take girls for slaves? Or don't you care whether or not they join? I know of two girls and more who will leave the union if I do not get a satisfactory answer. I shall drop out myself ... Maybe you have forgotten that once you used to work in the bush and complained also. So why do you not have an increase for the girls from your last meeting in Toronto? Every man in this camp is opposed to this dirty move.

The editor admitted that the complaints were 'certainly well taken and will be one of the main problems to be rectified next year.' Later the *Timberworker* made special efforts to respond to the needs of 'the girls in the kitchen.'[54]

Although most of the content of the newspaper concerned matters relating directly to collective bargaining, grievance handling, certification, and organization, the Lumber and Saw also dealt with broader, more political issues. It took stands that placed the union pretty much within the mainstream of the Canadian labour movement in domestic politics. Far more controversial were the positions on foreign affairs. Before 1949 the *Timber-*

worker had little to say about foreign policy. But by mid-1949, following Canada's entry into NATO, the LPP had sharpened its criticisms and stepped up its peace campaign; the Lumber and Saw followed suit. Three northern Ontario locals sent delegates to the founding convention of the Canadian Peace Congress in 1949. And local 2995 sent an unsuccessful resolution on nuclear disarmament to the TLC convention in Calgary.[55]

The positions taken by the union leaders' positions on foreign affairs ran directly counter to Liberal government policy and public opinion in general. Along with parallel statements by leftists in other unions, they fuelled the drive of powerful anti-Communist forces within the labour movement. Spurred by authorities and the media, as well as the sensational Gouzenko disclosures on Soviet spying in Canada, public opinion in the late 1940s and early 1950s grew increasingly uneasy about, and intolerant of, what was seen as Soviet aggression abroad and Communist subversion at home. As several studies have shown, the North American labour movement was deeply affected by this Cold War environment. Long before the late 1940s, non-Communists and Communists within the Canadian trade unions had been awkward allies, if not bitter rivals fighting for power and influence. With the spread of Cold War ideology, however, the Communists' rivals had an added incentive to cleanse the image of the labour movement to ensure its legitimacy, and they found it much easier to garner support for such a campaign. In the United States the enormous power of the anti-communists was made abundantly clear in 1947 with the passage of the Taft-Hartley Act which restricted many of labour's hard-won rights and required union officials to file noncommunist affidavits. Indirectly the Taft-Hartley Act strengthened anti-Communists on this side of the border as well. By 1951 leftist leaders had been ousted from positions of power within a host of union organizations in Canada, and where they proved too powerful to be dislodged, their unions were expelled from the CIO and from Canada's major industrial-union centre, the Canadian Congress of Labour (CCL).[56]

Naturally the Lumber and Saw's leaders lent their support to the defence of their leftist allies in the labour movement. During the spectacular and bloody battles between the Communist-led Canadian Seamen's Union (CSU) and its enemies, the *Timberworker* gave the CSU constant support. As Cold War tensions mounted, however, Lumber and Saw delegates found themselves in an increasingly untenable position within an overwhelmingly hostile congress. Bruce Magnuson, an LPP electoral candidate who sat on the executive of the Lumber and Saw, the Port Arthur Trades and Labour Council, and the Ontario Federation of Labour, came under particularly fierce fire in the Lakehead press and at the 1949 TLC convention where he was denied a seat. By 1951 the Port Arthur Trades and Labour Council had unseated leftist delegates from three unions, including Dan MacIsaac, president of Lumber and Saw local 2786. Clearly it was only a matter of time before the Communist leaders would face unbearable pressure to leave their positions within the Lumber and Saw itself.[57]

In most unions from which Communists were ousted, the impetus came from rival union officers, rather than the rank and file: the Lumber and Saw was no exception. The great majority of unionized bushworkers appear to have remained unmoved by, or were even aware of, the upper-level rivalries. Senior leaders of the Brotherhood, in particular Andy Cooper, Ontario's member of the General Executive Board, took the initiative to expel Lumber and Saw leftists. No doubt Cooper was a willing executioner, for his own conservative union philosophy had long conflicted with the views of the leaders of the Lumber and Saw. Yet given Brotherhood policies, the expulsion of the bushworkers' left-wing leaders was virtually inevitable. The Carpenters executive was one of the most conservative and vehemently anti-Communist in North America. Its journal, *The Carpenter*, had boasted in 1947: 'It is no secret that organizations like the Brotherhood have done more to combat Stalinism in this country than any other group, not excluding the FBI.'[58] What is surprising, is that the leftists in Lumber and Saw had been permitted to hang on for so long. Perhaps unskilled workers in remote northern Ontario camps had been simply overlooked by the Carpenters executive in Indianapolis. Or perhaps Cooper had been reluctant to oust the Lumber and Saw leaders on the grounds of Communism, out of fear the membership would rally in support of their democratically elected officials. In any case, as happened in several other unions, the Brotherhood used other pretexts for expelling the leftists in Lumber and Saw.

Cooper's chance came following the signing of the 1950 collective agreement. Lumber and Saw negotiators had overlooked a change management had slipped into the agreement. Any union officer wishing to visit a camp now had to carry authorization from General Representative Andy Cooper. As the *Timberworker* pointed out, inadvertently the negotiators had given Cooper 'a veto power.' Cooper quickly moved to exercise that veto. Charging that elected officers were misusing their authority, Cooper lifted the credentials of several officials of locals 2786 and 2995 in October 1950. Marc Leclerc, for example, had his removed after a company executive had complained that, contrary to the collective agreement, he had advised the men at one camp to leave for another. Numerous meetings at camps and locals passed resolutions protesting Cooper's actions, but with little effect.[59]

Cooper and the international executive moved even more decisively a few months later. On 4 May 1951 Cooper and four other out-of-town international officers, armed with an Ontario Supreme Court injunction, marched into the Port Arthur offices of the north's largest Lumber and Saw local, no. 2786, and seized control of its affairs and property. Charging 'misappropriation of Union funds,' a pretext used against leftists in other unions, the Brotherhood placed the local under trusteeship. Rumours spread that Magnuson had used union funds to finance a trip to California. And citing *Timberworker* articles on peace and foreign policy, Brotherhood officials publicly declared that, contrary to the Carpenters' constitution, the ousted leaders had used union funds for political purposes.[60]

With these dramatic moves, long-time Communist leaders, such as Bruce Magnuson, Harry Raketti, A.T. Hill, Marc Leclerc, Harry Timchishin, and Jack Quinn, were deposed. Their places were filled by international officers and a mixed bag of Brotherhood appointees who lacked not only a knowledge of the logging industry, but in many cases union experience as well. A Lumber and Saw business agent of the mid-1950s has said that three-quarters of these initial appointees were 'taxi drivers and pimps – and an absolute disgrace to the union movement.'[61]

Only one month after Cooper's seizure of local 2786, the former officers and their supporters from across the north held meetings and elected officers to preside over a new organization, the Canadian Union of Woodworkers (CUW). (In so doing they were following the earlier example of British Columbia where the Woodworkers Industrial Union of Canada had been formed in 1948.) Marc Leclerc became president, Bruce Magnuson, the English-language editor of its organ *The Woodworker*, and various other former Lumber and Saw activists served on the executives of the three locals that had their offices in Port Arthur, Timmins, and Sudbury. Through LPP ties, the CUW brought in Quebec's fledgling L'Union des Bucherons, which became local four of what was known in Quebec as the Union Canadienne des Travailleurs du Bois.[62]

The new union tried to appeal to Ontario and Quebec woodsworkers by opposing all forms of 'Yankee imperialism,' by pledging absolute rank-and-file control and full local autonomy, and by stressing the need to fight not only for economic goals, but also for 'the democratic rights of labor,' and the 'international solidarity of working people.'[63] It is difficult to determine whether such issues had a wide appeal among bushworkers, for the new union never had a real opportunity to test its support.

Unfortunate timing and strong opposition from the Brotherhood, employers, and the government prevented bushworkers from democratically choosing between the Lumber and Saw and the Canadian Workers. The latter union had been hastily pulled together in June 1951 so that the left could build support and defeat Cooper's bid to renew the master agreement in August. But in the off-season there were simply too few bushworkers who could be rallied to support the new union. When organizers tried to enter those camps that were operating in the summer of 1951, they found their way blocked by Ontario Provincial Police officers who, in response to complaints from the forest companies, arrested the unauthorized organizers. As *The Woodworker* put it, the Ontario government had permitted 'Yankee corporations to use its police force ... to keep Canadian union organizers from organizing workmen on Canadian soil.'[64] Naturally the big operators preferred to deal with Cooper than with the left-led Canadian Woodworkers.[65] Certain observers later charged there was a very close understanding between the general representative, a Conservative, and Earl Rowe, the president of Great Lakes Paper, chief spokesman for woods operators in collective bargaining negotiations, and a former leader of the provincial Conservative Party.[66] Certainly the Canadian Woodworkers failed to gain any support when they asked the Ontario Labour Relations Board and the Conservative government at Queen's Park to consult the bushworkers about their union preferences and to delay Cooper's signing 'contracts behind the backs of the bushworkers themselves.'[67] In the negotiations Cooper requested, and received, far less than the Canadian Woodworkers were demanding. Yet Cooper and Lumber and Saw did win some modest wage increases and, even more significantly, improvements in union security. This contract would make it all the easier for Cooper to hold onto the bulk of the province's woodworkers.

Shortly after the new agreement had been signed, the Canadian Woodworkers folded. Although the former Lumber and Saw leaders had enjoyed considerable support from Ontario's bushworkers, it was impossible to motivate the great majority who, having never taken much interest in union affairs, simply stayed with the organization that the companies recognized. By the fall the Canadian Woodworkers were penniless and beaten. 'Our tactics were mistaken,' Magnuson said much later. 'We had the government, the employers and the international against us, and it was in between seasons. It was impossible ... We had to drop it.'[68] It is unlikely that better tactics would have brought about a substantially different result. With the coming of the Cold War, the Communists' days in the Brotherhood were numbered. In 1951 they ended. Gone were many of the pioneers of the bushworkers' union who had worked with such dedication to organize the industry. Yet in the years ahead a new leadership would take up the woodsworkers' fight.

EXPANSION UNDER NEW LEADERS

While the forced departure of the Communist leaders marked a drastic change in the executive of the Lumber and Saw in the decades ahead the organization's business agents and officers would continue to pursue the same pragmatic approach that had long characterized the day-to-day operations of the union. After 1951, as the forest industry expanded and the supply of woods labour decreased, this approach would pay off handsomely.

It did not take long for Ontario's bushworkers to acquire a group of effective, hard-working, new leaders. Most of the men Cooper had hurriedly appointed in 1951 soon quit their jobs. The task of building a new staff fell to Cooper's most capable appointee, Bill Sawyer, a former mill office employee of the Spruce Fall Power and Paper Company. Although he lacked woods and union experience, he brought a business-like commitment to his job, and he hired some first-rate organizers. Foremost among them were Lothar Bode, a recent German immigrant and outspoken socialist, Bode's brother-in-law, André Wellsby, and Tulio Mior, a veteran Canadian-born woodsworker of Italian descent. Bode has recalled the initial hostility of many bushmen who regarded the new organizers as 'Cooper's men.' In fact, Cooper did not fully trust the crew Sawyer had hired, and he did everything possible to block their taking the Port Arthur local out of trusteeship. It was not until 1953 that they regained control of the local, and they succeeded in doing so only by appealing directly to the international president.[69] Whatever Cooper's doubts, the employers approved of the new men. 'I speak on behalf of all the companies that you have a splendid clean organization,' Earl Rowe told union leaders in 1953. 'We appreciate doing business with you.'[70] Despite such unprecedented accolades, the new men were never stooges to Cooper nor to any operator. They appear to have run an efficient, democratic organization and, after a brief trial period, enjoyed solid support from the membership. More cautious than their predecessors in raising political issues, the new leaders nevertheless urged support for the CCF and its successor, the New Democratic Party (NDP).

Union business continued much as before. A reading of the *Ontario*

Bushworker, the Lumber and Saw's monthly newsletter of the 1950s and 1960s, shows that the leaders still tussled with the same kinds of problems when handling grievances, organizing an ethnically diverse work force, and penetrating sawlog camps. In the more favourable economic and labour-market conditions of the 1950s, however, the union expanded with unprecedented rapidity. It has been estimated that the number of union-ized bushworkers in Ontario increased from less than 2,000 at the time of the disruptions in 1951 to an all-time high of about 16,000 in 1957. During the same period the number of forest companies under contract increased from twenty-four to fifty-two, as many additional lumber firms signed agreements.[71]

While the shift towards labour scarcity in the post-war woods is the chief reason why the union gained leverage and numbers, the changing work force also played a part. Many of the new recruits to the bush during the 1950s were New Canadians who had come to Canada with their own young families, or who hoped to establish permanent homes and families here. They contrasted markedly to the dwindling numbers of old-time lumberjacks, the bachelors who had long made up a significant proportion of the professional bushmen. Renowned Canadian painter and one-time Ontario pulp cutter, William Kurelek remarks on this change in his book *Lumberjack*. 'The lumberman's philosophy,' says Kurelek, 'was supposed to be work hard, save up, then go to town ... and, in a few days or weeks, let the women and the taverns clean out your pockets.' However, he found in 1951 that most of his camp mates were, as he puts it, 'new immigrants, who had come to Canada after World War II. They, like myself, were earning stakes; and they meant to invest theirs in families, homes or small businesses once they came out of the woods.' Keenly interested in maxi-mizing their incomes, such men were willing to join the Lumber and Saw because the union promised better wages, protection, and relevant ser-vices in a strange country. Whereas only a few years before woodsworkers had balked at paying monthly union dues of a couple of dollars, by the mid-1950s members agreed to raise dues to twenty-five dollars. Of course, they could better afford the higher dues. Weekly earnings of Ontario woodsworkers had climbed substantially in the late 1940s and early 1950s (see Appendix 6). As wages improved, the Lumber and Saw gained a reputation for 'delivering the goods,' which had a snowballing effect on union membership.[72]

In addition to providing for higher wages, from the mid-1950s contracts increasingly contained other provisions favourable to the union: seniority, the union shop, and a system of timber classification which reduced the arbitrary authority of foremen by setting higher rates for sub-standard strips. And each year the companies agreed to provide a higher level of camp standards. The one significant set-back of the period was the breakdown of industry-wide bargaining in 1953. Operators cited the diversity of forest conditions and the increasingly diverse methods of logging as the reasons for their failure to agree to a master contract.[73] Thereafter, the union had to deal separately with each company. However, the task was soon simplified by the development of pattern bargaining, whereby Abitibi usually set the industry standard. Wildcats, some of them occurring at crucial moments during contract negotiations, helped the union wring concessions from reluctant operators.[74] As in most industries during the 1950s, Ontario's bushworkers made substantial gains without resorting to lengthy strikes.

It was not until 1963 that a major strike erupted in the northern Ontario logging industry. On 14 January about 365 employees of the Longlac division of Kimberly-Clark and 1,150 Spruce Falls employees in the Kapuskasing area walked out illegally in protest of conciliation delays and the employers' refusal to grant the terms won at Abitibi. In the Kapuskasing area, a district with an unusually large number of settlers who cut pulpwood on private lands, the strike became extremely bitter. Violence and sabotage occurred as non-union settlers ran picket lines and continued to deliver their pulpwood to the Spruce Falls depots. Events climaxed at Reesor Siding where settlers had piled wood. Although union leaders warned against violence, in the early hours of 10 February about 400 strikers set out to dismantle the wood piles. Having pushed their way through a small police cordon, the strikers were about to scatter the wood when settlers armed with shotguns emerged from a nearby shack. They opened fire, cutting down more than a dozen strikers. Three were killed. In less than one week's time, the shocked and dispirited strikers agreed to compulsory arbitration and a return to work. Police charged nineteen settlers with intent to maim. After protests, the charges were increased to non-capital murder. However, no one was convicted. The most that Lumber and Saw could do was raise an impressive monument at Reesor Siding to honour the memory of the three victims.[75]

The dramatic and tragic developments of 1963 demonstrated that the province's woodsworkers were still capable of the kind of intense militancy that characterized the bushworkers of an earlier era. Yet 1935 marked a definite break in the history of labour relations in this industry because in that year not only had Communist activists opted to work within the mainstream of North America's trade-union movement, but the Ontario government with its Industrial Standards Act had taken a step towards the encouragement of collective bargaining. Thereafter, labour relations developments in the Ontario logging industry roughly paralleled the course of change in most Canadian industries. In the Ontario bush, as elsewhere, Communist leaders contributed substantially towards building an industrial union movement in the 1930s and 1940s, even though they worked within an industrial affiliate of the craft-based Brother of Carpenters and Joiners, rather than within the new CIO unions.

After decades of failed attempts to build industrial unions in Canada generally, and in the Ontario woods in particular, breakthroughs finally came in the mid- and late-1940s as unionists struggled to make their wartime gains permanent. During the post-war expansion, workers in the Ontario logging industry made steady gains in terms of wages, conditions, and job and union security, though they did so under non-communist leaders and by working within the legal confines of a rules-laden collective-bargaining system. After years of such gains, the socialist goals of old-time bushworker activists were no closer, but at least wages and working conditions had improved spectacularly. For woodlands managers, the higher costs of the new arrangements appeared threatening enough. During the 1950s, 1960s, and 1970s, employers would search long and hard for new logging techniques and other means to halt this spiral. Their innovations would, in turn, bring Ontario's loggers and their union new opportunities and new challenges.

8

Management responds:
new recruits, camp improvements,
and training schemes

In the years immediately following World War II woods operators and senior executives in Ontario's forest companies faced an unfamiliar conundrum. They were relieved to find that peace soon brought demands for lumber and for pulp and paper products. Veterans on both sides of the Canadian–American border wanted houses, and with help from the governments they were purchasing new homes at a rapid pace. This boom was good news for Ontario lumbermen. In the mean time, North American consumers who had delayed purchasing goods through the long years of the depression and war now scrambled to buy products that advertisers paraded before the public – good news for newsprint producers who scurried to meet the demands of Canadian and U.S. publishers. As the years passed Canadian forest-products firms grew more confident that the demand for their products would remain very strong.

Lumbermen and their counterparts in pulp and paper, however, had grave doubts about northern Ontario's ability to take advantage of the booming markets. For one thing, the competition was getting stiffer. Ontario operators watched as lumber and new pulp and paper operations in British Columbia took an increasing share of the markets in Canada and the United States. And they had deep misgivings about the rise of the pulp and paper industry in the southern United States, which threatened Ontario's markets in New England, New York, and Ohio. Both these competing regions enjoyed cost advantages because of their larger diameter trees, faster-growing and denser forests, and newer, more productive mills. The southern producers were also conveniently located for eastern consumers[1] and had a seemingly bottomless supply of cheap labour.

If competition in product markets appeared forbidding, the Ontario forest industry confronted even more alarming developments in the area of timber supplies. Lumbermen and paper company executives alike feared their mills might become starved for wood. They attributed this post-war crisis to two problems: first, a shortage of suitable trees growing in accessible locations, and secondly, a shortage of men willing to cut and haul trees.

The problem of inadequate timber resources had long troubled industry executives. In the pine-sawlog sector a serious timber famine had developed by World War I, and lumbermen had to make do with inferior stands and less valuable species. In the pulpwood sector, as early as 1918 woodlands officials complained about the rising costs of harvesting timber in hard-to-reach locations. These problems had become acute by the late-1940s, as the Kennedy Commission on Forestry made clear. Howard Kennedy, himself an industrial forester, sharply criticized government and industry for recklessly squandering forest resources. High grading during the manpower shortages throughout World War II had been especially destructive.[2] Post-war operators had to pay the price. That meant working over previously cut stands, taking the second- and third-rate timber. It also meant building roads into remote sites and improving streams deep in the backwoods. All of this cost the companies.

Equally alarming to cost-conscious forest executives was the growing shortage of bushworkers. 'The question of woods labour and, consequently wood supply, has been,' said Howard Kennedy in 1946, 'the nightmare which has most consistently disturbed the rest and contentment of every executive in the Pulp and Paper Industry and every woods operator in eastern Canada for the past five years.' Before World War II Ontario woods employers had been able to draw on plenty of low-priced seasonal labour. But men – especially experienced woodsmen – were no longer offering the industry their labour power in the same numbers. 'The older generation is passing on and the youth are not in sufficient numbers filling the gaps,' W.R. Beatty, chairman of the White Pine Bureau of the Canadian Lumberman's Association, lamented in 1946. The following year a Woodlands Section report concluded that 'we are fast approaching the "point of exhaustion" of labour supply – if it has not already been reached.'[3]

Logging operators attributed the labour shortages to several factors. First, the neat dovetailing of labour requirements among seasonal industries had broken down. A 1950 study undertaken by the logging industry showed that the preceding dozen years had seen an average annual net migration away from Canada's farms of some 50,000 people. Since agriculturalists cut about half the timber harvest in Ontario, operators regarded rural depopulation as an alarming trend. And as one analyst noted in 1955, 'with the higher farm incomes in recent years, the urgency of need for supplementary winter work became weaker.' Similarly, fewer construction workers were available to the post-war logging industry. According to the Canadian Lumbermen's Association, this was the result of 'continued efforts of the construction industry to make as many operations as possible year-round.'[4]

Secondly, lumbermen insisted that federal social legislation introduced during the war, such as unemployment insurance and the baby bonus, had reduced the number of construction and general labourers willing to work in winter lumbering operations. Whereas once such men had turned to woods jobs 'to fill an empty belly,' they now shunned the industry and depended on government benefits.[5]

Thirdly, during the boom years of the war many bushworkers had found secure jobs with firms such as International Nickle in Sudbury and Algoma Steel in Sault Ste Marie. Still other woodsworkers, for example Joe Sarazin of Blind River, had gained valuable training as enlisted men during the war. Although Sarazin loved logging, the training he received overseas enabled him to become a mechanic and open his own garage. He never returned to the bush. In short, *Timber of Canada* concluded in October 1946: 'The blunt fact must be faced that Canadian labor is shying away from hard work and from inconveniences such as living away from home.' Altogether, these developments amounted to a fundamental change in the labour market – one that would have profound consequences for the entire logging industry.[6]

With the labour shortages, employers found production costs soaring. In order to maintain the flow of logs to the mills, companies had to attract men by offering higher wages and providing better – and more costly – camp conditions. Wages ran especially high in Ontario, partly because of the success the Lumber and Sawmill Workers Union had in collective bargaining. Yet the increases were not the only reason for rising labour costs. Some operators maintained that costs were increasing because productivity had fallen with the influx of greenhorns.[7] Moreover, with labour so scarce, woodsworkers were jumping at ever-accelerating rates. Between 1943–4 and 1950–1 on average a bushworker in eastern Canada stayed at a job a mere 43.7 days, and the figure was decreasing sharply.[8] One study showed that for every 100 men hired in the pulpwood sector, 'thirteen of the original 100 do not stay more than a week on the job, fifty do not complete one month's work.'[9] This instability was emphasized in a letter written in November 1948 from the division manager of the Great Lakes Lumber and Shipping Company at Fort William to the president: 'To-day

Camps 16 and 10 . . . are in motion, but are still not fully manned. We have sent some six bus loads into the area but invariably 50% or more are returning to the city within a day or two, with the result that there are [only] some fifty men at Camp 16 and thirty at Camp 10.'[10] High turn-over meant increased recruiting costs, lower productivity, more accidents, and mounting transportation and boarding expenses. Since labour accounted for more than half of the total costs for raw material in the logging industry, operators knew that higher expenditures would mean substantially greater production costs.

For executives eager to attract investment, and for woodlands managers charged with maintaining the flow of wood to mills, the shortages of low-cost timber and woods labour amounted to alarming problems. Without innovations, production costs would continue to sky-rocket. Yet given the competitiveness of the post-war market-place, these increases could not easily be passed on to consumers. Instead profits were threatened.

Yet woods operators were not discouraged. Immediately after the war they set about to overcome their problems, moving aggressively in a number of directions. First, they sought to expand their labour pool by encouraging immigration and facilitating the entry of new immigrants, particularly refugees from eastern Europe. Secondly, they tried to reduce turn-over and retain men in their camps by improving conditions and making it possible for them to commute to their jobs. And thirdly, woodlands management attempted to increase the productivity of their men. Companies developed training programs for woodsworkers and upgraded the supervisory skills of foremen. The industry also renewed efforts to mechanize logging.

NEW RECRUITS

Throughout World War II, woods managers had wondered about the possibility of post-war shortages of bush workers. With the victory in Europe in the spring of 1945, the industry's long-term labour needs remained uncertain. But the managers were sure of one thing: the repatriation of thousands of prisoners of war would result in an immediate labour shortfall in the Ontario bush. While the 8,000 POWs working in Ontario forests had sometimes posed disciplinary problems and operators differed in their assessments of their efficiency, none doubted that the departure of the POWs could prove crippling. Furthermore, operators expected a shortage of civilian replacements – in the spring of 1946 some were already experiencing difficulties finding enough men. Such a shortage, woods managers feared, might provide an opportunity for would-be strikers. And so, in an effort to avoid wood shortages and a resurgent union, operators set out to draw on new immigrants in the time-honoured fashion.[11]

At a meeting in September with the Ontario Regional Advisory Board of the federal Department of Labour, forest company officials won support for a resolution urging that Ottawa 'consider a policy of selective immigration from Great Britain and other countries of northern Europe, of men calculated to fit into our economy and climate and willing to work in the industry.' The industry and the board were on record for a return to an ethnically selective, open-door immigration that had characterized Canadian policy until the onslaught of the depression.[12]

In taking such a stand, employers were joining a rising chorus of voices in support of increased post-war immigration. Employers wanted to increase the labour supply and the number of consumers, while vocal pro-refugee groups hoped to sponsor kin and respond to the pleas of the victims of persecution and the devastation wrought by the war. There was, however, a significant number of Canadians who feared that unemployment would soar, or that Canada's ethnic mix would be altered by the arrival of large numbers of newcomers many of whom might be Jewish.[13]

In the end the proponents of increased immigration won out. In January 1947 the Canadian cabinet approved the admittance of selected classes of displaced persons to meet labour needs 'in particular, in the mines and forests.'[14] Plans for bringing in woodsworkers, and parallel schemes for the movement of agriculturalists and other groups, were administered by the Department of Labour and modelled on the 1946 'bulk movement' of Polish veterans who had fought alongside the Allies during the war.[15]

Employers were to assess their labour needs, and then, through the newly created Woods Labour Committee, make formal requests to the Department of Labour for specific numbers of immigrants. Labour officials passed these requests to selection teams in Europe. Forest industry representatives there worked with officials from the Canadian government and the International Refugee Organization to select appropriate woodsworkers – preferably men with logging experience. Applicants deemed suitable were informed about wages and conditions in logging camps, given a rigorous physical examination, and asked to sign a contract with one of the participating companies. Employers offered twelve-month employment with bed, board, and wages provided at local standards and rates. The United Nations Relief and Rehabilitation Administration paid the cost of passage to Halifax, and the forest companies covered transportation charges in Canada unless the employee quit before completing his contract. (If that happened the employee was required to reimburse the employer, although few, if any, ever did so.) After the contract had expired, the immigrant was free to do as he pleased. In five years he could apply for Canadian citizenship.[16]

For penniless refugees, the program provided an escape from the uncertainties and endless waiting in European camps. To men like Luka Radulovich, a soldier from Yugoslavia who had spent a total of seven years in prisoner-of-war and refugee camps, the scheme meant a chance to come to 'democratic Canada,' a land he believed had greater opportunities than countries in South America and Africa, which were the only other countries open to him.[17] Displaced persons from various work and education backgrounds quickly became adept at providing selection officers with the information that would open the door to Canada, so eager were such men to reach North America. For woods employers, the plan offered at least a short-term solution to the anticipated labour shortages. Although by 1947 the pulp and paper companies had already been forced to sign a contract with the Lumber and Saw Mill Workers, the operators knew the influx of refugees might prove useful in weakening the bargaining position of the newly recognized union. This wider purpose became clearer as the program got under way.

In preparation for the 1947–8 operating season, woods employers began flooding the Department of Labour with orders for refugees. By 31 October 1947, they had made requests for 5,330 men. Ontario operators – from the small contractor to the big corporations – clamoured for young, healthy, refugee woodsmen. Beginning in August, ships carrying 700 or 800 woodsworkers arrived at Halifax every two or three weeks.[18]

Upon arrival most refugees responded to their woods jobs in ways similar to most other greenhorns in the industry. When Luke Radulovich first saw the wet ground and crowded bunkhouses at his Spruce Falls camp north of Kapuskasing, he said to himself, 'I'm sorry I didn't stay in the DP camp!' But he, Estonian Vello Hansen, and several Lithuanians all remember being amazed at the abundance of food available – a situation in such sharp contrast to the acute food shortages they had known in Europe. According to Radulovich, the Serbian, German, and French-Canadian ethnic groups kept to themselves, both on the job and in the bunkhouse where each group had its own poker table. Like many newcomers to the camps, these displaced persons found the camp routine boring. But because of their different cultural backgrounds and superior education, they took the trouble to set up volleyball games and practise javelin throwing, 'much to the amazement of the lumberjacks.' At one camp a

Lithuanian conservatory-trained singer even succeeded in forming a choir among his camp mates.[19]

When W.G. McAndrews, a representative from the Department of Labour visited the northern Ontario logging camps in November 1947, he found the majority of woodsworkers 'succeeding very well and well contented.' Nevertheless, he reported that some refugees had become dissatisfied soon after arriving, a situation he attributed to the selection teams in Europe who had painted 'too rosy a picture.' Furthermore, the refugees had 'misunderstood' the wage rates.[20] As inexperienced piece workers, it seems likely that in many cases their production – and incomes – fell below the levels they had been led to expect.[21] Also of concern were their many accidents. By the end of November 1947, less than three months into the first season, Pranas Zeknys had been killed by a blow from a cable attached to a bundle of logs at a camp run by the J.J. McFadden Lumber Company, and Joseph Janula had been crushed to death by a falling tree on an operation of the Gillies Brothers.[22]

Forest-industry employers at first regarded the refugee scheme as an overnight success. By October 1947 the Ontario woods labour market was flooded. Logging operators could rely on large numbers of refugees and pick and choose from among other bushworkers, a situation fraught with dangers for union activists. However, it soon became apparent that companies had greatly over-estimated – or exaggerated – the numbers of immigrants they would need to meet their fall labour requirements. As it turned out, a disappointing harvest in the prairies prompted agriculturalists to seek woods work in greater numbers than the operators had anticipated. Although large numbers of prairie harvesters needed winter work, the National Employment Service (NES) was forced to curtail its recruiting drive in the west. NES officials in northern Ontario reported a labour surplus 'so great' that even many experienced Canadian woodsmen had to be turned away by forest companies. Logging operators quickly realized that they would be better off selecting employees from among the experienced woodsmen on their doorstep rather than paying the railway fares of men unfamiliar with Canadian conditions. In October 1947 woods employers cancelled orders for refugees, including those for the 1,120 men already on their way to Canada. Immigration and Labour officials then had to scramble to find these men jobs on the railways or in the mines.[23]

Although the labour scheme of 1947 had proven largely unnecessary as far as the industry's immediate needs were concerned, logging operators could at least be heartened by reports of the anti-Communist views of the newcomers. When bureaucrats and employers met together at Port Arthur in December 1947, a government official who had toured twenty-five northern Ontario camps where displaced persons were working reported: 'Elements of Communism were to be found in practically all the bush camps and it was gratifying to note that the DPS were an excellent counter-influence.' Another Department of Labour investigator described some of the political tensions in the camps, citing, for example, an incident in which a foreman from the Brompton Pulp and Paper Company hurled abuse at the displaced persons, calling them 'bandits, fascists and murderers.'[24] Old-timers, too, recall these kinds of conflicts. A Lithuanian who worked in a Great Lakes Paper camp remembers: 'In our camp there were at least seven Ukrainians – old immigrants – communists, all of them. We couldn't get along with them at all. They called us Nazis and Hitler's dogs. There were misunderstandings and even fistfights.' Contemporary Canadian newspapers tended to look favourably on the 'patriotic role' played by displaced persons in the 'battle against communism.'[25]

The anti-communism of the refugee woodsmen had a special meaning in the Ontario logging industry where Communists had long been the driving force behind the woodsworkers' union. Their presence threatened the solidarity and survival of the Lumber and Sawmill Workers Union. Some of the refugees refused to have anything to do with the union on the grounds that it was 'communistic.' Luka Radulovich remembers that when union organizers came to the Spruce Falls Power and Paper camp in 1948, the French Canadians were eager to participate, but his fellow Serbian refugees, who constituted the majority, succeeded in keeping the union out of the camp. Although the Lumber and Saw urged members to avoid conflicts with refugee workers and welcome them into the union, it voiced strong opposition to the Canadian refugee policy. The union's Joint Council for Northern Ontario called for tripartite manpower planning to avoid unemployment and it objected to admittance procedures that favoured 'our wartime enemies and fascist collaborators, while discriminating against our wartime allies and foes of fascist aggression.'[26]

It soon became apparent that the displaced persons were not a very serious threat to the Lumber and Saw. Many refugees quickly made it clear that they would insist on the best possible wages and treatment from employers. Kazimieras Daunys recalls that when displaced persons employed by the McChesney Lumber Company of Timmins discovered nearby woodsworkers were being paid more, the refugees promptly struck and won an increase. According to another Lithuanian, when refugee woodsworkers at camp 305 of the Great Lakes Paper Company realized one of their own was being given bad cutting strips, the refugees staged a walk-out and not only gained justice, but also much appreciated encouragement from the union.[27]

The threat represented by the displaced persons eased in the union's view because of the refugees' rapid abandonment of the industry. Much to the disappointment of woods managers, the displaced persons soon showed a willingness to defy Canadian authorities and woods employers by breaking their contracts and high-tailing it to the cities. A 1951 study of mobility rates of displaced persons in logging, mining, and construction showed that those in pulpwood logging were the least likely to stay at their jobs. The report's author concluded that in the pulp and paper industry the bulk labour scheme had been 'a double failure,' because not only had the industry 'failed to add a durable body of workers to its labour force but the part leaving during the first three months probably represent a direct financial loss to the companies concerned.' Lakehead lumberman Eddie Johnson, who had brought in 325 displaced persons, complained privately in 1948: 'This labour was unskilled and inexperienced when it came to us and involved us in considerable operating difficulties and resulted in expensive operations.'[28]

The displaced person scheme marked the most dramatic attempt by Ontario forest companies to flood the post-war labour pool with immigrants. Despite its failure, employers continued to apply to Immigration authorities for new recruits and to draw on recent arrivals such as the refugees from the Hungarian revolution in 1956. And once again the Lumber and Saw expressed concern about the political ideas of the immigrants and their limited knowledge of the 'Canadian way of life' and of 'labour relations.'[29] Throughout the 1960s and 1970s forest employers showed less concern about the ethnicity of recruits. The Great Western Timber Company sent representatives to Portugal in 1974 to recruit loggers for its Savant Lake operations, and Pearson Lumber Company contacted the Fort Frances offices of Canada Manpower regarding the possibility of recruiting in the Caribbean.[30] Manpower officials, however, criticized the 'assumption by industry that highly skilled workers [could] be imported through immigration procedures in the numbers required, instead of trained here.'[31] Indeed, federal policies constrained the employers' ability to import labour. While some new immigrants continued to find jobs in the logging camps, recruitment abroad was a much less significant part of management's production strategy in the 1960s and 1970s. The forest industry's failure to flood the woods labour market with immigrants forced company officials to look to other means for overcoming the persistent post-war problems of labour shortages and rising labour costs.

BETTER LIVING

Immediately after World War II, woods managers in eastern Canada began to take a long, hard look at living conditions in the logging camps. In 1946 the industry sponsored its first major study of camp design because 'the need for improvement with regards to the kind and cost of housing for men in camps has been generally recognized throughout the industry.'[32] The recognition of the need to improve camps came in part because of union pressure. By focusing on better living conditions during the successful 1946 strike, the Lumber and Saw had alerted management to the need for change. Continuing union pressure during collective bargaining and grievance hearings also brought results. And occasional wildcat strikes, such as the three-day strike in 1956 in which more than 500 Great Lakes employees protested against sanitary conditions, kept employers on their toes. The growing fears of labour shortages also compelled the companies to respond. In the tight post-war labour market, operators attempted to entice men to the bush by offering what the industry called 'city conditions in the bush.'[33] By the late 1970s management and labour both looked back with pride on a transformation in camp conditions for which each party claimed credit.

The shift away from the traditional log buildings had begun during World War II. At that time many companies discovered that it was more cost effective to move their camps rather than build them from scratch in each new location. In the mid-1940s the dominant trend was skid-mounted, portable camp buildings constructed of lumber and designed to house about eight to sixteen men. However, operators encountered problems with these camps. Such buildings had to be small so that available vehicles could pull them along winter logging roads. Each building required its own stove that had to be stoked and supplied with cordwood. And the Lumber and Saw's victory in 1946 meant many additional little buildings had to be provided because double-decker bunks had been eliminated.[34]

In an effort to find an equally attractive but cheaper alternative, operators began building large, semi-permanent and centrally heated buildings constructed of panels that could be knocked down and salvaged. A camp constructed by the Pigeon Timber Company near Lake Nipigon at the end of the war was the first such camp in all of eastern Canada. The 64-man prefabricated building had a central section and four wings. The central part contained hot showers, wash basins, and flush toilets. A single oil furnace provided even heat to the entire structure. Two of the wings contained the men's sleeping quarters, which included single cots, overhead lockers, and a wall plug for the men's lamps and radios. The other two wings housed the office, kitchen, and dining facilities, as well as reading and recreation rooms. These amenities were far superior to those in the surrounding district, a fact which compelled competitors to upgrade their camps.[35]

Late in the decade, however, companies were finding it prohibitively costly to move even panel camps. Consequently the industry began constructing central camps for 350 men who could be bussed daily to their work sites. A growing network of logging access roads, made necessary as the forests retreated from convenient rail and water routes, facilitated the movement of men from camps to work areas. Yet while these roads made possible the transition to central camps, they did not cause the shift. As one woods manager admitted, central camps were 'a natural outcome of post-World War II efforts to attract labour by camp improvement.' In order to provide 'more comfortable and attractive quarters,' it was essential to make 'operating economies': central camps permitted savings of furnace and cooking fuel, as well as reductions in cookhouse, cleaning, and supervisory staff. A 1963 study showed that while a conventional camp for 350 men would cost the equivalent of $24,000 per year to operate for a period of twenty-one years, central camp costs would run only $10,700 annually.[36]

During the post-war period operators moved towards prefabricated construction. When Abitibi chose to build an 18,000-square foot, two-storey structure as a central camp in its Smooth Rock Falls Division in the late 1950s, the company called for tenders. Most of the structure was built at Beaupré, Que., by Beau-Fab Ltd and assembled in northern Ontario.[37] In the 1960s and 1970s many operators purchased or leased a type of mobile-home. By the 1970s many logging camps looked like trailer parks with their rows of long, narrow aluminum buildings, complete with television antennas.

Although improved camp facilities became the norm throughout the entire Ontario logging industry, the camps run by jobbers remained below standard. By the 1955-6 operating season, the camps of the J.J. McFadden Company had flush toilets, hot and cold running water, and electricity, but the camps operated by the firm's jobbers were of rough construction, heated by wood stoves, and lacked flush toilets. Contractors continued to rely on other means, such as a personal following, to attract and retain woodsworkers.[38]

By the 1950s most woods employers found it increasingly necessary to provide recreational facilities. Virtually all company camps had rooms with ping-pong tables, dart boards, and card tables. Most operators had contracts with film distributors so that movies could be shown in each camp at least once a week. In December 1967 the editor of the *Woodlands Review* summed up the industry's predicament: 'We must ... develop an acceptable atmosphere if we are going to attract any men.'

Various companies opted for different approaches to maintain their recreation facilities. Longlac Paper left the organization of activities to employees. Perhaps because the company had succeeded to a large extent in de-seasonalizing operations, their permanent woods employees had taken the trouble to set up softball teams and horse-shoe pitches, while in some camps the men had clubbed together to provide themselves with billiard tables and pinball machines. Ever since 1951, the woodsworkers of Marathon Paper Mills had managed their own recreation hall which was equipped with a refreshment booth, pool table, and a movie screen. The men had even laid hardwood floors in their hall. The Lumber and Sawmill Workers Union also became active in overseeing recreation halls, for this was a way of both providing the services members desired while maintaining a day-to-day presence in the camp. By 1956 Lumber and Saw local 2995 proudly reported that it had established thirty canteens and placed fifteen television sets in logging camps in the Cochrane area.[39]

Recreational life also changed in the late 1950s with the coming of new policies and practices regarding liquor and beer. For decades provincial authorities had prohibited the consumption of alcohol in logging camps and employers had enforced their own strict rules on the matter, usually firing any man unfit for work. Believing the penalties to be overly harsh, Lumber and Saw leaders sought to curb the employers' arbitrary power. The opportunity came in 1958 when Marathon Paper built the first logging camps with two-man rooms and individual lockers. The union's lawyer took the matter to the Liquor Control Board of Ontario, pleading that, since these woodsmen no longer lived in 'dormitories' and each man had his own locker, they should be entitled to consume liquor at their place of residence – the logging camp. The board agreed and soon lockers and liquor spread throughout the industry. Management rules still compelled employees to be fit for work, but gradually the union and the companies worked out arrangements whereby repeat offenders were not fired but allowed to keep their seniority standing and apply for sick benefits, long-term disability pay, or addiction treatment. The attitudes towards alcohol and alcoholism in the logging camps came to reflect approaches found more generally throughout Ontario society.[40]

Post-war improvements in the variety of camp fare and in the set-up of cookhouses were nearly as dramatic as the changes in buildings and recreational life. At last logging operators began to provide their men with well-balanced meals and a wide variety of foods. Pressure to move in this direction came in part from the Lumber and Saw, which bargained for specific food items. By 1955 collective agreements contained clauses such as the following: 'There shall be no substitute for butter'; 'fruit juice will be supplied for breakfast only, each day'; and 'there shall be coffee breaks in the morning, afternoon and evening; coffee and cakes to be provided by the Company in the cookery.'[41] Most woods managers had found that they had to provide a much greater range of foodstuffs than they had in the past to retain men. In 1953 one official explained that it paid his company to supply fresh milk to their employees. 'The milk is trucked in specially-built ice containers,' he said, 'and while it is more expensive than powdered or canned milk it is considered to be an important labour stabilizer and worth the extra cost.'[42] Improved logging access roads made it easier for the companies to bring in foodstuffs on a regular basis, just as technological advances in refrigeration permitted enhanced camp diets.

Improvements in the cookhouse were only indirectly related to the skills of the cooks. In post-war decades cooks suffered a decline in status and pay relative to production workers. In the inter-war period cooks had been paid more than twice the monthly rate of teamsters but the differential decreased steadily to a point in the mid-1960s when their pay rates were equal (see Appendix 8). In part, the declining place of the cooks in the pay hierarchy was related to the appearance of new kitchen equipment, prepared foods, and closer supervision, all of which undercut their skills and autonomy. Increasingly companies hired commissary officials – management personnel charged with ensuring adequate nutrition at minimal cost. Such officials attributed the increased variety of camp fare to their own scientific appreciation of the nutritional needs of a healthy, productive work force. Acting through the Nutrition Committee of the Woodlands Section, first formed in 1943 in an effort to deal with wartime rationing and shortages, commissary personnel and food and equipment suppliers began in 1953 to meet annually at Feeding Conferences. Usually several papers on nutrition were given by experts in the field. The purpose of the exercise was crystal clear: 'To have a "contented" crew, we must have good food because a contented crew is a productive one,' declared one commissary official at the first conference.[43]

Evidence suggests that nutrition and health probably did improve in at least the bigger camps as a result of the new approach.[45] However, its introduction cost the employers plenty. Commissary officials turned to mechanization as a means to keep a lid on rising costs in the cookhouse. Propane gas stoves, electric refrigerators, and small appliances such as mechanical potato peelers appeared in camp kitchens. The forest companies also introduced pre-packaged mixes and convenience foods. The most effective cost-cutting innovation was the shift from sit-down meals to cafeteria plans. Because cafeterias eliminated cookees, woods officials reported they had been able to make savings of 15 to 25 per cent, the amount increasing with the size of the camp.[45]

In their drive to offer appealing, nourishing meals at minimal cost, commissary officials brought about a significant change in the way of life in the woods camp. Gone were the crude dining halls in which the entire camp sat down to heaps of food prepared on the cook-stove and served by cookees balancing ten plates on an arm. Now as the logger entered the fluorescent-lit cafeteria, he picked up a tray, took his place in line, and made his selection from an array of options that included plenty of iceberg lettuce and hot-house tomatoes.

Alongside these various changes in camp life came a quite different approach to cutting costs and attracting stable staffs – the forest village. Woodsworkers and their families could live together year-round in small, semi-permanent villages located in the heart of timber operations on company property or crown land. Rather than building camps, companies constructed small homes and rented them to employees. Men such as Abitibi's Jack Auden insisted that the stable, sedentary work force of married men would produce more wood at cheaper cost. Howard Kennedy in his Royal Commission *Report* of 1946 also called for operator-sponsored forest communities that would help 'to reverse the flow of rural citizens, stabilize woods labour and provide a nucleus of well trained woods workers.'[46]

A few forest villages were established in the 1950s. In 1956 C.R. Binger of Ontario and Minnesota Pulp and Paper reported that his company had built 170 houses in its timber limits, enough housing for 42 per cent of the woods staff. Not only had this system cut the costs of supervision but company statistics showed that family men cut 11.1 per cent more wood, had higher daily earnings ($15.68 compared to $11.97), and fed themselves and their families for the same amount that, as piece workers, they would have paid for board in a logging camp. When the Quebec-born Dubreuil brothers began logging in Algoma in the late 1950s, they built a sawmill town deep in the forest. Dubreuilville, a closed company town, had housing not only for mill employees, but also for loggers. The company even rented motel-type accommodation to single men. However, the forest village concept never caught on in northern Ontario.[47]

Before pulpwood operators and lumbermen became convinced of the feasibility of the forest village, the expanding network of all-weather logging roads made it possible for significant numbers of woods employees to commute to work from established centres where many owned their own homes. By 1960 Spruce Falls Pulp and Paper found that nearly one quarter of the firm's wood was cut by employees who travelled daily from homes in Kapuskasing and smaller communities along Highway 11. In the late 1950s the Dryden Paper Company improved their logging roads radiating out of Dryden in order to facilitate the trucking of logs and to permit employees to live in town. By 1976 approximately 61 per cent of Ontario's pulpwood operations were run on a commuter basis.[48]

While the services and facilities of forest communities marked an improvement over those available in bush camps, they nevertheless remained far below the level offered in cities. Very few women found jobs in isolated forest communities. Left behind by husbands who worked in the bush and enjoyed hunting and fishing trips in their spare time, many women and children in these remote towns complained about the lack of services and encouraged the men to quit their jobs and look for work in the cities. A 1977 study, conducted by G.H.U. Bayley for the Canadian Council on Regional Development, a group advising the federal minister in charge of the Department of Regional Economic Expansion, pointed to these kinds of problems and suggested they were the cause of a manpower shortage in the Ontario woods. The study concluded: 'Labour turnover and reluctance of local people to work in timber harvesting and silvicultural management would be reduced if community services were improved.'[49]

By the mid-1970s, various forest companies operating in Ontario and Quebec were considering using air transport so they could draw on well-serviced urban dwellers for even the most remote logging chances. Several firms looked into using Short Take-Off and Landing aircraft. In 1974, when the expanded operations of Kimberly-Clark required an additional 450 woodsworkers, company officials examined the possibility of using helicopters to transport commuters, even though the proposition appeared to be expensive. The first firm in eastern Canada to introduce air transport was the Canadian International Paper Company, which used a DC-3 aircraft to carry bushworkers to and from the northern logging sites in its St Maurice Division. According to a company spokesman, the service had succeeded in attracting trained men to northern camps, stabilizing the labour force, increasing production, and improving employee morale.[50]

Of course, many commuters still had to spend week nights in logging camps. By the late 1970s the company camps that remained were more spacious, brighter, and offered much more privacy to the individual. Collective agreements required humidifiers in the men's rooms, air-conditioning in the cookhouses and colour television in the recreation rooms. In the Thunder Bay district one Great Lakes camp offered each employee his (or her) own room complete with bed, closet, desk, carpeted floor, textured ceiling, and sliding windows. In a roofed courtyard the company had built recreation facilities where employees could play horse-shoes, darts, and ping-pong year round. And the company had plans to construct indoor volleyball and basketball courts. As D. Burn, a Great Lakes official, explained to an International Labour Organization meeting, the company had developed facilities 'in response to the changing conditions and expectations of the modern woodsworkers.' The 'better educated and better qualified' loggers of the 1980s 'have higher expectations than seasonal loggers of years ago.'[51] Such improvements also illustrate the stronger bargaining position of unionized, trained workers in remote areas where labour was in short supply. After all, many woodsworkers in the 1930s had expected better camp conditions than they had found, but there was little they could do to persuade employers to provide such conditions. Fifty years later loggers expected still more – and they had the clout to get it.

Altogether, these post-war management schemes to retain loyal, productive employees by making living arrangements more attractive amounted to a new development in woodlands operations. The impetus behind earlier attempts at camp reform had come chiefly from outside the industry – from social reformers, radical unionists, and provincial sanitary officials. In some respects post-war developments more closely resembled the strategy pursued earlier by managers of pulp and paper mills who had been leading innovators in the early twentieth-century movement known as welfarism.[52] Improving productivity and promoting employee loyalty were central features of both the earlier mill towns and the post-war camp improvements. In the later period, however, management put much less emphasis on morality – on trying to improve the worker as a person. And rather than trying to undercut the appeal of the unions, forest companies introduced improvements partly to meet the demands of the Lumber and Sawmill Workers Union. Furthermore, when developing their package of attractive innovations, woods operators selected carefully, taking only those options that appeared suited to their own peculiar needs.

During the 1940s, 1950s, and 1960s, when woods managers discussed how to reduce labour turn-over, they expressed no interest whatsoever in providing employees with fringe benefits such as pensions and life insurance. They saw this kind of plan as impractical in such an unstable industry.[53] Of course, during this same period forest employers had to contribute to the government benefit schemes – the Ontario Hospital Insurance Plan, Unemployment Insurance, the Canada Pension Plan, and Workmen's Compensation. But because these schemes were portable and universal, they did little to encourage steady employment. In fact, woods managers frequently complained that Unemployment Insurance encouraged men to stay at work only the minimum number of weeks necessary to collect benefits. It was not until the 1970s, that forest companies began to offer benefit packages. Under pressure from the Lumber and Sawmill Workers Union which was seeking parity with mill employees, the pulp and paper firms provided group benefits such as dental plans, life insurance, and long-term disability. To qualify, employees had to work only 65 days, a length-of-service requirement that would have done little to encourage stability. Clearly, when it came to employee-welfare schemes, woods operators gave a decided preference to improvements in accommodation, transportation, and recreation.

TRAINING FOR EFFICIENCY

As part of their post-war response to rising costs, woods employers increasingly turned to training programs, which they hoped would improve productivity. Such measures grew directly out of the industry's experiences during the war. Because the war industries and the military had siphoned off many experienced woodsworkers, operators were left with an unusually large proportion of greenhorns which heightened the need for training. 'The industry generally,' explained one woods manager, Gordon Godwin in 1942, 'is unable to obtain sufficient choppers for its needs this year, and in many cases, in greater numbers than is usual, the men engaged are without prior experience in woods work.' Godwin's address, entitled 'Increasing Worker Efficiency,' went on to explain that 'the training of labour, good business in peacetime, is essential in wartime.' As the war proceeded, the federal government promoted Job

Instruction Training (JIT) as a solution to the greenhorn problem through-out Canadian industry. The principles behind JIT, first developed by the U.S. military, involved breaking down each job into discrete tasks and then teaching each one in turn. A survey by the Woodlands Section showed that by January 1944, seven of twenty companies were offering JIT courses to members of their woodlands staffs. These methods continued to pro-vide the basis for instruction in the post-war period.[54]

Forest companies became far more committed to training in the decade following the war. As a 1955 review of the activities of the Labour Training Committee of the Woodlands Section pointed out, 'practically every com-pany' was by then carrying out some type of organized training program, 'a complete reversal of conditions that existed in the mid-forties.' There were several reasons given for this trend. First, greenhorns made up a growing proportion of the work force. Secondly, as new mechanical equip-ment became available, even experienced woodsmen needed instruction. Thirdly, the signing of collective agreements introduced new responsibili-ties to foremen who knew nothing of such matters as grievance proce-dures. As C.C. Wright of Spruce Falls Power and Paper explained, 'han-dling grievances and dealing with union committees are new problems to many supervisors and guidance is required.' And finally, managers had at last awakened to the idea that safety instruction could reduce woods accidents and their costs.[55]

Companies adopted various approaches to training. At first, woods managers saw it as a simple matter of instruction in technique. During the war, the Woodlands Section issued cartoon-illustrated booklets explaining how to file a saw, fell a tree, or treat horses. And in co-operation with equipment manufacturers such as Sandvik Saws and Caterpillar Tractor, companies held courses at central points for selected employees who were then expected to pass on their knowledge. It soon became apparent, how-ever, that not everyone had the ability to instruct his men or his peers. In recognition of this fact, the industry began producing training films that featured expert instructors. At the same time, the emphasis shifted to training supervisors and foremen, who could then provide expert on-the-job instruction. The Woodlands Section's JIT course was geared to training supervisors in their 'five needs: knowledge of the work, knowledge of responsibilities, skill in improving methods, skill in leading, and skill in instructing.' It also amounted to an attempt to centralize control over training methods – on every page of the manual, instructors were told 'DO NOT DEVIATE.'[56]

Training advocates soon realized that many foremen lacked the basic education necessary to carry out the program. Though in the past, literacy had never been a requirement of the job, it was now necessary for foremen to be able to read instruction manuals and keep records on the progress of those receiving the instruction. By 1954 it was generally agreed that companies no longer promoted bushworkers to supervisory jobs, but instead 'more and more we're looking to professionally-trained men to fill supervisory positions.'[57]

The results of training were debated among woods managers, because it proved very difficult to demonstrate the connection between improved productivity and training. To the frustration of the keen advocates of long-term training, the enthusiasm of managers grew only when manpower shortages became particularly acute. At all times the older foremen resisted re-education for themselves. One commentator believed that such men feared their shortcomings would be uncovered. He also noted a pattern in which supervisors demonstrated a reluctance to let the men 'know too much in case some young squirt gets his job.'[58]

The move towards formal training programs amounted to a significant development in the industry. Though individual workers were no doubt pleased to learn more efficient techniques that would enable them to increase piece-work earnings, job-instruction schemes nevertheless signalled the decline of informal, worker-initiated training. Previously bushworkers had learned from their co-workers, now they also were taught by supervisory personnel. This change represented a modest erosion of the bushworkers' autonomy.

At the same time, though the foreman took on additional responsibilities that reinforced his authority over his men, he did so as the field representative of an increasingly formalized and centralized management structure. Foremen themselves had been subjected to corporate training programs that sometimes exposed their inadequacies. As a result, managers had rewritten the job descriptions of their foremen and had altered recruitment patterns. No longer could even the most competent, but illiterate bushworker, expect to be promoted to the rank of foreman. At least in the larger firms that stressed the instruction function of the foreman, personnel departments were urged to recruit foremen who would be, in the words of one operator, 'capable of development, of going ahead.'[59] Rather than being the top rung on the job ladder, the foreman's position was now the lowest rung on the management ladder. C.C. Wright of Spruce Falls Power and Paper underlined the point in 1954. 'We feel,' he declared, 'that every supervisor, to be effective and to be the kind of man we want in our organization, must feel that he is part of the management team.'[60]

This transition in the foreman's role was part of a general transformation that occurred unevenly throughout industry in North America. As U.S. historian Sandford Jacoby has observed, in most work places the 'once-powerful foreman' became 'subjected to sharp pressures from above and below. Personnel managers crimped his prerogatives and took responsibilities away from him. Union grievance procedures and collective bargaining stripped him of much of his authority.'[61] Though the woods industry had been comparatively late in adopting this approach, by the mid-1950s the bush camp foreman had lost some of his autonomy – his control over the men in his isolated kingdom. Now his ties to the central woodlands office were stronger because supervisory and instruction methods were set down and he had to look to the central office for his own career advancement.

Woods managers in the decades after World War II had initiated several innovations. They had found new recruits abroad, altered the living arrangements of loggers, and experimented with training programs. All along, however, there were managers who doubted the value of such schemes, who wondered whether more costly facilities really did stabilize labour and whether job instruction actually increased productivity. Many such sceptics looked to another solution to productivity and manpower problems: mechanization.

9

Management responds: mechanization

At the end of World War II mechanization enthusiasts within the Ontario logging industry had reason to believe that progress might be made at last. In preceding years, as Ivar Fogh of Canadian International Paper noted in 1945, 'mechanization made practically no progress for the simple reason that plenty of men were available to swing all the axes, push all the bucksaws and drive all the horses that were required to produce the steadily increasing quantities of logs and pulpwood each year.'[1] But as Fogh and his counterparts in other firms realized, the manpower situation in the bush had changed fundamentally by the mid-1940s as traditional labour pools evaporated. To make matters worse, remaining timber supplies were less accessible and more remote, adding to logging costs. Managers had become convinced that in order to keep mills supplied it was essential to increase substantially the productivity of woods employees.

In 1949 W.A.E. Pepler, the new manager of the Woodlands Section, set the demanding goal of 'changing the present two man-days per cord to one or two cords per man-day.'[2] To achieve such an objective managers knew that a great deal more was necessary than a simple reorganization of existing methods or improvements in training programs. Operators would have to substitute capital for labour and introduce mechanized logging methods suited to the northern environment. Thanks to the tight labour situation and booming product markets, officials in woods departments found it easier to persuade executives and owners to provide the capital for developing and purchasing such equipment. They also hoped that recent technological breakthroughs in such fields as light engines, hydraulics, and diesel equipment had increased the potential for innovation in logging.

Although increasing productivity remained the major rationale for management's drive towards mechanization, advocates marshalled other arguments as well. Some hoped that by introducing new logging methods, forests could be 'utilized' more closely. Mechanical systems, it was maintained, might make it economically feasible to harvest small trees and less-desirable species, and to discover new ways to process and make use of 'the so-called waste material in the form of slash and cull.'[3] Some supporters of mechanization were foresters who linked new methods with the objective of 'sustained yield operations.' In his 1951 study, *Stability as a Factor in Efficient Forest Management*, Alexander Koroleff argued that it was essential for the industry to find new logging methods that would 'deseasonalize' operations, thereby permitting employers to build a 'permanent, competent and contented' labour force which could operate a well-managed forest *ad infinitum*.[4] And finally, some advocates of the new techniques insisted that mechanization was necessary because the industry's suppliers had lost interest in meeting the shrinking demand for horses and hardware.

During the post-war period, cutting and skidding, the logging phases that had hitherto defied the efforts of mechanization enthusiasts, were most dramatically affected by innovations. Changes were also occurring in the transport of wood from the bush roads to the mill. Ontario logging operators were replacing their iced haul roads with all-weather roads, and their sleighs with large diesel trucks. The Ontario government and the forest industry were extending the logging roads as well, linking them to the growing highway system of the north. By the late 1960s river driving had virtually vanished from the province and by 1974 the Ministry of Natural Resources and the forest industry were together maintaining 11,894 miles of access roads.[5]

In making the shift to trucking, the industry's major challenges were to raise the necessary capital for purchasing trucks and other equipment, and to mobilize the government, which built and maintained many of the new logging access roads and the provincial highways used by the loggers. As a mainstay of the northern Ontario economy, the forest industry had little difficulty winning political and bureaucratic support for road building. Woods managers justified these new expenditures to their company executives on the grounds that the truck haul would minimize the industry's dependence on unpredictable weather and hence ensure a steadier supply of wood to the mills, which in turn would reduce the costs of maintaining huge stockpiles. The roads also meant improved access to the forests, an advantage in fighting fires and in attracting a steady work force of commuters.[6] Dramatic as the consequences of these changes were, they required few technological innovations because trucks and loading equipment were already on the market in the 1940s. Cutting and skidding were the areas where engineers would seize the opportunities for bold innovation.

POWERSAW PERFORMANCE

The first major innovation to hit Ontario's post-war logging industry was the one-man gasoline-powered chainsaw. During the inter-war years, the Woodlands Section had tested various chainsaws, all of which had to be operated by two men. But these tools had proven impractical in the small timber of Ontario. World War II developments had a substantial impact on powersaw design. Demand for chainsaws increased as the Canadian army found uses for the tools and as the west coast logging industry experienced labour shortages. In the 1930s nearly all chainsaws were built in Germany by Stihl, which also held important patents. After the outbreak of hostilities, these patents became meaningless, and so a few North American companies such as Industrial Engineering Ltd of Vancouver began manufacturing improved versions of the Stihl chainsaw. Meanwhile, wartime developments in the aircraft industry led to advances in light-metal and air-cooled engines. By the end of the war such innovations had enabled saw manufacturers to reduce substantially the weight of saws. In 1945 Industrial Engineering produced the Beaver, a thirty-pound chainsaw driven by an air-cooled, two-cylinder, one-and-a-quarter horsepower engine. Since one man could operate the Beaver, the pulpwood industry in eastern Canada thought it might be an answer to their problems.[7]

Initial tests of the Beaver, conducted by the Cutting Tool Committee of the Woodlands Section, disappointed woods managers. Because the carburettor had to be kept upright, the saw could not be used for felling, only for bucking. Even then, there were problems with starting it in cold weather and test models 'were not operated without breakdown long enough to produce a real test.'[8] In the late 1940s various powersaw manufacturers made improvements, the most important of which was a new carburettor design that enabled sawyers to turn the powersaw in any direction when felling or bucking. By 1949 reports from the Woodlands Section showed that a pulpwood cutter with experience using a chainsaw increased his daily productivity by 190 per cent over that when he worked with a bucksaw. But when a test group of inexperienced men cut pulpwood with a chainsaw they produced only 14 per cent more than bucksaw users. After taking into account the increased cost of purchasing and maintaining a chainsaw, it was estimated that this amounted to a real productivity increase of only 5 per cent.[9] By 1951, however, tests suggested that woodsworkers using chainsaws might expect to improve their output by as much as 30 per cent. And the advantage grew larger as machines improved.[10]

Yet even during the period 1949–52, when productivity gains were still unimpressive, Ontario chainsaw sales soared. Sales representatives for powersaw manufacturers found eager consumers among the province's bushworkers. Woodsmen were discovering that it took far less effort to operate a chainsaw than a bucksaw. In 1951 Alistair Grant, a Precision chainsaw salesman, reported that bushworkers were 'really sold on power-saws,' because even if sawyers using chainsaws cut no more wood, the men preferred them because the work was 'easier and they enjoyed it more.' As a result men were staying at their jobs longer, and thus increasing their earnings. According to Grant some 3,000 Precision powersaws were in use in Canadian pulpwood operations, 95 per cent of the saws having been purchased by the bushworkers themselves.[11]

Few forest companies supplied employees with powersaws free of charge because managers believed that the temperamental saws would receive the necessary care only when the men owned them. Moreover, managers realized that they did not need to tie up company capital in powersaws as long as each cutter was willing to pay the $200 to $400 price tag. At the beginning of the 1950s many bushworkers were willing to do so; by the mid-1950s virtually all cutters had abandoned their bucksaws and had purchased, or were renting, chainsaws. By then woodsworkers knew that not only were the new tools less exhausting to cut with, but newer, more reliable models enabled fellers to improve their earnings significantly.

For their part, woods managers in the early 1950s were pleased with the new chainsaws, mainly because they had reduced the amount of recruiting required. Productivity had increased, while the rate of turn over had been slashed. For these reasons, managers were willing to help employees arrange financing for their saw purchases. Nevertheless, by 1951 managers were expressing disappointment that 'at present there is not much money in it for the companies.' It had proven impossible 'to reduce the piecework rate for the [powersaw] owners and thus penalize them.' Such officials looked hopefully towards the future. 'We feel that if we encourage the use of the saws, providing it does not cost us more than normally, in the long run, some day we will be able to base part of our piece-rate work rates on their performance.'[12] As it turned out, continuing labour shortages and a vigilant union prevented companies from actually lowering the cutter's piece rates.

Thus, the first major technological innovation in post-war logging had come from the combined efforts of the Woodlands Section, saw manufacturers, forest firms, and bushworkers themselves. By supervising site trials of chainsaws and publicizing developments in the field, the Woodlands Section had not only stimulated interest in, and increased awareness of, the new tools, but it had also encouraged saw makers to undertake improvements that would make the saws better suited to Ontario conditions. Once the advantages of the new chainsaws were apparent, the diffusion of the tool was largely the result of sales campaigns by tool manufacturers. Forest companies sometimes helped employees finance their purchases, but it was the manufacturers and bushworkers themselves who were chiefly responsible for the widespread use of the chainsaw because they had the most to gain. Logging operators benefited indirectly; but the chainsaw had failed to decrease production costs dramatically. In order to achieve more substantial cost-cutting breakthroughs, managers would have to look elsewhere.

FROM TRACTOR TO SKIDDER

Immediately after World War II, woods operators began directing considerable attention toward mechanizing the skidding phase where the horse seemed such an obvious anachronism. Operators hoped that by introducing a mechanical skidder they could lengthen skidding distances, reduce labour expenses, and eliminate much of the costly road building. But logging engineers had a great deal of difficulty finding such a machine, even as the need for such a substitute became greater.

In searching for a mechanical skidding device, operators first turned to the crawler-tractor, a vehicle long deployed on the sleigh haul. It was a machine with proven off-road capabilities and drawing power far in excess of even the biggest teams of Percherons. Enthusiasts pointed out that tractors could operate on wet, soft ground where horses could not walk.[13] Moreover, it was a simple matter to adapt the crawler-tractor to skidding purposes. On the rear of each tractor woods mechanics or tractor manufacturers could mount a motorized winch designed to draw cables with attached chokers, or loops of cable that resembled a hangman's noose. Just as the skidding teamster had secured the logs to his horse by means of chains, so might the tractor-operator jump down from his machine and fasten the chokers to his load.

Immediately after the war, Marathon Paper Mills, Ontario Paper Company, and Abitibi acquired crawler-tractors and began experimenting with various winching arrangements. Having found it was best to lead the cable from a height, their engineers had a steel arch with a fairlead welded to the tractor. Before long, major tractor manufacturers such as Massey Ferguson and Caterpillar were producing special logging models with winches and arches. By the beginning of the 1960s, companies had become even more innovative. The Drott Manufacturing Company of Wasau, Wisc., replaced the front blade of its tractors with a hydraulic-powered grapple loader capable of picking up a half-cord of pulpwood bolts in its giant claws and 'forwarding' them to the road. Other companies soon began to manufacture forwarders, as this type of vehicle came to be called. In 1961 Robin-Nodwell Company of Calgary, an equipment manufacturing firm which specialized in off-road track vehicles for use in the sub-Arctic, introduced the Muskeg, a self-loading forwarder well suited to soft terrain. Developing these kinds of skidders and forwarders required little in the way of sophisticated engineering; it was largely a matter of combining existing components.[14]

Despite such improvements, woods managers remained far from satisfied with the crawler tractor. In a survey conducted in 1948–9 the Mechanical Hauling Committee of the Woodlands Section found that the horse remained 'the prime mover for practically all wood moved less than two miles from the stump and compete[d] with mechanical hauling up to four miles.' And even the section's mechanical engineer had to admit in 1951 that the horse was 'still at an advantage in moving loads over very low-standard haulways.'[15]

At the Woodlands Section's annual meeting in 1953 dissatisfied company personnel formed the Committee on Tractors to study tractor design and determine what refinements were needed. A survey of twenty-nine member companies showed that the firms had a long list of complaints about the mechanical durability of the tractors. Particularly troublesome were the tracks, which tended to break down frequently, especially on rocky ground, and which were costly to repair. Because of these and other problems, not to mention the price tag of several thousand dollars, operating costs in most mechanized operations exceeded those where horses had been retained. Therefore, some companies such as Marathon Paper Mills abandoned the crawler-tractor for skidding, although most operators continued to rely on them to a limited extent.[16]

Discouraged by the poor record of the crawler-tractor, many logging operators planned to continue to depend on horses. However, two developments made this increasingly more difficult. First, in 'hot logging operations' – where logs were skidded as soon as the trees had been felled – the higher productivity of the new chainsaws of the early 1950s made it impossible for the teamster and his skidding horse to keep up with the increased pace of operations. As one operator explained in 1958, a new 'bottleneck' had developed and the 'horse then became the limiting factor.'[17] Secondly, as the work horse disappeared from the agricultural and transportation industries, lumbermen and pulpwood operators found it nearly impossible to secure an adequate supply of horses. In 1951 the Woodlands Section reported that the horse population of Canada had been declining at a rate of 100,000 a year since 1944, and the average age of logging horses was rising, with an estimated 13 per cent decline in horse productivity in less than a decade.[18] As the era of the work horse drew to a close, logging operators were also finding it more difficult to hire qualified teamsters and buy supplies of harnesses, collars, and other essential paraphernalia. Don Whitman, who ran a hardwood operation based in North Bay, recalls that in the mid-1950s, 'horses were still the best thing for skidding logs.' But after 1955 Cochrane-Dunlop Hardware in North Bay stopped stocking harnesses, and so 'you had to order them in, and it could take weeks.' Consequently, Ontario operators, large and small, were 'forced to mechanize.'[19]

Forest companies began looking to wheeled tractors or skidders as a possible alternative. One of the first to experiment with skidders was the woodlands department of KVP. As one KVP official explained, in the mid-1950s the company had been experiencing 'very stiff competition from pulp producers in the Southern States and the West Coast,' and so executives had decided to mechanize skidding operations in an attempt 'to increase labour productivity.'[20] Inspired by the example of the logging industry in the southern United States which brought in tractors from nearby farms, KVP put a few models of wheeled tractors through trials on the firm's timber limits near Ramsey, Ont. Based on these experiments, the company purchased three Blue Ox skidders, manufactured by the Logging Division of the Four-wheel Drive Auto Company of Clintonville, Wisc.

The Blue Ox was an open-cab, four-wheel drive vehicle powered by a 97-horsepower engine. The tires had been specially designed to withstand punctures, and to minimize damage from the forest floor the machine had eighteen inches of ground clearance as well as protective plates on its underside. Like the crawler-tractors used in logging, the Blue Ox had an arch, a fairlead, and a winch mounted at the rear. During 1956–7, the first season of operations at Ramsey, KVP used the skidders in an 8,000-cord operation to move tree-length logs in various types of terrain and forests. Company officials were pleased with the results, which showed that the skidder could be cost effective under quite varied conditions – in the selective cutting of mixed stands, as well as in clear-cutting operations where trees were of either large or small diameters. Snow to depths of three feet did not hinder performance, although 'light blow sands proved somewhat of a hindrance,' and 'swamp areas defied this method of operation during summer months.'[21]

Encouraged by KVP's reports, a number of companies began replacing horses with wheeled skidders. Thanks in part to the effective salesmanship of Archie Keen of A.M. Keen Equipment, the Ontario distributor of the Blue Ox, that machine remained the most popular. Other equipment manufacturers also entered the field, including Timberland Machines of Woodstock, Ont., which manufactured the Timberskidder. More extensive use of the wheeled skidders revealed their advantages and limitations. In comparison with crawler-tractors, the skidders could travel faster and they had a superior availability record, as well as low maintenance costs. However, crawler-tractors could negotiate steeper slopes, work in a wider range of ground conditions, and carry heavier loads. The chief limitation of the skidder was its wide turning arc, a great handicap in the boulder-strewn Shield country. The skidder was also cheaper to maintain than a crawler tractor, but it had a far higher initial cost. Woods managers concluded that neither machine represented a satisfactory piece of skidding equipment for the Canadian Shield.[22]

In fact, the development of a more efficient skidding vehicle had been underway for some years. At the field meeting of the Woodlands Section in 1950 a unique Mechanization Committee had been formed. Breaking with the past, corporate members of the new group agreed to contribute substantial funds to finance the development of logging equipment and pool their resources and talents. Canadian International Paper played a dominant role in the new group, although Gordon Godwin of Ontario Paper also brought considerable resources. After assessing the most promising fields of development, the committee decided to direct much of its attention to producing a skidding vehicle designed specifically for use in the boreal forests of eastern Canada. Within three years the group was experimenting with a prototype articulated skidder. Instead of the skidder's body being constructed of one solid structure as had been the case with wheeled skidders in the past, the articulated vehicle was made of two sections hinged at the centre. The wheels could not be turned; the skidder was steered by powerful hydraulic arms that swung the sections to either side on the central pivot. Such a machine would have a very small turning arc, and by wiggling back and forth, it could duckwalk across muskegs and through deep mud. The articulated concept had been known for forty years, but post-war engineering advances in hydraulic power systems enabled the committee members to adapt the idea to the industry's needs.[23]

In 1955 the members expressed their enthusiasm for the articulated machine's performance in field trials. The Bonnard Marx IV demonstrated that an articulated skidder was the answer to the problems of power and manoeuvrability on the Shield. Nevertheless, the committee reported that the Bonnard needed numerous improvements that would require a great deal of costly tinkering. Having already spent $250,000 on the project, corporate executives withdrew their financial support. The committee was forced to sell the patent rights to an interested buyer – Clark Equipment of Benton, Mich. This firm, which had considerable experience in manufacturing construction equipment, refined the Bonnard and marketed their version, calling it the Clark Pulpwood Logger 75, or PL 75.[24]

In 1957 and 1958 Clark's new PL 75 was put to the test in northern Ontario by the Ontario Paper Company, which used the machine to skid bundles of four-foot wood. Initial trials revealed a number of mechanical weaknesses that Clark spent considerable funds trying to correct. The next season officials from Ontario Paper were delighted with the results. At the same time, Great Lakes Paper began testing the PL 75 with a hydraulically powered grapple attachment designed to move their eight-foot wood. Tests showed the PL 75 had good potential even in black spruce swamps, a type of terrain that had hitherto defied attempts at tractor skidding. Despite these promising trials, however, Clark Equipment lost interest. Apparently the firm's executives believed they could make more money with their construction equipment as the U.S. government undertook a major highway development program.[25]

In the mean time other equipment developers had been working along similar lines. On the west coast the Garrett Enumclaw Company of Enumclaw, Wash., produced a similar articulated skidder which was tested for the first time in eastern Canada in November 1959. Dryden Paper Company put a Garrett Tree Farmer through trials 'in country ranging from poor to excellent skid chances.' Dryden's D. Wilson praised the Tree Farmer and concluded: 'low fuel consumption, inexpensive tires, absence of springs, a simple chain drive system, low rigging repair cost and excellent manoeuvrability make the Garrett Tree Farmer an attractive competitor to the present system of skidding tree lengths with horses.'[26] Hoping to profit from the market opportunities in eastern Canada, Canadian Car of Fort William, a division of Hawker-Siddeley Canada, Ltd, began to manufacture the Tree Farmer at the Lakehead in the early 1960s.

A few years earlier, however, firms in eastern Canada had also begun work on perfecting the concept of the articulated skidder pioneered by the Mechanization Committee. During the 1958–9 operating season, the Quebec-based Canadian International Paper Company began experimental work on a machine that could transport the eight-foot pulpwood cut in its Manawaki Division. The designers took a Bonnard Mark IV Logger and added a grapple to the front and a log-carrying platform at the rear. After initial trials the plans were handed over to Dowty Equipment of Canada, Ltd, which produced the Dowty Forwarder at its Ajax, Ont., plant in 1963. It was a self-loading machine that could carry pulpwood bolts on the rear section of the articulated vehicle, as well as a half cord in its grapple. This kind of machine had an obvious appeal for many logging operators because they would need to make few adjustments to their existing logging systems. Most operators in eastern Canada had long relied on the 'shortwood system' where fellers bucked trees into bolts at the stump. With the Dowty Forwarder, such bolts could be efficiently moved long distances to central landings. When using skidders like the Tree Farmer, bolts had to be bundled before they could be skidded or operators had to switch to a tree-length logging system. As it turned out, few Dowty Forwarders were ever manufactured. However, the concept was adopted by other firms, including Canadian Car and Volvo, which produced articulated forwarders as well as skidders.[27]

The best-selling articulated skidder of the 1960s was developed and manufactured in Woodstock. The Timberjack was the brainchild of two local men with no formal engineering training: Bob Simmons, a former west coast logger, and Wes McGill, an equipment salesman. Their financial backing came from Vern King, an entrepreneur with diverse business interests. In the early 1950s under the name Timberland Machines, the team had produced comparatively simple logging equipment, and by the late 1950s they were successfully marketing the rigid-frame Timberskidder. Yet ever since the articulated concept had been developed by the Mechanization Committee, McGill and Simmons had been working on an articulated model. The breakthrough came in 1960 when they produced their first Timberjack, a small articulated skidder. Because Timberland Machines lacked the capital to set up a production line for the new skidders, the firm was sold to a U.S. equipment company, Ellicott Dredge, and so the Timberjack was manufactured by Timberland-Ellicott Ltd at Woodstock.[28]

The Timberjack was a run-away success. It was highly dependable (advertisements trumpeted that the machines were available to operate 98 per cent of the time), manoeuvrable in most types of terrain encountered in the Shield, and its low, accessible cab made it comparatively easy for the skidder-operator to do his own choking. In 1962 Arthur Michell estimated that by switching from horses and crawler tractors to Timberjacks, Kimberly-Clark could knock $2.05 off the cost of producing each cord of pulpwood, a saving of nearly 7 per cent. By 1964 the manufacturer was building several hundred Timberjacks a year and selling them not only to the pulpwood industry in eastern Canada but also to the lumber sector, and to U.S. forest operations. But to meet rising demands and develop a number of different models, the firm needed a large infusion of capital. And so in 1967 it became a division of the giant Eaton Corporation, a U.S. firm which already produced some of the component parts for the Timberland skidders. That year, Timberjack, as the firm was now called, claimed to have 65 per cent of the Canadian skidder market. Sales were indeed brisk: the number of articulated skidders used in eastern Canada increased from 62 in 1960 to 2,160 in 1965 and 3,550 in 1969.[29]

The development of the wheeled skidder stands as an intriguing example of how the attention of innovating woods managers became focused on a particular path of technological change. Economic historians and historians of technological change have long puzzled over the reasons firms have chosen to make particular changes in techniques, when a host of other cost-saving alternatives was available. Nathan Rosenberg has suggested that since a firm cannot explore in all directions at once, 'threats of deterioration or the actual deterioration from some previous state are more powerful attention-focussing devices than are vague possibilities for improvements.' According to Rosenberg, firms are more likely to be motivated by such developments as: a state of technological disequilibrium caused by a change in one component of an integrated system; labour strikes that managers regard as intolerable intrusions into their decision-making domain; and 'reductions or curtailments of traditional sources of supply.'[30]

During the early 1950s Ontario woods operators had their attention drawn to problems in skidding because of a disequilibrium in their logging system and a curtailment of supplies. Gasoline chainsaws had quickened the pace of cutting, thereby creating a bottleneck in the skidding phase. In the mean time, the declining horse population and the lack of related equipment resulted in inconveniences and underlined just how out of step with the times skidding horses had become. As a result, equipment manufacturers and a special committee of the Woodlands Section had concentrated on developing an appropriate substitute for the horse. By the mid-1960s, the horse had disappeared from Ontario logging operations.

In attempting to halt their rising costs and solve production problems, Ontario woods operators indirectly played a part in encouraging mechanization in logging regions throughout the world. In 1966 the Technical Commission of the World Forestry Congress reported: 'The scarcity and rising costs of labour are everywhere leading to efforts to reduce the costs of operations by mechanization and by economies of scale.' Ontario operators had led the way by example, and that lead had given Ontario logging equipment manufacturers an edge on competitors. By 1980 exports amounted to approximately 70 per cent of total sales by Timberjack. Ontario-made equipment was skidding logs in the United States, South American, and Africa.[31]

TOWARDS INTEGRATED SYSTEMS

Not all logging operators in Ontario saw chainsaws and skidders as successful solutions to their production problem. More theoretically oriented logging engineers had been insisting all along that in order to increase productivity drastically, the industry needed to do much more than find mechanical substitutes for traditional methods. In a major statement on mechanization first prepared in 1949, W.A.E. Pepler, then manager of the Woodlands Section, and its forest engineer, Bruce McColl, maintained that cost savings would be greatest – perhaps as high as 50 per cent – if logging engineers could eliminate much of the material handling between steps in the logging process. They noted that in sixteen-foot operations logs were bucked by cutters, loaded onto skidding horses by a teamster, unloaded, piled at the skidway, reloaded onto sleighs, and finally unloaded from sleighs at the dump. Woods manager J.O. Wilson estimated in 1947 that altogether, in moving a single cord of wood, the equivalent of two tons of wood had to be lifted by hand. This was heavy, slow work – the pace being governed by the speed at which workers toiled. What the logging industry needed, said some engineers, was a new system that would not only reduce the amount of handling but also allow management and their machines to set a faster, steadier, and more predictable production pace. According to Pepler and McColl, 'Continuous mechanical pulpwood production based on the pace-setting characteristics of continuous material handling systems and multi-operation processing equipment, presents by far the best way in which to reduce the cost of producing at the stage between the stump and the final landing.' Here was the now influential voice of the professional logging engineer, applying principles long followed by his papermill counterpart.[32]

In pursuing the approach outlined by Pepler and McColl, logging operators and engineers followed two routes. Some took their lead from west coast loggers and sought to move logs from the stump to a central processing yard by means of a suspended wire cable and winch. Others tried to develop multi-processing vehicles that could either fell trees and transport them, or fell the trees, process them into logs, and transport the logs from the stump area. Both strategies involved the co-operation of woods management staffs and equipment manufacturers, as well as a good deal of costly trial-and-error experimentation.

In North America skidding or hauling timber by means of a long cable and powerful winch dates back to 1881 when California Redwood logs were first 'cable yarded' by steam-driven winches or donkeys. In eastern Canada logs were not cable yarded until the late 1930s when Abitibi began tinkering with cable systems in the black spruce swamps so prevalent in their Iroquois Falls limits. However, the west coast equipment which they tried had proven too heavy, and executives had failed to appropriate funds for equipment development. As A.H. Burk, KVP woods manager, explained in 1957, 'it was not until after World War II, when labour costs had increased substantially that cable yarding as a method of moving timber was given definite impetus.'[33] At that time Abitibi and Marathon Paper were committed to adapting cable techniques to their northern Ontario operations. Before long, responsive equipment manufacturers and the Woodlands Section were publicizing the idea and other forest companies were experimenting with cable systems.

No firm in eastern Canada became as thoroughly committed to cable yarding as Marathon Paper, which by 1949 was skidding virtually all its wood by cable. Immediately after the war, P.V. Lemay, Marathon's woods manager, decided that the firm's logging operations should be undertaken along unconventional lines. The company planned the harvest on what their foresters said was a sustained-yield basis, and it set up permanent camps. This made it possible to offer superior camp facilities and attract a more stable work force. At the same time Lemay decided to mechanize all skidding and hauling operations. Rather than have the fellers buck the trees into short logs at the stump, he planned to make bolts by mechanical means at central locations. In 1946 he introduced a kind of semi-portable sawmill or slasher to cut tree-length logs into bolts. Marathon's slasher consisted of a gasoline-powered circular saw mounted on a trailer that could be pulled by diesel tractor into a bush clearing or intermediate landing. Initially tree lengths were skidded to these landings by means of newly purchased crawler-tractors. But because of their poor performance Lemay began in the 1946–7 season to experiment with cable yarding.[34]

Marathon tried various yarding engines and winches, but the company found that west coast models were too heavy to move on crude bush roads. Therefore, in conjunction with a veteran American logging equipment firm, Lidgerwood Equipment, the forest firm developed the Marathon Logger, a powerful but lighter yarding machine that relied on a 100-horsepower gasoline engine. Marathon called for tenders and Timberland Machines won the job of manufacturing the Logger. At about the same time Marathon's logging department was working at improving the design of its slashers, turning, for instance, to a truck-mounted, fully mobile unit. By September 1949, when the Cable Yarding Committee of the Woodlands Section held its first meeting at Marathon's Stevens, Ont., operations, the company was running what became known as eastern Canada's first fully mechanized logging system.[35]

In 1949 Marathon's Planning Committee divided the limits into 'set-ups' of about twenty acres a piece. Since the forest averaged twenty-five cords to the acre, the plan was to yard 500 cords to a central area for piling. From five to ten felling strips were laid out in a radial pattern centred on the yarding area. After fellers had a head-start, a crew brought the yarding machine into the central area and set it up. A loop of cable was run from the yarder winch up a fifty-foot high, A-frame structure through a block at the top and then out to another block in the stump area. Crew members in the bush would hook tree-length logs onto the cable. When the engine was put in forward gear, the logs were lifted off the ground and hauled through the air to the yarding area where they were released and bunched by bulldozer so as to form a fan shape around one side of the yarder. After all the wood in a set-up had been brought forward and the yarder taken to another site, a second crew arrived with a slasher, positioning it in the centre of the semi-circle of logs. The tree lengths were then fed up to the slasher, cut by its circular saw and then fed automatically onto waiting trucks for the haul to the mill. In a single season Marathon would handle about 32,500 cords at sixty-five set-ups.[36]

Several other firms introduced similar systems, though none was as complete as the Marathon model. By 1957 approximately 20.4 per cent of the pulpwood harvest in eastern Canada was moved by cable yarders; 90

per cent of this activity took place in Ontario.[37] However, eastern Canadian operators never practised yarding on a wider scale, largely because setting up the equipment at each site was time-consuming and costly. It made economic sense to yard wood only when the number of cords per acre was unusually high or where steep slopes prevented moving logs by any other means. And once the articulated skidder came on the market, several firms dropped their yarders and purchased the new machines. Some managers, such as Ken Carlisle of Abitibi's Iroquois Falls Division, continued to believe yarding systems were effective.[38] But others, such as Bruce McColl who had initially seen the yarder and slasher as major steps towards a fully mechanized system, came to regard cable yarding as a failure. Although cable skidding reduced the amount of handling, the preliminary steps of felling and bunching still involved much hand labour – even with the chainsaws of the 1950s.[39]

LUMBERING GIANTS

In the late 1950s several logging engineers who were committed to the concept of multi-operational equipment began working on machines that would complement cable yarding or wheeled skidders. The Yarding Committee of the Woodlands Section had long recognized the need to assemble bunches of tree-lengths so that skidding equipment could be loaded to full capacity. This need was particularly acute in the north's many sparsely treed areas.

The first to tackle this problem was Rudy Vit, a logging equipment specialist from Quebec North Shore Paper. As he explained, studies made by the Yarding Committee had convinced him that it was 'difficult to justify the construction of a machine for bunching purposes only, particularly under conditions found on the north shore of the St Lawrence and in the boreal forest generally.' Therefore, he began working on a unit that would 'incorporate three or more phases.' In August 1959 at the field meeting of the Woodlands Section at Baie Comeau, Que., Vit unveiled the Vit Feller Buncher, a machine he designed that had been manufactured by Bombardier Snowmobiles, Ltd of Valcourt, Que. The Feller-Buncher was a compact, heavy-track vehicle (in fact, a Bombardier Muskeg) with special claw attachments, two hydraulically driven chainsaws, and a rear carrying platform. The machine moved up to a tree, gripped it with the hydraulic claws, and then notched it using one chainsaw and felled it with the other. By using the jaws, the operator could load the tree onto the rear platform. The process was repeated until the machine was fully loaded with the equivalent of about one cord of wood. Finally the tree-lengths would be unloaded in a spot convenient for skidding. Vit's idea was to have skidders transport the tree-lengths to a central landing where his Bombardier Processing Unit, also introduced at the same meeting, would convert trees into logs and chips. The Processing Unit was a large, immobile device for limbing, cutting trunks into bolts, and chipping the slash.[40]

A number of operators tested Vit's equipment. In northern Ontario trials in 1961, KVP found that, although the Feller-Buncher could fell and bunch 2.3 cords per productive hour, it was available only 196 of the 304 test hours. Most of the frequent breakdowns were caused by weaknesses in the felling components, although there also were the familiar difficulties of track maintenance on rocky ground. Even greater problems showed up with the Processing Unit: its immobility, several temperamental motors, and the considerable number of personnel required to operate it. In the end Bombardier constructed only eleven Vit Feller Bunchers, six of which were sold in France.[41]

Marathon Paper Mills, long a leader in the mechanization field, also sponsored the development of a harvesting vehicle. Marathon's equipment designers, Dick Harkness and Olle Oleson, came up with the ingenious idea of limbing and topping trees, using the standing tree as a structural support for equipment. Their concept was developed further by an engineering consultant, Bob Larson, and Hiabob Hydraulics, Ltd. At the 1962 field meeting Larson unveiled the Larson Harvester. The basic vehicle was a large heavy-track machine with a hydraulically controlled arm which had a reach of twenty feet. Fixed to the end of the arm was a 65-foot telescopic mast and the limbing and felling devices. From inside the cab of the vehicle, an operator placed the limbing mast against the tree and limbed it with a device that travelled up the mast to a point where a shearing mechanism topped the tree. Finally, as the tree was grasped by the claws, it was felled by a hydraulic shearing head resembling a giant pair of scissors.[42]

Because Larson lacked the capital to turn his Harvester into a production model, the project was taken over by the Beloit Corporation of Beloit, Wisc., an established manufacturer of pulping, paper-making, and sawmill machinery. Although the firm produced forty Beloit Harvesters, it abandoned the project after a few years, writing off losses estimated at tens of millions of dollars. Operators found the Beloit, which weighed 62,000 pounds and had a 5,000-pound mast tacked onto the end of its long arm, was too heavy and awkward to manoeuvre in rugged country. The machine could only be operated efficiently in dense 'stands that were above average size for eastern Canada.'[43]

In 1961 Canadian International Paper Company (CIPC) revealed its equipment development projects. At the field meeting of the Woodlands Section, the giant Quebec-based firm demonstrated its Busch Combine, a machine developed by T.N. Busch in the southern U.S. operations of the parent company, International Paper. This 9.25-ton wheeled vehicle could fell trees, feed them through a limbing and slashing attachment, and transport a half-cord of eight-foot bolts in its rear carrier. Due to stability problems and insufficient ground clearance for the Shield country, as well as difficulties in felling frozen wood, the Busch Combine never gained acceptance in Canada. That same year D.D. Hamilton of CIPC announced the results of a three-year project he had headed to develop 'a high-speed machine which would remove limbs and bark from a full tree, scale the volume of the bole, and cut it in to lengths.' The plan was to use the Arbomatik roadside processor with a feller-forwarder, a machine that would fell trees and carry the full tree – branches and all – to the Arbomatik. In fact, Canadian International opted to pool its resources and talents with two other Quebec-based paper firms, Quebec North Shore and St Anne Paper. The joint organization, Logging Research Associates, attempted a number of ambitious projects with considerable financial backing from the three firms.[44]

The commitment of funds for research and development in the woodlands harvesting and processing field by the pulp and paper companies helped convince equipment manufacturers in the late 1960s that the forest industry was at last getting serious about mechanization. As enthusiasm mounted, the Canadian government established a program to provide technical and other assistance to interested innovators. Numerous firms specializing in construction, mining, and paper-making equipment began work on woodlands machinery. Even though most of these companies were American-owned, design and manufacturing usually took place in Canadian branch plants, and the products were tested on timber limits in eastern Canada. Innovators believed that the region's boreal forests offered better prospects for heavy harvesting equipment than the even more varied forests of the Great Lakes–St Lawrence region or areas further south, where trees were still less uniform and where selective cutting rather than clearcutting prevailed.[45]

Most equipment manufacturers worked out joint development programs with a pulp and paper firm operating in Ontario or Quebec. In some cases the forest company made no financial commitment and instead simply arranged to purchase pre-production models, test them for quality, and suggest modifications. Naturally machinery makers disliked taking all the risk, especially since the forest companies derived so much benefit from using successful machines. (According to one expert, the forest company stood to benefit by as much as four times the amount gained by the manufacturer.)[46] In other cases, however, joint agreements required that both parties actively participate in all aspects of research and development. If the results proved successful, the forest company had the option of purchasing the more productive equipment at cheaper prices, and sooner, than its competitors. According to a study undertaken in 1971 by the Canadian Department of Industry, Trade and Commerce entitled *Mechanization in the Forest*, this second type of joint program had become widely accepted among large forest companies and manufacturers. It resulted in the bigger logging operators 'increasingly improving their competitive advantage over small companies.'[47] While the study provided no proof for this statement, there can be little doubt that all the major pulp and paper firms operating in Ontario had the financial strength to opt for the so-called 'fully mechanized systems' ahead of virtually all the much smaller pulpwood contractors and sawlog operators. Gradually even many of these poorer cousins were tempted by the growing array of impressive equipment on the market. For instance, Oliver Korpela, a Chapleau lumberman and pulpwood contractor, says he had no compelling reason to purchase a harvester, but it had become 'the thing to do.'[48]

Perhaps the most amazing of the new machines was the Koehring Short-Wood Harvester, produced jointly by Koehring, a Milwaukee-based, construction equipment firm, and Waterous, a Brantford, Ont., manufacturer of pulping and other equipment. Koehring had begun work on the harvester in 1963 and after much redesign Dryden Paper began testing the pre-production model in 1969. The following year Koehring offered a $133,000 Short-Wood Harvester that had been built to shear, top, limb, accumulate, and forward eight-foot pulpwood. The first models were huge – 33-feet long by 15-feet wide – and heavy – 80,000 pounds plus a payload of 30,000 pounds. By 1977 the machine had been strengthened so it weighed even more – 104,000 pounds plus a load capacity of 56,000 pounds. Despite its gargantuan proportions, the vehicle was remarkably manoeuvrable in the Shield country because of the articulated frame and giant, eight-foot diameter, low-pressure tires.[49]

The Koehring Harvester had a feller head mounted at the end of a hydraulic arm with a forty-foot reach. Without moving the vehicle itself, the harvester-operator could fell all suitable trees within a radius of forty feet, a great advantage in the many sparse stands of the north. (In dense stands of small-diameter trees, Koehring-Waterous offered their multi-tree option, a cutting head that could grasp and fell several small-diameter trees at once.) Having felled the tree, the operator then used the arm and claws to pass it, butt first, to the fully automated limbing and shearing tower fixed to the middle of the harvester. Trees entering the top of the tower, emerged at its base in the form of partially barked, eight-foot bolts which were then automatically stuffed through a spring-loaded gate into a cradle at the rear of the vehicle. The harvester could accumulate three cords before the carrier had to be emptied by means of a grapple attachment. One operator, sitting inside the cab, performed all these operations which had once required the work of a whole crew.

Although this remarkable machine had a number of supporters and sold well, many equipment designers rejected the short-wood concept. They held that it was best to perform as many functions as possible under more controlled conditions away from the stump. Furthermore, it was found that when one part of a Short-Wood Harvester broke down – and many of the newly developed components were subject to frequent breakdowns – the entire logging system was paralysed. Thus, the trend in the 1970s was towards less integrated systems. Various pieces of powerful tree-length handling equipment came on the market. While some of the new felling machines were mounted on crawler tracks others were articulated, wheeled vehicles. All used a long hydraulic arm with a cutting shear attachment so that they could cut many trees before having to move. Some were designed as Feller-Bunchers, equipment that simply felled trees and bunched them in readiness for skidding or forwarding by some other machine. Others, known as Feller-Forwarders, not only felled the trees but carried them to a roadside landing. There processing equipment might be used to limb and top the trees, cut them into boils, or chip almost the entire tree and blow the chips into waiting container trucks. Debates raged among engineers and other woods personnel who differed in their assessments of the productivity and cost-effectiveness of the various pieces of harvesting equipment. Some operators continued to rely on the less capital intensive chainsaw and skidder combinations. Increasingly woodlands departments of pulp and paper firms used computer programs to help them compare costs of various machines and systems and to analyse how best to organize production under various conditions.[50]

ASSESSING THE TRANSITION

Woods operators looked back with pride on their post-war innovations, certain that their efforts had resulted in substantial labour savings which in turn had helped keep costs in line. Unfortunately, because of the lack of access to runs of cost data, it is impossible to measure precisely any one piece of equipment's impact on productivity. Moreover, in virtually every operation there were different combinations of equipment and organizational structures, and widely varying forest conditions. With the spotty data available, it is impossible to control factors such as ground conditions, stand densities, crew size, and payment systems – all of which could substantially affect production levels.[51]

It is clear that in the post-war period productivity increases in logging were substantial. Naturally, harvesters offered the most dramatic savings of labour. R.C. Bjerklund of Great Lakes Paper Company reported in 1965 that with their Beloit harvesters it required nine man-days to produce 100 cords in comparison with forty-four man-days in a chainsaw and skidder operation. Cost savings amounted to 38 per cent. In a 1970 advertisement Drott Manufacturing Company held that with its Feller-Buncher one man did the work of twelve skilled sawyers with power saws. By the late 1970s Koehring Canada was reporting that two Short-Wood Harvesters, operated by an eight-man crew, on a round-the-clock basis, six days a week over a nine month period, had produced 29,000 cords of wood, 'mostly delivered onto trucks at roadside.' Thirty years earlier it would have taken approximately three camps of 100 men each to produce a similar volume of wood in seven months. Of course, none of these reports took into consideration supervisory and maintenance costs which ran far higher with the new, fully mechanized systems.[52]

Aggregate statistics point to similarly dramatic changes. Before 1945 total annual capital invested in machinery and equipment in the Canadian logging industry never exceeded $37,100,000 (in 1961 dollars); by 1960 the figure had increased to $125,000,000 and by 1970 it reached $621,800,000.[53] In 1963 Alexander Koroleff produced data to show that in 1949–50 mechanical expenses accounted for 17.6 per cent of total logging costs in eastern Canada; by 1959–60 they amounted to 43.2 per cent.[54] In Ontario the average production of pulpwood per man-hour increased 45 per cent in the ten-year period 1954–5 to 1964–5, that is, even before harvesters had penetrated the market.[55] No wonder Gordon Godwin of the Ontario Paper Company suggested to his fellow woods managers that 'the next time the inquisitors in the executive suite' threatened a squeeze through the 'corporate wringer,' the woods official might say to his president: ' "Sir, do you realize that in 1945 wood was 31 per cent of the total product value for our industry and thanks to the good work of men like me, that figure came down to 26 per cent in 1965?" '[56] Ontario operators could crow especially loudly. As a Canada Manpower study in 1965 showed, wood costs in this province were the lowest in eastern Canada, even though labour costs per hour stood about 40 per cent above the average.[57] Productivity increases continued apace; by 1980 reported man-hours worked in the Ontario logging industry were 17.7 per cent lower than they had been in 1965, even though output had increased by 4.2 per cent.[58]

While the woods manager could evaluate the new methods used in logging operations strictly in terms of productivity increases, the historian must cast a wider net and assess the case of woods mechanization in the context of historical findings about the processes of invention and innovation. Historians of technology point to a few key features of the general pattern of technological change in the industrial era.

First, they note that breakthroughs and innovations 'tend to cluster in time, largely in relation to the patterns of economic growth and factor price trends.'[59] Certainly developments in Ontario logging confirm this point. The quite sudden post-war industrial revolution in the woods occurred at a time when product markets were booming and the costs of labour soaring. The pressures favouring change were reinforced by engineering breakthroughs in such fields as light metals, air-cooled motors, hydraulic equipment, and diesel engines.

Secondly, these historians find that 'inventions and innovations tend to cluster in geographic locations and diffuse outward from these innovation centres.' The Ontario region was just such a dynamic centre. Within eastern North America, Ontario's unusually high post-war labour costs provided an early push towards mechanization. The presence of large-scale operators also facilitated the transition, for such firms not only had the financial resources to invest in research and development and to make equipment purchases but, as Pepler and McColl noted, they had the most to gain from 'quantity production methods.' During the next decade the contrast between northern Ontario and the northeastern United States was heightened; while the new harvesters worked comparatively well in the more uniform boreal forests where clear-cutting (felling all trees in an area) prevailed, they proved ill-suited to the mixed stands in New England, where selective cutting was necessary.[60]

Thirdly, historians of technological change observe a twentieth-century trend towards corporate research and development.[61] In the post-war period the inventive genius of individuals in the logging industry was strongly reinforced by corporate-sponsored research and development programs conducted systematically within firms that could be expected to profit from the discoveries.

Fourthly, historians have begun to reassess the Canadian contribution to technology. Commentators once lamented the conservatism and lack of inventiveness among Canadians, or recounted the opportunities Canadians let slip through their fingers. Now scholars looking more closely at specific industries have begun to find considerable evidence of creativity, particularly in the adaptation of technologies to Canadian needs. A fine example of this new approach is Diane Newell's *Technology on the Frontier*, which traces 'the successful adoption of new technology to the particular economic and engineering circumstances associated with the newness or frontier nature of Ontario mining to 1890.'[62] Similar patterns are evident in the case of post-World War II Ontario bush operations. Much of the new logging equipment included components designed and manufactured in the United States, and development here was sometimes conducted by American branch plants. Nevertheless, Canadians did considerable on-site testing and refining to arrive at designs appropriate for forest conditions on the Shield. As Canadian historians of technology emphasize, this kind of transfer of technique is itself a creative process, and ultimately, 'the ability to adapt is as critical as the ability to originate.'[63] Ontario's woods operators and logging engineers were well ahead of the historians; for many years they had been expressing great pride in their willingness to innovate, in the impressive array of new machinery, and in their success in checking the cost spiral.

10

Mechanized bush work

The mechanical breakthroughs of the post-war period dramatically transformed labour processes in Ontario's logging industry. During the 1950s and 1960s especially, woodsworkers experienced a dizzying pace of technological change as they abandoned their axes and hand saws for ever-more powerful tools and equipment. With little exaggeration one Ontario publication commented in 1964: 'Today's mechanical operations are making the legendary feats of Paul Bunyan look like those performed by a 97 pound weakling.'[1]

Since the publication in 1974 of Harry Braverman's insightful *Labor and Monopoly Capital*, the protracted and often heated debate on the labour process has focused on the issue of control at the workplace. Crucial to Braverman's analysis is the triumphant quest of management in the twentieth century for greater control over workers and work processes. According to Braverman, as scientific management or Taylorism has gained greater sway, capital has succeeded in deskilling workers both technically and intellectually. The essential principles of scientific management, first given coherence by Frederick W. Taylor at the end of the last century, called for the separation of 'conception and execution.' Engineers and other managerial personnel analysed jobs, subdivided tasks, and planned production flows while workers carried out the simplified, routinized, and hence boring and degrading tasks. Braverman also maintains that throughout the twentieth century capital has applied these basic principles with increasing rigour in more and more workplaces.[2]

In the forest industry of Ontario woods managers and logging engineers sometimes spoke explicitly about their interest in enhancing management's control over the pace of production, but generally they maintained they were responding to a host of pressures, including increasing competition in product markets, production bottlenecks, or rising costs related to labour shortages, instability, and unionization. Certainly these reasons appear to have been compelling enough for management to turn to mechanization strategy. It is nevertheless possible that, perhaps even unwittingly, managers pursued only those kinds of innovations that enhanced their own power and control at the expense of the autonomy and skills of production workers. British labour sociologist Barry Wilkinson has recently argued that when employers insist they are forced to innovate to remain competitive, or when they make arguments about the efficiency of new techniques, they may really be serving to mystify the true nature of the new technology and to 'justify or make legitimate, choices which are essentially political.' Hidden agendas, or at least the real consequences of change, may differ from the declared objectives of management. Wilkinson points out: 'Engineers may, perhaps innocently, simply not conceive of themselves as advancing political interests on behalf of themselves or the managers of the firms taking up the technology.' And yet he adds, the engineers' values and 'model of man' inevitably shape their choices.[3]

FELLING WITH CHAINSAWS

With the arrival of the one-man chainsaw the atmosphere in woods operations changed dramatically. Suddenly the air was pierced by the deafening roar of powersaws tearing through wood at a frantic pace. The feller now toiled amid the swirl of sawdust and exhaust fumes. Yet as long as horses continued to do the skidding, only certain aspects of the feller's job altered drastically.

After the arrival of the chainsaw, pulpwood operators did little to reorganize the work process; the pulp cutter continued to work alone on his timber strip. More reorganization occurred in the sawlog sector, because the two-man crosscut saw was replaced by the one-man powersaw and fellers lost their partners. Thus sawlog felling operations came to resemble those of the pulpwood sector. In both parts of the industry, piece work remained the most prevalent form of payment. Supervisors rarely appeared in the timber strips, allowing cutters to continue to enjoy considerable discretion in carrying out their tasks. Independence remained a vital characteristic of these woodsworkers.

Most of the skills that fellers had traditionally required were still needed in chainsaw operations. Filing was just as difficult to learn – and as rewarding for piece workers. The early chainsaw models had teeth resembling those of a bucksaw, and so there was little the experienced filer needed to learn. In the 1950s, however, saw manufacturers introduced new, more effective cutting teeth which did require some adjustment.[4] For the most part, the bushworker's operating skills also remained fairly constant. A good feller still had to be able to size up a tree and control its descent in order to avoid dangers and to facilitate subsequent steps. As Wayne Lennox, a journalist who worked in the Ontario bush during the 1970s, notes:

A skillful lumberjack attempts to fell each tree with regard to informal scheme; quite often though many trees simply do not conform to the feller's strategy, as every tree presents its own particular combination of the characteristics that affect felling. While nothing can be done about some of these trees and they must be felled where they will, some lumberjacks can "draw" a tree so that it will at least fall in an acceptable spot. Drawing a tree causes it to swing to the right or left of its normal path of descent as it is falling. To do this, and other techniques, a feller must master such tricks of the trade as holding the corner, or cutting the throat. When a difference of a few feet can often mean much wasted time getting the tree out of the bush, these skills become quite important.[5]

The forest, in all its diversity, still presented challenges that fellers of the post-war period had to meet using essentially traditional skills. This was especially true in the selective-cutting operations in the sawlog sector, where knowledge of the forest and sound judgment in selecting rot-free timber remained at a premium.

Similarly, chainsaw users had to contend with dangers long familiar to old-timers. Drunken sailors, widow-makers, foolcatchers, and the like, remained a part of the woodsworker's vivid lexicon because they still represented a threatening part of the job. In 1981 a woodcutter in north-western Ontario explained some of the dangers in powersaw operations: 'You have to be careful that you don't cut your tree completely off because once you cut your tree off, you have no control over it. It's completely loose and can go anywhere. You have to watch that very closely. You have to watch other trees standing near you, especially the dry ones. There's lots of dry trees in the bush. They can come down at any time. That causes a lot of accidents.'[6]

Of course, powersaws did result in some changes. One obvious difference between manual saws and powersaws was the new tool's higher cost, which in most instances was borne by the worker himself. In the late 1940s when forest companies began experimenting with powersaws, the firms supplied employees with the new tools. But bosses soon discovered that because the chainsaws were so prone to breakdowns, downtime could be kept to reasonable levels when the sawyer owned his own powersaw and hence had a stronger incentive to avoid equipment abuse and to learn how to keep it running.[7] Forest employers left it up to the men to choose between using manual tools supplied by the company or powersaws which cost $200 to $400. Because piece-work earnings rose dramatically with the purchase of the chainsaws of the 1950s, nearly all the men selected them.

In a sense, chainsaw ownership amounted to a step in the direction of small-scale, independent production. Yet it was only a small step; bushworkers who owned chainsaws were still essentially employed wage-earners. They worked on company-owned timber limits, were paid at piece rates set mainly through collective bargaining and in response to the vicissitudes of the labour market, and they sold their labour subject to the time constraints and overtime provisions of the collective agreement. As such, these employees differed substantially from settler-cutters who harvested wood on private lands, and who contracted to supply companies with set amounts of wood at prices partly determined by market competition. Moreover, purchasing a chainsaw did not entail a huge outlay of cash. Even in the early 1950s a bushworker could buy one out of the wages earned during one or two seasons. In later years, as powersaw prices declined and wages increased, it became even easier. (In 1959 a McCulloch chainsaw sold for $199.95; daily earnings of cutters averaged $16 to $23.)[8] Because of the comparatively high earnings of Ontario cutters, powersaw salesmen initially concentrated their sales drive in the province, resulting in a faster diffusion of the new tool in Ontario than elsewhere in Canada.[9]

A second change brought by the powersaw was the bushworker's increased need for mechanical skills. To keep a chainsaw running, it was necessary to have some knowledge of motor maintenance and repair. In the early 1950s, when few people were familiar with the new tool, and when the saws were more prone to breakdowns, equipment manufacturers and forest companies provided instruction in chainsaw use, maintenance, and repair. According to the master collective agreement, employers were required to stock parts for at least two popular chainsaw brands and provide storage and repair sheds for the use of chainsaw owners. In order to keep their saws in running condition and to minimize the delays involved in waiting for a mechanic, chainsaw users relied chiefly on their own skills with a wrench and screwdriver.[10]

The arrival of powersaws also affected the woodsworker's health and safety. Using a chainsaw was far less physically exhausting than felling with a bucksaw and it became possible for sawyers to stay at their occupation until much later in life. Nevertheless, because powersaws could cut through wood so fast, piece workers tended to fell many more trees in a day, which increased the amount of back-breaking piling that had to be done. William Ritokoski, a physically powerful Finn who immigrated to Algoma in the early 1950s, recalls that he worked very hard to produce three cords a day with a bucksaw; after purchasing a chainsaw he worked very hard to produce five cords a day. In the end Ritokoski was just as exhausted, though better rewarded.[11]

The speed and power of chainsaws also made them more dangerous tools than their predecessors. Just as a chainsaw could tear through wood in a flash, so could it rip through flesh. According to the Ontario Pulp and Paper Makers Safety Association, only 2 per cent of disabling logging accidents involved machinery in 1946, but a decade later the proportion had increased to more than 15 per cent; 103 of the 257 'mechanical accidents' involved powersaws.[12] Veteran bushworker Elmer Johnston, testifying in 1960 before the Ontario Royal Commission on Industrial Safety, emphasized that 'power saws are now a big cause of accidents.' He noted their tendency to kick back, causing injuries because 'often safety switches don't work.'[13]

As a result of the increased speed at which trees could be felled, it was all the more important that fellers carefully check for hazards before beginning to saw. When using a bucksaw, for instance, the feller could often hear a problem developing overhead and jump clear of falling timber or deadwood. Little could be heard over the din of the chainsaw, and there was less time to escape. According to some experts, piece work increased the dangers because loggers paid on an incentive basis were shown to take less care and time in checking for hazards and in planning escape routes.[14] In order to reduce injuries and compensation costs, employers and provincial authorities encouraged Ontario loggers to wear more safety equipment, such as steel-toed boots, hard hats, ear muffs, and specially-made padded pants.[15] Despite such precautions logging remained one of the most dangerous occupations and powersaws one of the job's major hazards. Chainsaw accidents numbered 468 in 1973 and 206 in 1980. Many of these were very serious. During the period 1950–80, there were 491 fatalities in Ontario logging operations. Even in the late 1970s and early 1980s, forestry still competed with mining for the highest fatality rate in the province. In 1981, for instance, the fatality rate per million man-hours was 0.40 for forestry, 0.26 for mining, and 0.02 for manufacturing.[16]

Equally alarming, though initially less obvious, was the occupational disease known to loggers as white finger, which was caused by chainsaw vibration. Beginning with a numbness in the fingers, it sometimes resulted in the permanent loss of use of the hand. Medical authorities estimated that by 1980 about one quarter of Canada's loggers suffered from white finger.[17] In the 1960s and 1970s chainsaw manufacturers increasingly offered saws with reduced vibration levels, but the problem persisted. To combat white finger, some other countries set limits on the number of hours a forest worker could operate a chainsaw. In the USSR, for instance, it was 'ordered for the safety of the forest worker that he should use one-man powersaws 2.5 hours/shift maximally. Interruptions are necessary.'[18] Under the collective agreement in Ontario, powersaw operators worked eight hours per shift; it was not uncommon for piece workers and contractors in non-union operations to work twelve-hour shifts.

Clearly, then, the chainsaw brought some disadvantages with it. Generally, the new tool contributed to lighter work and the possibility of higher piece-work earnings, without any significant erosion of skills or autonomy. Rather than deskilling the job, the feller's range of technical expertise actually increased as he became his own mechanic. Yet it would be wrong to romanticize about the satisfaction woodsmen derived from their new-found skills. Repairing a chainsaw in a bitter arctic wind, or amid a swarm of blackflies, is extremely unpleasant. Wayne Lennox surmises: 'It is likely that every logger has, at one time or another, kicked, thrown, clubbed or battered pernicious chainsaws.'[19]

POWER SKIDDING

Throughout Ontario's forests during the post-war period, the whine of chainsaws was increasingly accompanied by the deep, throaty roar of power skidders. The long-familiar, easy rhythms of horses, as well as their distinctive odours, quickly gave way to the faster, tireless pace of skidders and the stench of diesel fumes. Many woodsworkers and their bosses would mourn the passing of what Bert Styffe, a Lakehead pulpwood contractor called 'the romance and serenity' of the horse era. 'We hate to see the horses go,' John Pringle, a Spruce Falls supervisor remarked in 1966 as the company eliminated its last horse. 'But they are outdated. They represent a productivity factor that is just too low for us.' For woodsworkers the arrival of the skidder would have far greater consequences than had the coming of the chainsaw.[20]

In order to get the most out of their large investments in skidding and forwarding equipment, logging operators had to reorganize their production systems in several ways. First, they opted for what they called year-round operations. Because of the large amounts of capital tied up in the skidders, management had a strong incentive to minimize the amount of idle time when equipment was unproductive and depreciation charges had to be met. Unlike horses, which were most effective at skidding on snow-covered ground, the powerful new machinery could also operate in the summer and fall. Only during the spring season when the ground was wet and soft were skidders left idle and their operators laid off. The year-round capabilities of the skidders also had the advantages of stabilizing the labour force and regularizing the flow of wood to the mills.

Secondly, operators increasingly turned away from the cut-and-pile methods to hot logging ones, where wood was removed from the stump area by skidders as soon as the trees were felled and then quickly trucked to the mill. Hot logging helped to ensure a more even demand for woods-workers, a steadier supply of wood to the mills, smaller stockpiles, and lower inventory costs.

Thirdly, Ontario operators tended to move from short-wood operations to tree-length logging. According to one expert, 90 per cent of the pulpwood in eastern Canada was cut into short lengths at the stump in 1951, whereas two decades later 80 per cent was skidded to the roadside or landing in tree-lengths.[21] Most operators had found that it was cheaper to move tree-lengths with a skidder, which was less expensive to purchase than the short-wood forwarder with its hydraulic grapple attachment. And it was usually cheaper to cut wood into required lengths at the roadside or at the mill where conditions were easier to control and where high-speed slashers could be used. Altogether, this shift towards the year-round, hot-logging of tree-lengths would have sweeping consequences for Ontario woodsworkers.

When bosses integrated skidders into their operations, the rhythms of woods work altered profoundly. Most obviously, as work was de-seasonalized, to a large extent the labour market became more permanent. No longer did a significant proportion of the woods work force look to logging as a means to earn 'fast money' in a few weeks. The largest part of the work force was chiefly made up of professional woodsworkers, who had a long-term commitment to their occupation and were less likely to jump. Loggers came to resemble more closely the mainstream of Ontario's post-war labour force. Like factory and mill workers, woodsmen in some operations had to work afternoon and grave-yard shifts because managers discovered that by operating their costly new equipment on a round-the-clock basis, they received a better return on their investment. Shift work and year-round operations meant new limitations for the loggers. In a paper presented to the World Forestry Congress in Madrid in 1966, C. Ross Silversides, a logging development engineer for Abitibi, said: 'With mechanization must come discipline of work. The steady pattern of the day's work, the week's and the year's which is accepted for the most part by a worker in a developed economy, is often repugnant and strange to a forest worker who formerly worked at his own pace, often intermittently, and was to a degree a relatively free man.'[22] For generations most woodsworkers had been employed by large firms. But it was not until the arrival of the skidder in the 1950s and 1960s that many loggers were confronted with the management-imposed rhythms of industrial work.

The woodsworker's independence, his control over his job, and his ability to pace his work were also altered by management's insistence on team work in mechanized operations. No longer did the cutter or teamster work at his own pace. In mechanized operations, the feller, skidder-operator, and sometimes a chokerman and a log-maker, formed a crew whose members had to co-ordinate their work. The make-up of the crew depended on the availability of equipment and on the supervisor's assessment of the natural conditions and the men's abilities. The boss usually set up crews with an eye to keeping the costly skidder operating at full capacity. When felling conditions were good and skidding distances long, a skidder-operator might work with only one cutter. If skidding distances were short, it might require two or three cutters to keep him supplied. Usually the skidder-operator did his own choking, but when they were in short supply a chokerman might be assigned to do the job so as to maximize the machine's daily output. In 'fully hot operations' the crew would also include log-makers at the roadside. They converted tree lengths into logs, either by bucking them with chainsaws or by operating a mechanical slasher, and loaded them onto waiting trucks. This kind of operation called for maximum co-ordination. But because a delay in one area could wreak havoc throughout the system, not all operators preferred such a highly integrated set up.[23]

In these new logging systems, the individual had less control over the pace of his work. In the past the teamster had been limited by the strength, endurance, and speed of his horse. When a horse took a rest, so too did the teamster. By contrast, the skidder needed no rests, and so there were no natural breaks for the operator to enjoy. In hot-logging operations the system itself forced workers to keep up with the skidder or slasher. Bushworkers now scrambled to supply skidders with logs and to feed the hungry slashers. This integration was a step towards what labour economist Richard Edwards calls 'technical control,' where management takes advantage of the pace-setting characteristics of machinery.[24]

Although the equipment did much to set the pace, management also hired far more front-line supervisors to help co-ordinate skidder and slasher crews, to ensure each member kept up the pace, and to tend quickly to breakdowns. As an added stimulus to high productivity, many bosses implemented some form of incentive pay system. Usually this took the form of a bonus paid to the team when its output exceeded certain levels, crew members splitting the bonus on an agreed-upon formula. Since an individual's pay now depended in part on how hard and efficiently his team mates worked, loggers came under peer pressure to maintain an appropriate pace. W.J. Windebank of Dryden Paper observed in 1963 that logging had suddenly become 'a closely-integrated *group* enterprise. Laws of group behaviour that didn't apply are at work now.'[25]

Managers differed in their assessments of just how much control the worker in a mechanized operation had over his output; consequently officials also disagreed on how to pay workers. In the 1960s most companies reduced their reliance on piece-work and incentive systems. By 1967 the Spruce Falls Power and Paper Company paid 50 per cent of its workers on a piece-rate basis, 45 per cent on day rates and 5 per cent were salaried. Some companies, such as Great Lakes Paper, eventually hired all their woodsworkers on an hourly basis.[26] Management proponents of time-wage payments held that in mechanized operations the worker had so little control over his productivity that piece-work made no sense. One observer went so far as to maintain that it was destructive. 'An important justification for piece work in the past,' commented sociologist Camille Legendre, 'was that the period of operations was short and, because productivity was directly dependent on the workers, there was a need to rush them.' But once productivity depended more on machinery and operations became year-round, what appeared desirable was 'not so much feverish agitation of [a] few months as a sustained and regular progress [of] a longer period.' Advocates of day work also held that incentive payments increased equipment abuse, as well as the number of accidents, thus raising total production cost.

Some managers disagreed with this viewpoint and insisted that an incentive pay system worked. A 1965 study of skidder-operators in eastern Canada concluded that some 40 per cent of the variation in productivity among operators was due to skill and motivation. A later study of wheeled skidding showed that variations in bonuses had an effect on worker attitudes and consequently on productivity that 'was both important and measurable.'[27] Perhaps because of these kinds of findings, in the 1970s many companies reverted to the piece-work system or put more emphasis on a bonus. Still others believed that the highest productivity rates and lowest levels of machinery downtime were achieved when the incentive system was taken to the extreme, and operators who owned their skidders were hired on a contract basis. This arrangement became prevalent in smaller, non-union operations where worker resistance to it was the weakest.[28]

Whatever the payment system, managers hoped that crew members in the new group operations would help each other to maximize their crew's output and earnings. In a report on the successful introduction of articulated skidders in 1962 at Consolidated Paper, E.S. Cadenhead described to his fellow woods managers just how co-operative crew members had been: 'At times, the driver reached the feller before the load was prepared in which case he left his machine and helped choke. As he was paid for the number of cunits he skidded, he was as interested in high production as the rest of the gang. Co-operation was excellent between gang members.' Similarly, Earl Craig, an Ontario member of the Forest Producers Accident Prevention Association, found it 'enlightening to observe an experienced crew ... felling and ... winching as a team. Every move is planned and executed to maximize efficiency and safety. They are constantly alert to assist each other and make the tasks easier.'[29]

In order to work effectively as a team, skidder-operators had to acquire a number of skills. Some of the basics remained little changed from the days of horse skidding. Like the teamster, the machine operator had to determine an appropriate size of load, attach the logs quickly, and then select the most direct route that avoided obstacles. This last task had become considerably more difficult with mechanization. Because skidders and forwarders were far wider and moved much faster than their equine predecessors, equipment operators had to learn to respond very quickly to obstacles. And whereas horses had been used chiefly on snow-covered, frozen ground, skidder operators had to learn to manoeuvre their heavy machines through deep mud and muskegs. It took experience to identify the type of muskeg over which the skidder could safely travel and to duckwalk the machine across soft terrain.[30]

Because of the similar skills required in horse and mechanized skidding operations, some of the old-time teamsters were able to make the transition to the new methods. Others lacked driving and mechanical skills and simply could not adjust to the new ways. They tried to find jobs in pockets of the industry that were slow to mechanize, or they looked for choring jobs in the camps.[31] But most of the men who applied for woods jobs after the mid-1950s had some experience driving and maintaining cars, trucks, or heavy equipment. They nevertheless had to hone their skills to the special requirements of bush work. In driving a skidder, productivity depended to a large extent on the speed at which an operator could manoeuvre his vehicle around rocks, fallen or standing trees, ditches, streams, large stumps, and steep slopes. In a report from the Forest Engineering Research Institute of Canada (FERIC) entitled *Higher Travel Speeds for Off-Road Logging Vehicles*, engineering consultant John Radforth observed in 1978: 'Travel speed of a vehicle through a field of obstacles is obviously highly dependent on the driver's skill. If the driver has acquired a good feel for the steering response of the vehicle and for the vehicle width and encroachment, and has learned to judge very precisely and quickly the distances between the vehicle and an obstacle, then he can react quickly as new obstacles appear in his path to adjust the travel direction of the vehicle. An inexperienced driver needs more time to make his steering decisions and must acquire this time by slowing down the vehicle.'[32] Obviously, it took a good deal of time to learn how to operate a skidder at optimal levels. While the average training course for skidder-operators was only four weeks, even someone experienced in equipment handling and with good reflexes needed far longer than one month to acquire the necessary expertise.[33] According to a supervisor at Great Lakes Forest Products, it took 'ten years to get really proficient at it so that you can do a steady, everyday pace, and not be too hard on yourself.' To perform efficiently a skidder-operator had to learn 'the tricks of the trade,' such as cutting 'down your choking time by using your machine more.'[34]

In addition to these operating skills, skidder-drivers needed at least a modicum of mechanical experience in order to keep their machines running. Woods employees of the large companies were well served by trained mechanics who took on all the big repair jobs. At the other end of the spectrum were piece-workers who had to learn the mechanic's trade so they could avoid costly delays waiting for a repairman to appear in some isolated spot. But managers expected all skidder-operators to be able to perform minor repairs such as clearing a frozen fuel line. In a dramatization, Wayne Lennox describes what it was like to have to do such a job at dawn on a bitterly cold day:

He returned to the skidder, unhinged the protective motor shield so that he could get at the fuel line, and unbolted it from the pump, the icy wrench leaving a white cold-burn across his hands and fingers. Wriggling himself into the space between the huge tire and the frame, he grasped the fuel line and placed his lips over the end. He sucked hard, drawing a mixture of fuel, ice and debris into his mouth. Quickly he turned and expelled the foul fluid, spitting several times in an attempt to clear the taste that, regardless of his efforts, would linger most of the day. He had to repeat this procedure a number of times until he obtained a mouthful of clear fuel. Hoping that the line would remain ice-free now, he reattached it to the pump.

'God, what a way to make a living!' he declared to no one in particular.[35]

Because so many different skills were required to operate and maintain a skidder, managers raised the question of appropriate training. Some companies preferred to hold to the industry's traditional approach, leaving training to the workers themselves. Woods manager Bill Thom explained in 1965 that at Kimberly-Clark they had not 'found it necessary to institute formal training programmes for machine operators' because they had 'built up a nucleus of trained men, who in turn have trained others as the number of machines has increased.'[36] Other managers grasped the opportunity provided by the introduction of the new equipment to establish management-designed training schemes for skidder-operators. Marathon Corporation and Dryden Paper set up formal courses to instruct new men and upgrade veteran employees. At Dryden the emphasis was on training supervisors in managerial and operating skills since supervisors were so much more important in skidder operations, and they, too, lacked mechanical knowledge. Eventually most firms took advantage of federal and provincial funds and programs in order to train skidder-operators.[37] According to one manager whose company had participated in such a program in 1965, the training course had 'added materially in the acceptance of wheeled skidding as an integral part of our operating method and contributed toward enhanced relations with our labour force.'[38] Equipment manufacturers also provided some training, and they issued illustrated manuals for operators. Detailed operating instructions are an indication that logging jobs were beginning to feel the influence of what Richard Edwards refers to as 'bureaucratic control,' the pervasive rules-oriented form of control pioneered by certain very large corporations.[39]

The skidder-operating manuals also demonstrated some of the dangers involved in handling skidders, as well as some of the skills operators required. Drivers of Hawker-Siddeley's Tree Farmers were instructed to:

DRIVE slowly over rough terrain and steep grades.

DROP the load if the front wheels leave the ground when skidding logs uphill.

NEVER winch-in a heavy load at an extreme angle. Any machine can be tipped over if improperly used.

NEVER free-wheel at high speed. When engine r.p.m. drops you will not be able to steer.

ALWAYS winch to load up to the arch otherwise it may hand-up and overturn the skidder.

TAKE CARE not to tip the machine over frontwards when travelling downhill.[40]

It took practice to know the meaning of such terms as 'an extreme angle,' or 'a high speed.'

Tipping over a fast-moving skidder was an obvious danger, but much less apparent were the dangers of vibrations, jolting, and high noise levels. Until the late 1970s, engineers who designed logging vehicles gave little or no thought to operator comfort and health. Referring to Ontario's first popular skidder, the Blue Ox of the 1950s, one observer later commented: 'The concept was good but each operator who stayed with the machine for a period of time ended up in the hospital with injuries to the spinal column.'[41] Twenty years later, sore backs brought on by jolting skidders remained a major complaint of operators. In 1978 a consulting engineer found that, although the roughness of the ride was a strong impediment to increasing off-road travel speeds and corrective technology was 'widely and easily available,' engineers had made 'no conscious efforts ... to use springs and dampers to tune out a rough ride.'[42] Designers of skidders had instead counted on low-pressure tires to cushion the ride. But the tires magnified oscillations in such a way as to increase the health hazard. The frequencies of the vibrations transmitted to the operators were so high they made the driver's internal organs resonate, causing discomfort and eventually 'serious physical harm.'[43] Noise levels were also high enough to cause deafness. A representative of Clark Equipment admitted in 1974 that much diesel equipment in the past had been excessively noisy, in part because mufflers were 'gutted so operators would "appreciate" the power.'[44] In 1975 when FERIC tested the FMC 200 BG Grapple Skidder made by Ford, it found that noise levels inside the operator's cab considerably exceeded permissible limits set by the United States Department of Labor. They also discovered that temperatures in the enclosed cab were uncomfortably high. When the thermometer registered seventy-two Fahrenheit outside, inside it soared to ninety-eight degrees.[45] Even as the awareness of 'human factors' increased in the late 1970s, equipment manufacturers continued to build skidders that were uncomfortable as well as dangerous to operate, forcing drivers to run the vehicles at less than optimal speeds.

The coming of the wheeled skidder had advantages and disadvantages for woodsmen. Companies now offered steadier work, even the possibility of a life-time career as a skidder-operator. Moreover, no clear-cut deskilling process had occurred. Jobs opened up for highly skilled mechanics, and skidder-operators needed a knowledge of terrain types in order to duck-walk across muskeg, as well as excellent driving skills to operate their equipment at acceptable speeds. Such skills could not be acquired over-night, and expertise came only after several years. However, the new jobs had their drawbacks, serious back injuries being one of the most obvious. In addition, while the stabilization of employment promised security for some men, to others it brought new disciplines, more exacting and unfa-miliar work rhythms. Team work and somewhat closer supervision restricted the freedom of loggers to set their own pace. Yet the job had still not been fully routinized. Woods managers could never easily control scattered work groups in an ever-changing forest environment.

LEVERS AND JOYSTICKS

By the time harvesters and other large pieces of processing equipment began to rumble through the Shield country of northern Ontario, bush operations had already undergone a profound change. The familiar logger's call – Timber-r-r! – had long been drowned out by the shriek of chainsaws and the roar of skidders. Although the arrival in the 1960s and 1970s of the harvester was scarcely audible, the gigantic new machines made a vivid impression. These monsters with their enormous tires, forty-foot arms, mammoth claws, and huge cutting shears, towered above forest workers. The transformation in the nature of the logger's job could not have been more striking; less obvious were the continuities.

When woods managers introduced harvesters they reorganized work processes only minimally. Similar to the skidders, the enormous new machines could be run on a nearly year-round basis. Indeed, in the case of these far more costly vehicles, managers had an even stronger incentive to see them used round-the-clock, and so they came equipped with powerful floodlights that enabled harvesting to continue throughout the night.

The trend towards closer supervision not only continued but was car-ried a step further in fully mechanized operations. Managers believed that their investments were best protected when supervisors were on hand to pressure workers to maintain a fast pace, restrain abuse of equipment by operators, and attend quickly to any production snags. Because of the high depreciation charges, downtime was much more costly in these capital-intensive logging systems. Thus, in one of the first fully-mechanized operations, management assigned two supervisors to every four or six operators.[46] Though supervision was usually less intense in later years, cabs came equipped with two-way radios so that supervisors could maintain close contact and mechanics could be immediately informed of a breakdown. Improved communications and closer supervision meant that harvester-operators enjoyed substantially less autonomy than had their counterparts in traditional logging systems. Reinforcing this trend were group pressures similar to those encountered earlier by skidder-operators. Drivers of all the big machines, with the exception of Short-Wood Harvesters, had to make certain that other team members, such as skidder- and slasher-operators, were supplied with trees so that the productivity of the whole team could be maintained.

With the arrival of the huge equipment, personnel officers began looking for woods employees with new kinds of characteristics. No longer were powerful muscles and an iron constitution essential where diesel engines and hydraulic pumps did the heavy work. In 1976 FERIC published a major study, *Performance Variations among Logging-Machine Operators*. After testing a number of tree-shear operators, the investigators found that physical fitness did not significantly affect the productivity of operators. The physical characteristics that counted were 'visual depth perception' and 'manual dexterity.' Depth perception affected 'the operator's skill in planning the sequences of felling, in driving from one tree to the next, and in positioning the shear accurately on the tree to be felled.' Manual dexterity was 'presumably associated with an operator's ability to co-ordinate visual information with arm and hand movements.'[47]

Because of the new emphasis on dexterity and perception, employers in the late 1970s began to consider hiring women to operate heavy logging equipment. By 1980, however, Ontario forest companies had hired at most a half-dozen female harvester-operators. Yet the arrival of these women suggested that in the future employers might draw heavily on the large pool of underemployed women living in resource towns.[48] Not surprisingly, in their glossy magazine advertisements, equipment manufacturers began to feature eye-catching female operators who were also supposed to convey the impression that the intimidating new machinery was easy to operate.[49]

To the untrained eye, the harvester cab with its dozens of gauges, and its levers, pedals, and joy sticks appears almost as complicated as a jet plane's cockpit. The Hawker-Siddeley Tree Processor, for example, had a cab with a swivel seat permitting access to a front console with four large levers, a brake pedal, and clutch, and to a rear console with ten levers, four foot pedals, and numerous buttons and knobs. In order to complete one cycle of operation, the driver of an early-model harvester had to go through twenty-two distinct but co-ordinated movements in a period of fifteen seconds.[50] Obviously it took training and experience to operate these machines efficiently, even in the case of the Short-Wood Harvester with its fully automated limbing, barking, and bucking components. In an early report on the Koehring Short-Wood Harvester, the equipment evalu-ator observed: 'The Harvester is a complex piece of machinery that requires a high degree of operating skill to produce pulpwood at an eco-nomical cost. Operator selection and training is important. A training period of five to ten weeks is required, depending on the skill and past mechanical equipment experience of the trainee.' More than a decade later, a FERIC report on tests conducted at Atikokan and Ignace on the new Hohn Pulp/Logger II showed the productivity was 'very dependent on the capability, experience and motivation of ... operators. Since it normally requires several months for each operator on the Hohn to become fully proficient, there should be planned continuity of operators.' In their inves-tigation of tree-sheer operators, P.L. Cottell and his team had found that the equipment operators and personnel officers agreed that experience affected output. On the basis of test results, Cottell reported that an operator with one year of experience cut approximately seven trees per hour more than an operator with only a month on the machine. On aver-age operators cut 115 trees per hour.[51]

Notwithstanding the fact that operators needed considerable job-learn-ing time, the kinds of skills they required were not as specialized as those of the men working in more conventional cut-and-skid systems. Operators of the new equipment needed less knowledge of the forest and the envi-ronment. When clear-cutting with a harvester, the logger applied the same techniques to fell all species. So powerful were the big machines that variations in trees, ground conditions, and weather meant little. Rather than having to learn how to dodge small obstructions or duckwalk across muskeg, the mighty harvesters roared ahead unimpeded. And the broad-based nature of the skill required by the machine operator was evident from the fact that equipment users in the construction and mining indus-tries snapped up trained harvester-operators. This had advantages, as well as drawbacks, for forest employers. They could attempt to draw on a pool of experienced men whose training had been paid for by others, though managers frequently complained that there were too few such men. Conversely they found that often the men they had trained moved to jobs in other industries.[52]

Woods managers faced even greater employee-training and retention problems with the highly skilled mechanics who were employed to maintain and repair the new equipment. Knowledgeable mechanics were prized by managers because the complex harvesters, with their many hydraulic pumps and elaborate electrical systems, were prone to breakdown, and downtime costs were high. In 1971 it was estimated that maintenance and repairs accounted for about 46 per cent of the total operating costs of the harvesters. Woods managers developed elaborate preventive maintenance programs, using computers to help co-ordinate maintenance schedules and the supply of parts. Yet as a Department of Industry, Trade and Commerce study noted, forest companies found that their experienced mechanics were 'not always able to maintain more complex equipment such as harvesters.' Since it proved extremely difficult to attract highly specialized mechanics to remote camps, the bigger forest firms introduced programs designed to upgrade the skills of existing employees, instructing them in the intricacies of diesel engines and automatic transmissions, hydraulic and electrical systems. Thus, some very well paid, highly skilled jobs opened up in logging as a result of the introduction of the new machines.[53]

In addition to the new kinds of skills needed by forest workers, there were also substantial changes in the working environment. Since harvester-operators worked in enclosed cabs, drivers were not exposed to the same kinds of dangers and discomforts that had long been associated with logging. Sitting in a cab, the operator was well protected from sharp cutting tools, falling timber, and the weather. The major safety hazard was the danger that the big vehicles would roll over into a ditch or tumble when felling on a steep slope. As it turned out, however, serious accidents were few. More common were injuries sustained by mechanics while making repairs on hard-to-reach parts, high above the ground, especially in bitterly cold weather when equipment was encrusted with ice.[54]

When the new harvesters first appeared in the 1960s, woods managers were enthusiastic about the superior working conditions their woods employees would enjoy. 'Heaters in winter, fans in summer, portable air-conditioning units, insecticides, lighting systems, etc. can, as far as the worker is concerned, turn night into day and winter into summer,' declared one observer in 1966. In fact, it was not until the late 1970s and the 1980s that managers began to realize that equipment designers had given too little attention to operator comfort. In 1981 a manager recalled: 'Machine operation improved many a job, but it never became a guarantee for a good working environment. Instead of getting wet by the rain, the operator got overheated in a poorly ventilated cabin. Instead of heavy-lifting outside, he got day-long bad vibrations from going back and forth with the machine. Instead of walking all day, he ended up standing all day because he could not see to operate the machine while sitting.' Equipment designers began to apply the principles of ergonomics to the design of appropriate seating and to the layout of instrument panels. Similarly, employers were finding that in order to attract skilled repairmen to the bush, improved repair facilities were needed. Great Lakes Paper not only built well-lit and heated portable garages, but the company also introduced a large nylon tent so that broken-down harvesters could be enclosed and repairmen provided with heat.[55]

DESKILLING?

By the 1970s woods work in Ontario more closely resembled modern factory production than it had at any time in the past. Managers had devised new tools and equipment, and deployed them in integrated series so that the wood might move smoothly, on a year-round basis, from stump to mill. With the arrival of the new machinery, management had redesigned jobs so that woodsworkers had less control over the pace of work. Rather than depending on the strength of men and horses, employers relied much more heavily on powerful pieces of equipment, team work, and closer supervision of employees. Most striking of all was the appearance of the Short-Wood Harvester which resembled an entire production line on wheels and included fully automated components.

By several tests, woodsworkers' jobs were not deskilled. As we have seen, many loggers continued to enjoy considerable autonomy on the job, and they exercised some discretion in performing their tasks. Especially in operations where selective cutting was the practice, the chainsaw operator needed knowledge and sound judgment in order to size up his cutting chances. Though supervision had become closer, the work force remained scattered and thus difficult to observe. In terms of the technical requirements of the job, much reskilling had taken place. Harvester-operators needed great dexterity and keen perception to get the most out of their machines. The time for job training had not been reduced to a matter of hours or days; basic training courses lasted several weeks, and it generally took much longer than that to become proficient. And the status of the occupation had certainly not declined. Ontario woodsworkers had traditionally done what was perceived to be unskilled work; now that their machine-operating and repair skills were valued by woods employers and in demand in other industries, loggers had become skilled employees. What happened in the Ontario logging industry was not so much a straightforward trend toward deskilling, but a complex process of job redesign that involved trade-offs in terms of autonomy, technical skill, and status, and a considerable amount of reskilling.

In many respects the pattern described here conforms to the growing consensus about deskilling that has begun to emerge in the recent literature on the labour process. A host of case studies of various industries have stressed the complexity of labour-process transformations in general, and changes in skill levels in particular.[56] Richard Edwards has argued that 'accumulation must be seen as simultaneously deskilling and reskilling the labour force. Rather than the simple one-way process that Braverman describes, we must recognize this more complicated two-way process.'[57] To the question 'What happened to skill in the twentieth century in Canada?' Craig Heron and Robert Storey reply in part: 'Certainly the decentralized occupational mix was invariably more complex than a simple thesis of deskilling and "proletarianization" would indicate.'[58] Whatever their dreams may have been, managers in a number of diverse industries failed to eradicate all traces of skill. This was clearly the case in Ontario logging.

11

Bushworkers respond to mechanization

In a 1918 issue of *Lumberjack Bulletin*, a publication of the Industrial Workers of the World, there appears a story entitled 'Tall Timber Tales,' in which Lumberjack Joe tells a greenhorn about some of the contraptions he has seen during his long days in the woods. Among them was 'a 90 foot Improved McCormick Reaper and Harvester with 15 foot blades as sharp as razors.' When Paul Bunyan hitched his old blue ox onto it, he 'mowed down every tree in Kansas.' That machine cut trees close to the ground, trimmed them clean, bundled the logs, and ground up the tops into patent breakfast food. 'We made a million dollars every day,' says Joe, 'and were known all over the country as great philanthropists because all the breakfast food we didn't feed to the ox and the crew we sent down to be given away to the hungry lumberjacks on the breadline.' Like all effective Wobbly propaganda, this story ended with an uplifting message. Lumberjack Joe goes on to describe 'the latest thing in machinery in the woods ... A motor chain saw which will cut down a thirty inch tree in two minutes, and cut it low without waste.' Joe predicts that this machine will make Wobbly members 'faster than all the speeches of the delegates ... If every Wobbly were jailed tomorrow, the machine would produce a fresh crop of revolutionary industrial unionists within a year.'[1]

Many of Joe's predictions turned out to be dead on the mark. Eventually the chainsaw did prove to be a remarkably efficient tool. Technological change did eliminate jobs in the industry; from a seasonal work force of nearly 40,000 in the late 1940s, the Ontario woods labour force was less than 10,000 full-time employees in 1980. And Paul Bunyan's Improved McCormick Reaper and Harvester bears an uncanny resemblance to a Short-Wood Harvester. But was Joe correct about the connection between mechanization and worker protest?

Students of the labour process have tended to polarize around the issue of what role, if any, worker resistance has played in shaping the pace or direction of technological and other changes on the job. In *Labor and Monopoly Capital*, Harry Braverman emphasizes capitalist hegemony and portrays capital's campaign for control at the point of production as a victorious march that was virtually unaffected by resistance from labour.'[2] Fellow Marxist Richard Edwards has criticized Braverman for constructing a model in which, 'Unions play no role, and there is no class struggle.'[3] Edwards maintains that the workplace is, in fact, a 'contested terrain,' where managers and workers through negotiations and conflict play a crucial part in shaping the course and consequences of managerial strategies.

A WARM RECEPTION

Overwhelmingly, woodsworkers and their union spokesmen welcomed the new logging equipment and many of the new methods. Indeed, throughout the entire post-war period, Lumber and Saw leaders gave enthusiastic support to woods mechanization. In 1948, on the eve of the introduction of substantial innovations, the union's *Ontario Timberworker* wondered about technologically induced unemployment, but then proceeded to speculate: 'Mechanization will make for a better and greater production and will reduce the amount of heavy labour in industry.' Twelve years later the *Ontario Bushworker* observed that mechanization was 'rapidly making progress and showing signs of improvements of productivity, lower costs and higher wages.' The publication even went so far as to claim some of the credit for bringing about technological change: 'The Union has done its part to bring about this change to mechanical operators. Even increasing wages slowly, put a prohibitive price tag on old types of piecework cutting operations. This no doubt helped to encourage the industry to look for better and more modern methods.' And looking back from the vantage point of the early 1980s, former Lumber and Saw leader Tulio Mior observed that Ontario workers had 'accepted new methods easily' and mechanization had been 'quite painless.'[4]

The bushworkers' widespread acceptance of mechanization can be partially explained by the timing of the transition. Radically new logging methods hit the industry in the period from the late 1940s to the late 1960s, a time of great optimism about the promise of technology. Certainly unions in North America frequently expressed concern about the connection between automation and unemployment. But they did not question the value of technology *per se*, and in most years jobless rates remained low while the economy boomed. Moreover, in comparison with manufacturing industries, mechanization came late to logging; by the post-war period, workers had perhaps become resigned to the fact that they lacked the power to prevent the spread of new techniques.

There were also more specific reasons for the general acceptance of new methods by Ontario bushworkers. In order to understand why the transition to mechanical methods was so smooth, it is necessary to examine how workers perceived the changes, how the union sought to protect its members from any adverse effects, and how the peculiar labour market of the bush affected the outcome.

Woodsworkers accepted the technological changes in large part because their earnings increased as new methods became more widely practised. The size of their wage packet had always been a key priority. Many, who were recent immigrants eager to get off to a good start in Canada, believed the new tools and methods could help ensure that their days spent in bush camps were financially rewarding. In the case of the chainsaw, almost all woodsworkers in the 1950s soon perceived that by purchasing one they could increase their output and hence their piece-work earnings. As one veteran logger recalls, even the relatively awkward powersaws of the early 1950s were 'quite a thing for us at the time ... You could do more; you could produce more and limb easier. Everybody was for it.'[5] With the arrival of slashers, skidders, and harvesters, workers and the Lumber and Saw were able to use their considerable bargaining power to ensure that wages and piece-rate earnings would not drop. According to the collective agreement, when a new piece of equipment was introduced, workers were put on a daily wage for thirty days until management and the union had negotiated an acceptable piece rate.[6] Occasionally a manager would deplore the fact that it was impossible to reduce wage rates in the new logging systems: 'Union agreements make it difficult for companies to profit from the introduction of machinery,' said one official in 1962.[7] Yet managers had to be content with indirect cost savings resulting from increased productivity levels.

Another attractive feature of pay rates during the period of mechanization was the trend towards decreasing differentials – the wage rates of the lower-paid workers rose (see Appendix 8). The wage gap between teamsters (later skidder-operators) and the better-paid cooks and blacksmiths had been narrowing for decades. In 1926 the pay rate for blacksmiths was 181.2 per cent higher than that of teamsters, and cooks received 212.3 per cent more than skidder-operators. By 1946 the percentages were 64.8 and 59.6 respectively. By 1965–6 there was only a one cent-an-hour difference between the pay rate for skidder-operators and blacksmiths; a cook received just 1.2 per cent more than a skidder-operator.

These figures suggest that over time the hierarchy of jobs in the logging industry had been decidedly flattened, an impression that is reinforced by the data in Appendix 10. By the 1980s there was only a narrow range of pay rates among monthly woods employees. The highest paid workers – the lead mechanic, welder, and carpenter – received $12.58 per hour; the lowest paid worker – the fire patrol man and general labourer – $10.01, a differential of 25.7 per cent. Unfortunately we do not have information about how many people were employed in each of the categories listed, but it is safe to assume that few worked in the very highest- or very lowest-paid positions. The great majority were equipment operators, truck drivers, and people in logging positions, where rates ranged from a low of $10.26 to a high of $11.03, a differential of just 77 cents an hour or 7.5 per cent. It is evident that in the woods industry in northern Ontario a major objective of the post-war labour movement – narrowing pay differentials – had been set.

Mechanization was also a fairly smooth process because the new logging machinery tended to alter job content in ways that bushworkers liked. Nobody mourned the elimination of bullwork. Woodsworkers had never enjoyed the sheer drudgery of back-breaking tasks such as piling; diesel and hydraulic equipment swept away such horrors. 'It is the bullwork of piling that turns most men away from this type of work,' wrote Lloyd M. Lein in 1948. He went on to say that officials from Marathon Paper had found 'since their [mechanized] units got into production, they have no trouble at all getting men to work on the slasher and are able to select the type of men they require.' In the 1960 daily journal of a foreman from Gillies Brothers operating in the Temagami area there is a revealing entry: 'Go to pole camp, inspect cut. Find it slow. Chainsaws having difficulties in procuring parts. Men [too] spoilt by work with machinery, very very unwilling and leasy to cut with swede saws, prefer to stay idle in camp missing earnings. A very sad impression.' Woodsmen were just as eager to abandon their horses. 'I'm sure a fellow operating a skidder now would not go back to skidding with horses,' declared Leon Pond, a woods superintendent from Kimberly-Clark in 1965. 'We have a list of cutters who have applied to become operators and truck drivers.'[8]

Woods mechanization also involved little outright deskilling. In many of the new jobs woodsworkers retained aspects of their traditional skills – such as sizing up a tree and planning the cut – while also acquiring highly valued mechanical skills. When interviewed at Vermillion Bay in 1981 Jake

Hildebrand said that although he had been a woodcutter for thirty years, he was still learning things on the job. Moreover, he expressed great pride in his craft. 'When you work as a team,' said Hildebrand, 'one guy will know exactly ... what the other guy's going to do. It comes with experience and ability. When they call you a professional woodcutter, they mean it. You got to have lots of ability. It's just like a carpenter. A carpenter is a professional and so is a woodcutter. You can't learn that in one day.'[9]

Harvester-operators may have found their work repetitive, closely watched, and nerve-racking, but employers rarely ran short of men willing to train as operators. When companies first introduced harvesters there was a great deal of prestige attached to operating the big, powerful machines – the muscle cars of the bush. Equipment operators and mechanics alike took advantage of the training offered by forest companies because it could also open doors in construction and mining. Employees also snapped up chances to work with harvesters because, in an effort to maximize returns from the costly equipment, companies paid top wages to operators and repairmen. However, by the time Abitibi and the Lumber and Saw signed their agreement in 1980, wheeled skidder-operators received $10.52 per hour; Koehring harvester-operators, $11.03; and class A mechanics, $12.48 (see Appendix 10). Indeed, the vast majority of production workers at Abitibi in the mechanized logging operators were paid in the range of $10.50 to $11 and the production labour force still lacked a steeply graded hierarchy.

Although woodsworkers did not welcome the particular hazards associated with mechanized operations, old-timers were only too familiar with the danger that lurked in the forest and they responded to the new hazards in a customary way. On the basis of his experiences during the 1970s, Wayne Lennox describes how loggers continued to project a machismo, devil-may-care image:

Every feller has a healthy respect for the possibility of injury or death, but among lumberjacks there is seldom any preoccupation with this aspect of the job. In fact, a certain defiance of the dangers is often apparent, a 'catch-me-if-you-can' attitude that sometimes borders on the foolish ... [The] feeling of defiant satisfaction in missing a 'close one' is evident in the tales of escape from the forest's cripplers and killers, tales that are common in conversations around lunch fires or in the camps.[10]

Perhaps this outlook helps to account for the low priority Lumber and Saw officials gave to health and safety issues. When the Ontario government drafted the regulations to be applied under the new Loggers Safety

Act of 1963, the union lobbied hard to ensure that the act would not override the less rigorous safety provisions contained in collective agreements. Union officials won assurances that there would be '*no* increase in job content for pieceworkers' who would '*not* be required to remove any more chicots, etc., than they did in the past.' The union also defeated a proposal that would have compelled loggers 'to wear any and all safety apparel furnished by the Company which could be anything from hard hats to nylon knee protectors to goggles.' In conforming with the collective agreement, only hard hats in the bush and life preservers on the river drive would be required. As in other logging regions, Ontario bushworkers resisted wearing equipment they believed was not only constraining and hence potentially dangerous, but also in conflict with their masculine self-image.[11]

The quite painless transition to new logging methods can also be explained by the favourable reception bushworkers and their union gave to the greater stability of employment that accompanied mechanization. Steady income and permanent homes had long been a demand of the labour movement in the bush. Certainly during the 1950s the union persistently urged stabilization. In 1957 the *Ontario Bushworker* attributed job instability to management's lack of planning: 'The opening and closing of camps, the maintenance of roads, which are not used for years, the construction of roads which are only used once and then left to deteriorate, are all facts which cause doubts of the efficient and economical management of bush operations. From our point of view this unstable forest production has even more serious factors than just a lack of economy: it deprives the majority of us of a stable income and a permanent home.' Looking back on the post-war period, Tulio Mior reckoned that increased stability of woods labour had been largely a result of the union's breakthrough in 1955 that brought effective seniority clauses to the collective agreement which were then backed up by the unions' persistent efforts to see them fairly applied. After 1955 workers could be reasonably certain that they would be recalled after a layoff and so they were much more likely to establish permanent homes in the north. Most men preferred to reside near operations and commute to work like people in other industries. Mior did not see this shift as a management strategy, but rather a result of a union objective that 'the companies didn't fight hard.'[12]

Certainly after the mid-1950s large numbers of woodsworkers took advantage of seniority provisions and the commuting option. By the early 1970s union members with high seniority held the great majority of jobs in commuter operations. At the Lakehead, for instance, many such members lived in Thunder Bay and worked in the garages of Abitibi's Woodlands Division located on the outskirts of the city. In all the more accessible logging operations of the north, the work force was more sedentary and older. In contrast to earlier complaints about the youthfulness of the labour force, some employers now even went so far as to complain that these commuter operations were manned by workers who were too elderly.[13]

The possibility of bushworker resistance to the technological changes of the immediate post-war years was also lessened by the nature of the woods labour market. Although jobs were lost as employers introduced labour-saving equipment, there was no need for mass layoffs. High levels of labour turn over in the late 1940s and early 1950s meant the bosses rarely had to fire employees. As a study for the federal Department of Manpower and Immigration later noted, 'the level of voluntary quits is so high in this industry that it would be possible to theoretically reduce the woods labour force to zero in the space of twelve months without laying off a single individual.'[14] The fact that fewer and fewer men were offering their labour to woods employers also removed another pressure. Because of the shrinkage of job opportunities, no doubt some men did suffer, especially those who quit in the spring, expecting to be rehired as usual in the fall. But before 1955, the year when the major forest companies began to recognize seniority, and long after 1955 in non-union operations, former employees had no direct claim on their previous job and no ready means to organize against their former employers.

During the mid-1950s the Lumber and Saw was becoming more powerful and hence more effective in dealing with some of the effects of management's mechanization strategy. The union took three approaches to protecting its members. First, it sought strong seniority provisions in the collective agreement. Not only was seniority a means of limiting the arbitrary actions of employers, it was also a way of dealing with the threat of lay-offs because of the introduction of labour-saving techniques. It is not clear why forest company negotiators agreed to the much-improved seniority provisions. Perhaps managers were merely bowing to the strength of the union – they realized that seniority would help stabilize the labour force – or they saw it as a way of warding off possible protest from redundant employees. Whatever the reason after 1955 unionized operators were obliged to inform employees who were laid off about job openings and re-hire them according to seniority.[15]

Secondly, beginning in the fall of 1960 the Lumber and Saw made a strong push to reduce the work week from forty-eight hours to forty with no loss in pay. As the *Ontario Bushworker* explained, the work force had shrunk drastically in the period 1956–60, making it essential: 'to spread the available employment out to more workers. We are not opposed to the introduction of new machines and [techniques] but we say "You must not throw so many people on the scrap heap of unemployment just because you wish to introduce these new machines." We say our workers must be protected and they must derive some benefits out of increased production because of the introduction of these machines.' Because they feared a loss of income, not all union members supported job-sharing and a shorter work week. Nevertheless, the union succeeded in winning a forty-four-hour week in 1960 and a forty-hour week a few years later, a pattern found in most Canadian industries at the time. This union achievement did not, however, reduce the hours worked by non-unionized men, most of whom continued to toil for long hours to maximize their piece-work earnings.[16]

A third Lumber and Saw approach to cushioning the effects of techno-logical change involved the demand for transfers and retraining. Even after the union won strong seniority provisions, there was no protection for those whose jobs became redundant and who lacked the skills required to perform the remaining jobs. This absence became a particularly acute problem when management introduced harvesters. Some chainsaw and skidder-operators found themselves laid off, but they did not know how to operate harvesters. Management wanted to pick men it believed were most suited to the new type of work. But the union insisted that seniority prevail. Beginning in 1967 any employee affected by new methods and equipment was guaranteed, subject to seniority provisions, a job with the company. If he or she required training then it had to be provided at the company's expense.[17]

In various ways, then, the union sought to protect bushworkers from some of the adverse effects of technological change, and thus it helped make the transition to the new methods easier.

RESISTANCE

Despite the general acceptance by woodsworkers of the new technology and methods, it would be wrong to see the process of mechanization as having been problem free. Certainly woods managers did not view it that way. They were only too aware that the success of their strategy was intimately tied up with industrial relations. In addition to the constraints the union placed on management through the clauses negotiated in collec-tive agreements, employers also had to confront initial hostilities to new equipment, the problems of persistently high quit rates and absenteeism, and a concerted attack by the Lumber and Saw on employers who sought to induce or compel woodsworkers to supply their own heavy equipment.

Like most people who are forced to change their work practices, woodsmen acted with apprehension and some hostility when new equipment appeared on the job. Even chainsaws which had been introduced by equipment salesmen rather than woods managers, were at first eyed with suspicion, especially since early models frequently broke down. A forestry student from the University of Toronto who visited the Longlac Paper operations in 1948 found that piece workers who had purchased Precision chainsaws had become disillusioned with them. Because the men could not keep their saws in working order they had lost money using the new tools.[18] In *Lumberjack* William Kurelek describes with some smugness the failure of early-model chainsaws at his northern Ontario camp:

A few students arrived, armed with new gadgets called 'power chain saws.' Flamboyantly, they gave a demonstration behind the bunkhouse to us lowly swedesawyers of how the chain ripped through a fallen log like a piece of butter. They couldn't wait to get on their strips to start making money ...

For a week or so, we swede-sawyers saw columns of blue smoke rising out of the forest where the get-rich-quick guys were at it; and we heard the terrific racket that scared all the forest creatures away ... [Those] early chain-sawyers ran into so many snags, they gave up in disgust, packed up their machines and returned to the city. A few lucky ones, like myself, inherited the partly chewed up work strips and partially filled log piles.[19]

When management first brought in new equipment such as skidders, harvesters, and processors, labour disputes sometimes erupted over the setting of fair piece rates or bonuses. At one Spruce Falls camp in 1957, for instance, a wildcat strike occurred when the company replaced horses with John Deere tractors and set piece rates at such a low level that the men were convinced their earnings would decline. The strikers insisted that the company return to horses which it did after a seven-day disruption.[20]

Management observers noted that workers, as well as their immediate supervisors, were sometimes suspicious of new harvesting equipment. Each new machine was regarded as 'just another head office toy.'[21] Ivar Fogh, chief engineer at Canadian International Paper, warned about the dangers of resistance: 'Unfortunately, but probably inevitably ... the industrial revolution in the woods has introduced a new type of change, namely one initiated by a staff specialist who often does not have the intimate contact with the working groups in the woods allowing him to fully understand their points of view and their motivations. This type of change is very apt to bring on symptoms of resistance such as persistent reductions in output, increases in numbers of "quits" and the vociferous expression of a lot of reasons why the change will not work.' It was also reported that workers paid on an incentive basis sometimes sabotaged trials of new equipment when they believed the innovation might disrupt production for even a short while. It would appear, however, that none of these protests had any serious long-term effect on the course of managerial strategy.[22]

Much more serious and costly a problem for the companies in the long run was the continuing propensity of woodsworkers to quit their jobs or take unscheduled holidays. Despite mechanization and the move towards greater labour stability, manpower shortages continued to loom large in the Ontario logging industry. C.R. Day, director of Industrial Relations Services for the Canadian Pulp and Paper Association, reported that in the fall of 1972 woodlands operators in eastern Canada had faced 'a critical shortage of manpower' and very high turn over rates, a situation he found 'totally irreconcilable with the high rate of unemployment then being experienced in Canada.'[23] Four years later the Ontario Forest Industries Association reported a manpower shortage of 3,000. Throughout the 1970s, much to the alarm of managers, woodsworkers in remote locations continued 'to move on to greener pastures at more or less regular intervals.'[24] It was not surprising that many skilled mechanics avoided jobs that required fiddling for hours with a temperamental carburettor in howling gales. And managers realized that in at least one way, mechanization had actually increased the propensity of workers to quit their jobs: the skills of heavy equipment operators, mechanics, and other tradesmen enabled them to find work in other industries.[25]

Labour's instability not only added to production costs as it had done in conventional logging systems, but in the fully mechanized operations, the workers' propensity to jump also wreaked havoc on production schedules and cost projections. In order to make harvesters a paying proposition, it was essential that they be operated continuously. Downtime costs ran very high and production costs rose dramatically when there were disruptions. The continual training of new employees, as well as equipment damage caused by greenhorns, also added to management's problems. In 1971 G.K. Seed, logging development engineer at Great Lakes Paper, argued: 'Investment in woods equipment has reached such proportions that operations can't be stopped without serious loss. Further, the job has become so skill demanding that it is difficult to satisfy operational requirements through substitution. It is essential to minimize absenteeism.'[26]

Managers perceived, however, that eliminating high turn-over and absentee rates among loggers in isolated locales would be extremely difficult. Most experienced men simply preferred to be closer to the bright lights. A sociologist working for the industry told woods officials that the kind of men who were attracted to such logging jobs found satisfaction in changing jobs frequently. In a study based on interviews with forest workers in British Columbia Philip Cottell observed: 'Security for these men lay in their mobility itself ... They took pride in the portability and variety of their skills, and ability to "do anything" and be a "jack of all trades". It was frequently said that: "I could quit here Friday night and have another job to go to Monday morning".' Cottell concluded there were psychological barriers to stabilizing the woods work force. Whether or not his analysis was correct, there can be no doubt that geographical isolation cushioned loggers from job market competition, thus enabling them to continue with their customary habits.[27]

This behaviour and the migration of trained woods labour to other industries, acted as a constraint on managers who admitted that harvesters were therefore neither as productive nor as reliable as management had hoped. Because of the high quit rates, actual costs ran far above those projected by employers. Consequently, to ensure a continuous supply of wood to the mills, managers found it was best to deploy skidders as well as harvesters. Inadvertently, then, the behaviour of bushworkers had limited the freedom of management to deploy the labour-saving technology it might otherwise have preferred. Woodsworkers had helped preserve jobs and keep open the choice between working with skidders or harvesters. They played a crucial part in shaping the direction and pace of innovation in the Ontario forest industry.

In contrast to this instance of unwitting worker resistance to management's tactics, opposition to owner-operated skidders amounted to a definite counter-offensive. When Ontario's forest employers began introducing skidders in the mid-1950s, some firms encouraged their employees to purchase their own machines. The principle was familiar to bushworkers; for decades a small proportion of teamsters had brought their own horses to the logging camps, and in the 1950s nearly all Ontario loggers purchased their own chainsaws. By permitting employees to purchase skidders, some woods managers hoped that their firms could avoid the large outlays of capital needed to mechanize skidding operations. And as in the case of temperamental chainsaws, management expected owner-operators would take greater care to maintain their skidders and work harder to maximize their returns. By opting for owner-operators, companies could avoid paying most employee benefits, a substantial saving. In 1971 it was estimated that fringe benefits cost between 17.1 and 22.3 per cent of the woods payroll.[28]

In order to make owner-operating an attractive proposition, companies set special, higher piece-rates for such employees. The higher rates proved appealing to many forest workers, some of whom were able to arrange bank loans to help finance the purchase of the costly new vehicles. In non-unionized lumbering operations bosses insisted that skidder-operators either buy or rent their machines. But because of the Lumber and Saw's opposition, until the late 1970s there were almost no owner-operated skidders in the pulpwood sector nor in the larger sawlog operations.

The union's resistance to owner-operating dates from the mid-1950s, when numerous union members working in Ontario pulpwood operations began to purchase skidders. The Lumber and Saw immediately warned members of the dangers of such a system and fought it through collective bargaining. In April 1956, for example, the *Ontario Bushworker* reported that members employed by the St Lawrence Corporation at Beardmore had purchased John Deere tractors, a development that presented 'a problem to the men who bought them and to all others of the Union.' Consequently, union leaders prevented members from using their equipment. A few months later the Northern Ontario District Council of the Lumber and Saw issued a statement explaining the union's position. According to the council, skidder or tractor owners discriminated against their fellow workers in several ways. First, since tractor skidding was new to many companies and 'nobody knew how they were going to turn out, the Companies obligingly gave these tractor owners the better bush.' Other employees had to work in poor stands where their productivity, and their piece-work earnings, suffered. Secondly, since the owners invested 'a substantial amount of money in their equipment and owe[d] several dozen payments, in most cases, they expect to be hired first and laid off last, irrespective of their seniority.' Members with higher seniority would then be 'put out of work in the most discriminating way possible.' Thirdly, the council maintained that in labour negotiations, the companies would say owner-operators ' "are already earning so much money, how come you are still looking for a wage increase?" The companies purposely overlook the point that these owners invested thousands of dollars in order to earn a few bucks more.' In the end, employees would have an added weapon to keep down the wage rates of ordinary employees.[29]

Beginning in 1958, the Lumber and Saw was able to use its leverage to negotiate contract clauses prohibiting the spread of owner-operating. In subsequent years forest firms occasionally tried to re-introduce the practice in unionized operations. Spruce Falls and Kimberly-Clark, for instance, tried to bring about a return to owner-operating in 1959, but they backed down when the union threatened to strike during the short, winter hauling season.[30] Only at the Ontario and Minnesota Pulp and Paper Company did the Lumber and Saw fail to wipe out owner-operating.

Throughout the late 1950s, the union had found Ontario and Minnesota a particularly tough opponent. And in 1959 the company used its power as the only major employer in a large district of northwestern Ontario to force the union to allow employees who had already owned skidders to continue to operate them on company limits. According to Lumber and Saw sources, the understanding was that when these owner-operators resigned or retired, they would be replaced by men who could operate company-owned equipment. Since the owner-operators were union members, Lumber and Saw negotiators did not see the situation as dangerous. And indeed, for a number of years the company lived up to the agreement.[31]

In 1978, however, Ontario and Minnesota abruptly changed its policy on skidder ownership. According to union leader Tulio Mior, new executives with new ideas arrived at the firm in the 1970s. They were appointed by the top executives of Boise Cascade Corporation, which in 1965 had purchased the company's mills and timber leases in Ontario. (In late 1978 the name of the operations in Ontario was changed to Boise Cascade, Canada, Ltd, a wholly owned subsidiary of the giant, u.s.-based multinational forest firm which had extensive holdings in North, South, and Central America.)[32] In 1978 Ontario woods managers for Boise, perhaps inspired by the success of owner-operating in the firm's holdings outside the province, began to encourage some of its employees in the Fort Frances area to purchase the company's skidders. Initially the company wanted some unionized woods employees on day wages and some working as owner-operators on piece work.

Boise officials insisted that the firm had to improve its competitive position and that owner-operating offered 'the only way around costs of harvesting ... which [were] the highest in North America.[33] Certainly in the late 1970s woods managers were complaining about high wages and costs in Ontario. While mechanization had enabled the province's pulp producers to remain competitive during the 1950s and 1960s, by the late 1970s Ontario operators seemed to be reaching the outer limits of cost-saving mechanical substitutes. Other producing regions in North America were catching up in the mechanization field. Thus, even though Reed Paper had failed in a 1976 bid to introduce owner-operating to its north-western Ontario operations, Boise officials thought they might do better.[34] After all, Boise's dominance of the labour market in the Kenora and Fort Frances areas gave it unusual leverage. It also had an advantage because of the exceptional 1959 contract clause which permitted some owner-opera-tors.

On 15 May 1978 Boise announced that it was offering employees in the Fort Frances area the opportunity to purchase company-owned skidders. Lumber and Saw leaders immediately voiced their opposition, informing the company that this was a violation of the collective agreement and warning members not to be 'bamboozled' by the spokesmen who were saying employees would increase their annual incomes by at least $10,000. All employees except Larry Andershuk abandoned plans to purchase equipment. In reply to Andershuk's purchase and the company's continu-ing attempts to sell its machines, Boise's employees began walking off the job on 5 July. Soon the strikers numbered 140 and the firm's logging operations were completely shut down. In October the strike spread to the Kenora operation.[35]

Boise asked the Ontario Labour Relations Board to rule the strike illegal. In a subsequent hearing, union leaders contended that the dispute was, in fact, a lockout, for Boise had broken the agreement by expanding the number of owner-operators, and by threatening employees who refused to purchase equipment. The board found that, while it was not obvious whether Boise had the right to increase the number of owner-operators during the life of the equipment, the strike was indeed illegal.[37] Union members, however, felt strongly enough about the issue that they contin-ued their strike. The company filed contempt charges against 100 of the strikers. They were found guilty in the Ontario Supreme Court on 26 July and fined $50 each, plus $25 for each additional day they remained off the job. Shortly thereafter the sheriff at Fort Frances began serving writs to every bank in the area ordering the withdrawal of $150 from the bank accounts of about fifty strikers. The determination of both parties became obvious, and so began the months of bitter confrontation. Before long the small Fort Frances detachment of Ontario Provincial Police was expanded to 141 men. In January 1981 on the basis of evidence accumulated during raids on offices, homes, and from wire-taps, the police charged twelve unionists with conspiracy to commit mischief, which the police said was related to about $2,000,000 in property damage. In the mean time, the small town of Fort Frances was torn apart by a battle which one journalist likened to 'a civil war in that brothers and cousins [found] themselves on opposing sides.'[37]

Throughout the dispute Boise tried to convince its employees that purchasing company skidders and switching to piece work were attractive financial propositions. Not only would the company's competitive position be improved by the supposedly greater efficiency of piece workers but employees would make an average of $32,000 annually instead of $22,000. Furthermore, employees could buy the used skidders at $6,000, a price far below the cost of a brand new machine. But there were stipulations: during the first year the complete cost of the skidders would have to be paid; the machines could be used only on Boise's operations; and they could not be sold.[38]

The union dubbed this a disastrous offer that would render employees virtual 'slaves to their machines.' According to the Lumber and Saw, the company's skidders were old and in need of constant repair which would cost owner-operators a great deal of time and money. In turn, these expenses would eat into supposedly increased earnings, as well as precious leisure time. After a year the used skidders would be irreparable, and each operator would have to purchase a new machine at a cost of about $55,000. The owner-operator would also have to buy a powersaw, fuel tank, and probably a truck – altogether a huge financial outlay requiring bank loans. While payments might be made as long as work was steady and interest charges not too onerous, there was no guarantee that such conditions would prevail. If Boise laid off the workers, a real possibility given changing demands for pulpwood, then the owner would have to find other work. This could be costly if the skidder had to be trucked a long distance. If no work could be found, or when an employee went on strike, he would have to maintain his bank payments or risk losing his skidder. Houses used as collateral might also be lost. Naturally, when confronted with the possibility of losing his investment and his home, a worker would hesitate to exercise his legal right to strike. In the final analysis, the Lumber and Saw perceived Boise's strategy as an attack on the union itself. While owner-operators as well as regular employees would be union members, their interests would conflict. Boise could play one group off against the other: divide and conquer was the corporation's implicit strategy.[39]

By taking on the Lumber and Saw on this issue, Boise undoubtedly encountered stronger opposition than it expected from such a small labour organization. It was more than a year before operations were stabilized, another year before the last pickets packed up, and the bitterness lingered much longer. According to Boise Canada president, H.W. Sherman, at the end of the battle 'there were no winners. In fact everyone lost and lost a great deal.' This, of course, was a public relations ploy – part of an attempt to convince employees that 'confrontation solves nothing.'[40] The company thoroughly succeeded in its strategy of undermining the union, though not in the manner planned. Rather than having two groups of workers to play off against each other, Boise ended up hiring only owner-operators on a contract basis. It eliminated the union from its woodlands.

In the early 1980s it was not yet clear whether other major companies would attempt to follow Boise's move to owner-operating. Managers had to consider the costs of taking on the feisty Lumber and Saw. Although the union lost the strike, it had fought hard and long, utterly disrupting production for months and souring labour relations throughout the company's operations for a much longer period.[41] Woodlands officials also had to assess carefully whether owner-operators could provide an assured source of wood supply to their mills. If too many owner-operators were driven out of business by high interest rates and erratic employment, then the wood supply might be endangered. In addition, some woods managers preferred the status quo because they feared that owner-operating would disrupt established management practices.[42]

Ontario woodsworkers were by no means alone in facing this kind of aggressive employer strategy. In the harder economic times of the 1970s, contracting out became a favourite management tactic for reducing costs and undercutting union power.[43] Within the resource sector, the essentials of owner-operating have been widely applied, not only in the forest but also in fishing. In his discussion of the Atlantic coastal fisheries, Wallace Clement points to the importance of 'dependent commodity production,' where the fisherman works independently, in control of his labour power and owning his own fishing gear, and yet he is dependent on loans and on a non-competitive processing firm to purchase his catch. This system is promoted because 'it can ensure a source of produce yet absolve capital from the risks of weather, natural disaster, or stock depletion; the need to invest (without guaranteed returns through interest) in the first stage of production; and, most important, the requirement to supervise labour. The final point includes the cost of direct supervision, recruitment of a labour force, development of skills and training, and reliance on producers to "exploit" themselves and their families by working long hours and engaging in intensified labour.'[44] There are obvious parallels between the Atlantic fisheries and Ontario logging, where some businessmen have also sought to avoid the high risks associated with the weather and to minimize capital expenditures and the problem of supervising a dispersed work force.

CAPITALIST HEGEMONY OR CONTESTED TERRAIN?

By the time the Boise strike had ground to a halt in the fall of 1979, it was evident that the responses of bushworkers to post-war technological change were complex. Loggers and their union expressed enthusiasm for most of the new machines and methods, not only because they were part of a North American culture that celebrated the triumphs of technology, but also because in the logging industry, mechanization appeared to bring higher wages, lighter, steadier work, and portable new skills. Yet woodsworkers also forced managers to adjust their plans. By insisting on seniority clauses, retraining provisions, and a reduced work week, the Lumber and Saw gained concessions from the corporations and thus helped to establish rules and structures that gave some protection to its members. On the job, workers and even supervisors acted with initial hostility to some new developments, forcing managers to find different ways to handle the introduction of new techniques and operating methods. Moreover, significant numbers of bushworkers continued to quit or absent themselves from their jobs. Such behaviour increased production costs, particularly in the most capital-intensive operations, and it had a sobering effect on those managers advocating a major transition to harvesters and other pieces of huge equipment. Furthermore, the Lumber and Saw steadfastly resisted the attempts by some employers to introduce owner-operating.

Who, then, has the more appropriate model for describing the process of technological change in Ontario logging: Braverman, who stresses management's hegemony, or Edwards, who emphasizes the role of workers in resisting and reshaping the pace and direction of labour-process transformation? Since there is abundant evidence to show that the behaviour of woodsworkers impeded management's freedom to proceed with innovations in preferred ways, it is apparent that the model proposed by Edwards more accurately describes the overall pattern in the Ontario woods. However, the temptation to exaggerate the power of workers to influence developments must be resisted. For the most part, technology had been developed or introduced by corporate executives with corporate objectives in mind. Management, though impeded by worker resistance, had pursued its strategy with considerable success. Woodsworkers and their union had never even so much as demanded, much less won, a fundamental restructuring of the labour process. Indeed, they had welcomed most of the changes. Contrary to the 1918 predictions of Lumberjack Joe, woods mechanization had not produced 'a fresh crop of revolutionary industrial unionists.'

Conclusion

In the boom years at the turn of the twentieth century, increasing numbers of investors and politicians, prospectors and miners, and logging operators and woodsworkers began to discover new opportunities in northern Ontario's rich storehouse of natural resources. The railway mania of the early 1900s had opened vast new territories to the woodsman's axe. New pulping and papermaking technologies and a growing demand for newsprint encouraged entrepreneurs to develop the vast boreal forests. They breathed new life into Canada's venerable timber industry.

Although much was changing in the New Ontario when twentieth-century operators came to exploit the northern woodlands, they conducted their logging campaigns along traditional lines – relying heavily on labour-intensive, conventional logging methods. Simple tools and equipment – axes and handsaws, canthooks and sleighs – were powered by the muscles of men and horses. Strong backs and specialized skills learned on the job were the major attributes of the armies of men who invaded the woods each autumn. In assembling their crews, woods employers enjoyed the advantage of being able to draw on large numbers of out-of-work immigrant sojourners from construction projects, countless cash-hungry farmers and their sons and hired hands, and thousands of professional bushmen who, each September, shouldered axe and saw, as part of the seasonal rhythm of their working lives. Together these men formed a highly unstable labour force, not only because the work was seasonal, but also because so many bushmen jumped their jobs in search of better conditions or to blow off steam. Employers tried to entice steady, productive workers to their camps by providing first-rate meals. But few operators paid attention to the standards of comfort and cleanliness in their camps, building crude, temporary structures intended to be used only as long as the timber held out within walking distance of the site.

Before the end of World War II the attempts of various groups to improve or change logging methods and camp conditions proved largely unsuccessful. Social reformers, whether from Frontier College or the public health department, failed to effect a complete transformation of camp conditions and frontier life. Woods managers, troubled by the primitiveness of logging techniques, banded together in the Woodlands Section of the Canadian Pulp and Paper Association to discover mechanical improvements over hand and horse. But they made little headway in finding substitutes adequate for the freezing temperatures and rough country of northern Ontario. Bushworkers, too, banded together, forming unions that struggled for better pay and conditions on the job. They fought dozens of strikes under the direction of Finnish radicals, but seldom won permanent advances.

All of this changed drastically in the two decades following World War II. The woodsworkers' union won recognition from most major employers in the north. Incomes increased sharply. Employers built more attractive camps complete with recreational facilities. And many men commuted to work from northern towns and cities. More dramatic still, a technological cyclone swept through the industry. Equipment manufacturers and woodlands departments devised new logging tools and vehicles powered by hydraulic pumps and internal-combustion engines. Management reorganized work routines in an effort to increase productivity in their now more capital-intensive logging operations. A quarter century after the war, the woodsworker of the 1940s would have felt thoroughly lost amid the deafening roar of feller-bunchers, forwarders, and mobile slashers.

In examining and explaining these transformations, this book has drawn upon literature from several fields and sought to enhance our understanding of such matters as the regional development of northern Ontario, Canadian labour history, and changes in the labour process.

In important respects, the woodsworkers' transition mirrors wider transformations in the development of the regional history of northern Ontario. The lumberjack has long helped to define the image of the north; a tough, masculine outdoorsman, experienced in the real, natural world, he is the quintessential northerner. Like workers from other popularly celebrated occupations, the early bushworker was a bunkhouseman. His mobility, and the ephemeral woods camp, had their parallels in the railway navvies with their box-car dwellings and in fortune-seeking miners with their temporary shacks at the booming settlements of Cobalt, Elk Lake, and Gowganda. Their rollicking, rootless way of life became a dominant theme in early regional development. Yet these sojourners had only a limited impact on the communities of the north. Once the trees had been cut, the tracks repaired, or the mother-lode exhausted, the bunkhousemen moved on. Eventually this way of life faded into the shadows. By the 1960s woodsworkers were settling down and commuting loggers became permanent members of northern towns and active contributors to community life. In the course of the past half-century, the north generally has moved well beyond its frontier past. Expressing pride in his adopted region, historian Matt Bray of Laurentian University writes:

Today Northern Ontario is a fully defined place populated by men and women of diverse ethnic origins who are genuine northerners, either by birth or adoption. The transitional phases of unsettled immigrants shifting from one area to another or leaving altogether have ended. Northerners are now born, raised, and educated from kindergarten to community college or university graduation in both of Canada's official languages. They enter a work force that has become infinitely more varied and complex, and they enjoy theatre, the arts, and other cultural activities as well as a wide range of outdoor recreational opportunities, all without leaving the north.[1]

In addition to revealing something of the regional development of the north, this study has also sought to fill in a neglected chapter in Canadian labour history. It demonstrates the possibilities for reconstructing the working experiences and way of life of one group among the so-called unskilled. By such an exercise we can see that the wide range of tasks performed by this particular group of unskilled workers required a great deal of technical expertise and knowledge. In noting the prevalence of jumping and the employers' attempts to stabilize their work forces, we glimpse but one part of a widespread pattern of protest in unorganized industries. We also explore an aspect of class relations that takes place independent of, or even in the absence of, articulate working-class leaders with a strategy for change.

The institutional labour history of Ontario bushworkers falls into two periods. During the first phase, which lasted from World War I to early 1935, radical Finnish immigrants took the lead in organizing unions that sought not only to improve pay and conditions but also to build mass support for revolutionary change. In a long series of bitter confrontations with employers, the unionists seldom won victories. Worker solidarity was less than complete and the powerful employers remained absolutely determined to resist the demands of a radical union leadership which they believed was dangerous and did not represent the membership. Apart from sending police into picket-line battles, the government played little part in these turbulent labour relations. During the second phase, which began in 1935 with the Communists' decision to move into affiliates of the American Federation of Labor, the union focused on establishing collective-bargaining and relying on it to bring about higher pay rates, job security, and fairer treatment for members. In this period the government took a much more active part, vigorously promoting the transition to collective bargaining. Although labour historians have tended to ignore the provincial Industrial Standards Act of 1935 and the work of the federal War Labour Board, in the logging industry these measures were crucial in bringing the parties together to negotiate pay and other matters. Full-scale bargaining came only in 1946 when most major woods employers signed a central collective agreement for the first time. Thereafter the Lumber and Saw won significant advances in wages, higher camp standards, union security, seniority provisions, and a system of timber classification that eliminated some of the abuses of former days.

The experience of the Ontario bushworkers' union both parallels and diverges from patterns in other industries. Ethnic and immigrant cohesiveness laid a base for unionism in the logging sector as it did in other industries, such as the garment trade, where Jews were crucial, or coal mining in Cape Breton, where Scots played a pivotal role. Radicals and union leaders in all these industries shrewdly perceived that workers could be mobilized through their ethnic community contacts, and that the immigrants' sense of ethnic 'fellow-feeling' could contribute towards the development of union or class consciousness. In company with other so-called unskilled workers, the Ontario bushworkers faced enormous structural hurdles in their struggle to win recognition. Foremost among their problems was the relative ease with which employers could find replacements for striking employees, a factor that long delayed union recognition. In the United States, industrial unionists made significant progress in the mid-1930s during the era of the New Deal, but the birth of a powerful industrial union movement in Canada had to await World War II. With the coming of wartime militancy and the new government labour policies of the mid-1940s, Ontario's organized bushworkers triumphed at last. Their achievement of formal collective bargaining coincided with breakthroughs in many other Canadian industries.

Woodsworkers in Ontario broke with dominant patterns, however, when they chose to adhere to a peculiar union structure. Outside the crafts, most workers built their own industrial unions. Loggers in British Columbia and the Pacific northwest broke away from the Lumber and

Sawmill Workers Union to form the International Woodworkers of America, an affiliate of the Congress of Industrial Organizations. But Ontario bushworkers remained in their separate industrial-based locals within the broader structure of a craft union, the United Brotherhood of Carpenters and Joiners, itself an affiliate of the craft-dominated American Federation of Labor and the Trades and Labour Congress of Canada. The province's radical Lumber and Saw leaders made strange bedfellows with the self-consciously conservative, craft-union officials of the parent organization; the Brotherhood's expulsion of the leftists in 1951 was virtually inevitable during the Cold War. Whether their fate would have been any different in an industrial union is a moot point, the left-wing leadership of British Columbia's International Woodworkers of America was also ousted. Under non-Communist officers, Lumber and Saw locals in northern Ontario gained a reasonable degree of autonomy within the Brotherhood, perhaps because the loggers' interests were so remote from the concerns of the craft-minded executive of the International. The province's woodsworker had found a suitable, though unusual, place in the labour movement.

Throughout this book, the transition in work processes has held centre stage. In part, this study is intended as a critique of labour-process analysts who have been tempted to generalize too widely about a management's deskilling strategy. The analysts are too ready to posit a model that pits capitalists armed with a plan to undermine worker autonomy against employees who consciously resist such a program. It is important to look closely at the intentions of those who introduced new techniques. At the most immediate level, the motivations of innovators may vary widely. In the case of the gasoline chainsaw, management did little to encourage its adoption; equipment salesmen jumped at a market opportunity among cutters who were eager to increase their piece-rate incomes. But woods managers did give priority to the development of the skidder because the slow pace of the horse had created a bottleneck between the mechanized cutting and hauling operations. Only the efforts to develop fully mechanized logging systems represent an attempt by managers to adopt pace-setting technology based on the automated assembly line. There is, however, a secondary level at which all these changes can be assessed, and from this perspective a clear, overall pattern to mechanization can be discerned. After World War II, rising labour costs, associated with reductions in labour supply and the growing leverage of workers in the industry, threatened the success of firms during the period of booming product markets. The over-riding concern of woods managers was to halt the spiral of labour costs. As a motivating factor behind the drive towards mechanization, deskilling was very much in the background.

At the same time it is important to distinguish between the intentions of innovators and the results of their activities. An equipment-development engineer may give little thought to reducing worker autonomy on the job, but his design may incidentally have such an effect. When engineers set out to design efficient skidders, they were preoccupied with maximizing manoeuvrability and traction. Nevertheless, effective implementation of the new equipment involved a shift towards team work and hence a partial erosion of worker independence on the job.

In assessing transformations of work processes, it is also imperative to appreciate the various forms that worker resistance can take. The most obvious, of course, are the concerted campaigns of unions to block management plans for change. The Lumber and Sawmill Workers Union fought long and hard against attempts to introduce or expand owner-operated skidders because union leaders perceived them as an attempt to undercut the power of their organization. Less readily apparent are patterns of worker behaviour that are not intended as outright resistance. On remote logging sites, the high quit rates of equipment operators undermined the cost-saving purposes of the big new equipment of the 1970s. Unwittingly woodsworkers checked the expanded use of Short-Wood Harvesters. This form of resistance was no less powerful for being unintentional.

The findings presented here reinforce Stephen Wood's point that 'deskilling ... must be located in a context which is far broader than Taylorism, and certainly more complex than a straight managerial conspiracy.'[2] A central contention of the present study is that management decisions regarding the choice of technique and the organization of work are the result of a complex, historical process of negotiation with labour; these negotiations are, in turn, profoundly shaped by labour and product markets, as well as by the wider socio-economic climate, and they take place within particular material environments.

The importance of the material environment is especially clear in the case of resource industries. It proved exceedingly difficult to find appropriate techniques for logging in the north, with its changing seasons, bitter winter temperatures, and rugged terrain. Ideally, equipment needed to have sufficient flotation to travel on spongy muskeg and yet be durable enough to withstand the severe jolts experienced in moving across rock outcroppings. Forest conditions also created difficulties for managers eager to supervise woodsmen closely. In order to overcome this problem, and that of predicting and stabilizing costs in an outdoor environment, woods managers turned to piece-rate payment systems and owner-operating.

These kinds of managerial problems and attempted solutions form part of a wider pattern in the resource sector. Whether it is mining companies trying to devise equipment suitable for varying thicknesses of ore bodies or fish-processing firms attempting to control the cost of their raw products, nature has intervened, creating challenges for managers and prompting certain types of solutions. Historians have long recognized the importance to Canadian development of the resource sector, but they have not yet fully appreciated the consequences of this dominance for patterns of social development at the workplace. Factors related to the natural environment and to the characteristics of the staple itself have resulted in late mechanization, continuing limitations on management's control over workers, and a tendency to opt for incentives such as piece rates or some form of 'dependent commodity production,' along the lines of owner-operating. Thus Canada, a country heavily dependent on resource exploitation, has experienced work-related transformations in ways that differ from countries where the manufacturing sector dominates.

Because the historian is preoccupied with change, with laying bear the dynamics of past developments, there is a strong temptation to exaggerate the extent of transition and underplay continuities. In the case of the social history of Ontario's logging industry, that temptation is certainly great because the historian must rely on documents provided by men living through the dizzying changes – commentators who highlighted the breaks from the past. At the World Forestry Congress in 1966, C. Ross Silversides, then director of Woodlands Development at Abitibi, reflected on the process of change sweeping through Canada's woodlands: 'With the introduction of increased mechanization into the logging industry there will be profound changes with regard to the labour force involved. The changes are of many kinds and will have far reaching effects. Karl Marx himself wrote "Social relations are closely bound up with production processes. In acquiring new productive processes, men change their mode of production and in changing their mode of production they change their ways of earning a living – they change all their social relations".'[3] Yet in the end, the sweeping technological changes that management introduced into the bush did not thoroughly alter social relations. New techniques certainly did not herald a new era of workers' control of production. Innovations were introduced by managers to meet corporate objectives. Bosses remained bosses and bushworkers remained bush-workers. Certainly seasonal jobs had been superseded by more permanent employment opportunities. Bullwork gave way to machine operating – though the dangers and machismo remained. Crude camps were replaced by far more comfortable lodgings or home life. And the boss's authority was now tempered by the union. These developments were the result – though by no means the end result – of the continually evolving relationship between bushworkers and their bosses.

Appendix 1

Primary forest products in Ontario

		1906	1926	1936
Sawlogs				
Pine	FBM	674,800,465	192,810,559	109,920,800
Other	FBM	66,945,987	130,223,500	33,189,959
Boom and dimension timber				
Pine	FBM	29,517,482	7,499,079	3,614,500
Other	FBM	8,507,487	2,023,630	2,469,083
Square timber				
Pine	Pieces	11,851	N/A	N/A
Other	Pieces	267	N/A	N/A
Waney pine	Pieces	N/A	3,307	N/A
Pile timber	FBM	648,609	762,256	480,013
Cord Wood				
Hardwood	Cords	5,458	6,947	28,298
Softwood	Cords	14,085	49,526	105,552
Tan bark	Cords	12,270	3,111	40
Railway ties	Pieces	1,740,442	1,827,496	753,077
Posts	Cords	1,805	Pieces 83,009	73,955
Telegraph poles	Pieces	8,094	13,471	N/A
Shingle bolts	Cords	9	N/A	N/A
Head bolts	Cords	4,352	N/A	N/A
Car stakes	Pieces	591	N/A	22,209
Pulpwood	Cords	84,961	642,774	604,587
Lagging	Pieces	N/A	2,171	200

		1956	1966
Logs and bolts	1,000 FBM	830,944	496,401
Pulpwood	Cords	3,740,811	4,574,961
Fuelwood	Cords	719,104	747
Poles and piling	Number	99,037	847
Round mining timber	Cords	16,450	8,307
Fence posts	Number	978,950	164,753
Fence rails	Number	66,000	N/A
Wood for charcoal	Cords	17,000	N/A

SOURCE: Ontario, Department of Lands and Forest, Appendix, 'Statement of Timber,' *Annual Reports* 1906, 1926, 1936; Canada, Statistics Canada, *Logging*, 'Estimates of Forest Production, by Products and by Provinces' 1956, 1966

Appendix 2

Comparison of primary forest production between Ontario and Canada, 1925–80

Year	Ontario (A)	Canada (B)	A as a percentage of B
1925	581,452	2,227,785	26.1
1930	581,369	2,477,787	23.5
1935	408,226	1,933,450	21.1
1940	466,226	2,664,365	17.5
1945	453,756	2,692,200	16.8
1950	516,361	3,023,465	17.1
1955	542,031	3,280,020	16.5
1960	541,329	3,293,311	16.4
1965	567,131	3,660,669	15.5
1970	593,315	4,287,890	13.8
1975	502,000	4,070,470	12.3
1980	591,279	3,804,343	15.5

SOURCE: Statistics Canada, *Canadian Forestry Statistics, revised 1974*; Statistics Canada, *Logging 1975*, and *Logging 1980*

Appendix 3

Reported number of camps and number of woods employees living in camps, 1919–20, 1961–62

Season	Camps	Employees
1919–20	528	22,447
1920–1	796	21,370
1921–2	N/A	N/A
1922–3	596	28,834
1923–4	751	28,598
1924–5	673	31,387
1925–6	N/A	N/A
1926–7	504	24,516
1927–8	425	17,047
1928–9	440	21,000
1929–30	250	13,000
1930–1	N/A	N/A
1931–2	N/A	N/A
1932–3	214	4,825
1933–4	282	11,184
1934–5	406	14,550
1935–6	410	17,543
1936–7	557	23,140
1937–8	382	28,148
1938–9	385	21,832
1939–40	339	22,947
1940–1	431	28,857
1941–2	548	31,558
1942–3	535	28,883
1943–4	446	20,711

Season	Camps	Employees
1944-5	527	21,728
1945-6	627	23,471
1946-7	640	32,661
1947-8	720	37,466
1948-9	710	37,578
1949-50	700	33,053
1950-1	598	29,450
1951-2	712	37,299
1952-3	624	34,642
1953-4	518	25,232
1954-5	482	25,313
1955-6	462	24,115
1956-7	451	23,914
1957-8	420	21,404
1958-9	284	16,684
1959-60	337	16,110
1960-1	268	16,411
1961-2	301	15,360

SOURCE: Ontario, Department of Health, *Annual Report*, 1919-31, 1934-63; Department of Lands and Forests, *Annual Report*, 1932-6

Note: Declining numbers in the 1950s and 1960s indicate both a fall in the numbers actually employed and the trend towards commuter operations which reduced the number of men living in camps.

Appendix 4

Production workers in the logging industry, 1963–80

Year	Number of production and related workers		Man-hours ('000)	
	Ontario	Canada	Ontario	Canada
1963	9,562	53,921	23,186	123,146
1964	9,599	55,882	23,250	127,359
1965	9,595	53,992	23,244	122,571
1966	9,662	54,317	23,384	123,650
1967	8,969	51,004	21,718	115,876
1968	7,853	45,187	19,005	102,000
1969	8,487	46,847	20,500	104,946
1970	8,246	44,814	19,635	100,235
1971	6,900	40,126	16,080	88,740
1972	6,598	40,363	15,861	89,599
1973	7,677	49,573	17,292	105,082
1974	8,225	50,733	18,543	108,321
1975	6,616	45,533	14,865	97,662
1976	6,307	42,185	12,802	83,917
1977	7,035	41,804	14,324	83,192
1978	8,099	45,944	16,562	91,554
1979	8,096	48,301	16,572	96,238
1980	8,015	45,826	16,692	90,653

SOURCE: Canada, Statistics Canada, *Logging* 1965–80

Note: A note in the original source states: 'large quantities of wood are produced in operations that do not qualify as "establishments" (accounting units) belonging to the "logging industry" as defined in the revised Standard Industrial Classification. Thus the "logging industry" does not include: 1. Logging operations conducted by sawmill establishments (not maintaining separate records for their logging operations); 2. farm woodlot operations; 3. any logging operations producing less than 60 M cu. ft. per annum.' *Logging* 1965 (Ottawa 1967) 5. The total number of production workers actually employed would have been somewhat higher than these figures indicate. A study by the Ontario Ministry of Natural Resources estimated that actual woods employment in 1978 was 9,569 (*The Forest Industry in the Economy of Ontario* [Toronto 1981] Table 2).

Appendix 5

Monthly logging wages for choppers in Ontario, 1911–20

Year	Example 1 ($)	Example 2 ($)
1911	30–35	32
1912	35	35
1913	33	35
1914	300	26–28
1915	28	20–24
1916	40	35–40
1917	50	50
1918	50	60
1919	60	65
1920	75	75

SOURCE: Canada, Department of Labour, *Wages and Hours of Labour in Canada*, Report no. 1 (Ottawa 1921)

Appendix 6

Logging wages in Ontario, 1921–52

Year	Choppers/ sawyers ($)	Blacksmiths ($)	Cooks ($)	Teamsters ($)	General hands ($)	River drivers ($)
1921	70	125	125	70–75	60	65–70
1922	26–32	85	100	26–32	26–32	40–45
1923	35–40	90	90–100	35	35	60
1924	40–45	90	100–125	45–50	45	65
1925	30–35	100	100	30–35	30	50
1926	35–40	90	100	30–35	26–30	40–50
1927	35–40	75–85	100	35	30–32	40–50
1928	35	80	100	35	30–35	40–50
1929	35	75–100	100	35–40	30–35	50
1930	35	100	90–100	38	26–32	40–50
1931	26–30	75	90	30	22–25	40
1931–2	24	70	75	24	22	40
1932–3	N/A	N/A	60	24–35	22	30
1933–4	30–35	75	75	36	35	30
1935	35	75	75–90	35–40	N/A	48
1936	30	75	100	30	N/A	58
1936–7	35–38	75	75–100	45	N/A	2.75[1]
1937–8	45	75	100	42–45	N/A	2.75[1]
1938–9	42.50	75	100	45	N/A	3.00[1]
1939–40	45	85	100	50	N/A	3.00[1]
1940–1	50–55	N/A	N/A	55	N/A	N/A
1943	3.29[1]	4.08[1]	3.76[1]	2.67[1]	2.53[1]	3.81[1]
1944	2.88[1]	4.63[1]	4.22[1]	2.90[1]	2.88[1]	3.84[1]

Year	Choppers/ sawyers ($)	Blacksmiths ($)	Cooks ($)	Teamsters ($)	General hands ($)	River drivers ($)
1945	3.22[1]	5.06[1]	4.90[1]	3.08[1]	2.88[1]	3.92[1]
1946	3.36[1]	5.53[1]	5.13[1]	3.07[1]	N/A	4.07[1]
1947	3.87[1]	5.55[1]	5.03[1]	3.93[1]	N/A	5.03[1]
1948	7.95[2]	6.05[1]	5.62[1]	10.00[3]	N/A	5.19[1]
1949	9.69[3]	6.35[1]	5.71[1]	10.66[3]	N/A	5.02[1]
1950	7.89[2]	6.81[1]	6.59[1]	N/A	N/A	7.44[4]
1951	9.41[3]	6.93[1]	6.52[1]	N/A	N/A	N/A
1952	11.44[3]	7.92[1]	7.34[1]	12.90[3]	N/A	N/A

SOURCE: Canada, Department of Labour, *Wages and Hours of Labour in Canada 1921–52*

Note: All wages shown per month except where noted: 1 – per day; 2 – piece work; 3 – piece work without board; 4 – per day without board.

Appendix 7

Productivity of choppers for a 165,000-cord operation, 1935–6

Class	Number of choppers	Percentage	Average production per man-day	Percentage of wood cut per class	Earnings per man-day
1	727	23.4	2.67	37.7	$3.42
2	863	27.7	2.16	34.1	2.74
3	817	26.3	1.80	21.1	2.28
4	425	13.7	1.46	6.4	1.83
5	150	4.8	1.05	0.6	1.32
6	52	1.7	0.65	0.1	0.84
7	72	2.4	nil	nil	nil
	3108	100.0	2.14	100.0	2.72

SOURCE: J.O. Wilson, 'Some Aspects of the Woods Labour Problem,' Canadian Pulp and Paper Association, Woodlands Section, *Report 77* (1937)

Appendix 8

Wage differentials among Ontario woodsworkers

Year	A Teamster/ skidder operator ($)	B Blacksmith ($)	Percentage that B is greater than A	C Cook ($)	Percentage that C is greater than A
1926	32.00/mo	90.00	181.2	100.00	212.5
1936	30.00/mo	75.00	150.0	100.00	233.3
1946	3.07/da	5.06	64.8	4.90	59.6
1955–6	10.84/da	12.63	16.5	12.63	16.5
1965–6	20.32/da	20.40	0.4	20.57	1.2

SOURCES: Canada, Department of Labour, *Wages and Hours of Labour in Canada*, 1926, 1936, 1946; Collective Agreement between Abitibi Power and Paper Company Ltd, Lakehead Woodlands Division and Lumber and Sawmill Workers Union Local no. 2693, 1955–6; Collective Agreement between Abitibi Power and Paper Company Ltd, Lakehead Woodlands Division and Lumber and Sawmill Workers Union Local no. 2693, 1964–6

Appendix 9

Ontario logging strikes, 1926–35

Locality	Starting date	Ending date	Demands and results	Number of employees	Striker days
Port Arthur	16/09/26	08/11/26	Increased wages and improved working conditions. Compromise	700	26,300
Northern Ontario	24/09/72	??/11/27	Increase in wages. In some cases employers complied with demands and in others attempted to replace the strikers.	10	50
Timmins district	01/12/27	07/12/27	Increase in wages and changes in conditions. Partially successful	70	240
Cochrane district	28/06/28	21/07/28	Increase in wages. Terminated in favour of woodworkers	850	8,500
Cochrane	15/10/28	?	Increase in wages	300	4,500
Onion Lake	28/06/29	04/03/30	Increase in piece rates and monthly rate. Compromise	200	5,060
Thunder Bay district	14/10/29	18/12/29	Increase in wages. Terminated in favour of employers	800	20,000

Locality	Starting date	Ending date	Demands and results	Number of employees	Striker days
Nipigon district	28/12/31	09/02/32	To secure dismissal of workers not joining in previous strike. Replacement of workers. Terminated in favour of employers	100	1,700
South Porcupine	04/06/32	27/06/32	Increase in piece rates. Terminated in favour of employer	37	500
Nipigon district	10/06/32	31/07/32	Increase in wages, reduction in board, and improved working conditions. Replacement. Terminated in favour of employer	225	4,000
Nipigon district	29/06/32	31/07/32	Increase in piece rates. Terminated in favour of workers	600	600
Nipigon district	18/07/32	19/07/32	Increase in wages from $0.30 to $0.35 per hour. Terminated in favour of workers	50	50
Allanwater	10/11/32	14/10/32	Wage increase and reduction in rate for board. Replacement. Termination in favour of employer	17	50
Three Nations and Hoyle	08/12/32	23/01/33	Wage increase and reduction in rate for board. Compromise	125	4,310
Long Lac	21/12/32	24/12/32	Increased wage rate. Terminated in favour of workers	110	330

Locality	Starting date	Ending date	Demands and results	Number of employees	Striker days
Atikokan and Abiwan	20/02/33	31/03/33	Wage increase, improved working conditions, and recognition of union. Terminated in favour of employer	40	500
Onion Lake	05/06/33	21/06/33	Increase in wage rates and reduction in rates for board. Compromise	1,300	18,000
Onion Lake	15/09/33	26/09/33	Change in working conditions. Compromise	140	1,400
Kapuskasing	01/11/33	08/11/33	Wage increase, reduced rate for board, and recognition of camp committees. Terminated in favour of workers.	450	2,900
Thunder Bay district	01/11/33	18/12/33	Wage increase, reduced rate for board, and improved camp conditions. Compromise	1,500	48,000
Hearst	08/11/33	27/11/33	Increased wages, reduction in hours and rate for board, and recognition of camp committees. Compromise; partially successful	123	1,900
Cochrane district	13/11/33	16/12/33	Wage increase, reduction in hours and rate for board, and recognition of camp committees. Compromise	500	10,000

Locality	Starting date	Ending date	Demands and results	Number of employees	Striker days
Fort Frances	26/11/33	31/12/33	Wage increase and improved camp conditions. Workers replaced. Terminated in favour of employer	240	6,000
Timmins	04/12/33	20/12/33	Increased wages. Replacement. Terminated in favour of workers	140	2,000
Chaplean district	03/01/34	03/01/34	Increase in wage rates and improved working conditions. Terminated in favour of employer	50	50
Chaplean district	15/01/34	31/01/34	Increase in wage rates and improved conditions. Terminated in favour of employer	500	3,000
Sault Ste Marie district	26/01/34	27/01/34	Increase in wage rates	70	140
Hearst	03/04/34	15/05/34	Increased wages. Terminated in favour of workers	75	2,775
Kapuskasing	05/04/34	07/04/34	Increased wages and reduced hours. Terminated in favour of employer	500	1,500
South River	16/04/34	31/05/34	Increased wages. Terminated in favour of employer	150	3,000
Strickland	08/06/34	??/07/34	Increased wages and recognition of camp committee. Terminated in favour of employer	52	1,100

Locality	Starting date	Ending date	Demands and results	Number of employees	Striker days
Kapuskasing	04/07/34	12/07/34	Increased wages. Terminated in favour of employer	200	1,000
Cochrane and Ansonville district	05/09/34	31/10/34	Increased wages, reduced hours, improved conditions, and recognition of union. Terminated in favour of employer	500	23,000
Thunder Bay district	18/09/34	26/09/34	Increased wages and improved conditions. Terminated in favour of employer	400	3,000
Sault Ste Marie	03/10/34	13/11/34	Increased wages, reduced hours, improved conditions, and recognition of camp committees. Terminated in favour of employer	900	20,000
Sioux Look-out	01/11/34	11/12/34	Increased wages, reduced hours, and improved conditions. Compromise	45	1,400
Nipigon district	19/06/35	25/06/35	Increased wages. Compromise	2,100	20,000

SOURCE: Canada, Department of Labour, *Labour Gazette*, 1927–36

Appendix 10

Wage schedule: hourly-rated employees Abitibi Paper Company Ltd, Lakehead Woodlands Division (1 Sept. 1980 to 31 Aug. 1981)

Hourly rate ($)	Classification
	Equipment operators
11.32	Crane operator (with certificate)
11.20	Bulldozer operator A
11.03	Crane operator (without certificate)
11.03	Koehring Waterous Harvester operator
10.93	Logma Delimber operator
10.80	Bulldozer operator B
10.78	Koehring Waterous Harvester operator (in training)
10.75	Feller-buncher operator
10.75	Nesco Processor operator
10.75	Yabo 30–40 Cruzaire operator (and with felling head)
10.67	Drott Front End and Overhead Loader operator
10.67	Power grader operator
10.66	Shortwood-forwarder operator
10.66	Hydraulic loader operator (on slasher)
10.66	Mechanical slasher operator
10.66	Pettibone Super 30 operator
10.62	Mechanical-skidder operator (crawler type)
10.61	Grapple-skidder operator
10.61	Wheeled-skidder operator (Michigan with cord grapple)
10.61	Flail operator
10.52	Mechanical-skidder operator (wheeled type)
10.47	Winch operator
10.33	Compressor operator

Hourly rate ($)	Classification
10.35	Machine operator (newly hired trainee)
10.26	Tractor operator (general)
10.21	Power-saw operator (non-productive)
10.06	Pump operator
	Truck drivers
10.75	Self loader
10.74	Hauling multiple trailers (in excess of 102 inches in width)
10.64	Tandem-axle hauling trailer (in excess of 102 inches in width)
10.59	Float
10.59	Tandem-axle hauling trailer
10.54	Trailer, four wheel drive
10.47	Snow plowing
10.46	Tandem Axle
10.33	Warehouse
10.26	Single Axle, hauling on body
10.26	Bus driver
10.18	Snowmobile operator
	Logging positions
10.75	Powderman
10.52	Bucker, piler, tree-length skidding
10.52	Chokerman, tree-length skidding
10.52	Feller, limber, tree-length skidding
10.52	Tree planter
10.47	Saw tailer, mechanical slasher
10.26	Toploader
10.21	Camp, dam, and bridge construction worker (experienced)
10.15	Helper, crane operator
10.07	Jackhammer driller
10.05	Dumpman
10.05	Helper, bulldozer, tractor
10.01	General labourer
	Maintenance and repair
12.58	Lead carpenter

Hourly rate ($)	Classification
12.58	Lead mechanic
12.58	Lead welder
12.48	Mechanic, class A-1
12.23	Mechanic, class A
12.23	Bodyman mechanic, class A
12.23	Machinist, class A
12.23	Carpenter, qualified
12.23	Welder, class A
11.40	Bodyman mechanic, class B
11.40	Machinist, class B
11.40	Mechanic I
11.40	Welder I
11.10	Electrician
10.83	Mechanic II
10.83	Welder II
10.37	Tire repairman
10.32	Mechanic helper, class A
10.32	Welder helper, class A
10.32	Welder helper
10.28	Handyman
	Camp service personnel
11.21	Cook (over twenty men)
11.00	Cook (one to twenty men)
10.82	Baker
10.82	Second Cook
10.21	Bullcook or choreboy
10.04	Cookee
10.01	Fire patrol man

SOURCE: Collective Agreement between Abitibi Paper Company Ltd, Lakehead Woodlands Division and the Lumber and Sawmill Workers' Union, local 2693, 1980–2

Note on sources

Some of the sources used for this study are unusual and deserve comment. I relied heavily on the reports of the Woodlands Section of the Canadian Pulp and Paper Association. In the period 1927-79 the section published nearly 3,000 reports, ranging from one page mimeographs offering tips on such topics as, 'How to Make Picaroons from Discarded Axe Handles' (no. 1986 [1951]) to substantial, printed analyses by highly trained specialists. The Woodlands Section assigned each of the reports an index number. Some of the studies were widely circulated through publication in the *Woodlands Review*. Others contain comparatively confidential information or opinions and were thus intended to be used only by management personnel. For instance, included among the reports are the verbatim minutes of meetings where managers frankly discussed labour policies. Nevertheless, all the reports were routinely sent to the Faculty of Forestry Library at the University of Toronto. I consulted them there.

Also useful were the Logging Reports written by Forestry students at the University of Toronto. Nearly every year, from 1909 to 1964, third-year students made field trips to logging camps located throughout Canada, though most were comparatively near at hand in northern Ontario. The students spent about one week in two or three camps in an area, observing and photographing operations, interviewing personnel, and collecting data on all aspects of the logging campaign. The students - sometimes as individuals, sometimes in teams - submitted detailed reports. The best of these contain great amounts of precise information about such matters as: food supplies, cost breakdowns, the dimensions of camp buildings, and forest conditions before and after cutting. They are illustrated with drawings of equipment, photographs of men at work and maps showing camp buildings, logging-road networks, and types of forests. Some also quote the views of operators on various subjects or record the students' own opinions and assessments. Scholars pursuing local or lumber company histories might find excellent data in these reports. Most are available in the University of Toronto Archives, Faculty of

Forestry collection. Some reports from the period 1939 to 1955 are in the faculty's library.

I also had the privilege of examining records in private collections. Mr C. Ross Silversides, now of Prescott, Ont., granted me access to his vast and valuable collection of materials on logging. As a forest engineer who worked in both the private and public sectors, Mr Silversides had access to an enormous range of materials, many of which he has carefully preserved and filed. Mr Tulio Mior, for many years president of local 2786 of the Lumber and Sawmill Workers Union, gave me access to dozens of files in the union's Thunder Bay offices. It was there that I found the best run of collective agreements, as well as the union's *Ontario Bushworker*. Other labour papers, such as the *One Big Union Bulletin*, *Le Travailleur/ The Worker*, *Lumber Worker*, and *Ontario Timberworker* are available on microfilm from the Labour Canada Library in Hull, Que. The newspaper *Metsätyöläinen*, translated from Finnish to mean 'The Lumber Worker,' is part of the Finnish Organization of Canada collection at the Public Archives of Canada. The following notes indicate the most pertinent sources that I consulted.

Notes

ABBREVIATIONS

AO	Archives of Ontario
CL	*Canada Lumberman*
CPPA	Canadian Pulp and Paper Association
CR	Commission records, Ontario
DH	Department/Board of Health records, Ontario
DL	Department of Labour records, Ontario and federal
FFC	Faculty of Forestry collection, University of Toronto Archives
FOCC	Finnish Organization of Canada collection
FERIC	Forest Engineering Research Institute of Canada
IR	Immigration Branch records, Ontario
ITC	Industry, Trade and Commerce, Federal Department of
Le T/Wkr	*Le Travailleur/The Worker*
LR	Logging Reports
LSWUF	Lumber and Sawmill Workers Union files
Metsa	*Metsätyöläinen*
MHSO	Multicultural History Society of Ontario
OB	*Ontario Bushworker*
OBUB	*One Big Union Bulletin*
OHC	Oral History Collection, Multicultural History Society of Ontario
OLRB	Ontario Labour Relations Board
OT	*Ontario Timberworker*
PAC	Public Archives of Canada
PPMC	*Pulp and Paper Magazine of Canada*
PPRIC	Pulp and Paper Research Institute of Canada
SLF	Strikes and Lockouts files, Public Archives of Canada

TC	*Timber of Canada*
UTA	University of Toronto Archives
Wkr	*Worker*
WR	*Woodlands Review*
WS	Woodlands Section, Canadian Pulp and Paper Association

INTRODUCTION

1 Pierre Berton, *Hollywood's Canada* (Toronto 1975) 80. On Paul Bunyan, see especially Edith Fowke, 'In Defence of Paul Bunyan,' *New York Folklore* 5 (Summer 1979) 43-51. On Joe Monteferrand, see Donald MacKay, *The Lumberjacks* (Toronto 1978) 35-40; Bernie Bedore, *Tall Tales of Joe Mufferaw* (Toronto 1979). On the mythology of the north, see Carl Berger, 'The True North Strong and Free,' in Peter Russell, ed., *Nationalism in Canada* (Toronto 1966) 3-26; Cole Harris, 'The Myth of the Land in Canadian Nationalism,' in ibid., 27-46.

2 There are no reliable series of statistics on the size of the Ontario woods workforce prior to 1963 (for 1963-80, see Appendix 2). Because of the difficulties involved in getting reliable data on remote, shifting, seasonal woods operations, the Dominion Bureau of Statistics did not publish runs on the logging workforce of eastern Canada. The Canadian census was taken in June, during the off-season in logging, and so available data are almost useless for eastern Canada. Nor did the Ontario Department of Lands and Forests keep a running count of woodsworkers. The best series available comes from the Ontario Board of Health (later the Department of Health). From 1919-20 it published an annual count of employees in woods camps in the unorganized districts or wilderness areas beyond the limits of local administration, where health officials had certain responsibilities - as discussed in chapter 5. In all likelihood these numbers underestimate the size of the workforce (see Appendix 1), for there were some camps within the organized districts, and many smaller operators did not report fully to health authorities.

3 Ontario, Ministry of Natural Resources, Timber Sales Branch, *The Forest Industry in the Economy of Ontario* (Toronto 1981), 36-7

4 Thomas L. Cox et al., *This Well-Wooded Land: Americans and Their Forests from Colonial Times to the Present* (Lincoln, Neb. 1985). For a brief look at logging in Quebec before 1940, see René Hardy and Normand Séguin, *Forêt et société en Mauricie: La formation de la région de Trois-Rivières 1830-1950* (Montreal 1983); for post-war Quebec see Camille G. Légendre, 'Organizational Technology, Structure and Environment: The Pulp and Paper Logging Industry of

Quebec,' PH D thesis, Michigan State University 1977. A first-rate examination of the timber industry in early nineteenth-century New Brunswick is Graeme Wynn, *Timber Colony: A Historical Geography of Early Nineteenth Century New Brunswick* (Toronto 1981). A useful exploration of the current scene in British Columbia is Patricia Marchak, *Green Gold: The Forest Industry in British Columbia* (Vancouver 1982).

5 For Canada, see especially Craig Heron and Robert Storey, eds., *On the Job: Confronting the Labour Process in Canada* (Kingston 1986).

6 Harry Braverman, *Labor and Monopoly Capital: The Degradation of Work in the Twentieth Century* (New York 1974). For useful contributions and critiques of the debate, see Heron and Storey, *On the Job*; David F. Noble, *Forces of Production: A Social History of Industrial Automation* (New York 1984); Craig Littler, *The Development of the Labour Process in Capitalist Societies: A Comparative Study of the Transformation of Work Organization in Britain, Japan and the U.S.A.* (London 1982); David M. Gordon, Richard Edwards, and Michael Reich, *Segmented Work, Divided Workers: The Historical Transformation of Labor in the United States* (Cambridge 1982); Richard Edwards, *Contested Terrain: The Transformation of the Workplace in the Twentieth Century* (New York 1976); Stephen Wood, ed., *The Degradation of Work?: Skill, Deskilling and the Labour Process* (London 1982); Andrew Zimbalist, ed., *Case Studies on the Labour Process* (New York 1979); Michael Burawoy, *Manufacturing Consent: Changes in the Labour Process under Capitalism* (Chicago 1979), 'Toward A Marxist Theory of the Labour Process: Braverman and Beyond,' *Politics and Society* 8:3–4 (1979), and *The Politics of Production: Factory Regimes under Capitalism and Socialism* (London 1985); Andrew Herman, 'Conceptualizing Control: Domination and Hegemony in the Capitalist Labour Process,' *Insurgent Sociologist* 11:3 (1982); Craig Littler and Graeme Salamen, 'Braverman and Beyond: Recent Theories of the Labour Process,' *Sociology* 16:2 (1982); Richard Price, 'The Labour Process and Labor History,' *Journal of Social History* 8:1 (January 1983) 57–75.

7 On Canada's nineteenth-century crafts workers, see Gregory S. Kealey, *Toronto Workers Respond to Industrial Capitalism* (Toronto 1980); Wayne Roberts, 'The Last Artisans: Toronto Printers, 1896–1914,' in Gregory S. Kealey and Peter Warrian, eds., *Essays in Canadian Working Class History* (Toronto 1976); Wayne Roberts, 'Artisans, Aristocrats and Handymen: Politics and Unions among Toronto Skilled Building Trades Workers, 1896–1914,' *Labour/Le Travailleur* 1 (1976) 92–121; Bryan D. Palmer, *A Culture in Conflict: Skilled Workers and Industrial Capitalism in Hamilton, Ontario, 1860–1914* (Montreal 1979); Craig Heron, 'Crisis of the Craftsman: Hamilton's Metal Workers and the Early Twentieth Century,' *Labour/Le Travailleur* 6 (Autumn 1980) 7–48; Paul Craven and Tom Traves, 'Dimensions of Paternalism: Discipline and Culture in

Canadian Railway Operations in the 1850s,' in Heron and Storey, *On the Job*
47–74; Gregory S. Kealey, 'Work Control, the Labour Process and Nineteenth-
Century Canadian Printers,' in ibid. 75–191. On mass-production workers, see
Wayne Roberts, 'Toronto's Metal Workers and the Second Industrial
Revolution,' *Labour/Le Travailleur* (Autumn 1980) 49–72; Craig Heron, 'Hamilton
Steelworkers and the Rise of Mass Production,' Canadian Historical
Association, *Historical Papers* 1982, 103–32; Craig Heron and Robert Storey,
'Work and Struggle in the Canadian Steel Industry, 1900–1950,' in their book
On the Job 210–44; and Heron's forthcoming book, *Working in Steel: The Pre-CIO
Years*. On workers in resource industries, see Wallace Clement, *Hard Rock
Mining: Industrial Relations and Technological Change at Inco* (Toronto 1981).

8 Classic works by staple historians include A.R.M. Lower's three major studies:
Settlement and the Forest Frontier in Eastern Canada (Toronto 1936); *The North
American Assault on the Canadian Forest: A History of the Lumber Trade between
Canada and the United States* (New York 1938); *Great Britain's Woodyard: British
America and the Timber Trade, 1763–1867* (Montreal and Kingston 1973); Harold
A. Innis, *The Fur Trade in Canada: An Introduction to Canadian Economic History*
(New York 1930), *The Cod Fisheries: The History of an International Economy*
(Toronto 1940), and *Essays in Canadian Economic History* (Toronto 1956).

9 The strengths and weaknesses of ethnic history are discussed in Roberto
Perrin, 'Clio as an Ethnic: The Third Force in Canadian Historiography,'
Canadian Historical Review 64:4 (December 1983) 441–67; Robert Harney, 'The
State of Canadian Ethnic History,' paper presented to the Canadian Historical
Association annual meeting, 1984.

10 Gender conscious studies of the workplace include Cynthia Cockburn,
Brothers: Male Dominance and Technological Change (London 1983); Gail Cuthbert
Brandt, ' 'Weaving It Together': Life Cycle and the Industrial Experience of
Female Cotton Workers in Quebec, 1910–1950,' *Labour/Le Travailleur* 7 (Spring
1981) 113–26; Mercedes Steedman, 'Skill and Gender in the Canadian Clothing
Industry, 1890–1940,' in Heron and Storey, eds., *On the Job* 152–76; Graham S.
Lowe, ''Mechanization, Feminization, and Managerial Control in the Early
Twentieth-Century Canadian Office,' in ibid. 177–209; Paul Willis, *Learning to
Labour: How Working Class Kids Get Working Class Jobs* (London 1977), and his
'Shop Floor Culture, Masculinity and the Wage Form,' in John Clarke, Charles
Critche, and Richard Johnson, eds., *Working-Class Culture: Studies in History and
Theory* (London 1979) 185–98.

CHAPTER 1 Northern Ontario and the forest industry

1 Bess Harris and R.G.P. Colgrove, eds., *Lawren Harris* (Toronto 1969) 39

2 Cole Harris, 'The Myth of the Land in Canadian Nationalism,' in Peter
  Russell, ed., *Nationalism in Canada* (Toronto 1966) 27–66; Graeme Wynn, 'Notes
  on Society and Environment in Old Ontario,' *Journal of Social History* 13 (1979)
  49–65; George Altmeyer, 'Three Ideas of Nature in Canada 1893–1914,' *Journal
  of Canadian Studies* 11 (1976) 21–36; Carl Berger, 'The True North Strong and
  Free,' in Peter Russell, ed., *Nationalism* 3–26; James Doyle, 'The Image of
  Northern Ontario in English Canadian Literature,' *Laurentian University Review*
  8 (1975) 103–16; A.R.M. Lower, *The North American Assault on the Canadian Forest:
  A History of the Lumber Trade between Canada and the United States* (Toronto 1938)
3 On the geography of the Shield, see John Warkentin, ed., *Canada: A
  Geographical Interpretation* (Toronto 1968); J. Lewis Robinson, *Concepts and
  Themes in the Regional Geography of Canada* (Vancouver 1983) ch. 7; A.R.M.
  Lower, *Settlement and the Forest Frontier in Eastern Canada* (Toronto 1936) ch. 1;
  Iain Wallace, 'The Canadian Shield: The Development of a Resource Frontier,'
  in L.D. McCann, ed., *Heartland and Hinterland: A Geography of Canada*
  (Scarborough 1982); L.P. Chapman and M.K. Thomas, *The Climate of Northern
  Ontario* (Toronto 1968).
4 Lower, *Settlement*; Roman Brozowski, Keith Topps, and David Rees,
  'Agriculture and Settlement,' in Matt Bray and Ernie Epp, eds., *A Vast and
  Magnificent Land: An Illustrated History of Northern Ontario* (Sudbury and
  Thunder Bay 1984) 109–26; Benoit-Beaudry Gourd, 'La colonisation des Clay
  Belts du nord-ouest québécois et du nord-est ontarien,' *Revue d'histoire de
  l'Amerique-francaise* 27 (September 1973) 234–56; Peter N. Sinclair, 'Strategies of
  Development on an Agricultural Frontier: The Great Clay Belt, 1900-1950,'
  PH D thesis, University of Toronto 1980
5 This description of the forest follows J.S. Rowe, *Forest Regions of Canada* (Ottawa
  1972). See also Canada, Department of Frontier and Rural Development, *Native
  Trees of Canada*, 6th ed. (Ottawa 1966).
6 James A. Larsen, *The Boreal Ecosystem* (New York 1980); Jamie Swift, *Cut and
  Run: The Assault on Canada's Forests* (Toronto 1983) ch. 1; Clifford E. Ahlgren and
  Isobel F. Ahlgren, 'The Human Impact on Northern Forest Ecosystems,' in
  Susan L. Flader, ed., *The Great Lakes Forest: An Environmental and Social History*
  (Minneapolis 1983) 33–51
7 On forestry in Ontario, see Richard S. Lambert with Paul Pross, *Renewing
  Nature's Wealth: A Centennial History of Lands, Forests and Wildlife Administration in
  Ontario, 1763–1967* (Toronto 1967) 117–249, 390–423; H.V. Nelles, *The Politics of
  Development: Forests, Mines, and Hydro-electric Power in Ontario, 1849–1941*
  (Toronto 1974) 182–214; J.W.B. Sisam, *Forestry and Forestry Education in a
  Developing Country* (Toronto 1982); A. Paul Pross, 'The Development of a Forest
  Policy: A Study of the Ontario Department of Lands and Forests,' PH D thesis,

University of Toronto 1967; K.J. Rea, *The Prosperous Years: Economic History of Ontario, 1939–1975* (Toronto 1985) 186–92. For Canada, see Donald MacKay, *Heritage Lost: The Crisis in Canada's Forests* (Toronto 1985); R. Peter Gillis and Thomas R. Roach, *Lost Initiatives: Canada's Forest Industries, Forest Policy and Forest Conservation* (New York 1986).

8 Michael S. Cross, 'The Dark Druidical Groves: The Lumber Community and the Commercial Frontier in British North America, to 1854,' PH D thesis, University of Toronto 1968, 127–31; Douglas McCalla, 'The Timber Trade and Upper Canadian Development, 1822–42: A Working Paper' (1985)

9 R.G. Albion, *Forests and Sea Power: The Timber Problem of the Royal Navy, 1652–1862* (Cambridge 1926); A.R.M. Lower, *Great Britain's Woodyard: British America and the Timber Trade, 1763–1867* (Montreal and Kingston 1973); Graeme Wynn, *Timber Colony: A Historical Geography of Early Nineteenth Century New Brunswick* (Toronto 1981) 28–30; W.T. Easterbrook and Hugh G.J. Aitken, *Canadian Economic History* (Toronto 1956) 191–3

10 Wynn, *Timber Colony* 26–8

11 Ibid., ch. 5; A.R.M. Lower, 'The Trade in Square Timber,' in W.T. Easterbrook and M.H. Watkins, eds., *Approaches to Economic History* (Toronto 1967) 28–48; Lower, *Great Britain's Woodyard* pt. II; William L. Marr and Donald G. Paterson, *Canada: An Economic History* (Toronto 1980) 61–73. Business arrangements in the early timber trade need further study, but they are touched on in Sandra Gillis, 'The Timber Trade in the Ottawa Valley, 1806–54,' National Historic Parks and Sites manuscript report no. 153 (Ottawa 1975). Wynn describes the New Brunswick case in *Timber Colony*, ch. 5. The commercial structures of the Quebec timber trade of the second half of the nineteenth century are examined in John Keynes, 'The Dunn Family: Two Generations of Timber Merchants at Quebec, 1850–1914,' paper presented to the Canadian Business History Conference, Trent University, Peterborough, Ont., May 1984.

12 Lower, *Great Britain's Woodyard* 166

13 On Ontario regulations, see Thomas Southworth and A. White, 'A History of Crown Timber Regulations from the Date of the French Occupation to the Year 1899,' in Ontario, Department of Forests, *Annual Report* 1907; Lambert and Pross, *Renewing Nature's Wealth* ch. 4; Nelles, *Politics of Development* ch. 1.

14 Cross, 'Dark Druidical Groves,' 302–10 and his article 'The Lumber Community of Upper Canada, 1815–1867,' *Ontario History* 52 (1960) 213–33; Grant Head, 'An Introduction to Forest Exploitation in Nineteenth Century Ontario,' in J. David Wood, ed., *Perspectives on Landscape and Settlement in Nineteenth Century Ontario* (Toronto 1975) 88–91; Lower, *North American Assault* 89–147; W.E. Greening, 'The Lumber Industry in the Ottawa Valley and the

American Market in the Nineteenth Century,' *Ontario History* 72 (1970) 134–6; James Elliott Defebaugh, *History of the Lumber Industry of America* vol. I (Chicago 1906) 172–8

15 Charlotte Whitton, *A Hundred Years A-Fellin': The Story of the Gillies on the Ottawa* (Ottawa 1943) 72; W.P.T. Silva, 'The Southern Georgian Bay Region, 1895–1961: A Study in Economic Geography,' PH D thesis, University of Toronto 1966; Lower, *North American Assault* 174–5; W.R. Wightman, *Forever on the Fringe: Six Studies in the Development of Manitoulin Island* (Toronto 1982) 84–8; Gwenda Hallsworth, ' "A Good Paying Business": Lumbering on the North Shore of Lake Huron, 1850–1910, with Particular Reference to the Sudbury District,' MA thesis, Laurentian University 1983; Robert C. Johnson, 'Logs for Saginaw: The Development of Raft-Towing on Lake Huron,' *Inland Seas* 5 (1949) 37–44, 83–90, and his 'Logs for Saginaw: An Episode in Canadian-American Relations,' *Michigan History* 34 (1950) 213–33; W.G. Rector, *Log Transport in the Lake States Lumber Industry, 1840–1918* (Glendale 1953) 166–70; W.R. Williams, 'Big Tugs and Big Rafts: A Story of Georgian Bay Lumbering,' *Inland Seas* 3 (1947) 11–16

16 Nelles, *Politics of Development* 62–80, and his 'Empire Ontario: The Problems of Resource Development,' in Donald Swainson, ed., *Oliver Mowat's Ontario* (Toronto 1972) 189–210; Christopher Armstrong, *The Politics of Federalism: Ontario's Relations with the Federal Government* (Toronto 1982) 35–42

17 Ontario, Department of Crown Lands, *Annual Report 1899*, ix

18 See note 16 and Albert Tucker, *Steam into Wilderness: Ontario Northland Railway, 1902–1962* (Toronto 1978) 1–49; Jamie Benedickson, 'Temagami and the Northern Ontario Tourist Frontier,' *Lakehead University Review* 11:2 (February 1979) 43–70; Peter Oliver, *G. Howard Ferguson: Ontario Tory* (Toronto 1977) 67–71, 110–28; Charles W. Humphries, *'Honest Enough to Be Bold': The Life and Times of Sir James Pliny Whitney* (Toronto 1985) 145–50.

19 Public Archives of Manitoba, MG 9Ab, J.A. Mathieu interviewed by Bruce Harding, 4 Aug. 1957 (transcript). See also Lower, *North America Assault* 117.

20 Ontario, Ministry of Natural Resources, Timber Sales Branch, *The Forest Industry in the Economy of Ontario* (Toronto 1981) 10–13; Lakehead University, *Economic Future of the Forest Products Industry of Northern Ontario* (Thunder Bay 1980) 62; ITC, *Review of the Canadian Forest Products Industry* (Ottawa 1978) 53

21 Ontario, Royal Commission on Forestry, *Report* (Toronto 1947) 41; ITC, *Review* 43; Lakehead University, *Economic Future* 21

22 Ontario, Department of Crown Lands, *A Statement Concerning the Extent, Resources, Climate and Industrial Development of the Province of Ontario, Canada* (Toronto 1901) 84. On promoters' hopes, see also Ontario, Department of Crown Lands, *Annual Report 1899*, viii, x, 14, and the department's *Land*

Settlement in New Ontario (Toronto 1903); *Report of the Survey and Exploration of Northern Ontario, 1900* (Toronto 1901); *PPMC*, June 1919; *Monetary Times* (Toronto), 26 Feb. 1897, 6 May 1911.

23 Trevor J.O. Dick, 'Canadian Newsprint,' 1913-1930: National Policies and the North American Economy,' *Journal of Economic History* 42 (September 1982) 662; Paul Rutherford, *A Victorian Authority: The Daily Press in Late Nineteenth-Century Canada* (Toronto 1982) 24–35; George Carruthers, *Paper Making* II, 673; John A. Guthrie, *The Newsprint Paper Industry: An Economic Analysis* (Cambridge 1941) 47–55; Lambert and Pross, *Renewing Nature's Wealth* 250–3; Nelles, *Politics of Development* 84–7, 102–7; James M. Gilmour, 'The Economic Geography of the Pulp and Paper Industry in Ontario,' MA thesis, University of Toronto 1964, 31–3

24 On Clergue, see especially Nelles, *Politics of Development* 56–62, 82–3; Margaret Van Every, 'Francis Hector Clergue and the Rise of Sault Ste. Marie as an Industrial Centre,' *Ontario History* 56 (1964) 191–202; Alan Sullivan, *The Rapids* (rpr. Toronto 1972); Duncan McDowall, *Steel at the Sault: Frances H. Clergue, Sir James Dunn and the Algoma Steel Corporation, 1901–1956* (Toronto 1984)

25 Guthrie, *Newsprint Paper Industry* ch. 3; L.E. Ellis, *The Print Paper Pendulum: Group Pressure and the Price of Newsprint* (New Brunswick, NJ 1960); Nathan Reich, *The Pulp and Paper Industry in Canada* (Toronto 1926?)

26 *Northern Ontario: Its Progress and Development under the Whitney Government* (Toronto 1914?) 6

27 Tom Traves, *The State and Enterprise: Canadian Manufacturers and the Federal Government, 1913–1931* (Toronto 1979) 30–50

28 Wallace Clement, *Continental Corporate Power: Economic Linkages between Canada and the United States* (Toronto 1977) 91; Herbert Marshall, Frank Southard, Jr, and Kenneth W. Taylor, *Canadian-American Industry: A Study in International Investment* (rpr. Toronto 1976) 36

29 Gilmour, 'Economic Geography,' 334; Robert E. Ankli, 'The Canadian Newsprint Industry, 1900–1940,' in Bruce R. Dalgaard and Richard K. Vedder, eds., *Variations in Business and Economic History: Essays in Honour of Donald L. Kremmer* (Greenwich, Conn. 1982) 9–25. The expansion of the Canadian pulp and paper industry in the 1920s is summarized and put into context by John Herd Thompson with Allen Seager, *Canada, 1922–1939: Decades of Discord* (Toronto 1985) ch. 5.

30 Traves, *State and Enterprise* 77–85; Nelles, *Politics of Development* 444–59; Guthrie, *Newsprint* ch. 5. See also Lloyd G. Reynolds, *The Control of Competition in Canada* (Cambridge, Mass. 1940); V.W. Bladen, *An Introduction to Political Economy* (Toronto 1944) 162–83. The wider context is summarized in Thompson and

Seager, *Decades of Discord* ch. 9 and covered more thoroughly in A.E. Safarian, *The Canadian Economy in the Great Depression* (Toronto 1970).

31 Charles Vining, *Newsprint Prorating: An Account of Government Policy in Quebec and Ontario* (Montreal 1940); Nelles, *Politics of Development* 410–64; on Abitibi's reorganization, see Ontario, Royal Commission of Inquiry into the Affairs of the Abitibi Pulp and Paper Company Ltd., *Report* (Toronto 1946).

32 Canadian Pulp and Paper Association, *Reference Tables, 1961* (Montreal 1962) table 39; capacity increase calculated from Table 1:2, Lakehead University, *Economic Future of the Forest Products Industry of Northern Ontario* (Thunder Bay 1980) 9

33 Lakehead University, *Economic Future* 7, 81–121; see also Gilmour, 'Economic Geography,' 43–4.

34 ITC, *Review* 35

35 Lakehead University, *Economic Future* 15–18, 45–9; Forestry Study Group, *The Outlook for the Canadian Forest Industries* (Ottawa 1957) 135

36 Alfred D. Chandler, *The Visible Hand: The Managerial Revolution in American Business* (Cambridge, Mass. 1977) 243

37 Calculated from Canada, Dominion Bureau of Statistics, *The Lumber Industry, 1927* 51 and *The Pulp and Paper Industry, 1927* 49

38 Chandler, *Visible Hand* 243. On Canada, see Graham S. Lowe, 'The Rise of Modern Management in Canada,' *Canadian Dimension* 14:3 (December 1979) 32–8.

39 *Pulp and Paper Canada: Annual and Directory 1982* (Montreal 1982); Philip Mathias, *Takeover: The 22 Days of Risk and Decision that Created the World's Largest Newsprint Empire, Abitibi-Price* (Toronto 1976)

40 ITC, *Review* 140. Using Statistics Canada data, the Canadian Paperworkers Union found higher proportions of foreign ownership; see Canadian Paperworkers Union, *The Forestry, Pulp, Paper and Allied Industries: Characteristics and Developments* (Toronto 1980) 76–7.

41 See *Post's Pulp and Paper Directory 1980* (San Francisco 1981) for details on all firms.

42 See two studies prepared for Ontario, Royal Commission on the Northern Environment: Lakehead, *Economic Future*; Canadian Paperworkers, *Forestry*. See also ITC, *Review*; Canada, Ministry of the Environment, *A Forest Sector Strategy for Canada* (Ottawa 1981); Science Council of Canada, *Canada's Threatened Forests* (Ottawa 1983).

43 Lakehead, *Economic Future*, s-18

44 ITC, *Review* 8; Frazee cited in Swift, *Cut and Run* 10

CHAPTER 2 Seasonal labour force, 1900–1945

1 On Ontario sawmill technology, see especially CL, 1 Jan. 1905. On sawmills elsewhere in eastern Canada, see Graeme Wynn, *Timber Colony: A Historical Geography of Early Nineteenth Century New Brunswick* (Toronto 1981) ch. 4; Barbara R. Robertson, *Sawpower: Making Lumber in the Sawmills of Nova Scotia* (Halifax 1986). On science and technology in Canadian pulp and paper mills, see James Hull, 'Science and the Canadian Pulp and Paper Industry, 1903–1933,' PH D thesis, York University 1985.

2 On combined and uneven development, see especially Raphael Samuels, 'Workshop of the World: Steam Power and Hand Technology in Mid-Victorian Britain,' *History Workshop* 3 (1977) 6–72.

3 Ellwood Wilson cited in *PPMC*, October 1918

4 An exception to the general pattern of winter camp operations was the case of the settlers who cut pulpwood on their homesteads or on private lands near their farms. They lived at home, rather than in camps, and they were independent commodity producers, not wage earners. While they sold some of their wood to Ontario pulp and paper firms, they – or intermediaries – exported much of it to American mills because the fibre-hungry Americans offered higher prices than Ontario mill managers. The history of the settler-cutter deserves a full study, but it can be glimpsed in A.R.M. Lower, *Settlement and the Forest Frontier in Eastern Canada* (Toronto 1936); Canada, Royal Commission on Pulpwood, *Report* (Ottawa 1924); Tom Roach, 'Private Pulpwood Cutting in Northeastern Ontario: Its Organization after the First World War,' paper presented to the Ontario Historical Society annual meeting, 1983, and his 'Farm Woodlots and Pulpwood Exports from Eastern Canada,' in H.K. Steen, ed., *History of Sustained Yield Forestry* (Santa Cruz, Calif. 1984) 202–10. An excellent primary source is PAC, Royal Commission on Pulpwood, 'Evidence,' vols. 6–9.

5 General descriptions of logging in the nineteenth century may be found in A.R.M. Lower, *The North American Assault on the Canadian Forest: A History of the Lumber Trade between Canada and the United States* (Toronto 1938), ch. 4; J.W. Hughson and C.C.J. Bond, *Hurling Down the Pine*, 2nd ed. (Old Chelsea, Que. 1965); Charlotte Whitton, *A Hundred Years A-Fellin': The Story of the Gillies on the Ottawa* (Ottawa 1943); George S. Thompson, *Up to Date, or the Life of a Lumberman* (Peterborough 1895?); Donald MacKay, *The Lumberjacks* (Toronto 1978); Chris Curtis, 'Shanty Life in the Kawarthas, Ontario, 1850–1855,' *Material History Bulletin* 13 (Fall 1981) 39–50; Wynn, *Timber Colony* 54–86; Thomas R. Cox et al., *This Well-Wooded Land: Americans and Their Forest from Colonial Times to the Present* (Lincoln, Neb. 1985) 51–90.

6 Canada, Dominion Bureau of Statistics, *Operations in the Woods* 1919, 233-4; AO, CR, RC 18 B-109 vol. 6, 'A Brief for Presentation to the Ontario Royal Commission on Forestry by the Pulp and Paper Association on behalf of the Pulp and Paper Industry of Ontario,' 1946

7 Judith Fingard, 'The Poor in Winter: Seasonality and Society in Pre-Industrial Canada,' in Michael S. Cross and Gregory S. Kealey, eds., *Pre-Industrial Canada, 1760-1849* (Toronto 1982) 62-78; Ruth Bleasdale, 'Class Conflict on the Canals of Upper Canada in the 1840s,' *Labour/Le Travailleur* 7 (1981) 9-39

8 Dennis Guest, *The Emergence of Social Security in Canada* (Vancouver 1980) 18-28; James Struthers, *No Fault of Their Own: Unemployment and the Canadian Welfare State, 1914-1941* (Toronto 1983) 3-15

9 Donald Avery, 'Canadian Immigration Policy and the "Foreign Navvy",' Canadian Historical Association, *Historical Papers* 1972, 135-56. On immigration to Canada in the early twentieth century, see Donald Avery, *"Dangerous Foreigners": European Immigration, Workers, and Labour Radicalism in Canada, 1896-1932* (Toronto 1972); Norman Macdonald, *Canadian Immigration and Colonization, 1841-1903* (Toronto 1968); Robert F. Harney, 'Commerce of Migration,' *Canadian Ethnic Studies* 9 (1977) 42-53; Anthony W. Rasporich, *For a Better Life: A History of Croatians in Canada* (Toronto 1982) 29-48; Mabel Timlin, 'Canada's Immigration Policy 1896-1910,' *Canadian Journal of Economics and Political Science* 26 (1963). On the wider context, see Charlotte Erickson, *Emigration from Europe 1815-1914* (London 1976); Philip Taylor, *The Distant Magnet: European Emigration to the U.S.A.* (New York 1971).

10 Struthers, *No Fault* 6

11 On migratory workers, see Edmund Bradwin, *The Bunkhouse Man* (Toronto 1972); Rasporich, *Better Life* 52-135; Bruno Ramirez, 'Brief Encounters: Italian Immigrant Workers and the CPR, 1900-30,' *Labour/Le Travail* 17 (Spring 1986) 9-28; A.R. McCormack, 'The Blanketstiffs: Itinerant Railway Construction Workers in Canada, 1896-1914' (Ottawa, National Film Board/National Museum, Visual History Set, 1975) and his *Reformers, Rebels, and Revolutionaries: A History of the Western Canadian Radical Movement, 1899-1919* (Toronto 1977) 98-117; Leonard C. Marsh, 'The Mobility of Labour in Relation to Unemployment,' *Papers and Proceedings of the Annual Meeting of the Canadian Political Science Association* 3 (1931) 7-31. On urban, seasonal unemployment, see Terry Copp, *The Anatomy of Poverty: The Condition of the Working Class in Montreal, 1897-1929* (Toronto 1974); Michael J. Piva, *The Condition of the Working Class in Toronto - 1900-1921* (Ottawa 1979); Bruno Ramirez, 'Workers without a "Cause": Italian Immigrant Labour in Montreal, 1880-1930,' paper presented to the Canadian Historical Association, Annual Meeting 1984.

12 Struthers, *No Fault* 3. On the problems of unemployment statistics, see Udo

Sautter, 'Measuring Unemployment in Canada: Federal Efforts before World War II,' *Histoire Sociale/Social History* 15 (November 1982) 475–87.

13 Cecilia Danysk, 'Farm Workers and Agricultural Development: Changing Conditions of Agricultural Labour in the Prairie West, 1900–1930,' paper presented to the Canadian Historical Association, Annual Meeting 1984; C. Ross Silversides collection, Prescott, David L. McFarlane, 'The Labour Force of the Eastern Canadian Woods Industry' (typescript 1955?). See also Lower, *Settlement*. On the agro-forest economy, see Normand Séguin, *La conquête du sol au 19ᵉ siècle* (Sillery 1977) and his 'L'économie agro-forestière: Génèse du developpement au Saguenay au 19ᵉ siècle,' in his *Agriculture et colonization au Québec* (Montreal 1980) 195–264; Gérard Bouchard, 'Démographie et société rurale au Saguenay, 1851–1935,' *Recherches Sociographiques* 19 (1978) 7–31; Chad Gaffield, 'Boom and Bust: The Demography and Economy of the Lower Ottawa Valley in the Nineteenth Century,' Canadian Historical Association, *Historical Papers* 1982, 172–95; René Hardy and Normand Séguin, *Forêt et société en Mauricie: La formation de la région de Trois-Rivières 1830–1930* (Montreal 1984).

14 Lower, *Settlement* and Wynn, *Timber Colony* provide pertinent information, though their arguments are different from those presented here. For other resource industries, see Robert J. Brym and R. James Sacouman, eds., *Underdevelopment and Social Movements in Atlantic Canada* (Toronto 1979); James Sacouman, 'Semi-Proletarianization and Rural Underdevelopment in the Maritimes,' *Canada Review of Sociology and Anthropology* 17 (1980) 232–45; *Journal of Canadian Studies* 19:1 (Spring 1984) special issue on fisheries; Peter R. Sinclair, *From Traps to Draggers: Domestic Commodity Production in Northwestern Newfoundland, 1850–1982* (St John's 1985).

15 Allan Greer, 'Fur-Trade Labour and Lower Canadian Agrarian Structures,' Canadian Historical Association, *Historical Papers* 1981, 197–214 and his *Peasant, Lord, and Merchant: Rural Society in Three Quebec Parishes, 1740–1840* (Toronto 1985) ch. 7

16 Canada, Dominion Bureau of Statistics, *Operations in the Woods*, 1919, 28–9

17 Ken Collins, *Oatmeal and the Eaton's Catologue: The Dryden Area – The Early Days* (Dryden 1982) 119

18 UTA, FF, LR #51, J.W. Johnson and L.R. Seheult (1926–7)

19 Joseph-Alphonse Desjardins, *Le bûcheron d'autrefois: Vie et travaux de l'ouvrier de la forêt* (Sudbury 1980) 36 (Desjardins wrote these memoirs in the early 1920s). On surviving the off-season in the Finnish communities in the Thunder Bay district, see Chris Kouhi et al., eds., *A Chronicle of Finnish Settlement in Rural Thunder Bay* (Thunder Bay 1976); Mark Rasmussen, 'The Geographic Impact of Finnish Settlement on the Thunder Bay Area,' MA thesis, University of Alberta 1975. See also the files of public health nurses who visited such men, AO, DH,

RG 10 3A1 Historical Files, Field Work, Rainy River District, 1926.

20 AO, Royal Commission records, RG 18 B-109 vol. 6, 'A Brief for Presentation to the Ontario Royal Commission on Forestry by the Pulp and Paper Association on Behalf of the Pulp and Paper Industry of Ontario,' 1946. Published census materials and Dominion Bureau of Statistics data are not helpful here.

21 *CL*, 1 May 1903, 1 Mar. 1907, 1 Nov. 1908

22 Ibid.; 15 May 1916, 15 Nov. 1919; United Church of Canada Archives, Methodist Church records, Home Mission, 'Report of the Board of Home Missions, 1921'

23 PAC, IR, RG 27 vol. 230 file 127304, 'Arrivals at Quebec, September–November 1923'

24 *CL*, 1 Dec. 1923

25 Ibid.; 15 Nov. 1913; CPPA, WS, 'Questionnaire Returns,' WSI B67 1929. See also L.A. Nix, *Woods Labour* (Montreal 1939).

26 UTA, FF, LR #54, G.R. Lane, R.E. Smith, A.W. Goodfellow (1921)

27 On ethnic hierarchies, see Bradwin, *Bunkhouse Man* ch. 4; Howard Palmer, 'Reluctant Hosts: Anglo-Canadian Views of Multiculturalism in the Twentieth Century,' in R. Douglas Francis and Donald B. Smith, eds., *Readings in Canadian History: Post-Confederation* (Toronto 1982) 123–39; Palmer, *Immigration and the Rise of Multiculturalism* (Toronto 1975); J.S. Woodsworth, *Strangers within Our Gates* (rpr. Toronto 1972); Robert England, *The Central European Immigrant in Canada* (Toronto 1929).

28 CPPA, WS, 'Efficiency and Stability of Woods Labour in Eastern Canada,' WSI B60 (1930)

29 Ibid.; AO, DL, RG 7 II-1 vol. 6 'Replies to Questions Relating to Employment of Foreign-born Workers' 6

30 Nix, *Woods Labour* 7; student report cited *CL*, 1 Sept. 1916

31 *CL*, 15 June 1911; Canada, Indian Affairs Branch, *Annual Report* 1900–30; W.R. Wightman, *Forever on the Fringe: Six Studies in the Development of Manitoulin Island* (Toronto 1982) 139, 156–9

32 AO, OHC, Impi Kanerva interview

33 Varpu Lindstrom-Best, 'Central Organization of the Loyal Finns in Canada,' *Polyphony* 3:2 (Fall 1981) 97–103

34 CPPA, WS, 'Questionnaire Returns,' 1929

35 Ontario, *Report of the Ontario Commission on Unemployment* (Toronto 1916) 122

36 AO, MU 7252, Collins Inlet Lumber Company records, C.W. Pitt to Thomas Kirby, 19 Aug. 1898

37 Sandford M. Jacoby, 'The Development of Internal Labour Markets in American Manufacturing Firms,' in Paul Osterman, ed., *Internal Labour Markets* (Cambridge, Mass. 1984) 47–53

38 AO, DL, RG 7 II-1 vol. 2, H.C.H. to W. Riddell, 19 Jan. 1919. Bill Plaunt interviewed by author, Sudbury 1982; UTA, FF, J.D. Gilmour, Rat Portage Lumber Company, 1909

39 *CL*, 1 May 1903; AO, DL, RG 7 V-1 vol. 2, 'List of Agencies under Licence, 1919'

40 AO, DL, RG 7 V-1 vol. 2, H.C.H. to W. Riddell, 19 Jan. 1919; Ontario, *Report of Unemployment Commission*, 122; AO, DL, RG 7 II-1, vol. 2 'Northern Inspection Trip,' 26–9 Nov. 1917

41 AO, DL, RG 7 II-1, vol. 2, 'Northern Inspection Trip,' 26–9 Nov. 1917

42 *CL*, 15 Mar. 1918; CPPA, WS, *Convention Proceedings* 1930, 103

43 AO, DL, RG 7 II-1, 'Inspection of Employment Agencies, Ottawa,' 12 Nov. 1917; *PPMC*, 24 Oct. 1918

44 Udo Sautter, 'The Origins of the Employment Service of Canada, 1900–1920,' *Labour/Le Travailleur* 6 (Fall 1980) 90–112. On recruitment of harvesters, see W.J.C. Cherwinski, 'The Incredible Harvest Excursion of 1908,' *Labour/Le Travailleur* 5 (Spring 1980) 57–79; John Herd Thompson, 'Bringing in the Sheaves: The Harvest Excursionists, 1890–1929,' *Canadian Historical Review* 54:4 (1978) 467–89. AO, DL, RG 7 V-1 vol. 2, 'Employment Service Report, 1918–20.'

45 AO, DL, RG 7 II-1 vol. 1, Mr Appleton to W. Riddell, 14 Apr. 1920. Within a decade, immigrants were reported to show no hestitation in using the Employment Service offices throughout the north (see RG 7 II-1 vol. 6, 'Replies to Questions Relating to Placement of Foreign-born Workers,' 9–10).

46 The *CL* admitted as much, 1 July 1918. Pulpwood contractor Thomas Falls believed foreigners avoided government offices during the war because they thought they 'would be kept track of for military purposes.' (AO, DL, RG 7 II-1 vol. 1, Thomas Falls to W. Riddell, 13 Apr. 1920.) On the heavy-handed state during the war, see Robert Craig Brown, ' "Whither Are We Being Shoved?": Political Leadership in Canada during World War I,' in J.L. Granatstein and R.D. Cuff, eds., *War and Society in North American* (Toronto 1971) 104–19; on immigrant responses, see Avery, *Dangerous Foreigners* 70–6.

47 AO, DL, RG 7 II-1 vol. 21, 'Northern Inspection Trip,' November 1919; Alton Morse to W. Riddell, 13 Apr. 1920. In later years the Employment Service began advancing fares too (see AO, DL, RG 7 I-2 vol. 3, Roger Irwin to D. Croll, 6 Oct. 1936).

48 The *CL* frequently speculated on reasons for jumping, but the best analyses were provided in the late 1940s by WS researchers. See CPPA, WS, W.A.E. Pepler, 'Labour Turnover in Our Pulpwood Camps,' WSI 1013 (1949); Alexander Koroleff, *Stability as a Factor in Efficient Forest Management* (Montreal 1951) 18–20. For early studies of turnover in U.S. industry, see Sumner Slichter, *The Turnover of Factory Labor* (New York 1919); Frederick Brissenden and Emil Frankel, *Labor Turnover in Industry* (New York 1922).

49 *CL*, 1 Sept. 1901; 15 Jan. 1909; 1 Feb. 1918; 1 Sept. 1919
50 UTA, FF, LR #31, Gordon Cosens (1921). UTA, FF, LR #57, J.W. Johnson and L.R. Seheult, Abitibi Power and Paper Company, Ltd., 1926-7. On labour turnover as a form of protest among Canadian manufacturing workers see Craig Heron, 'Hamilton's Steelworkers and the Rise of Mass Production,' Canadian Historical Association, *Historical Papers* 1982, 121.
51 Canada, Department of Labour, *Labour Gazette* (December 1900) 172-3
52 *CL*, November 1881, February 1901
53 Ibid., December 1891
54 AO, MU 4144, A.E. Wicks Ltd. records, box 5, W.A. Delahey and W.J. Leclair to Charles Daly, 11 May 1944, Appendix A. These figures, based on replies to questionnaires from 27 companies, were prepared by the Ontario Forest Industries Association and presented by OFIA and the Canadian Lumbermen's Association to the Ontario Minister of Labour.
55 Michael J. Piva, *The Working Class in Toronto* 38
56 Bob Taylor, cited by Mackay, *The Lumberjacks*, 271; CPPA, WS, *Convention Proceedings* 1930
57 Arvi Tuuamen interviewed by author, Sault Ste Marie 1980. Similar views were expressed in the mid-1940s when woodsworkers' pay improved and Kirkland Lake mining companies had trouble securing labour. As one observer put it, men found logging 'more attractive on account of being outdoors rather than underground.' (AO, Royal Commission Records, RG 18 B-109 vol. 2, Testimony, Thunder Bay, Alex Harris, witness.) J.E. MacDonald, *Shantymen and Sodbusters: An Account of Logging and Settlement in Kirkwood Township, 1869-1929* (Sault Ste Marie 1966) 81
58 AO, J.P. Bertrand, 'Timber Wolves' (typescript 1961)
59 Bradwin, *Bunkhouse Man* 162

CHAPTER 3 Bush work, 1900-1945

1 AO, MHSO collection, Reino Keto papers. In all likelihood, Keto was the poet, and the incident is autobiographical. (Poem translated by Varpu Lindstrom-Best with author.)
2 UTA, FF, LR, #21, J.D. Gilmour (1909)
3 A.W. Bentley, 'Control Work in Forest Management,' CPPA, WS, WSI 434 (1928); C.R. Townsend, 'New Use of Aerial Photographs in Control of Logging Operations,' WSI 88 (1929); W. Kishbaugh, 'Cruising and Its Use in Logging,' WSI 21 (1931); F.R. Wilcox, 'Practical Means of Using Aerial Photography in Woods Operations,' WSI 22 (1933); Donald MacKay, *The Lumberjacks* (Toronto 1978), ch. 4. For examples of cruisers' reports, see AO, MU 1573, Edward E.

Johnson papers, Nipigon Cruise reports 1942, and MU 1580, Gull Bay Area
Cruises 1941. On forestry training, see H.V. Nelles, *The Politics of Development:
Forest, Mines and Hydro-Electric Power in Ontario* (Toronto 1974) 182-214; Paul
Pross, 'The Development of Professionalism in the Public Service: The
Foresters of Ontario,' *Canadian Public Administration* 10 (1967) 376-404; Peter
Gillis, 'The Ottawa Lumber Barons and the Conservation Movement, 1880-
1914,' *Journal of Canadian Studies* 9 (1974) 14-30; J.W.B. Sisam, *Forestry Education
at Toronto* (Toronto 1961); Richard Lambert with Paul Pross, *Renewing Nature's
Wealth: A Centennial History of Lands, Forest and Wildlife and Administration in
Ontario, 1763-1967* (Toronto 1967) 194-8.

4 UTA, FF, LR #21. On the fundamentals of logging, see older textbooks such as
Nelson Courtland Brown, *Logging: The Principles and Methods of Harvesting
Timber in the United States and Canada* (New York 1949).

5 Joe Mason, *My Sixteenth Winter: Logging on the French River* (Cobalt 1974) 7; AO,
MU 2140, transcript of Jack Campbell interview by John MacFie, 1963; AO, FF, LR
[no number] E.G. McDougall (1908); Joe Sarazin interviewed by author, Blind
River 1980

6 CPPA, WS, *Convention Proceedings* 1927, 'Report of the Committee on Organization and Administration'

7 UTA, FF, LR #21

8 L.A. Nix, *Woods Labour* (Montreal 1939)

9 AO, Gillies Brothers Lumber Company records, AA-3, vol. 4, D.A. Gillies to F.A.
Labelle, 17 Sept. 1918. See also D.A. Gillies to Exemption Board, 27 Nov. 1917;
CL, 1 Sept., 1 Nov. 1916.

10 Alton Morse interviewed by the author, Chapleau 1980. On the nicknames of
foremen, see L.M. Lein, 'The Supervisor – Yesterday and Today,' *Log Book* July
–August 1967.

11 Edmund Bradwin, *The Bunkhouse Man* (Toronto 1972) 163; Nix, *Woods Labour* 12

12 CPPA, WS, J.O. Wilson, 'Some Aspects of the Woods Labour Problem,' WSI 77
(1937); CPPA, WS, *Cutting Pulpwood: Efficiency of Technique* (Montreal 1941)

13 UTA, FF, LR #14, E.C. Manning and G.W. Bayly (1912)

14 Ibid. LR #37, N.M. Kensit (1923)

15 Ibid., LR #79 F.N. Wiley (1929)

16 See W.J. Carson, 'Mechanization of Woods Operations,' *CL*, 1 Aug. 1940

17 CPPA, WS, *Convention Proceedings* 1930, 105

18 J.D. Gilmour, 'Short versus Long Lengths,' CPPA, WS, *Convention Proceedings*
1927, 26

19 Arvi Tuuamen interviewed by author, Sault Ste Marie 1980; Ontario, Royal
Commission on Forestry, *Report* (Toronto 1947) 34

20 Mason, *Sixteenth Winter* 10; UTA, FF, LR #65, W.O. Faber, A.P. Macbean, A.B. Wheatley (1928)
21 *Globe and Mail*, 4 Feb. 1947; AO, CR, RG 18 B-109, Ontario Royal Commission on Forestry, 'Proceedings,' vol. 7, 204
22 CPPA, WS, C.D. Sewell, 'Opening Remarks, Symposium on Manpower Requirements in Selection and Training,' WSI 2342 (1965) 1–2
23 CPPA, WS, *Woodcutter's Handbook: How to Cut Pulpwood Safely without Greater Effort* (Montreal 1942) 5, 34
24 CPPA, WS, *Pulpwood Skidding with Horses: Efficiency of Technique* (Montreal 1943)
25 University of Toronto, Faculty of Forestry Library, LR [no number] D.E. Harrott and W. McBride (1955)
26 J.W. Sutherland, 'Horses in Woods Work: Their Care and Selection,' WSI 172 (1934) 3; CPPA, WS, *Pulpwood Skidding*, 12
27 Mason, *Sixteenth Winter* 14; CPPA, WS, *Pulpwood Skidding*
28 Mason, *Sixteenth Winter* 11
29 Sutherland, 'Horses in Woods Work,' 7–8. See also his 'Care and Stabling of Horses,' WSI 555 (1940).
30 Alton Morse interviewed by author, Chapleau 1980
31 *CL*, 1 June 1936, 1 Feb. 1938 (reprint of 1888 article)
32 R.J. Smith of Arnprior, cited in MacKay, *Lumberjacks* 111
33 'The Shantyboy's Song,' cited in MacKay, *Lumberjacks* 99
34 J.E. MacDonald, *Shantymen and Sodbusters: An Account of Logging and Settlement in Kirkwood Township, 1869–1928* (Sault Ste Marie 1966) 50
35 MacKay, *Lumberjacks* 111
36 See photographs in MacDonald, *Shantymen and Sodbusters* 52.
37 AO, MU 2140, transcript of Marshall Dobson interviewed by John MacFie, 1963
38 For details on the Bareinger brake, see Nelson Courtland Brown, *Logging-Transportation* (New York 1936) 172
39 CPPA, WS, *Pulpwood Hauling by Horse and Sleigh: Efficiency of Technique* (Montreal 1943)
40 CPPA, WS, *River Drive of Pulpwood: Efficiency of Technique* (Montreal 1946) 189; Frank Moran cited by MacKay, *Lumberjacks* 11
41 *Log Book*, July–August 1961
42 CPPA, WS, *River Drive*, 3–8
43 UTA, FF, LR #54, G.R. Lane, R.E. Smith, A.W. Goodfellow (1926)
44 UTA, FF, LR #28, J.A. Brodie and F.T. Jenkins (1922)
45 See, for example, AO, Madawaska Improvement Company, Ltd., papers, Minutebooks, 1888–1904; Benjamin F. Avery, 'Early Logging on the Spanish River' (Espanola, Ont.? n.d.).

46 MacDonald, *Lumberjacks* 90
47 Campbell interview transcript; Edith Fowke, *Lumbering Songs from the Northern Woods* (Austin 1970); see also William Main Doerflinger, comp., *Songs of the Sailor and Lumberman*, rev. ed. (New York 1972); M. Béland and L. Carrier-Aulien, *Chansons de voyageurs, coureurs de bois, et forestiers* (Quebec 1982)
48 CPPA, WS, *River Drive* 175. The Quebec disaster is described in CPPA, WS, Julian E. Rotherby, 'Safety in Woods Operations,' WSI B71 (1933) 4–5.
49 CPPA, WS, *River Drive* 8, 25
50 *CL*, 1 May 1930; Canada, Department of Labour, *Labour Gazette* (December 1903) 578; (March 1904) 926; (January 1906) 793
51 Rotherby, 'Safety,' 2–3. On the origins of the board, see Michael J. Piva, 'The Workmen's Compensation Movement in Ontario,' *Ontario History* 67 (1975) 39–45; Dennis Guest, *The Emergence of Social Security in Canada* (Vancouver 1980) 39–47.
52 CPPA, WS, *Convention Proceedings* 1927, 96
53 Canada, Department of Labour, *Labour Gazette* (February 1926) 145
54 Charles More, *Skill and the English Working Class, 1870–1914* (London 1980) 15
55 AO, CR, RG 18 B-109, Royal Commission on Forestry, 'Proceedings,' vol. 3, 155, 204. For further comments on the skills and image of the woodsworker, see Peter Neary, 'The Bradley Report on Logging Operations in Newfoundland, 1934: A Suppressed Document,' *Labour/Le Travail* 16 (Fall 1985) 203–4.
56 On skill, see especially Craig R. Littler, *The Development of the Labour Process in Capitalist Societies: A Comparative Study of the Transformation of Work Organization in Britain, Japan and the USA* (London 1982) 8–9; More, *Skill and the English* 15–26; Ken C. Kusterer, *Know-How on the Job: The Important Working Knowledge of 'Unskilled' Workers* (Boulder, Col. 1978).

CHAPTER 4 Cutting costs

1 Ellwood Wilson, 'Mechanical Logging and Practical Reforestation,' *PPMC*, 9 Dec. 1920
2 On the Progressive movement, see Samuel Hays, *Conservation and the Gospel of Efficiency* (Cambridge, Mass. 1959); Gabriel Kolko, *The Triumph of Conservatism* (Chicago 1963); James Weinstein, *The Corporate Ideal in the Liberal State, 1900–1918* (Boston 1968). On conservation and the role of foresters, see H.V. Nelles, *The Politics of Development: Forests, Mines & Hydro-Electric Power in Ontario, 1849–1949* (Toronto 1974) ch. 5; Peter Gillis, 'The Ottawa Lumber Barons and the Conservation Movement, 1880–1914,' *Journal of Canadian Studies* 9 (1974) 14–30; R. Peter Gillis and Thomas R. Roach, 'The American Influence on Conservation in Canada: 1899–1911,' *Journal of Forest History* 30 (October 1986)

160–74, and *Lost Initiatives: Canada's Forest Industries, Forest Policy and Forest Conservation* (New York 1986); Jamie Swift, *Cut and Run: The Assault on Canada's Forests* (Toronto 1983); Donald MacKay, *Heritage Lost: The Crisis of Canada's Forests* (Toronto 1985); A.F.J. Artibise and G.A. Stelter, 'Conservation Planning and Urban Planning: The Canadian Commission on Conservation in Historical Perspective,' in R. Kain, ed., *Planning for Conservation* (New York 1981) 17–36.

3 Carl Riordan is cited by Fred Stevens, 'The Section's First Sixty Years,' *Pulp and Paper Canada* 78:11 (November 1977) 22. Early reports are published in *PPMC*, 1918–23. Details regarding Koroleff's appointment may be found in CPPA, WS, *Convention Proceedings* 1927, 'Chairman's Report.'

4 *CL*, 15 Feb. 1918

5 Richard Edwards, *Contested Terrain: The Transformation of the Workplace in the Twentieth Century* (New York 1979) 113

6 Daniel Nelson, *Managers and Workers: Origins of the New Factory System in the United States, 1880–1920* (Madison 1975) 53. For Canadian examples, see Craig Heron and Robert Storey, eds., *On the Job: Confronting the Labour Process in Canada* (Kingston 1986).

7 Ralph Clement Bryant, *Logging: The Principles and General Methods of Operations in the United States*, 2nd ed. (New York 1923); *Wkr*, 1 July, 15 Sept. 1920; AO, CR, RG 18 B-109, Royal Commission on Forestry, Testimony vol. 2, 241–5, 337–9

8 *PPMC*, 1 Oct. 1913

9 UTA, FFC, LR #88, G.W. Munday (1936). Examples of scalers' tallies of the output levels of pieceworkers may be found in AO, MU 687 (Commercial Records #129) Oliver Kuursela papers.

10 L.A. Nix, *Woods Labour* (Montreal 1939) 17; CPPA, WS, *Pulpwood Cutting: Efficiency of Technique* (Montreal 1942) 9, 77

11 Alexander Koroleff, *Stability as a Factor in Efficient Forest Management* (Montreal 1951) 17

12 *Wkr*, 1 Aug. 1920; Lother Bode interviewed by author, Thunder Bay 1982; MHSO, OHC, Felix Lukkarila interviewed by A.-M. Lahtinen, 1978

13 Bill Plaunt interviewed by author, Sudbury 1982; William Kurelek, *Lumberjack* (Montreal 1974); A. Koroleff, *Woodcutter's Handbook* (Montreal 1942) 51

14 CPPA, WS, 'Efficiency and Stability of Woods Labour in Eastern Canada,' WSI B60

15 Ontario, Royal Commission on Forestry, *Report* (Toronto 1947) 37; AO, CR, RG 18 B-109, Royal Commission on Forestry vol. 18, 'Minutes of a Meeting of Operators, Kenora and Thunder Bay districts,' 18 June 1946

16 CPPA, WS, C.R. Townsend, 'New Developments in Logging Techniques,' WSI 590 (194?) 3; Joe Sarazin interviewed by author, Blind River 1980; Gerard Fortin and Boyce Richardson, *The Life of the Party* (Montreal 1984) 48; Bode interview;

Luka Radulovich (strip boss in 1947 at Spruce Fall Power and Paper Company) interviewed by author, Toronto 1985

17 CPPA, WS, 'Efficiency'; *OT*, 15 Feb. 1947

18 David M. Gordon, Richard Edwards, and Michael Reich, *Segmented Work, Divided Workers: The Historical Transformation of Labor in the United States* (Cambridge 1982) 141; Michael Burawoy, *Manufacturing Consent: Changes in the Labour Process under Capitalism* (Chicago 1979) ch. 5

19 For a thorough examination of the development of the alligator, see R. John Corby, 'The Alligator or Steam Warping Tug: A Canadian Contribution to the Development of Technology in the Forest Industry,' *Industrial Archaeology* 3:1 (1977) 15–33. For a vivid description of it in use, see the novel *Abitibi Adventure* (Toronto 1950) by Jack Hambleton (135–8); see also *CL*, 1 May 1893, 1 Jan. 1905; Brenda B. Lee-Whiting, 'The Alligator – Unique Canadian Boat, *Canadian Geographical Journal* 76 (January 1968) 30–3.

20 Corby, 'The Alligator,' 31–2; on productivity and problems in its measurement, see Corby, 24, and CPPA, WS, L.R. McCurdy, 'Report on a Survey of Tow-boats in Eastern Canada,' WSI 127 (1929); Plaunt interview.

21 William G. Rector, *Log Transportation in the Lake States Lumber Industry, 1840–1918* (Glendale 1953) 210; UTA, FF, LR [no number] James Johnson on the Hope Lumber Company (1909); Asa Williams, 'Logging by Steam,' *Forestry Quarterly* (1908) 5; UTA, Bernhard Fernow papers, vol. 4, Bernard Fernow to Judson Clark, 28 Oct. 1909

22 Ed Gould, *British Columbia's Logging History* (Saanichton 1975) 98–115; Robert D. Turner, 'Logging Railroads and Locomotives in British Columbia: A Background Survey and the Preservation Record,' *Material History Bulletin* 13 (Fall 1981) 3–20. On railways in the western Lakes States, see Frank A. King, *Minnesota Logging Railroads* (San Marino 1981); William G. Rector, 'Railroad Logging in the Lake States,' *Michigan History* 36 (1952) 351–62. See also John H. White, 'Industrial Locomotives: The Forgotten Servant,' *Technology and Culture* 21:2 (April 1980) 209–25.

23 *CL*, 1 Dec. 1929; Abitibi Power and Paper Company, *A Story in Pictures: An Illustrated Story of the Development of the Newsprint Paper Mill of the Abitibi Power and Paper Co., Ltd.* (Iroquois Falls 1924)

24 UTA, FF, LR #6

25 *CL*, 15 Dec. 1919; Rector, *Log Transportation* 239

26 *CL*, 1 Aug. 1902; Reynold M. Wik, 'Benjamen Holt and the Track-Type Tractor,' *Technology and Culture* 20:1 (January 1979) 95–6; *CL*, 1 March 1910, 1 Sept. 1911; Alton Morse interviewed by author, Chapleau 1980

27 Robert E. Ankli, H. Dan Helsberg, John Herd Thompson, 'The Adoption of the Gasoline Tractor in Western Canada,' in Donald H. Akenson, ed., *Canadian*

Papers in Rural History II (Gananoque 1980) 9–39; R. Bruce Shepard, 'The Roar of Tractors and Combines: Canadian Plains Agriculture in the Twenties,' paper presented to the Canadian Historical Association, Annual Meeting 1984; Reynold M. Wik, 'Some Interpretations of the Mechanization of Agriculture in the Far West,' *Agricultural History* 44:1 (January 1975) 73–83

28 *CL*, 1 Aug. 1917; Morse interview. (There is a short biography of A.L. Morse in Vincent Crichton, *Pioneering in Northern Ontario* [Chapleau 1977] 53–9.)

29 *CL*, 15 July 1937

30 Ibid., 15 June 1923

31 AO, Gillies papers, AB-7, D. Lunam to D.A. Gillies, 2 Apr. 1928; D.A. Gillies to Hugh White, 8 Nov. 1930; CPPA, WS, W.S. Carson, 'Training Woods Workers,' *Convention Proceedings* 1938

32 Ken Collins, *Oatmeal and the Eaton's Catologue: The Dryden Area – The Early Days* (Dryden 1982) 113–14, 171–2. On Osaquan and the Indian Lake Lumber Company, see also Elinor Barr and Betty Dyck, *Ignace: A Saga of the Shield* (Winnipeg 1979) 57–69.

33 *CL*, 15 Jan. 1913, 1 Dec. 1914, 1 Sept. 1916, 1 Aug., 15 Apr. 1919; 1 Sept. 1920; L.R. Seheult, 'The Use of Trucks in Logging Operations,' M SC Forestry thesis, University of Toronto 1935

34 CPPA, WS, G.E. LaMothe, 'Trucking Logs in Winter,' WSI 193 (1936); L.R. Seheult, 'The Use of Motor Trucks in Woods Operations,' WSI 187 (1932); L.R. Seheult, *The Motor Truck in Woods Operations* (Montreal 1937); W.K. Cox, 'Changes in Logging Costs in Diesel Tractors,' *CL*, 15 Aug. 1934

35 *CL*, 15 Aug. 1917

36 *CL*, 15 Nov. 1940; see also Koroleff, 'Use of Portable Motor Saws in Logging,' *Journal of Forestry* (October 1934) 742–8.

37 CPPA, WS, Alexander Koroleff, 'Portable Motor Saws and Their Applicability for Cutting Pulpwood in Canada,' *Convention Proceedings* 1930

38 CPPA, WS, Alexander Koroleff, 'Progress of Pulpwood Logging in Eastern Canada,' WSI B130 (1930). On the tests, see J.L. Kelly, 'Experimental Tests,' WSI B130 (1936); 'Recent Trials of the Dolmar Saw in Cutting Pulpwood,' WSI B132 (1936); 'Tests in Quebec,' WSI B134 (1936).

39 On powersaw developments in British Columbia, see Jim Wardrop, 'British Columbia's Experience with Early Chain Saws,' *Material History Bulletin* 21 (October 1977) 9–18; CPPA, WS, Logging Mechanization Committee, 'The Development of Portable Mechanical Saws for Felling and Bucking Timber,' WSI 733 (1944).

40 CPPA, WS, J.L. Kelly, 'Horses in the Pulpwood Industry,' WSI 1244 (1952)

41 CPPA, WS, B.J. McColl and W.A.E. Pepler, 'The Status of Mechanization,' WSI 1011 (1949)

42 AO, Gillies Brother Lumber Company records, AB-6, D.A. Gillies to Phoenix Manufacturing Company, 22 Nov. 1921. On early mechanization in British Columbia, see Gould, *Logging* 95–130; G.W. Taylor, *Timber: History of the Forest Industry in B.C.* (Vancouver 1975) 127–49. On the southern U.S., see Asa Williams, 'Logging by Steam,' *Forestry Quarterly* (1908); Arthur S. Michell, 'Analysis of Pulpwood Harvesting Techniques in North Carolina,' MSc Forestry thesis, Duke University 1951.

43 CPPA, WS, A. Koroleff, 'The Progress of Pulpwood Logging in Eastern Canada,' WSI B30 (1930); 'Analysis of Woods Operations,' WSI B37 (1933); 'Mechanical Logging,' WSI B52 (1937); and 'Economic Possibilities of Mechanized Logging,' WSI B54 (1938)

44 *PPMC*, 24 Oct. 1918; Koroleff, 'Progress of Pulpwood Logging'

45 CPPA, WS, *Convention Proceedings* 1932 (J.O. Wilson's comments in 'Discussion on Bucksaws')

46 CPPA, WS, G. Lemothe, 'Woods Labour Problems,' *Convention Proceedings* 1933; Koroleff, 'Relations between General, Woods, and Mill Management in Our Industry,' WSI 234 (1934); Douglas Jones, 'Co-operation,' WSI 952 (1947)

47 C. Ross Silversides, 'How Engineering Science Raised Woods Efficiency,' *Pulp and Paper Canada* 82:2 (February 1981) 42

48 Ibid., 33–8; H.R. Soderston, 'Booms, Chains and Wire Rope,' *PPMC* 32:7 (February 1932) 223–6, 239–40; CPPA, WS, W.E. Wakefield, 'An Investigation into the Various Factors Governing the Efficiency of Bucksaws,' *Convention Proceedings* 1932; Koroleff, 'Mechanical Tests of Efficiency of Bucksaws,' WSI B119 (1932); 'Instructions for Filing and Fitting Bucksaws,' WSI B122 and B123 (1932)

49 CPPA, WS, Koroleff, 'Manpower and Efficiency in Woods Operations,' WSI 688 (1942); *CL* 1 Oct. 1918

CHAPTER 5 In the camps

1 All references in this chapter to Magne Stortroen and Karl Brandvold are from M.E. Stortroen, *Immigrant in Porcupine* (Cobalt 1977) 1–22.

2 Ontario, Board of Health, *Annual Report* 1901, 40. On camboose camps, see Bernie Bedore, *The Shanty* (Arnprior 1975); Charles Macnamara, 'The Camboose Shanty,' *Ontario History* 5:2 (Spring 1959) 73–8. For comparisons with trends elsewhere, see Randall E. Rohe, 'The Evolution of the Great Lakes Logging Camp, 1830–1930,' *Journal of Forest History* 30:1 (January 1986) 17–28; René Hardy and Normand Séguin, *Forêt et société en Mauricie: La formation de la région des Trois-Rivières 1830–1930* (Montreal 1983) 115–20; Ed Gould, *Logging: British Columbia's Logging History* (Saanichton 1970) 135–46; P.H. Harrison, 'Life

in a Logging Camp,' *B.C. Studies* 54 (Summer 1982) 88–104.

3 UTA, FF, LR #21, J.D. Gilmour (1909)

4 W.R. Wilson, 'The Camp Clerk and Woods Labour Management,' WSI 1009 (1949) 2

5 Ralph Thomson, 'Where the North Begins' (typescript n.d.) 19–20

6 *CL*, 15 Aug. 1911, 15 Jan. 1928; Wilson, 'Camp Clerk,' 1

7 *CL*, 15 Jan. 1928

8 Arvi Tuuamen interviewed by author, Sault Ste Marie 1980; *CL*, 1 May 1928

9 UTA, FF, LR #21; 1 Oct. 1916. On camp improvements of the early twentieth century, see S.B. Detwiler, 'Comfortable Camps as a Means of Increasing Efficiency of Woodsworkers,' *Forestry Chronicle* 9 (1911) 15–17.

10 *CL*, 15 June 1937; Siami Hormavirta interviewed by author and Varpu Lindstrom-Best, Toronto 1980

11 Ontario, Board of Health, *Annual Report* 1922, 193; UTA, FF, LR #98, W.W. Adams (1942)

12 UTA, FF, LR #103, T.W. Hueston (1945); Ken Collins, *Oatmeal and the Eaton's Catalog: The Dryden Area – The Early Days* (Dryden 1982) 115

13 MHSO, OHC, Alva Korri interviewed by Lennard Silanpaa, 1977; J.E. MacDonald, *Shantymen and Sodbusters: An Account of Logging and Settlement in Kirkwood Township* (Sault Ste Marie 1966) 74

14 PAC, Frontier College papers, MG 28 I 124 vol. 36

15 On visits of pedlars and photographers to camps, see *CL*, 1 Mar. 1909. On priests in the camps, see Marcel Bréton, 'Les aspects réligieux chez les travailleurs de la forêt,' *Laurentian University Review* 19 (1978) 7–31; P. Joseph-Alphonse Desjardins, S.J., *Le bûcheron d'autrefois: Vie et travaux de l'ouvrier de la forêt* (Sudbury 1980); P.D. Martineau, 'Le ministre des chantiers,' Société Canadienne de l'Eglise Catholique, *Sessions d'Etude* 49 (1982) 59–68.

16 On major denominations and the lumberjacks, see United Church of Canada Archives, Methodist Missionary Society records, Home Department, vol. 2, 'Report of the Board of Home Missions and Social Service for 1921,' 7; *CL*, November 1881, April 1894, December 1898; *Sault Star*, 30 May 1907; F.N. White, *Gillmor of Algoma: Archdeacon Tramp* (Toronto 1967). On the history of the Shantyman's Christian Association, see *CL*, 1 Aug. 1910, 1 Apr. 1913, 15 Mar. 1917, 1 May 1918, 1 Oct. 1919, 1 Apr. 1920, 15 July 1921, 15 May 1928, 1 Jan. 1929, 1 Jan. 1931, 1 May 1936, 15 June 1938; Donald MacKay, *The Lumberjacks* (Toronto 1978) 251.

17 *CL*, 15 May 1929

18 New Brunswicker cited in MacKay, *Lumberjacks* 249; UTA, FF, LR #24, J.F. Turnbull et al. (1921)

19 Michael S. Cross, 'The Dark Druidical Groves: The Lumber Community and

the Commercial Frontier in British North America to 1854, PH D thesis, University of Toronto 1968, 194

20 A.R.M. Lower, *My First Seventy-Five Years* (Toronto 1967) 67

21 Joe Mason, *My Sixteenth Winter: Logging on the French River* (Cobalt 1974) 26; MHSO, OHC, Toivo Tienhara interviewed by Lennard Silanpaa, 1977 (translation by Varpu Lindstrom-Best)

22 Robert Marshall, 'A Contribution to the Life History of the Lumber Jack,' *PPMC*, 21 May 1931

23 For descriptions of 'Hot Hand,' see *CL*, 1 Dec. 1892; Mason, *Sixteenth Winter* 24; and for 'Hit Ass,' see James M. Hillis, 'Life in the Lumber Camp: 1883,' *Ontario History* 59 (Sept. 1967) 157–62. UTA, FF, LR #81, R.S. Young (1931)

24 Collins, *Oatmeal* 170

25 Joseph R. Conlin, ' "Did You Get Enough of Pie?": A Social History of Food in Logging Camps,' *Journal of Forest History* 25:3 (October 1979) 165–84; Ellard Connolly to Joseph A. Bradette, read into Canada, House of Commons, *Debates*, 28 Mar. 1934, 1916. On Quebec, see Hardy and Séguin, *Forêt et société* 124–6.

26 UTA, FF, LR #54 G.R. Lane, R.E. Smith, and A.W. Goodfellow (1924); *CL*, 1 Sept. 1916; A. Koroleff, 'Feeding of Lumberjacks,' WSI 66 (1932); J.V.G.A. Durnin and R. Passmore, *Energy, Work, and Leisure* (London 1967) 71–3, cited by Conlin, ' "Did You Get Enough of Pie?" ' 169

27 Confederation College Archives, Thunder Bay Labour History Project, Buzz Lein taped interview by Jean Morrison, 1975; verse cited in Carl Kauffmann, *Logging Days in Blind River* (Sault Ste Marie 1970); *PPMC*, 15 Mar. 1928

28 *OBUB*, 2 Apr. 1921; see also Michael Bennett, 'Rattlesnake Pork,' *Your Forests* 10:3 (Winter 1977) 16–20.

29 *CL*, 15 Nov. 1914

30 Ibid., 1 Apr. 1920; 1 May 1918

31 CPPA, WS, *Convention Proceedings*, 1932, 75; *CL*, 15 Feb. 1934; CPPA, WS, *Convention Proceedings* 1932, 77. See also J.W. Paterson, 'An Inquiry into Woods Diets,' in CPPA, WS, *Convention Proceedings* 1933; F.A. Harrison, 'Camp Diets,' WSI 460 (1936); J.E. Caron, comp. *Feeding Men in Camps: Manual of Commissary Practice* (Montreal 1934).

32 CPPA, WS, *Convention Proceedings* 1931, 35–6; Dr Paul L. Rivard, 'Balanced Camp Diet,' WSI 757 (1945); Dr L. Gibson and the PPRIC, 'Feeding in Logging Camps,' WSI 873 (1946)

33 Helvi Syrjä interviewed by author, Sault Ste Marie 1980; Shewfelt cited in MacKay, *Lumberjacks* 213–4

34 'Mentor,' 'Of the Salt of the Earth – The Cook,' *PPMC*, December 1933, 785–6; Lein interview

35 CPPA, WS, *Convention Proceedings* 1932, 76–7; UTA, FF, LR #21
36 Elsa Silanpaa interviewed by author, Sault Ste Marie 1980. On women in the
   North American forest industry, see also Dorothea Mitchell, *Lady Lumberjack*
   (Vancouver 1967) [the autobiography of an English immigrant timber
   contractor in the Thunder Bay region during the World War I era]; Anna M.
   Lind, 'Women in the Early Logging Camps: A Personal Reminiscence,' *Journal
   of Forest History* 19 (September 1975) 129–42.
37 Fitzpatrick cited in *CL*, 15 Feb. 1914. On Frontier College, see Eric Wilfred
   Robinson, 'The History of Frontier College,' MA thesis, McGill University 1960;
   George L. Cook, 'Alfred Fitzpatrick and the Founding of Frontier College,
   1899–1922,' *Canada: An Historical Magazine* 3:4 (June 1976) 15–17.
38 Alfred Fitzpatrick, *The University in Overalls: A Plea for Part-Time Study* (Toronto
   1920) 138–9; Edmund Bradwin, *The Bunkhouse Man* (rpr. Toronto 1972),
   especially 206–44. See also Marjorie E. Zavitz, 'Frontier College and
   Bolshevism in the Camps of Canada, 1919–1925,' MA thesis, University of
   Windsor 1974.
39 *CL*, 1 Mar. 1918, 1 Sept. 1918
40 Ibid., 1 Apr. 1918; see also 15 Mar. 1918.
41 Charles A. Hodgetts, 'Small Pox,' *The Sanitary Journal for 1905* (Toronto 1906)
   114–15; Ontario, Board of Health, *Annual Report* 1900, 42–3 and 1901, 40–1. On
   earlier epidemics and the lumber camps, see AO, DH, RG 10 1B4 vol. 464,
   Scrapbooks, item #50. On conditions in Quebec camps, see Hardy and
   Séguin, *Forêt et société* 120–4.
42 Hodgetts, 'Small Pox,' 115; On the public health movement, see Paul Adolphus
   Bator, ' "Saving Lives on the Wholesale Plan": Public Health Reform in the
   City of Toronto, 1900 to 1930,' PH D thesis, University of Toronto 1979, and his
   'The Health Reformer versus the Common Canadian: The Controversy over
   Compulsory Vaccination against Smallpox in Toronto and Ontario, 1900–1920,'
   Ontario History 75:4 (December 1983) 348–733; Heather Anne MacDougall,
   ' "Health is Wealth": The Development of Public Health Activities in Toronto,
   1834–90,' PH D thesis, University of Toronto 1981; Barbara Lazenby Craig,
   'State Medicine in Transition: Battling Smallpox in Ontario, 1882–1885,' *Ontario
   History* 75:4 (December 1983) 319–47.
43 The changes in regulations and enforcement problems are detailed in the
   Ontario, Board of Health, *Annual Report* 1902–20, but see especially 1902, 30;
   1906, 86–8; 1912, 486–93. Departmental correspondence also illustrates
   enforcement problems; see especially AO, DH, RG 10 1A1, vol. 2; 1B4 vols. 463–4;
   1B2a vol. 457. See also W.C. Miller, 'Why Compensation Costs Are Increasing
   in Ontario,' *CL* 15, January 1929.
44 Ontario, Board of Health, *Annual Report* 1917, 63. Details of conditions are in

AO, DH, RG 10 1B 2a vol. 457, George report, 7 Jan. 1916. Even the CL admitted
the need for stricter enforcement; see 15 May 1912.

45 See, for example, Ontario, Department of Health, *Annual Report* 1922, 240–55;
1927, 39.

46 *CL*, 15 Sept. 1923

47 *CL*, 15 Dec. 1922; see list of prosecutions, Ontario, Department of Health,
Annual Report 1920, 191–2. The regulations were published in ibid., 1921, 6–29.

48 For a vivid account of problems, see AO, DH, RG 10 1B 2a vol. 460, transcript of
trial, Fort William Police Court, 26 Jan. 1923. See also the reports of the
sanitary inspectors who visited Ontario logging camps, RG 10 1B 2a vols. 460–
3.

49 UTA, FF, LR #98, W.W. Adams (1942); LR #103, T.W. Hueston (1945); AO, CR, Royal
Commission on Forestry, RG 18 B109, vols. 6–9, 'Field Reports'; AO, MU 4144,
A.E. Wicks Ltd. records, box 5, Ontario Forest Industries Association file,
W.A.E. Pepler to F.E. Hull, 2 July 1943

CHAPTER 6 Bushworkers in struggle, 1919–1935

1 Egil Schonnig, 'Union-Management Relations in the Pulp and Paper Industry
of Ontario and Quebec, 1914–50,' PH D thesis, University of Toronto 1955;
William E. Greening, *Paper Makers in Canada: A History of the Paper Makers' Union*
(Cornwall 1952). On U.S. developments, see Robert H. Zieger, *Rebuilding the
Pulp and Paper Workers' Union, 1933–41* (Knoxville 1984) ch. 3. On the
willingness of pulp and paper managers to deal with mill unions, see Abitibi
Power and Paper Company's Directors' resolution of trade unions, Canada,
Labour Gazette (August 1924) 628; *Spanish River News*, 1920–25 (copies in Sault
Ste Marie and 149th Field Regiment R.C.A. Historical Society Archives).
Sawmill unionists made somewhat more headway on the West Coast, where
the political culture was different, labour in shorter supply, and operations
were more capital-intensive and less seasonal. See Harold Logan, *Trade Unions
in Canada* (Toronto 1948) 280; Carlos A. Schwantes, *Radical Heritage: Labor,
Socialism and Reform in Washington and British Columbia, 1885–1917* (Vancouver
1979) 153–4.

2 On Finland at this period, see L.A. Puntila, *The Political History of Finland, 1819–
1966* (Helsinki 1975) 123–48; D.G. Kirby, *Finland in the Twentieth Century*
(London 1979) 177–89, and his 'Revolutionary Finns in Finland and the
Origins of the Civil War 1917–18,' *Scandinavian Economic History Review* 24:1
(1978) 15–35; Anthony F. Upton, *The Finnish Revolution, 1917–18* (Minneapolis
1981); Hanna Soikkanen, 'Revisionism, Reformism and the Finnish Labour
Movement before the First World War,' *Scandinavian Journal of History* 3 (1978)

347–56; Varpu Lindstrom-Best, 'Defiant Sisters: A Social History of Finnish Women in Canada, 1890–1930,' PH D thesis, York University 1986, ch. 1. On Finnish emigration, see Reino Kero, 'Emigration from Finland to Canada before the First World War,' *Lakehead University Review* 9 (Spring 1976) and his *Migration from Finland to North America in the Years between the United States Civil War and the First World War* (Turku 1974); Keijo Virtanen, *Settlement or Return Finnish Emigrants (1860–1920) in the International Overseas Return Migration Movement* (Helsinki 1979); Varpu Lindstrom-Best, *The Finns in Canada* (Ottawa 1985).

3 On Finnish settlement and hall socialism, Varpu Lindstrom-Best, ed., 'Finns in Ontario,' special issue of *Polyphony* 3:2 (Fall 1981); Mauri Amiko Jalava, ' "Radicalism or a 'New Deal'?": The Unfolding World View of Finnish Immigrants in Sudbury, 1883–1932,' MA thesis, Laurentian University 1983; Lindstrom-Best, 'Defiant Sisters,' ch. 7; Peter V. Krats, ' "Sudburyn Suomalaiset": Finnish Immigrant Activities in the Sudbury Area, 1883–1939,' MA thesis, University of Western Ontario 1980, and his ' "Suomalaiset Nikkelialuella": Finns in the Sudbury Area, 1883–1939,' *Polyphony* 5 (Spring–Summer 1983) 37–48; Chris Kouki, ed., *A Chronicle of Finnish Settlements in Rural Thunder Bay* (Thunder Bay 1976); Ahti Tolvanen, 'Finntown': A Perspective on Urban Integration, Port Arthur Finns in the Inter-War Period: 1918–1939* (Helsinki 1985); M. Rasmussen, 'The Geographic Impact of Finnish Settlement on the Thunder Bay Area of Northern Ontario,' MA thesis, University of Alberta 1978. On the emigration of Tokoi, see PAC, IR, RG 76 C4682, 'Emigration from Finland 1893–1944'; Oskari Tokoi, *Sisu 'Even Through a Stone Wall': The Autobiography of Oskari Tokoi* (New York 1957).

4 Statistics are lacking, but this was the view of a perceptive observer, Akseli Rauenheimo, Finnish Consul at Montreal during the 1920s. See his 'Finnish Emigration to Canada: General Survey,' enclosed in a letter from Raunanheimo to F.C. Blair, 21 Nov. 1928 (PAC, IR, RG 76 vol. 25 651). See also Akseli Rauanheimo, *Kanadan-kirja* (Porvoo, Finland 1930).

5 Varpu Lindstrom-Best, 'Central Organization of the Loyal Finns in Canada, *Polyphony* 3:2 (Fall 1981) 81–90; Jalava, 'Radicalism,'; K.A. Iapuro, 'Regional Variations in Political Mobilization,' *Journal of Scandinavian History* 1 (1979) 215–42. On the radicalization of Finns in U.S. resource centres, see Paul George Hummasti, *Finnish Radicals in Astoria, Oregon, 1904–1940: A Story in Immigrant Socialism* (New York 1979); Arthur Puotinen, *Finnish Radicals and Religion in Midwestern Mining Towns, 1865–1914* (New York 1979) ch. 5, and his 'Copper Country Finns and the Strike of 1913,' in Michael G. Karni, Matti E. Kaups, and Douglas J. Ollila, eds., *Finnish Experience in the Western Great Lakes Region: New Perspectives* (Turku 1975) 143–55; A. Gedicles, 'The Social Organization of

Radicalism among Finnish Immigrants in Midwest Mining Communities,' *Review of Radical Economics* 8:3 (Fall 1976) 1–31; Auro Kostiainen, 'For or against Americanization? The Case of the Finnish Immigrant Radicals,' in Dirk Hoerder, ed., *American Labor and Immigration History, 1877–1920s: Recent European Research* (Urbana, Ill. 1982) 259–82.

6 A. William Hoglund, 'Breaking Religious Tradition: Finnish Immigrant Workers and the Church, 1890–1915,' in *For the Common Good* (Superior, Wisc. 1977) 23–64; Markku Suokonautio, 'Reorganization of the Finnish Lutherans in Canada,' *Polyphony* 3:2 (Fall 1981) 91–6; Lindstrom-Best, 'Defiant Sisters,' ch. 6; Yrjö Raivio, *Kanadan Suomalaisten Historia* vols. I and II (Vancouver and Thunder Bay 1975 and 1979)

7 Jalava, 'Radicalism,' 99–1126; Arja Pilli, *The Finnish-Language Press in Canada, 1901–1939: A Study in the History of Ethnic Journalism* (Turku 1982) 67–9; Taru Sundsten, 'The Theatre of the Finnish-Canadian Labour Movement and Its Dramatic Literature, 1900–1939,' in Michael G. Karni, *Finnish Diaspora I: Canada, South Africa and Sweden* (Toronto 1981) 77–92; Bruce Kidd, 'The Workers' Sports Movement in Canada, 1924–40: The Radical Immigrants' Alternative,' *Polyphony* 7:1 (1985) 80–8; Jim Tester, ed., *Sports Pioneers: A History of the Finnish-Canadian Amateur Sports Federation, 1906–1986* (Sudbury 1986); Mauri A. Jalava, 'The Finnish-Canadian Cooperative Movement in Ontario,' in Karni, *Finnish Diaspora I*, 93–100

8 Michael S. Cross, 'The Shiners' War: Social Violence in the Ottawa Valley in the 1830s,' *Canadian Historical Review* 54:1 (March 1973) 1–26; George Thompson, *Up to Date: Or the Life of a Lumberman* (Peterborough 1895?) 67–9. Thompson calls this the first strike by woodsmen (67). For an early twentieth-century example of woodsworkers' collective violence, see Livo Ducin (pseud.), 'Labour's Emergent Years and the 1903 Riots,' in *50 Years of Labour in Algoma* (Sault Ste Marie 1978) 1–18; primary sources for the same riots are in AO, Attorney-General's Records, RG 4 C-3 (1903) 1488. On the Knights of Labor and Ontario sawmill workers, see Gregory S. Kealey and Bryan D. Palmer, *Dreaming of What Might Be: The Knights of Labor in Ontario* (New York 1982) 84, 359–61; Edward McKenna, 'Unorganized Labour versus Management: The Strike at the Chaudière Mills, 1891,' *Histoire Sociale/Social History* 4 (1972) 186–211.

9 A copy of the union's constitution is available in PAC, FOCC, MG 28 V46 vol. 143:1. See also Ian Walter Radforth, 'Bushworkers and Bosses: A Social History of the Northern Ontario Logging Industry, 1900–1980,' PH D thesis, York University 1985, 222–3. On *Tyokansa*, see Pilli, *Finnish-Language Press* 67.

10 Thunder Bay Historical Museum and Archives, A.T. Hill papers, A.T. Hill,

'Historical Basis and Development of the Lumber Workers' Organization and Struggle in Ontario' (typescript 1952), his 'Autobiography' (typescript n.d.), and his 'Harry Bryan' (typescript n.d.)

11 John Wiita, 'A Finnish-American in Canada, 1918–23,' in J. Donald Wilson, 'The Canadian Sojourn of a Finnish American Radical,' *Canadian Ethnic Studies* 16:2 (1984) 108

12 Melvyn Dubofsky, *We Shall Be All: A History of the Industrial Workers of the World* (New York 1969); Robert L. Tyler, *Rebels of the Woods: The I.W.W. in the Pacific Northwest* (Eugene 1967); A.R. McCormack, 'The Industrial Workers of the World in Western Canada, 1905–1914,' Canadian Historical Association, *Historical Papers* 1975 167–90

13 Dubofsky, *We Shall Be All* 128–30, 209–20; Ralph Winstead, 'Evolution of Logging Conditions on the Northwest Coast,' *The One Big Union Monthly* 1:6 (August 1919), 20–9; Tyler, *Rebels of the Woods*; Industrial Workers of the World, *The Lumber Industry and Its Workers* (Chicago 1921?)

14 Dubofsky, *We Shall Be All* 360

15 Douglas Ollila, Jr., 'From Socialism to Industrial Unionism (IWW): Social Factors in the Emergence of Left-Labor Radicalism among Finnish Workers of the Mesabi, 1911–1919,' in Karni et al., *Finnish Experience*, 170

16 PAC, IR, RG 76 619 917093–102, Thomas Gilley to Secretary of the Immigration Department, 20 Jan. 1920 and 2 Nov. 1922. See also AO, OPPR, RG 23 E-30 1.6 for numerous reports on IWW activities in northern Ontario.

17 AO, OPPR, RG 23 E-30 1.6 Constable A.W. Symons to Supt. James E. Rogers, 5 April 1919.

18 *Metsa* 1927 #6 (transl.). On the Fist Press in general, see Varpu Lindstrom-Best, ' "Fist Press": A Study of the Finnish Canadian Handwritten Newspapers,' *Polyphony* 3:2 (Fall 1981) 65–73.

19 AO, OPPR, RG 23 E-30 1.6, translation of minutes of meeting, enclosed in James E. Rogers to A.W. Cawdron, 23 Apr. 1918, Commissioner Rogers to Cawdron, 23 Apr. 1918

20 Arja Pilli, 'Finnish Canadian Radicalism and the Government of Canada from the First World War to the Depression,' in Karni, *Finnish Diaspora I* 19–32; Hill, 'Basis,' 4

21 On post-World War I radicalism in Canada, see especially David J. Bercuson, *Fools and Wise Men: The Rise and Fall of the One Big Union* (Toronto 1978) 57–104; Gregory S. Kealey, '1919: The Canadian Labour Revolt,' *Labour/Le Travail* 13 (Spring 1984) 11–44.

22 Dorothy Steeves, *The Compassionate Rebel: Ernest Winch and the Growth of Socialism in Western Canada* (Vancouver 1977) 46; *British Columbia Federationist*

24 Jan. 1919; Gordon Hak, 'A Lost Opportunity: British Columbia's Loggers and the Lumber Workers Industrial Union, 1919–1922,' typescript, Department of History, Simon Fraser University 1986

23 Bercuson, *Fools* 135; *PPMC*, 8 Apr. 1920

24 Wiita, 'Finnish-American,' 111

25 On organizing at the Lakehead, see Lakehead University Archives, Finlandia Club collection, minutebook of the LWIU of the OBU, 7 Oct. 1919 (transl.). On holdouts, see AO, Jussi Palokangas collection, Algoma Line strike minutes 25 Oct. 1919 (transl.); AO, OPPR, RG 23 E-30 1.6, translation of minutes of Algoma Line strike committee meeting, 30 Aug. 1919, enclosed in Captain F.C. Flanagan to Inspector Perkins, 12 Sept. 1919.

26 Text of 'What the Workers of B.C. Have Done!' reproduced in *CL*, 1 Dec. 1919

27 'Proceedings,' in *LeT/W*, 1, 15 Oct. 1920

28 *LeT/W*, 1, 15 June, 1 Nov. 1920

29 *CL*, 1 Mar. 1920. On the Red Scare in Ontario, see Elliot Samuels, 'The Red Scare in Ontario: The Reaction of the Ontario Press to the Internal and External Threat of Bolshevism, 1917–1919,' MA thesis, Queen's University 1971

30 *LeT/W*, 15 May 1920

31 Ibid., 15 Oct., 15 Nov. 1920

32 Ibid., 15 May 1920. On strategy and tactics of militant industrial unionists, see A. Ross McCormack, *Reformers, Rebels and Revolutionaries: The Western Canada Radical Movement, 1899–1919* (Toronto 1977); Bercuson, *Fools* 150–2.

33 AO, DH RG 10 1A1 vol. 241, W. Cowan to Mr McCullough, 18 Mar. 1920, E. Guerbin to McCullough, 2 Sept. 1920. On the responses of the Department, see memos and reports in the above volume, as well as in vol. 261; see also Ontario, Department of Health, *Annual Report* 1920, 190–3.

34 *LeT/W*, 1 May, 1 Oct. 1920; *CL*, 1 Oct. 1920; *CL*, 1 Oct. 1922. Improved conditions are mentioned in the sanitary inspectors' reports in the Ontario Department of Health, *Annual Report* 1921–7.

35 *OBUB*, 20 Mar., 17 Apr., 1 Oct., and 6 Nov. 1920; *LeT/W*, 1 July, 1 Oct. 1920; Bercuson, *Fools* 169

36 *CL*, 15 Dec. 1920; UTA, RRC, LR #28, J.A. Brodie and F.T. Jenkins (1922). On conditions generally, see Bryan D. Palmer, *Working-Class Experience: The Rise and Reconstitution of Canadian Labour, 1800–1980* (Toronto 1983) 185–98; Ian Radforth, 'Organized Labour in Ontario during the 1920s,' MA major research paper, Graduate Programme in History, York University 1978.

37 Public Archives of Manitoba, Robert Boyd Russell collection, MG 10 A14-2 file 49, 'Proceedings of the 1923 OBU Convention'

38 On *Industrialisti*, see Pilli, *Finnish-Language Press* 120–5; on emigrés, see Wiita, 'Finnish-American,' 111.

39 Thunder Bay Finnish Canadian Historical Society Archives, newspaper clippings, *Industrialisti*, 21 Oct. 1975 (transl.). This article, 'The End of the Road,' is a history of the CTKL, and was printed in the last issue of *Industrialisti*. Developments within these organizations are well documented in the Lakehead University Archives, Finlandia collection, Minute Book of the LWIU of Ontario and OBU Support Circle's agitation committee, 20 Apr. 1923–28 Oct. 1925; Minute Book of the CTU Support Circle, 13 Jan. 1924–7 June 1926; Minute Book of the Industrial Union No. 120, 8 June 1925–19 Sept. 1928; Treasurers' Account Book, Port Arthur CTUK, 27 May 1925–4 Apr. 1929. (All of these are in Finnish.) Also in the collection are the English minutes of the IWW No. 120 Sudbury Branch Conference, 10–11 Apr. 1925.

40 Public Archives of Manitoba, Robert Boyd Russell collection, MG 10 A 14-2, file 49, Proceedings of the 5th OBU Convention, 2 May 1927

41 Hill, 'Basis.' On the origins of the Communist Party of Canada, see Norman Penner, *The Canadian Left: A Critical Analysis* (Scarborough 1977) 77–85; Ivan Avakumovic, *The Communist Party in Canada: A History* (Toronto 1975) 1–21; Ian Angus, *Canadian Bolsheviks: The Early Years of the Communist Party of Canada* (Montreal 1981) 1–80; *Canada's Party of Socialism* (Toronto 1982) 1–13; William Rodney, *Soldiers of the International: A History of the Communist Party of Canada, 1919–29* (Toronto 1968) 28–50.

42 K. Salo, 'The FOC as a Builder of the Lumber Workers Industrial Union of Canada' (transl.) in Toimituskomitea, ed., *Canada Suomaliainen Jäjestö 25 vuotta* (Sudbury 1936) 102–5

43 On the FOC, see Edward W. Laine, 'Finnish Canadian Radicalism and Canadian Politics: The First Forty Years, 1900–40,' in Jorgen Dahlie and Tissa Fernando, eds., *Ethnicity, Power and Politics in Canada* (Toronto 1981) 94–112; Edward W. Laine, 'The Finnish Organization of Canada, 1923–40, and the Development of a Finnish-Canadian Culture,' *Polyphony* 3:2 (Fall 1981) 81–90; William Eklund, 'The Formative Years of the Finnish Organization of Canada,' in Karni, *Finnish Diaspora I* 49–60; William Eklund, *Canadan Rakentajia: Canadan Suomalaisen Järjestön Historia vv. 1911–1971* (Toronto 1983).

44 *Metsa* 1926 #2 (transl.). On *Metsa*, see Pilli, *Finnish-Language Press* 213–15.

45 Ibid., 1926 #3, #5 (transl.)

46 Ibid., 1926 #2 (transl.), 1929 #1 (transl.)

47 Ibid., 1926 #3 (transl.)

48 MHSO, OHC, Edwin Suksi interviewed by Lennard Sillanpaa, 1977

49 MHSO, OHC, Edwin Suksi interviewed by author and Varpu Lindstrom-Best, Sudbury 1980

50 MHSO, OHC, Reino Keto interviewed by Varpu Lindstrom-Best, 1978 (transl.)

51 Lakehead University Archives, Finlandia collection, minutes of LWIU No. 120

meeting, 30 May 1926 (transl.). See also PAC, FOCC 143.18 minutes of the meeting in Liberty Hall, Sudbury 12 Mar. 1926. Hautamäki cited in *Wkr*, 2 Oct. 1926

52 Strike developments can be traced in PAC, DL, SLF, RG 27 vol. 337 76. Donations are reported in PAC, FOCC 143:3, LWIUC Financial Report, 1 Apr. 1926–20 Feb. 1927. Assessments given in *Wkr*, 13 Nov. 1926

53 PAC, DL, SLF, RG 27 341 193A & B; PAC, FOCC, 143:6, minutes of LWIUC delegates' meeting, 31 Mar. 1928 (transl.), minutes of the LWIUC convention, South Porcupine 6 Apr. 1929 (transl.), FOCC 143:8 minutes of the Area Committee Meeting for Northern Ontario, 9 Dec. 1928 (transl.), minutes of a meeting of Northern Ontario camp representatives, 29 Sept. 1929 (transl.)

54 PAC, DL, SLF, RG 27 344 98 various clippings; Hautamäki is criticized in *Industrial Worker*, 2 Nov. 1929; Hautamäki's reply is in *Wkr*, 11 Jan. 1930.

55 The strike and its long-term significance are examined in Satu Repo, 'Rosvall and Voutilainen: Two Union Men Who Never Died,' *Labour/Le Travailleur*, 8/9 (Autumn–Spring 1981–82) 179–302. The inquests are well documented in the files of Jacob L. Cohen, the lawyer representing the unionists. See PAC, Jacob L. Cohen Papers, MG 30 A94 vol. 1:10. On legal problems of Communists in Canada, see Lita Rose Betcherman, *The Little Band: The Clashes between the Communists and the Political-Legal Establishment of Canada, 1928–32* (Ottawa 1982); J. Petryshyn, 'Class Conflict and Civil Liberties: The Origins and Activities of the Canadian Labour Defence League,' *Labour/Le Travailleur* 10 (Autumn 1982) 39–46.

56 PAC, FOCC, 143:16 Report of the 8th Convention of the LWIUC, 3–5 May 1931 (transl.), 143:3 LWIUC Financial Report, 15 Apr. 1932–31 July 1932 (transl.), 143:14 Report of the Executive Committee of the L&AWIUC to the Annual Convention, Sudbury 27 Feb. 1932 (English minutes)

57 The Karelian episode is discussed in greater detail in Jalava, 'Radicalism,' 231–53; Reino Kero, 'The Canadian Finns in Soviet Karelia,' in Karni, *Finnish Diaspora I*, 203–14; Kaarlo R. Tuomi, 'The Karelian 'Fever' of the Early 1930s: A Personal Memoir,' *Finnish Americana* 13 (1980) 61–75. Its impact on the LWIUC is documented in PAC, FOCC, 143:6 Minutes of the LWIUC convention, Port Arthur, 7 Apr. 1920 (transl.); Minutes of the 8th Convention, 3–5 May 1931; 143:17 Minutes of the Timmins District meeting, L&WIUC, 10 Apr. 1930 (transl.).

58 PAC, FOCC 143:16 Minutes of the L&AWIUC convention 2–5 May 1931 (transl.)

59 On Bolshevization, see Jalava, 'Radicalism,' 194–208; Angus, *Canadian Bolsheviks* 296–301.

60 On the formation of the Workers Unity League, see Penner, *Canadian Left* 134–43; Avakumovic, *Communist Party* ch. 3; Angus, *Canadian Bolsheviks* 273–88; John Manley, 'Communism and the Canadian Working Class during the

Great Depression: The Workers' Unity League, 1930–1936,' PH D thesis, Dalhousie University 1984; and Ian Radforth, 'The Workers Unity League in Ontario,' PH D major research paper, Graduate Programme in History, York University 1978. From 1930 to 1932 the LWIUC was called the Lumber and Agricultural Workers Industrial Union of Canada (L&AWIUC), as the union set about to organize self-employed pulp cutters who were also farmers.

61 PAC, FOC 143:16 minutes of the L&AWIUC convention 2–5 May 1931 (transl.); on conflicts between the CPC and the Finns, see also AO, Attorney General's Department Records, CPC records, 10C 2001–4, General report on L&AWIUC convention, 1931, and 8c 0476–80 minutes of the CPC plenum 1931.

62 On attempts to reach English-speaking bushworkers, see 'Glimpses from Our History,' OT, 10 Mar. 1949. On party affiliation of Gillbanks, see AO, CPC records, correspondence 1A 0746.

63 Wkr, 17 June 1933; Canada, Department of Labour, Labour Gazette (June 1933) 685

64 PAC, DL, SLF, RG 27 355 52, Port Arthur New-Chronicle, 13 June 1933, Fort William Times-Journal 8 June 1933; 'Public Statement by Timber Operators,' in Port Arthur News Chronicle, 13 June 1933

65 Ibid., leaflet, 'Strikers Answer to the Public Statement of the Timber Operators,' n.d.; Wkr, 17 June 1933

66 Canada, Labour Gazette (December 1933) 1164, (February 1934) 107. Conference reports cited in OT, 'History,' May 1949.

67 Canada, House of Commons, Debates, 26 Mar. 1934, 1883–5

68 Ellard Connolly to James A. Bradette, 10 Feb. 1934, read into Canada, Commons Debates, 28 Mar. 1934, 1916–20

69 See newspaper clippings in PAC, DL, SLF, RG 27 vol. 358 127, 153, 166; vol. 359 file 7. Port Arthur News Chronicle 1 Dec. 1933.

70 PAC, DR, SLF, RG 27 353 166, Porcupine Advance, 16 Nov. 1933; Winnipeg Tribune (undated clipping); Metsa 11934 #1; Canada, Commons Debates, 12 Mar. 1934, 1415–17

71 Canada, Commons Debates 12 Mar. 1934

72 PAC, DL, SLF, RG 27 358, 153, Fort William Times Journal, 24 Nov. 1933

73 Ontario, Department of Lands and Forests, Annual Report 1934, 21–2; see also Richard S. Lambert with Paul Pross, Renewing Nature's Wealth: A Centennial History of Lands, Forest and Wildlife Administration in Ontario, 1763–1967 (Toronto 1967) 336–8; H.V. Nelles, 'Timber Regulation, 1900–60,' typescript 1965 (on file at Ontario Ministry of Natural Resources Library) 84–7.

74 PAC, DL, SLF, RG 27 365 218, unidentified clipping 7 Mar. 1934

75 Several CBU leaflets and newspaper clippings and reports on the CBU are in AO, DL, II-1 vol. 10.

76 Ibid., E. Hutchison to J. Marsh, 26 Sept. 1934. See *Wkr* attacks on CBU as a 'scab outfit,' in *Wkr*, 10 Nov. 1934, 25 Apr. 1935; see also attacks in *Metsa* 1934 #1.

77 AO, DL, RG 7 II-1 vol. 12, confidential report from OPP inspector Phil Walter on 'Proceedings of the LWIU'; Canada, Department of Labour, *Labour Organizations in Canada – 1934* reported a CBU membership of 878 in January 1934, 149; there are no data for 1935.

78 PAC, DL, SLF, RG 27 360 34 E.S. Noble to W.M. Dixon, 1 Mar. 1934; AO, OPPR, RG 23 E-105, 1.6 Inspector H. Gardner memo to Chief Inspector, 9 Apr. 1934 and Staff Inspector K to the Commissioner, 28 Apr. 1934

79 On these plans, see Canada, *Labour Gazette* (May 1934) 414, and RG 27 364 185, E.S. Noble to W.M. Dixon, 21 Aug. 1934; Lambert and Pross, *Renewing Nature's Wealth* 336; Nelles, 'Timber Regulation,' 85–8; UTA, FFC, LR #88 Cannon and J.H. Cooper (1936).

80 L.A. Nix *Woods Labour* (Montreal 1939) 12–15. On employee representation plans, see Bruce Scott, ' "A Place in the Sun": The Industrial Council at Massey-Harris, 1919–29,' *Labour/Le Travailleur* 1 (1976) 158–92.

81 *Wkr*, 12 Dec. 1934; see also 23 May 1935.

82 *OT*, 'History,' August 1949

83 PAC, DL, SLF, 364 209, Toronto *Daily Star*, 28 Sept. 1934

84 AO, DL, RG 7 II-1 vol. 12, L.A. Dent to J. Marsh, 25 Sept. 1934; L.A. Dent, 'Report of Conditions in the Woods,' L.A. Dent, 'Final Report,' 23 Oct. 1934. For a contrasting view of the strike, see AO, DL, RG 7 VIII-1 vol. 28, OPP District Inspector F.B. Creasy's memo, 15 Jan. 1935 and OPP Inspector A.H. Palmer's memo, 15 Jan. 1935. Strike developments may also be traced in PAC, DL, SLF, RG 27 364 209; Canada, *Labour Gazette* (October 1934) 908 and (November 1934) 997.

85 Livo Ducin (pseud.), 'Unrest in the Algoma Lumbercamps; the Bushworkers' Strikes of 1933–34,' in *50 Years*, 79–100. Strike developments can also be traced in PAC, DL, SLF, RG 27 365 228 and in the translations of dozens of *Vapaus* articles, contained in the Algoma University College Archives, Algoma Labour History Project collection, translations by Sandy Myllyperko.

86 AO, Palokangas papers, Scrapbooks, 1934; Working Class Organizations, Donations and Expenditures of the LWIU No. 120 Relief Committee, 28 Nov. 1934; or in *Metsa* 1934 #1

87 MHSO, OHC, Gertie Grönroos interviewed by Helena Doherty, 1979; *Vapaus*, 12 Nov. 1934 (transl. by Sandy Myllyperko)

88 Canada, *Labour Gazette* (August 1935) 725–6; PAC, DL, SLF, RG 27 370 90, Port Arthur *News Chronicle*, 20 June, 16 July 1935; *Wkr*, 4 July 1935; AO, Bruce

Magnuson papers, Scrapbook #1, Strike Bulletin, 18 July 1935

CHAPTER 7 Building the Lumber and Saw

1 In the mid-1930s the IWW No. 120 lumber workers' group in northern Ontario faded from sight; some IWW leaders did co-operate with the Communists in Lumber and Saw. A clearer understanding of the demise of the Wobblies would require a careful reading of the 'Canadian page' of the Finnish-language *Industrialisti*, published in Duluth, Minn.
2 Norman Penner, *The Canadian Left: A Critical Analysis* (Scarborough 1977) 138-42; Ivan Avakumovic, *The Communist Party in Canada* (Toronto 1975) 96-138; *Canada's Party of Socialism* (Toronto 1982) 83-7
3 Cited in 'Glimpses from Our History,' *OT*, 11 Nov. 1949
4 AO, I.M. Abella oral history collection, Bruce Magnuson interviewed by S. Penner, D. Chud, and D. Lake, Toronto 1971 and 1972; AO, Bruce Magnuson papers, Scrapbook #1
5 *Wkr*, 10 Dec. 1935
6 Ibid., 6 Feb. 1936
7 'History,' *OT*, 15 Dec. 1949. To be more precise, the AFL granted the local a federal charter in 1934, AFL-Sawmill Workers No. 19164, which soon became a Lumber and Sawmill Workers Union local (Canada, Department of Labour, *Labour Organizations in Canada* 1934, 194).
8 *Wkr*, 14 Jan. 1936, 28 Mar. 1936; 'History,' *OT*, 30 Dec. 1949
9 Walter Galenson, *The United Brotherhood of Carpenters: the First Hundred Years* (Cambridge, Mass. 1983) 252-8; Vernon Jenson, *Lumber and Labor* (New York 1945) 200-5
10 Galenson, *United Brotherhood*, 260-3; Jerry Lembcke and William M. Tattam, *One Union in Wood: A Political History of the International Woodworkers of America* (Madiera Park, BC 1984) 35-74
11 AO, Magnuson interview
12 On the ISA and particularly its sponsor, Arthur Roebuck, see T.C. Crossen, 'The Political Career of Attorney General Arthur Wentworth Roebuck, 1934-7,' MA thesis, University of Waterloo 1973; Neil McKenty, *Mitch Hepburn* (Toronto 1967) 102-3. For a different view of the importance of the ISA, see Mark Cox, 'The Dynamics of Conflict: Industrial Regulation and Management Rights in Ontario, 1930-1937,' York University PHD Research Paper, 1985. On Roosevelt's labour policies, see especially David Montgomery, 'American Workers and the New Deal Formula,' in his *Workers' Control in America: Studies in the History of Work, Technology and Labor Struggles* (Cambridge, Mass. 1980) 153-80; David

Brody, 'The New Deal and the Labor Movement,' in his *Workers in Industrial America: Essays on the 20th Century Struggle* (New York 1980) 138–45.

13 H.A. Logan, *Trade Unions in Canada* (Toronto 1948) 458–9. The Canadian Lumbermen's Association vigorously opposed the legislation, however. See AO, DL, RG 7 III-1 vol. 2, R.L. Sargent to A.W. Roebuck 29 Mar. 1935.

14 Cited in Toronto *Globe*, 15 Nov. 1934

15 Fine's early career may be traced in George Brown College Archives, Louis Fine papers, and in AO, I.M. Abella oral history collection, Louis Fine interview.

16 AO, DL, RG 7 VIII-1 vol. 32, Fine's memo 15 Jan. 1936

17 Ibid., minutes of meeting with representatives of bush workers, 6 Jan. 1935 [i.e. 1936]; minutes of meeting of timber operators, 6 Jan. 1936; minutes of meeting of timber operators and representatives of the bush workers, 6 Jan. 1936; Fine memo, 15 Jan. 1936

18 'History,' *OT*, 15 Dec. 1949; see also letters from various camps in AO, DL, RG 7 VIII-1 vol. 32.

19 AO, DL, RG 7 VIII-1 vol. 32, B. Magnuson et al. to L. Fine, September 1936, L. Fine to B. Magnuson et al., 16 Sept. 1936, and 'LSWU 2786 proposal for 1936 ISA agreement'

20 See correspondence and Ontario Provincial Police reports in AO, DL, RG 7 II-1 vol. 17; Port Arthur *News-Chronicle*, 27 Nov. 1936

21 AO, DL, RG 7 VIII-1 vol. 32, J.R. Patterson of the Logging Advisory Board to D. Croll, received 22 Sept. 1936 and J. Marsh to P. Heenan, 30 Sept. 1936

22 AO, DL, RG 7 II-1 vol. 17, correspondence in file 'Lumber Firms'

23 'History,' *OT*, 5 June 1950

24 Unless otherwise noted, this paragraph is based on AO, DL, RG 7 I-2 vol. 3, L. Fine to D. Croll, 25 Jan. 1937; 'History,' *OT*, 5 July 1950.

25 AO, DL, RG 7 VIII-1 vol. 32, minutes of meeting, 4 May 1937. This file contains a very few complaints.

26 AO, DL, RG 7 II-1 vol. 21, Constable T. Warren memo, 13 Jan. 1938. Similar memos are in the same volume.

27 AO, DL, RG 7 II-1 vol. 14, A. Locking to J. Marsh 18 Oct. 1937

28 Jeremy Webber, 'The Malaise of Compulsory Conciliation: Strike Prevention in Canada during World War II,' *Labour/Le Travail* 15 (1985) 57–88; Laurel Sefton MacDowell, 'The Formation of the Canadian Industrial Relations System during World War II,' *Labour/Le Travailleur* 3 (1978) 175–96 and her *'Remember Kirkland Lake': The History and Effects of the Kirkland Lake Gold Miners' Strike, 1941–42* (Toronto 1983) 3–35; Daniel Coates, 'Organized Labor and Politics in Canada: The Development of a National Labor Code,' PH D dissertation, Cornell University 1973. On the wider wartime context, see J.L. Granatstein,

Canada's War: The Politics of the Mackenzie King Government, 1939–45 (Toronto 1975).

29 Avakumovic, *Communist Party* 139–65; William Repka, *Dangerous Patriots: Canada's Unknown Prisoners of War* (Vancouver 1982) 121–6, 228–30; Reg Whitaker, 'Official Repression of Communism during World War II,' *Labour/Le Travail* 17 (Spring 1986) 135–66

30 AO, DL, RG 7 III-1 vol. 32, B. Magnuson and F. Cullick to H.O. Hipel, 27 Oct. 1939, L. Fine to J. Marsh, 27 Nov. 1939; AO, Magnuson collection, Scrapbooks, clipping, Port Arthur *News Chronicle*, 19 Feb. 1940

31 Eddie Johnson cited in Fort William *Times-Journal*, 30 Jan. 1940; AO, Magnuson papers, correspondence and scrapbooks detail Magnuson's experiences.

32 Canada, Department of Labour, *Labour Gazette* (July 1943) 904, (May 1944) 563–4. On conscientious objectors, see Thomas P. Socknet, *Witness against War: Pacifism in Canada, 1900–1945* (Toronto 1987) 5–42. Prisoners of war were paid 50 cents per day, the balance of their pay going to the receiver general of Canada. Wage rates were set 'somewhat below prevailing rates' on the grounds that the prisoners' productivity was lower (*Labour Gazette* [November 1943]).

33 An outline history of woods wage orders under the Regional War Labour Board for Ontario is AO, DL, RG 7 V-1(6) vol. 12, LSWU 2786 memo, 20 Apr. 1943.

34 Ibid., Henry S. Mosher of Newaygo Timber Company to L. Fine, 20 Aug. 1942

35 AO, DL, RG 7 V-1a vol. 2, L. Fine to J.C. Adams, 23 Feb. 1942; V-6 vol. 12, local 2786 memo, 20 Apr. 1943; VII-1 vol. 32, Regional War Labour Board Order 5963; V 1a-6, L. Fine to C. Daley, 24 July 1946

36 AO, MU 4144, A.E. Wicks Ltd. records, box 5, Ontario Forest Industries Association file, various memos, including 2, 11, 19 Oct. 1943; minutes OFIA Labour Committee meeting, Sudbury, 20 Oct. 1943; A.E. Wicks to W.C. Cain, 25 Apr. 1944

37 AO, RG 18 B-104, Records of the Royal Commission on the Sawlog Supplies of the Great Lakes Lumber and Shipping Ltd., testimony, Toronto, 17 Jan. 1944, 363. The speaker is Edward B. McGraw, Woodlands Manager, Ontario Paper Company.

38 AO, MU 4144, Wicks records, A.E. Wicks to W.C. Cain, 30 Mar. 1944, Report of the Manager of the Ontario Forest Industries Association for the period 15 Aug. 1943–3 Dec. 1943; W.A. Delahey and W.J. LeClair to Charles Daley, 11 May 1944

39 Stuart Marshall Jamieson, *Times of Trouble: Labour Unrest and Industrial Conflict in Canada, 1900–66* (Ottawa 1968) 302

40 AO, DL, RG 7 V-1a-6, L. Fine to C. Daley, 24 July 1946

41 AO, DL, SLF, RG 27 365, Port Arthur *News Chronicle*, 11 Oct. 1946; Confederation

College Archives, Thunder Bay Labour History Interview Project, Buzz Lein interviewed by Jean Morrison, 1972; PAC, DL, SLF, RG 27 365, Sault *Star*, 5 Oct. 1946; see also Ottawa *Citizen*, 17 Oct. 1946.

42 PAC, DL, SLF, RG 27 365, Fort William *Times-Journal*, 3 Oct. 1946; Port Arthur *News-Chronicle*, 8 Oct. 1946, C.R. Mills to Dep. Minister of Labour, 20 Nov. 1946; Toronto *Daily Star*, 12 Oct. 1946; AO, MU 849, W.A. Delaney diaries collection, 12 Oct. 1946

43 PAC, DL, SLF, RG 27 365, Fort William *Times-Journal*, 18 Oct. 1946; OPP Confidential Report on LSWU strike, 23 Oct. 1946, G.E. Charron (National Employment Service, Timmins) to Director of Labour Relations, 16 Oct. 1946; D.H. Merriwell (Brompton Paper Woods Manager) to Unemployment Commission, Port Arthur Office, 23 Oct. 1946; AO, Magnuson collection, Scrapbooks, n.p. *Daily Press*, 1 Nov. 1946

44 PAC, DL, SLF, RG 27 365, Port Arthur *News Chronicle*, 17 Oct. 1948

45 PAC, DL, RG 27 839 8-3-2-3-2 pt. 3, 'Report of the Woods Labour Committee,' 3 Oct. 1946, C.R. Mills to Deputy Minister of Labour, 20 Nov. 1946; *Canadian Tribune*, 7 Dec. 1946

46 The following companies signed the 1946 agreement: Abitibi (Toronto), Pulpwood Supply, Ripco Timber, Alexander-Clark Timber, Spruce Falls Power and Paper, Nipigon Lake Timber, Oscar Styffe, E.V. Woolings, Driftwood Lands and Timber, Marathon Paper Mills, Hammermill Paper, Great Lakes Paper, Ontario Paper, Sturgeon Lake Transportation, Northern Forest Products, Brompton Pulp and Paper, Northern Paper Mills, Newaygo Timber. In 1947 Ontario-Minnesota Paper, Northern Paper, Kimberly-Clark, and KVP also signed.

47 C. Ross Silversides collection, Prescott, minutes of Closed Meeting – Woods Managers, 29 Jan. 1947

48 Leo Panitch and Donald Swartz, 'Towards Permanent Exceptionalism: Coercion and Consent in Canadian Industrial Relations,' *Labour/Le Travail* 13 (Spring 1984) 133–56

49 Minutes of Closed Meeting, 29 Jan. 1947

50 *OT*, 5 Nov. 1947, 7 Feb. 1948

51 Ibid., 15 Dec. 1947

52 Ibid., 15 Jan., 30 May, 4 Dec. 1948, 30 March 1949, March 1950; For further examples of sawlog operators' opposition to unionism, see AO, MU 1581, Johnson papers, 'Missisagi Survey' by Dupuis and McClure, 16–20 Dec. 1949.

53 Ibid., 11 Sept. 1947

54 Ibid., 5 Nov. 1947, 5 Apr. 1948. (The *OT* letters-to-the-editor column was headed: 'Say what you want ... but say it!')

55 Ibid., May, August 1949; see also Magnuson's editorial on peace, 30 Dec. 1949.

56 On the Cold War and Canada, see Reg Whitaker, 'Fighting the Cold War on the Home Front: America, Britain, Australia and Canada,' *Socialist Register 1984* (London 1984) 23–67; R.D. Cuff and J.L. Granatstein, *American Dollars – Canadian Prosperity: Canadian–American Economic Relations, 1945–1950* (Toronto 1978); Robert Bothwell, Ian Drummond, and John English, *Canada since 1945: Power, Politics and Provincialism* (Toronto 1981) 104–8, 135–40; Robert Bothwell and J.L. Granatstein, eds., *The Gouzenko Transcripts: The Evidence Presented to the Kellock-Taschereau Royal Commission of 1946* (Ottawa n.d.). On labour's Cold War, see Irving Martin Abella, *Nationalism, Communism and Canadian Labour: The CIO, the Communist Party, and the Canadian Congress of Labour, 1935–1956* (Toronto 1973); Gad Horowitz, *Canadian Labour in Politics* (Toronto 1968) 85–161; Lembcke and Tattam, *One Union in Wood* 135–55. On developments in the U.S., see David Caute, *The Great Fear: The Anti-Communist Purge under Truman and Eisenhower* (New York 1978); Harvey A. Levenstein, *Communism, Anticommunism, and the C.I.O.* (Westport 1981).

57 *OT*, October–November 1949, February–March 1951

58 Cited in Galenson, *United Brotherhood*, 298.

59 *OT*, October–November 1950, 30 Jan. 1951, May 1951

60 Magnuson interview; AO, Bruce Magnuson papers, Scrapbook #10, daily press clippings, April–June 1951; 'Statement issued at Toronto press conference, 1 Aug. 1951,' 'Press Release,' issued by Magnuson, 2 Sept. 1951

61 Lother Bode interviewed by author, Thunder Bay August 1982

62 *The Woodworker/Travailleur des bois*, June 1951, July–August 1951. On BC, see Abella, *Nationalism*, 134–8; Lembcke and Tattam, *One Union in Wood*, 124–34. On Quebec, see Gerard Fortin and Boyce Richardson, *Life of the Party* (Montreal 1984) 149–50.

63 *The Woodworker*, July–August 1951

64 Ibid., June 1951

65 For a documented example, see AO, Edward E. Johnson papers, MU 1582, Jim N. Swinden to Eddie Johnson, 30 Nov. 1951, wherein operating manager Swinden explains to his boss a plan to avoid a democratic vote in their Great Lakes Lumber and Shipping Company camps. Swinden suggests that they have their mill agreement with Cooper's Lumber and Saw extended to cover woods employees, thus making it impossible for the Canadian Union of Woodworkers to organize in the logging operations.

66 Bode interview; Tulio Mior (president of LSWU local 2786, 1956–85) interviewed by author, Thunder Bay August 1982

67 *The Woodworker*, July–Aug. 1951; AO, Magnuson collection, Scrapbook #10, copy of telegram, Magnuson to P.M. Draper, Chairman Ontario Labour Relations Board, 8 Nov. 1951.

68 Magnuson interview
69 Bode interview; Mior interview; *OB*, Dec. 1953
70 Thunder Bay Historical Society Archives, Helmer Borg papers, Transcript of negotiations for renewal of 1953–54 Labour Agreement between the LSWU and the OFIA, 26 Aug. 1953, 15
71 Membership estimates are from the Mior interview. (Because the Lumber and Saw has no identity separate from the Brotherhood, *Labour Organizations in Canada* and other publications with union membership statistics have no data on the LSWU.)
72 William Kurelek, *Lumberjack* (Montreal 1974) n.p.; Bode interview
73 Thunder Bay Historical Society Archives, Borg papers, Transcript 1953–54 negotiations, 72–4
74 *OB*, 1 Feb. 1963; Bode interview
75 Published sources on the strike include Jamieson, *Times of Trouble* 412–4; Desmond Morton with Terry Copp, *Working People: An Illustrated History of the Canadian Labour Movement*, rev. ed. (Ottawa 1984) 240–2; D.L. Stein, 'Violence and Death Strike Ontario's Quiet North Country,' *Maclean's Magazine*, 23 March 1963. Other sources include PAC, DL, SLF, RG 27 3092 5; *OB*, 15 Feb. 1964. Similar clashes between contractors and union woodsmen are described in W.C. Osborn, *The Paper Plantation: Ralph Nader's Study Group on the Pulp and Paper Industry in Maine* (New York 1974).

CHAPTER 8 Management responds: new recruits, camp improvements, and training schemes

1 On the optimism of forest executives, see for example CPPA, Executive Board reports in *PPMC*, July, September 1945, January 1946. For examples of misgivings about competition from British Columbia and the South, see AO, MU 4144, A.E. Wicks Company Ltd. records, A.H. Dewolf to A.E. Wicks, 17 Feb. 1940.
2 Ontario, Royal Commission on Forestry, *Report* (Toronto 1947)
3 CPPA, WS, Howard Kennedy, 'Woods Labour,' WSI 823 (1946); R.S. Armitage, 'Training of Woods Labour and Personnel,' WSI 903 (1947)
4 David L. MacFarlane, cited by Alexander Koroleff et al., *Stability as a Factor in Efficient Forest Management* (Montreal 1951) 52; C.R. Silversides collection, Prescott, David L. MacFarlane, 'The Labour Force Problem of the Eastern Canadian Woods Industry,' unpublished paper, 1955; Canadian Lumbermen's Association brief to the Senate Committee on Immigration, cited in *TC*, June 1947

5 J.O. Wilson, 'Implementing the Forest Policy,' *Forestry Chronicle* 23:3 (September 1947) 203

6 *TC*, March 1946; Joe Sarazin interviewed by author, Blind River 1980; *TC*, October 1946. U.S. operators faced a similar predicament. See Fred C. Simmons, 'Mechanization of Forest Operations,' *TC*, November 1947.

7 Canada Lumbermen's Association, 'Report of the White Pine Bureau,' *TC*, March 1946

8 Koroleff, *Stability* 15

9 W.A.E. Pepler, 'Woods Labour in Eastern Canada,' cited in ibid. See also Pepler's other reports on turnover, CPPA, WS, WSI 904 (1947), WSI 964 (1948), WSI 1013 (1949), and a similar study by M.S.M. Hamilton, 'Study of Woods Labour Turnover,' WSI 1028 (1953).

10 AO, MU 1582, Edward E. Johnson papers, W. Earl Hunt to E.E. Johnson, 4 Nov. 1948

11 AO, CR, RG 18, Royal Commission on Forestry, B-109, vol. 6, 'Brief of the Ontario Forest Industries Association' and 'A Brief for Presentation to the Ontario Royal Commission on Forestry by the CPPA on behalf of the Pulp and Paper Industry of Ontario'; *PPMC*, October 1945; PAC, IR, RG 76 665 651615, G.H. McGee to G.V. Haythorne, 11 May 1946

12 PAC, DL, RG 27 839, 'Minutes of the Ontario Regional Advisory Board,' 30 Sept. 1946. On Canada's ethnically selective immigration policies prior to 1930, see especially Donald Avery, *'Dangerous Foreigners': European Immigrant Workers and Labour Radicalism in Canada, 1896–1932* ch. 4.

13 Irving Abella and Harold Troper, *None Is Too Many: Canada and the Jews of Europe, 1933–1948* (Toronto 1983) ch. 7. See also Gerald Dirks, *Canada's Refugee Policy: Indifference or Opportunism?* (Montreal 1977); Anthony W. Rasporich, *For a Better Life: A History of Croatians in Canada* (Toronto 1982) 52–6; and on post-war immigration to Canada, Freda Hawkins, *Canada and Immigration: Public Policy and Public Concern* (Montreal 1972); Alan G. Green, *Immigration and the Postwar Economy* (Toronto 1976).

14 PAC, William Lyon Mackenzie King papers, cabinet conclusions, 23 Jan. 1947, cited by Abella and Troper, *None Is Too Many* 247

15 Abella and Troper, *None Is Too Many* 217–24; Milda Danys, *DP: Lithuanian Immigration to Canada after the Second World War* (Toronto 1986) 67–90

16 PAC, DL, RG 76 230 127304 'Information for Workers Volunteering for Emigration on Canadian Logging Operations Northern Ontario'; A.H. Brown to G.V. Haythorne, 13 June 1947

17 Lukka Radulovich interviewed by the author, Toronto 1985

18 PAC, IR, RG 76 230 127304, C.E.S. Smith to C.R. Mills, 30 Oct. 1947; 'Report of the

Inspector at Halifax,' 16 Sept. 1947. For details on the selection of woodsmen, see Ian Walter Radforth, 'Bushworkers and Bosses: A Social History of the Northern Ontario Logging Industry, 1900–1980,' PH D thesis, York University 1985, 354–7.

19 Radulovich interview; Vello Hansen interviewed by the author, Sault Ste Marie 1980; Danys, *DP* 98

20 PAC, IR, RG 76 230 127304, Minutes of the Woods Labour Advisory Committee, 2 Dec. 1947

21 For a description of conditions, see PAC, IR, RG 76 230 127304, 'Information for Workers Volunteering for Emigration on Canadian Logging Operations Northern Ontario.' Complaints are voiced in *OT*, 4 July 1947, and PAC, IR, RG 76 230 127304, Minutes of the Woods Labour Advisory Committee, 2 Dec. 1947.

22 PAC, DL, RG 27 vol. 898, 89831–2, Minutes of the Immigration – Labour Committee, 17 Feb. 1948

23 PAC, IR, RG 76 127304, Minutes of the Woods Labour Advisory Committee, 22 Sept. 1947; C.E.S. Smith to C.R. Mills, 30 Oct. 1947; A. MacNamara to A.L. Joliffe, 20 Nov. 1947

24 Ibid., Minutes of the Woods Labour Advisory Committee, 2 Dec. 1947; RG 76 277 12623, Sharrer to W.W. Dawson, 22 Dec. 1947; Sharrer to J.H. Merrill, 18 Dec. 1947, cited in Danys, *DP*, 103–4

25 Edvardas Gumbelis interviewed by Milda Danys, White Rock, BC 1980, cited in Danys, *DP* 103; PAC, RG 27 vol. 898, clippings cited in minutes of the Immigration – Labour Committee, 9 Aug. 1949

26 Radulovich interview; *OT*, 4 July 1947

27 Kazimieras Dauyns interviewed by J.V. Danys, Toronto 1979, cited in Danys, *DP* 100; Dalys Vileita interviewed by Milda Danys, Tsewasseen, BC, 1980, cited in Danys, *DP* 102

28 C.R. Silversides collection, Prescott, Dr O. Hall, 'Displaced Persons in the Canadian Labour Force with References to Mining, Construction and Pulp and Paper,' typescript 1951; AO, MU 1575, Edward E. Johnson papers, E.E. Johnson to J.M. Conway, 6 July 1948

29 *OB*, 17 Dec. 1956

30 Silversides collection, Clifford Kearns to Dyer Hurdon, 18 Sept. 1974

31 Silversides collection, Canada Manpower, 'Recruiting and Retention of Employees – Forestry and Mining: A Case Study,' typescript 1974

32 CPPA, WS, C.R. Silversides, 'Design and Construction of Logging Camps: A Survey Conducted for the Pulp and Paper Research Institute of Canada,' WSI 879 (1946)

33 Wildcat strikes are described in *OB*, 16 July, 17 Dec. 1956; city conditions in Kennedy, 'Woods Labour,' and *WR*, November 1947.

34 Silversides, 'Design and Construction,' CPPA, WS, J.T. Walker, 'Camp Construction Trends at Smooth Rock Falls,' WSI 1967 (1960) 1–2
35 Silversides, 'Design and Construction'
36 CPPA, WS, I.F. Stewart, 'Central vs. Conventional Logging Camps,' WSI 2282 (1963)
37 Walker, 'Camp Construction Trends,' Stewart, 'Central vs. Conventional'
38 UTA, FFC, E.L. Kelly and F. Evert, 'Logging Report' (1956)
39 CPPA, WS, 'Recreation: A Panel Discussion,' WSI 1497 (1955); 'Report of the Field Meeting on Mechanical Hauling and Cable Yarding,' WSI 1225 (1951); OB, 3 Dec. 1956. By 1963 the union had lost interest in running canteens. See LSWUF, Abitibi-Lakehead file, Stevens to Mior, 22 Sept. 1963.
40 Erik Hautala interviewed by author, August 1982 Thunder Bay; LSWUF, minutes of Executive Meeting, LSWU local 2693, 25 Aug. 1967.
41 LSWUF, Abitibi–Lakehead Division: Master Agreements, 1955–6
42 CPPA, WS, 'Report of the Woodlands Section Feeding Conference, 18–23 Nov. 1953,' WSI 1352
43 Ibid.
44 CPPA, WS, Douglas L. Gibson, 'Survey and Report on Feeding in Logging Camps – 1952: A Resurvey of Nutrition of Woods Workers Prepared by the Woodlands Section,' WSI 1283 (1952)
45 CPPA, WS, G.H. Holland, 'Mechanized Camp Kitchens,' and 'Discussion,' in 'Report of the Woodlands Section Feeding Conference,' 1953; B.H.R. Brehaut, 'Cafeteria Experience in Woodlands Feeing,' in 'Report of the Woodlands Section Feeding Conference,' 1957
46 For Auden's views, see 'Obituary – Jack Auden,' Log Book July–August 1973. See also Anon., 'A Plan for Pulpwood Operations Based on Forest Villages,' in Koroleff, Stability, 107–9; Ontario, Royal Commission on Forestry, Report (Toronto 1946) 172.
47 C.R. Binger, 'Family Camps,' WR, February 1956; UTA, FC, J.W. Carter and G.C. Filton, 'Logging Report' (1963). On Dubreuilville, see also Sheila MacLeod Arnopoulos, Voices from French Ontario (Kingston 1982) 125–37.
48 'Company vs. Jobbers Camps: A Panel Discussion,' WR, May 1960; W. Morrison, 'Commuter-Camp Operations Result in Lower Woods Cost,' WR, August 1962; C.R. Silversides collection, Prescott, Logging Operations Group, Training Committee, 'Survey on Manpower and Training Needs,' 1977–8. On commuting and Newfoundland loggers, see Robert D. Peters, 'The Social and Economic Effects of the Transition from a System of Woods Camps to a System of Commuting in the Newfoundland Pulpwood Industry,' MA thesis, Memorial University of Newfoundland 1965.
49 G.H.U. Bayley, 'Government Policies and Progress Related to Forest

Management and Employment-Related Opportunities,' Report no. 5, Canadian Council on Rural Development, *The Relationship of Canada's Forests to Rural Employment and Community Stability* (Ottawa 1977). On the problems of women in the North, see also Lakehead University, *The Forest Industry in Northwestern Ontario: A Socio-Economic Study from a Social Planning Perspective* (Toronto 1981).

50 George L. McLeish, 'People Do Want to Work in the Bush,' *Pulp and Paper Canada*, May 1974; Peter Sandos, 'Can STOL aircraft be used to take woodsmen to work?,' *Pulp and Paper Canada*, March 1975; C.R. Silversides collection, Prescott, Clifford Kearns (Canada Manpower) to Dyer Hurdon, 18 Sept. 1974; Gordon Kelly, 'From City to Forest by Air,' *Pulp and Paper Canada*, September 1975

51 D. Burn, 'Living Accommodations for Forest Workers in Remote Areas,' in United Nations Economic Conference for Europe, Food and Agricultural Organization, International Labour Organization, *Seminar on Occupational Health and Safety: Applied Ergonomics on Highly Mechanized Logging Operations* (Ottawa 1981) 558-69

52 Eileen Goltz, 'Espanola: The History of a Pulp and Paper Town,' *Laurentian University Review* 6:3 (June 1974) 75-104; I.M. Robinson, *New Industrial Towns on Canada's Resource Frontier* (Chicago 1962) 40-53; Rex Lucas, *Minetown, Milltown, Railtown: Life in Canadian Communities of Single Industry* (Toronto 1971) 22-5, 192-220; Gilbert Stelter and Alan Artibise, 'Canadian Resource Towns in Historical Perspective,' in Stelter and Atibise, eds., *Shaping the Urban Landscape: Aspects of the Canadian City-Building Process* (Ottawa 1982). On welfarism in manufacturing industries, see Daniel Nelson, *Managers and Workers: Origins of the New Factory System in the United States, 1880-1920* (Madison 1975) 101-21; David Brody, 'The Rise and Decline of Welfare Capitalism,' in his *Workers in Industrial America: Essays on the Twentieth Century Struggle* (New York 1980) ch. 3; Stuart Brandes, *American Welfare Capitalism, 1880-1940* (Chicago 1976); Robert Ozanne, *A Century of Labour Management Relations at McCormick and International Harvester* (Madison 1967); Hellen Jones, 'Employees' Welfare Schemes and Industrial Relations in Inter-War Britain,' *Business History* 25:1 (March 1983) 61-75; Robert Storey, 'Unionization versus Corporate Welfare: The "Dofasco Way,"' *Labour/Le Travailleur* 12 (Autumn 1983) 7-43.

53 CPPA, WS, M.S.M. Hamilton, 'Study of Woods Labour Turnover,' WSI 1287 (1953); Roger Ferrange, 'Sociological Aspects of Woods Manpower Problems,' WSI 2417 (1967)

54 CPPA, WS, Gordon Godwin, 'Increasing Worker Efficiency,' WSI 644 (1942); Alexander Koroleff, 'Progress in Instruction of Woods Labour to Promote Efficiency,' WSI 716 (1944)

55 CPPA, WS, W.C. Harrison and C.C. Wright commenting in 'Symposium on Training,' WSI 1471 (1955)
56 Harrison in ibid.; 'Report of the General Meeting on Training in the Use of Mechanical Equipment,' in CPPA, WS, *Report of Summer Meeting, 1948*; CPPA, WS, *Job Instruction: Sessions Outline and Reference Material* (Montreal 1974)
57 CPPA, WS G.H. Morris, in 'Discussion of Woods Labour, General Session, Annual Meeting 1954,' WSI 1378 (1954)
58 Ibid.
59 Ibid.
60 C.C. Wright in 'Symposium on Training'
61 Sandford Jacoby, 'The Development of Internal Labor Markets in American Manufacturing Firms,' in Paul Osterman, ed., *Internal Labor Markets* (Cambridge, Mass. 1984) 55; see also Nelson, *Managers and Workers* chs. 3-4.

CHAPTER 9 Management responds: mechanization

1 *TC*, 1 Oct. 1945
2 CPPA, WS, *Convention Proceedings* 1949, 152-3. W.A.E. Pepler received his BSC Forestry from Toronto in 1922 and his MSC Forestry from Yale in 1926. After working for the Canadian International Paper Company he became manager of the Quebec Forest Industry Association in 1939 and manager of the Woodlands Section in 1949. At that time Alexander Koroleff became Director of Woodlands Research for the Pulp and Paper Research Institute of Canada. (*WR*, April 1959)
3 CPPA, WS, W.A.E. Pepler and B.J. McColl, 'The Development of Mechanical Pulpwood Logging Methods for Eastern Canada,' WSI 1325 (1953) 9
4 Alexander Koroleff, *Stability as a Factor in Efficient Forest Management* (Montreal 1951) 1-2
5 Ministry of Natural Resources, Timber Sales Branch, *The Forest Industry in the Economy of Ontario* (Toronto 1981) 76 *Log Book*, January-February 1971, March-April 1973
6 M.M. Dixon, 'An Appraisal of Present Hauling Trends in the Northern Clay Belt,' MSC Forestry thesis, University of Toronto 1956; Arthur S. Michell, 'Trends and New Developments in the Transportation of Wood in Eastern Canada,' *Forestry Chronicle* 29:4 (December 1953) 354-7; CPPA, WS, Mechanical Harvesting Committee, 'Report on Truck Problem Survey,' WSI 1825 (1958); James M. Guthrie, 'The Economic Geography of the Pulp and Paper Industry in Ontario,' MA thesis, University of Toronto 1965, 75-8
7 CPPA, WS, Logging Mechanization Committee, 'The Development of Portable Mechanical Saws for the Felling and Bucking of Timber,' WSI 733 (1944); Jim

Wardrop, 'British Columbia's Experience with Early Chainsaws,' *Material History Bulletin* 21 (1977) 9–18; C. Ross Silversides, 'Achievements and Failures – Logging Mechanization,' WSI 2619 (1972); T.B. Fraser, 'Testing Power Chain Saws on Pulpwood Operations,' WSI 733 (1945)

8 Fraser, 'Testing Power'

9 CPPA, WS, Hidola Levesque and G.E. Lamothe, 'Report on Use of Mechanical Saw,' WSI 1007 (1949)

10 CPPA, WS, T.M. Pond, 'Report on Power Saw Tests,' WSI 1139 (1951). On improvements to chainsaws, see Ellis Lucia, 'A Lesson from Nature: Joe Cox and His Revolutionary Saw Chain,' *Journal of Forest History* 25:3 (July 1981) 159–65. A study based on the company records of Anglo-Newfoundland Development of Newfoundland (where chainsaws were introduced later than in Ontario) shows that by 1956 bucksaw users averaged 1.59 cords per day, and chainsaw users 2.16 cords per day, or 35.8 per cent more. (J.P. Curren, 'The Process of Mechanization in the Forest Industries of Newfoundland,' MA thesis, Memorial University of Newfoundland 1971, 78)

11 CPPA, WS, B.A. Logan, 'The Proper Use of the Power Saw as a Cutting Tool – Panel Discussion,' WSI 1369 (1954)

12 Levesque and Lamothe, 'Report on Use of Mechanical Saw'

13 CPPA, WS, J.D. Morrison, 'Tractor Skidding,' WSI 1291 (1953)

14 CPPA, WS, Report of the Field Meeting on Cable Yarding held at Stevens, Ontario 20–22 Sept. 1949, WSI 1063 (1949) 2–3; K.W. Carlisle, 'Yarding at Iroquois Falls,' *WR*, October 1960; *WR*, August 1960; CPPA, WS, H.C. Walcom, 'The Nodwell R.N.S. Skidder,' WSI 2664 (1961)

15 B.J. McColl, 'Problems in Mechanical Hauling from the Stump,' *WR*, January 1951

16 CPPA, WS, 'Tractor Design and Development: A Panel Discussion,' WSI 1470 (1955); 'Small Crawler Tractor Problems and Their Solution,' WSI 1861 (1959); L.R. Seheult, 'The Use of Small Tractors in Logging,' WSI 2000 (1960); 'Report on Cable Yarding'

17 UTA, Arthur S. Michell papers W.S. Carlson, 'Notes of Speech to Yarding Committee Meeting,' 1958

18 Koroleff, *Stability* 54–63

19 Don Whitman interviewed by author, Callendar, July 1982. See also logging consultant Arthur S. Michell's reports in UTA, Michell papers, A.S. Michell, 'The Canadian Horse Population, paper prepared for Kimberly Clark, Longlac,' 4 Sept. 1958 and 'Cost Advantages of the Small Skidding Tractor,' 24 Aug. 1959.

20 CPPA, WS, J.R. Mackey, 'Wheeled Tractor Skidding of Tree Lengths,' WSI 11603 (1956)

21 Ibid.
22 C. Ross Silversides interviewed by author and Jamie Swift, Prescott 1982; WR, July 1959; CPPA, WS, J.F. Dunne, 'Timberland Timberskidder,' WSI 1856 (1960); 'Small Skidder Forum,' WSI 2140 (1962)
23 CPPA, WS, Annual Report 1957, 17; Gordon Godwin, ' "The Beginning of a Beginning," ' WSI 2479 (1968); Silversides, 'Achievements'; Arthur S. Michell, 'Mechanical Harvesting of Timber Crops,' Proceedings of the Royal Canadian Institute V:XI (1964). On the origins of the articulated vehicle, see Reginald M. Wik, 'Benjamen Holt and the Track-Type Tractor,' Technology and Culture 20:1 (January 1979) 12–13.
24 WR, June 1956; CPPA, WS, Annual Report 1957, 17; Silversides, 'Achievements'
25 G.A. Genge, 'Clark Logger – Final Report,' WR, July 1959; R.E. McKay, 'Michigan PL 75 on 1958 Operations,' WR, July 1959; Silversides interview
26 CPPA, WS, D. Wilson, 'The Garrett Tree Farmer,' WSI 1710 (1960) 1
27 CPPA, WS, A.J. Casey, 'Logging with the Dowty Forwarder,' WSI 2283 (1964); Canadian Car, 'Tree Farmer – Specifications'
28 Silversides interview; Wally Buchanan (Sales Promotion Manager, Timberjack Inc.) interviewed by Jamie Swift, Woodstock, 1981 (transcript); Timberjack Machines, Ltd., Timberjack: Continued Leadership in Skidder Design (n.p. 1966)
29 UTA, Michell papers, A.S. Michell, 'Analysis of Logging System for Longlac,' 1962; WR, June 1967; CPPA, WS, J.R. Hughes, 'Logging Operations in Canada – Review and Forecast,' WSI 2553 (1970); Buchanan interview. On the success of Canadian-made skidders in the world market, see also ITC, Mechanical Transport Branch, Mechanization in the Forest: Benefits and Opportunities (Ottawa 1972) 27.
30 Nathan Rosenberg, 'The Direction of Technological Change: Inducement Mechanisms and Focussing Devices,' Economic Development and Cultural Change 18:1 (October 1969) 1–24
31 Proceedings of the Sixth World Forestry Congress vol. II (Madrid 1966) 2120
32 Pepler and McColl, 'Development,' 6–17; J.O. Wilson, 'Implementing Forest Policy,' Forestry Chronicle 23:3 (September 1947) 206
33 CPPA, WS, B.J. McColl, 'Cable Yarding,' WSI 1056 (1949); A.H. Burk, 'Cable Yarding on Eastern Canadian Pulpwood Logging Operations: An Analysis of the 1957 Yarding Committee Questionnaire on Cable Yarding,' WSI 1769 (1958). Burk has an excellent bibliography on 'Cable Yarding Trends and History.'
34 CPPA, WS, P.V. Lemay, 'Logging at Marathon,' WSI 1055 (1949) 1–3
35 CPPA, WS, W.E. Mair, 'Marathon's Experience with High-Lead Cable Yarding,' WSI 1057 (1949)
36 Lemay, 'Logging at Marathon'
37 Burk, 'Cable Yarding'

38 'Report . . . on Cable Yarding' 3; Carlisle, 'Yarding at Iroquois Falls'
39 McColl, 'Cable Yarding'; Pepler and McColl, 'Development,' 16–17; CPPA, WS, 'Report on the Cable Yarding Situation' WSI 1864 (1960)
40 Rudolph Vit, 'Development of a Feller Buncher Skidder for Full Tree Logging Operations,' WSI 1946 (1960); WR, September 1959
41 CPPA, WS, D.C. Horncastle, 'Current Status of Multi-Processing Equipment,' WSI 2130 (1962); Silversides, 'Achievements'
42 'Report of the Summer Field Meeting,' WR, August 1962
43 Silversides, 'Achievements'
44 'Report of the Summer Field Meeting,' WR, August 1961; D.D. Hamilton, 'The Pulpwood Combine,' WR, June 1961; R. Rauzenhafer, 'The Arbomatik System,' WR, November 1967
45 Silversides, 'Achievements'; ITC, Mechanization 31
46 Silversides, 'Achievements'
47 ITC, Mechanization 31
48 Oliver Korpela interviewed by author, Chapleau 1980
49 CPPA, WS, W.R. Beatty, 'The Koehring KH III B Harvester,' WSI 1592 (1970); Koehring Canada Ltd., Koehring Woodlands Equipment: Strong on Performance (n.p. 1977)
50 S.A. Axelsson, Repair Statistics and Performance of New Logging Machines: Koehring Short-Wood Harvester (PPRIC Report no. 47, Montreal 1972); Jamie Swift, Cut and Run: The Assault on Canada's Forests (Toronto 1983) 138–9; D.C. Horncastle, 'Techniques for Analysis, Comparison and Choice of Harvesting Systems,' in C.R. Silversides, ed., Forest Harvesting, Mechanization and Automation (Ottawa 1974)
51 On problems with the meaning of 'productivity,' see Forestry Study Group, The Outlook for the Canadian Forest Industries (Ottawa 1958) 151–4; Duncan R. Campbell and Edward B. Power, Manpower Implications of Prospective Technological Changes in the Eastern Canadian Pulpwood Logging Industry (Ottawa 1966) 17–22.
52 'Mechanical Logging: A Panel Discussion,' WR, May 1965; Drott advertisement is in Canadian Forest Industries, June 1970; Koehring, Strong on Performance
53 Statistics Canada, Fixed Capital Flows and Stocks, 1927–1973 (Ottawa 1974) 121
54 CPPA, WS, Alexander Koroleff, 'New Approach to Collective Work Evaluations of Machinery Aggregations,' WSI 2051 (1963)
55 Hughes, 'Logging Operations'
56 Godwin, ' "The Beginning" '
57 Campbell and Power, Implications 17
58 Calculated from tables in Statistics Canada, Logging 1965 and 1980

59 Dianne Newell, *Technology on the Frontier: Mining in Old Ontario* (Vancouver 1986) 3

60 Ibid. 5; Pepler and McColl, 'Development'; CPPA, WS, D.A. Swan, 'Trends and Accomplishments in the Northeastern Pulpwood Industry,' WSI 2503 (1968); W.W. Hall, 'The Great Lakes-St. Lawrence Forest Region,' in Canadian Council of Rural Development, *The Relationship of Canada's Forests to Rural Employment and Community Stability* (Ottawa 1977); James Wesley McNutt, *Labour Relations in the Forest – A Half Century of Progress* (Toronto 1978) 2. See also International Labour Organization, Second Tripartite Technical Meeting for the Timber Industry, *General Report* (Geneva 1973) 17; CPPA, WS, W.S. Bromley, 'U.S. Southern Forest Developments,' WSI 2580 (1970); Boone Y. Richardson, 'Harvesting Mechanization and Automation in Northern Mountainous United States,' in Silversides, *Forest Harvesting*; Sam Guttenburg, 'Woods Labour Problems in American's South,' in ibid., CPPA, WS, 'Report of the Logging Field Meeting of the Woodlands Section and the Lake States Technical Committee of the American Pulpwood Association,' WSI 2301 (1964). Patterns were rather different in eastern Europe and the USSR; see Alexander Koroleff, *Mechanization in the USSR* 2 vols. (Montreal 1959); CPPA, WS, Jarolaw Halowacz, 'Forestry in the USSR: Resources, Industry and Production,' WSI 2473 (1968).

61 David F. Noble, *America by Design: Science, Technology, and the Rise of Corporate Capitalism* (Oxford 1977)

62 Newell, *Technology on the Frontier* preface; also, James Otto Petersen, 'The Origins of Canadian Gold Mining: The Part Played by Labour in the Transition from Tool Production to Machine Production,' PH D thesis, University of Toronto 1977; Donald MacLeod, 'Mines, Mining Men, and Mining Reformers: Changing the Technology of Nova Scotian Gold Mines and Colleries, 1858 to 1910'; Allan Skeoch, 'Technology and Change in Nineteenth-Century Ontario Agriculture,' MA thesis, University of Toronto 1976

63 B. Sinclair, N.R. Ball, and J.O. Petersen, eds., *Let Us Be Honest and Modest: Technology and Society in Canadian History* (Toronto 1972) 2

CHAPTER 10 Mechanized bush work

1 *Bush News*, July 1964

2 Harry Braverman, *Labor and Monopoly Capital: The Degradation of Work in the Twentieth Century* (New York 1974). Useful reviews of the debate include Richard Price, 'Theories of Labour Process Formation,' *Journal of Social History* 8:1 (January 1983); Steven Wood, ed., *The Degradation of Work?: Skill,*

Deskilling and the Labour Process (London 1982).

3 Barry Wilkinson, *The Shopfloor Politics of the New Technology* (London 1983). In his important work on the U.S. machine tools industry, David F. Noble has found evidence of a concerted drive by employers and engineers to maximize their control over work processes, even when this meant higher production costs. See his *Forces of Production: A Social History of Industrial Automation* (New York 1984).

4 CPPA, WS, Committee on Training of Woods Labour and Personnel, 'Review of Power Saw Manuals,' WSI 1353 (1953); 'The Proper Use of the Power Saw as a Cutting Tool: A Panel Discussion,' WSI 1369 (1954)

5 Wayne Lennox, *Ya Can't Holler 'Timber' With All That Racket!: Logging in Northern Ontario* (Cobalt 1979) 7

6 Jake Hildebrand interviewed by Jamie Swift, 1981, transcript

7 CPPA, WS, T.M. Pond, 'Report on Power Saw Tests,' WSI 1139 (1951). See especially the discussion that follows this paper, a transcript of which is appended to the report.

8 *WR*, June 1959; *OB*, 1 May 1959

9 Compare with the Newfoundland case as described in J.P. Curran, 'The Process of Mechanization in the Forest Industry of Newfoundland,' MA thesis, Memorial University of Newfoundland 1971.

10 'Proper Use of the Power Saw,' LSWUF, Master Agreement, 1955–6

11 William Ritokoski interviewed by author, Sault Ste Marie 1980

12 D.W. Gray, 'Accident Prevention in Mechanized Operations,' *WR*, January 1958

13 AO, CR, RG 18 B-125 vol. 7, Report of Hearings of the Royal Commission on Industrial Safety, Port Arthur, 28 Oct. 1960, 1716. See also ibid., vol. 5, 'Brief of the Northern Ontario District Council of the Lumber and Sawmill Workers Union,' 28 Oct. 1960.

14 Jamie Swift, *Cut and Run: The Assault on Canada's Forests* (Toronto 1983) 152–4; Keith Mason in 'The Effects of Piecework on Accident Rates in the Logging Industry,' *Journal of Occupational Accidents* 1:3 (1977) maintains that piecework does not increase accident rates. His findings have been challenged: see Charles E. Reason, Lois L. Ross, and Craig Patterson, *Assault on the Worker: Occupational Health and Safety in Canada* (Toronto 1981) 23–4; Joint Federal–Provincial Inquiry Commission into Safety in Mining and Mining Plants in Ontario, *Towards Safe Production* vol. 1 163–7.

15 James D. Nugent, 'Personal Protective Equipment Used by Forest Workers in Eastern Canada,' in C.R. Silversides, ed., *Proceedings of the International Union of Forest Research Organizations, Division 3: Forest Harvesting and Automation* (Ottawa 1974)

16 Ontario Advisory Council on Occupational Health and Safety, *Fifth Annual Report, 1981–82*, vol. I (Toronto 1983) 233. See also *Towards Safe Production* vol. II 15; Labour Canada, Occupational Health and Safety Branch, *Fatalities in Canadian Industry, 1969–78* (Ottawa 1980).

17 Swift, *Cut and Run* 155. See also *Abstracts of the Third International Symposium on Hand-Arm Vibration* (Ottawa 1981); A.J Bummer, *Chain Saw Vibration: Its Measurement, Hazard and Control* (Ottawa 1978).

18 C.R. Cermak, 'Forest Ergonomics in Eastern European Countries,' in Silversides, *Forest Harvesting* 51–60

19 Lennox, *Ya Can't Holler* 10

20 H.H. Bert Styffe, 'Whither Romance?' *Log Book* July–August 1962; *Ontario Logger*, February 1966

21 CPPA, WS, C.R. Silversides, 'Achievements and Failures in Logging Mechanization,' WSI 2619 (1972). See also Douglas D. Hamilton, 'Full-Tree Logging Methods and Machinery,' *Pulp and Paper Canada*, May 1980.

22 Gordon Godwin, 'The Impact of Modern Technology on Forestry in Canada,' *Forestry Chronicle* (December 1963) 450–1; CPPA, WS, 'Two Shift Logging: A Symposium,' WSI 2091 (1966); C.R. Silversides, 'The Influence of Mechanization on Harvesting and Transportation Methods,' *Proceedings of the Sixth World Forestry Congress* vol. III (Madrid 1966) 2804

23 CPPA, WS, 'Small Skidder Forum,' WSI 2140 (1962)

24 Richard Edwards, *Contested Terrain: The Transformation of the Workplace in the Twentieth Century* (New York 1979) ch. 7

25 W. Novak, *Some Forest Industry Thoughts on the Training of First-Line Supervisors* (FERIC Special Report 3, Montreal 1978); Silversides, 'Influence of Mechanization,' 2808. Windebank's comments are in CPPA, WS, 'Technical Change and Its Consequences on Woods Operations: A Symposium,' WSI 2217 (1963).

26 UTA, Arthur S. Michell papers, Spruce Falls Power and Paper Ltd. file, 1967; Tulio Mior interviewed by author, Thunder Bay 1982; CPPA, WS, Camille Legendre, 'Improving Productivity: Expensive Hardware, Better Qualified Workers, How about the Organization?' WSI 2661 (1973)

27 W.D. Bennett, H.I. Winer, and A. Bartholomew, *A Measurement of Environmental Factors and Their Effects on the Productivity of Tree-Length Logging with Rubber-Tired Skidders* (PPRIC Woodlands Report 22, Montreal 1965)

28 P.L. Cottell, H.I. Winer, and A. Bartholomew, *Alternative Methods of Evaluating the Productivity of Logging Operators: Report on a Study of Wheeled Skidding* (PPRIC Woodlands Report 37, Montreal 1971); UTA, Michell papers, Minutes of the 1976 National Meeting Logging Operations Group, Appendix C. See also CPPA, WS, Alex Bartholomew, 'An Incentive Plan for Harvester Operations, WSI 2731

(1977); P.R. Pickering, 'Carrot or Kick in the Pants?' WSI 2737 (1977).

29 CPPA, WS, E.S. Cadenhead, 'Small Wheeled Skidders,' WSI 2221 (1962); Earl M. Craig, 'Applied Ergonomics as a Means of Increasing Production Rates and Job Satisfaction,' in Silversides, *Forest Harvesting* 68–74

30 John R. Radforth, *Higher Travel Speeds for Off-Road Logging Vehicles* (FERIC Report Montreal 1978) 5–7; Norman W. Radforth, former Chairman of the Muskeg Subcommittee of the National Research Council Associate Committee on Geotechnical Research, interviewed by author, Parry Sound 1980

31 Bill Plaunt, Sudbury District lumberman, interviewed by author, Sudbury 1982

32 Radforth, *Higher Travel Speeds* 6

33 CPPA, WS, C.S. Miller, 'A Co-operative Training Project for Wheeled Skidder Operations, WSI 2372 (1965)

34 Don Harris interviewed by Jamie Swift, August 1981 (transcript)

35 Lennox, *Ya Can't Holler* 24

36 Cited in *Ontario Logger*, May 1965

37 D.A. Scott and P.L. Cottell, *Survey of Logger Training* (FERIC Technical Report 11, Montreal 1976)

38 Miller, 'Co-operative Training'

39 Edwards, *Contested Terrain* ch. 8

40 Canadian Car, Division of Hawker Siddeley Canada Ltd., *Operator's Manual – Tree Farmer: Power Shift Models* (n.p. 1970?) 15–16

41 D.V. Miles, 'Present Situation and Trends in Occupational Health and Safety,' in Silversides, *Forest Harvesting* 94–103

42 Radforth, *Higher Travel Speeds* 5

43 Ibid., 7; Silversides, 'Introduction' in his *Forest Harvesting*, 4–6

44 CPPA, WS, Richard Holton, 'Trends in Noise Suppression of Mobile Diesel Equipment,' WSI 2649 (1974). See also E.H. Reeves, 'Design of Logging Equipment for Operator Efficiency and Comfort,' draft copy in UTA, Michell papers; A.R. Howell, *Study of the Exposure to Noise of Operators of Mechanical Logging Equipment in British Columbia* (Ottawa 1974); Silversides, *Forest Harvesting* 239–332.

45 R. Legault and L.H. Powell, *Evaluation of the FMC 200 BG Grapple Skidder* (FERIC Technical Report 1, Montreal 1976)

46 CPPA, WS, W.F. Beatty, 'The Koehring KH III B Harvester,' WSI 2592 (1970)

47 P.L. Cottell et al., *Performance Variation among Logging Machine Operators: Felling with Tree Shears* (FERIC Technical Report 4, Montreal 1976) 20–2, 26–7

48 On the problems of employment opportunities for women in a forest economy, see Patricia Marchak, *Green Gold: The Forest Industry in British*

Columbia (Vancouver 1983) ch. 8; Elaine Pitt Enarson, *Woods-Working Women: Sexual Integration in the U.S. Forest Service* (Alabama 1984).

49 *WR*, August 1967; *Pulp and Paper Canada*, December 1976

50 D.C. Mason, 'The Effects of Changing Woodlands Operating Techniques on the Basic Job Characteristics of Woods Labour,' Pulpwood Production Manpower Conference, 1965, cited in Silversides, 'Influence of Mechanization,' 2807

51 Beatty, 'The Koehring'; M.P. Folkema and R. Levesque, *Evaluation of the Hohn Pulp/Logger II Limber-Slasher* (FERIC Technical Report 52, Montreal 1982); Cottel et al., *Performance Variation* 20

52 C.R. Silversides collection, Prescott, C.A. Kearns (Canada Manpower), 'Recruiting and Retention of Employees – Forestry and Mining (typescript 1974); CPPA, WS, Logging Operations Group, *Training Committee, Survey on Manpower and Training Needs* (Montreal 1977–8)

53 Silversides, 'Achievements and Failures'; CPPA, WS, G.K. Seed, 'The Machine Resource – Current Options,' WSI 2617 (1972); ITC, Mechanical Transport Branch, *Mechanization in the Forests: Benefits and Opportunities* (Ottawa 1972) 32

54 Kauko Turtiainen, 'Safety Hazards in Highly Mechanized Operations,' Forest and Agricultural Organization, *Seminar on Occupational Health and Safety and Applied Ergonomics on Highly Mechanized Logging Operations* (Ottawa 1981) 138

55 'Two Shift Logging'; S. Milling, 'Training and Development Needs of Forest Workers in the 80s,' *Pulp and Paper Canada*, April 1981; Forest and Agricultural Organization, *Seminar on Occupational Health* 202

56 See especially Andrew Zimbalist, ed., *Case Studies on the Labor Process* (New York 1979); Wood, *Degradation of Work?*; Craig Heron and Robert Storey, eds., *On the Job: Confronting the Labour Process in Canada* (Kingston 1986).

57 Richard Edwards, 'Social Relations of Production at the Point of Production,' *Insurgent Sociologist* 8:2–3 (1978) 109

58 Craig Heron and Robert Storey, 'On the Job in Canada,' in Heron and Storey, *On the Job* 28–9

CHAPTER 11 Bushworkers respond to mechanization

1 'Tall Timber Tales,' *The Lumberjack Bulletin*, 4 May 1918, rpr. in Joyce L. Kornbluh, ed., *Rebel Voices: An I.W.W. Anthology* (Ann Arbor 1964) 269

2 Harry Braverman, *Labor and Monopoly Capitalism: The Degradation of Work in the Twentieth Century* (New York 1974)

3 Richard Edwards, 'The Social Relations of Production at the Point of Production,' *Insurgent Sociologist* 8:2–3 (1978) 109; see also his *Contested Terrain:*

Transformation of the Workplace in the Twentieth Century (New York 1979). An insightful commentary on the debate is Richard Price, 'Theories of Labour Process Formation,' *Journal of Social History* 8:1 (January 1983) 57–75. See also David Stark, 'Class Struggle and the Transformation of the Labor Process: A Relational Approach,' *Theory and Society* 9:1 (January 1980) 89–130.

4 *OT*, 15 Apr. 1948; *OB*, May 1960, 17 Sept. 1956; Tulio Mior interviewed by author, Thunder Bay 1982

5 Jake Hildebrand interviewed by Jamie Swift, 1981 (transcript)

6 LSWUF, Master Agreement, 1955–6 and subsequent agreements

7 CPPA, WS, 'Small Skidder Forum,' WSI 2091 (1966)

8 UTA, Arthur S. Michell papers, drawer 6, Lloyd M. Lein, 'Mechanical Logging Operations as carried out at Marathan [sic] Paper Mills of Canada, Stevens – Ontario,' 26 June 1948; AO, Gillies Brothers Lumber Company records, AD-12, Temagami Journal, 5 Feb. 1960; *Ontario Logger*, June 1965

9 Hildebrand interview

10 Wayne Lennox, *Ya Can't Holler 'Timber' with All That Racket!: Logging in Northern Ontario* (Cobalt 1979) 11

11 *OB*, 15 Feb. 1964. See also PAC, CR, RG 18 B-125, Ontario Royal Commission on Industrial Safety, vol. 5, Exhibit #70, 'Brief of the Northern Ontario District Council of the Lumber and Sawmill Workers Union of the United Brotherhood of Carpenters and Joiners of America,' 28 Oct. 1960; Ontario, Royal Commission on Industrial Safety, *Report* (Toronto 1961) 7. On the masculine self-image of woodsworkers, see Geoffrey York, 'Woodsylore: Macho Culture Helps Loggers Conquer Fear,' *Globe and Mail*, 4 Apr. 1983, in reference to the research of Stuart Philpott.

12 *OB*, 4 Feb. 1957; Mior interview

13 C. Ross Silversides to author, 8 July 1982

14 Duncan R. Campbell and Edward B. Power, *Manpower Implications of Prospective Technological Changes in the Eastern Canadian Pulpwood Logging Industry* (Ottawa 1966) 108

15 LSWUF, Master Agreement, 1955–6 and subsequent agreements

16 *OB*, 25 Nov. 1965, 14 Oct. 1960. On Kimberly-Clark's attempts to benefit from such divisions, see an internal memo from the Superintendent of Industrial Relations, J.E.C. Pringle, 17 Aug. 1961 in UTA, Michell papers, Longlac file.

17 LSWUF, Master Agreements 1967–8

18 UTA, FFC, R.B. Laughlan, 'Logging Report: Longlac Pulp and Paper Company,' 1948

19 William Kurelek, *Lumberjack* (Montreal 1974) n.p.

20 *OB*, 18 Feb. 1957; UTA, FF, R.G. Lightheart, 'Logging Report,' 1957

21 H.I. Winer and M. Ryans, *Organizational Factors Affecting Trials of New Logging Machinery* (FERIC Special Report 10, Montreal 1980)

22 Ivar F. Fogh, 'Effects of Technical Change on Woods Operations,' *Forestry Chronicle* 44:1 (February 1968) 30–6; Winer and Ryans, *Organizational Factors*

23 CPPA, WS, C.R. Day, 'An Analysis of Woodslands Manpower,' WSI 2263 (1973). See also George McLeish, 'People Do Want to Work in the Bush,' *Pulp and Paper Canada*, May 1974; CPPA, WS, John A. Dawson, 'Manpower for Woods Operations,' WSI 2434 (1967); John S. Taylor, 'Woodlands Recruitment: Great Lakes Uses TV and Radio,' *Pulp and Paper Canada*, October 1974; CPPA, WS, D.A. Scott, 'The Use of Psychology in Logging Research,' WSI 2672 (1975); Henry Dealey, 'How to Recruit, Train and Retain Forest Workers, WSI 2657 (1975); Robert Neilson, 'Woodsworkers Can Be Recruited in the Cities,' WSI 2668 (1974); T.H. Ballantyne, 'Where to Get Wood Workers,' WSI 2673 (1975)

24 CPPA, WS, D.M. Johnson, 'The Manpower Situation,' WSI 2622 (1972). On labour turnover in mechanized operations, see Kenneth Pearce and George Stenzie, *Logging and Pulpwood Production* (New York 1972); D.A. Scott and P. Cottell, *Survey of Logger Training* (FERIC Technical Report 11, Montreal 1976).

25 Kearns, 'Recruiting and Retention,' 13

26 CPPA, WS, G.K. Seed, 'Machine Resource-Current Options' WSI 2617 (1972)

27 CPPA, WS, Philip L. Cottell, 'Why Work in the Woods?' WSI 2662 (1974). See also his *Occupational Choice and Employment Stability among Forest Workers* (New Haven 1974); and for Quebec in the 1950s, Gérard Fortier and Emile Gosselin, 'La professionalisation du travail en forêt,' *Recherches Sociographiques* (janv.–mars 1960) 33–60. Cottell's interpretation has been criticized in Patricia Marchak, *Green Gold: The Forest Industry in British Columbia* (Vancouver 1982) 116–17.

28 Johnson, 'Manpower Situation,' 2

29 *OB*, 16 Apr., 3 July 1956

30 Ibid., 10 Aug. 1959

31 Ibid., 18 Mar. 1957; Mior interview

32 *Moody's Industrial Manual 1979*, vol. I 256

33 W.J. Wesley cited in *Financial Post*, 10 May 1979. See also Ontario Labour Relations Board Report 1978 0658-78-U, 670

34 On the Reed strike, see University of Toronto, Industrial Relations Centre Library, Vertical Files, 'Lumber and Sawmill Workers Union.' On similar battles elsewhere, see especially W.C. Osborn, *The Paper Plantation: Ralph Nader's Study Group on the Pulp and Paper Industry in Maine* (New York 1974) pt. III.

35 W. Wesley to Tulio Mior, 15 May 1978, and Mior to Local 2693 members, 24 May 1978 in OLRB *Report* 1979 670-1

36 OLRB *Report* 1979 696-7
37 *Globe and Mail*, 4 Dec. 1980. Strike developments can be followed in the clipping files at the Ontario Ministry of Labour Library and the University of Toronto Industrial Relations Centre Library. See also Sue Vohanka, 'The Next Thirty-One Years Will Be the Hardest: The Woodcutters' Strike in Northern Ontario,' *This Magazine* (March–April 1980) 38-42 and her 'Update,' *This Magazine* (December 1980) 39-9; 'Lumber and Saw's Battle with Boise Enters Second Year,' *Ontario Labour* (September–October 1979) 8-9; C. Gilchrist, 'Boise Cascade: Kenora,' *Canadian Dimension* (May 1979) 20-2; Ian Radforth, 'The Roots of the Loggers' Strike at Boise Cascade, Canada, Ltd., 1978-80,' paper presented to the North American Labor History Conference, Wayne State University October 1982.
38 L.F. Lounden to Boise employees, 7 June 1978, in OLRB *Report* 1979 611
39 LSWUF, Local 2693, 'Review of the Strike of Woodlands Employees of Boise Cascade Canada, Ltd., 1978-9'
40 Cited in *Globe and Mail*, 9 Sept. 1979
41 Ontario New Democratic Party Research Office files, Queen's Park, Stephen Lewis and Robert Joyce to the Hon. Robert Elgie, 8 Mar. 1979
42 M.A. McKay, Vice President of Woodlands Operations, Great Lakes Forest Products, interviewed by Jamie Swift, August 1981 (transcript)
43 On contracting out internationally, see Frank Wilkinson, ed., *The Dynamics of Labour Market Segmentation* (London 1981).
44 Wallace Clement, 'Canada's Coastal Fisheries: Formation of Unions, Cooperatives, and Associations,' *Journal of Canadian Studies* 19:1 (Spring 1984) 9. See also Peter R. Sinclair, *From Traps to Draggers: Domestic Commodity Production in Northwestern Newfoundland, 1850-1982* (St John's 1985).

CONCLUSION

1 Matt Bray, 'The Place and the People,' in Matt Bray and Ernie Epp, eds., *A Vast and Magnificent Land: An Illustrated History of Northern Ontario* (Thunder Bay and Sudbury 1984) 16
2 Stephen Wood, ed., *The Degradation of Work?: Skill, Deskilling and the Labour Process* (London 1983) 22
3 C.R. Silversides, 'The Influence of Mechanization on Harvesting and Transportation Methods,' *Proceedings of the Sixth World Forestry Congress* vol. III (Madrid 1966) 2804

Index